Michael Alter, a dauntless researcher, has produced another invaluable polemical work that torpedoes the Christian hype about the alleged resurrection of Jesus. Thorough and insightful, *The Resurrection and Its Apologetics* joins Alter's previous volumes to puncture a perennial missionary argument.

–Rabbi Michael Skobac,
Director of Education, Jews for Judaism

Since C. S. Lewis' *Mere Christianity*, apologetics has been retreating to defend ever-diminishing territory. As its name suggests, "minimal facts apologetics" fights to hold the last smallest ground for Christian dogma; but with military precision and encyclopedic authority, Alter's new book seizes the final hill from apologetics, leaving it nowhere to stand and defeating it once and for all.

–Jack David Eller, PhD
Author of *Introducing Anthropology of Religion*

Michael Alter's new work represents a substantial contribution to the enduring debate over whether a historical Jesus was historically resurrected from the grave. This series takes us on a compendious and systematic tour through major historical and contemporary arguments that Christian apologists have used to support the historicity of the Resurrection, and rebuttals to each of those arguments that have been offered by skeptics and by Jewish and Muslim opponents. This work will serve as a useful survey and catalog of the reasons that have been given for belief and disbelief, for anyone who anyone interested in this critical foundation-stone of the Christian faith.

–Evan Fales, PhD
Author of *Reading Sacred Texts*

The first and abiding impression given by Michael J. Alter's study of the resurrection apologetic is one of intellectual integrity and an absolute commitment to fairness and accuracy. Add to that a critique that is based on prodigious scholarship and conducted with logical acumen, and you have a treatment of these controversial issues that is as close to definitive and authoritative as we are likely ever to get.

–Keith Parson, PhD
Author of *God and the Burden of Proof*

The Resurrection and Its Apologetics

The Resurrection and Its Apologetics

Jesus' Death and Burial
Volume One

Michael J. Alter

Foreword by Bruce D. Chilton

RESOURCE *Publications* • Eugene, Oregon

THE RESURRECTION AND ITS APOLOGETICS
Jesus' Death and Burial, Volume One

Copyright © 2024 Michael J. Alter. All rights reserved. Except for brief quotations in critical publications or reviews, no part of this book may be reproduced in any manner without prior written permission from the publisher. Write: Permissions, Wipf and Stock Publishers, 199 W. 8th Ave., Suite 3, Eugene, OR 97401.

Wipf & Stock
An Imprint of Wipf and Stock Publishers
199 W. 8th Ave., Suite 3
Eugene, OR 97401

www.wipfandstock.com

PAPERBACK ISBN: 979-8-3852-1750-2
HARDCOVER ISBN: 979-8-3852-1751-9
EBOOK ISBN: 979-8-3852-1752-6

Cataloguing-in-Publication Data

Names: Alter, Michael J.

Title: Book title : The Resurrection and Its Apologetics/ Michael J. Alter.

Description: Eugene, OR: Resource Publications, 2024 | Includes bibliographical references and index.

Identifiers: ISBN 979-8-3852-1750-2 (paperback) | ISBN 979-8-3852-1751-9 (hardcover) | ISBN 979-8-3852-1752-6 (ebook)

Subjects: LCSH: Jesus Christ—Resurretion—Controversial literature | Jesus Christ—Historicty | Conterapologetics | Title

Classification: BT482.A48 2024 (print) | BT482 (ebook)

Unless otherwise noted, Scripture quotations are from The Holy Bible, English Standard Version (ESV)®, copyright © 2001 by Crossway Bibles, a publishing ministry of Good News Publishers. Used by permission. All rights reserved worldwide.

To
Brandon, Sophie, Austin, and Summer

A Selection of Publications by Michael J. Alter

What Is the Purpose of Creation: A Jewish Anthology (Jason Aronson, 1991)

Why the Torah Begins with the Letter Beit (Jason Aronson, 1998)

The Resurrection: A Critical Inquiry (Xlibris, 2015)

A Thematic Access-Oriented Bibliography of Jesus's Resurrection (Resource Publications, 2020)

The Name Israel (Resource Publications, 2023)

Contents

List of Tables	xi
Foreword by Bruce Chilton	xii
Preface	xv
Acknowledgments	xxii
Segue	xxv
Caveat	xxix

1	Habermas and Licona's First Minimal Fact: Jesus Died by Crucifixion—An Overview	1
2	Jesus Was Not Brain-Dead While On the Cross	3
3	Problems with the Gospels and Acts	29
4	Problems with Josephus	32
5	Problems with Mara bar Serapion	83
6	Problems with Tacitus	86
7	Additional Problems with the Gospels	104
8	Problems with the Gospel of John and Jesus' Crucifixion	108
9	The Shroud of Turin	115
10	Medical Issues Continued	148
11	Islamic Theology and Jesus' Crucifixion—Did Jesus Die on the Cross?	154

12	Is Joseph of Arimathea Historical?	163
13	Was the Tomb Really Accessible?	184
14	Could the Disciples Preach an Empty Tomb in Jerusalem?	195
15	Why a Lack of Controversy Over the Tomb by the Public?	209
16	Why a Lack of Interest in the Tomb by Roman Leadership?	215
17	Why a Lack of Interest in the Tomb by the Jewish Authorities?	219
18	Was There Controversy About the Empty Tomb Among Jesus' Followers?	227
19	What Were the Consequences of an Empty Tomb?	231
20	Three Alternative Possibilities	242
21	Interactions with Christian Apologists	250
	Conclusion	254
	Bibliography	259
	Name Index	279
	Author Index	283
	Subject Index	288

List of Tables

2-1	Did Jesus Die While on the Cross?	7
4-1	Arguments About the Authenticity of the Testimonium Flavianum	36
4-2	Testimonium-Luke Comparison	41
4-3	Thirty-One English Correspondences Identified by Goldberg	44
4-4	Common Points of Contact Between the TF, the Nicene Creed, and the Apostles' Creed	50
12-1	Varying Details about Joseph of Arimathea	167
15-1	Selected Names of "Lost Books"	210

Foreword

In the torrent of current discussion of Jesus' Resurrection, Michael J. Alter has positioned himself strategically. The flood stage has reached a new apogee in recent years, as his bibliography reflects. His new book not only represents that cresting interest, but presses it forward.

Two factors have played a central role in promoting the rich controversy regarding the Resurrection that we are presently passing through.

Among established denominations of Christianity, the influence of the German theologian Rudolf Bultmann, long a dominant contributor until his death in 1976, has waned. Bultmann developed an existentialist argument that made the Cross of Jesus into the pivot of faith, such that a decision to take it on as a model of living aligned a person with Christ. Emphasis on the Cross in this sense tended to deflect attention from the Resurrection. Yet the emphasis of the New Testament and of early Christianity as a whole does not accord with any such deflection. They indeed portray Christ as crucified, but as the prelude to Christ as raised from the dead. A re-orientation was bound to come, especially as fashions of existentialism faded.

Fundamentalism has been the second and more obvious influence at this stage of the twenty-first century. Emerging in the United States at the end of the nineteenth century, this movement enumerated among its non-negotiable "Fundamentals" the proposition that Jesus was raised from the dead "in the same body" in which he died — that is, as physically resuscitated. The New Testament, like Second Temple Judaism, in fact speaks of the dead raising in a variety of ways, but Fundamentalism was concerned to insist on a single meaning of how Jesus rose, much as it would only tolerate one version of how he was conceived.

Established denominations and Fundamentalist groups largely went their own ways until the end of the Second World War, but the last decades of the twentieth century saw a profound change. Fundamentalism grew in influence, and denominations of Christianity once famous for their liberalism increasingly embraced Fundamentalist positions. During this period, for example, scholars who stood in the tradition of spiritual understandings of Jesus' Resurrection began to insist that faith required belief in "the empty tomb," a phrase that came to be used to speak even of texts in the New Testament that feature no such reference.

The combination of the two factors, the liberal loss of Bultmann's existentialism and the Fundamentalist hegemony in biblical interpretation, has resulted in a spate of apologetic works, including from authors who feature in Michael J. Alter's study: principally Gary R. Habermas and Michael R. Licona, with William Lane Craig also mentioned at crucial moments. The apologetic assertion of "facts" from the New Testament sometimes — and ironically — hinges upon allegedly reliable evidence from well outside the New Testament. That is a tacit admission that the New Testament is not as transparently factual as some apologists make it out to be.

Michael J. Alter is himself a kind of apologist, but of a different stripe from Habermas, Licona, and Craig. He openly sets out his own interpretative axioms, including the existence of God and the status of the Hebrew Bible as "God's revealed word" (p. 3). He also distances himself from the claim that Jesus was a purely mythic figure. But as an apologist, he problematizes claims of Jesus' physical Resurrection, starting in this book with the assertion, as if it were an established fact, that Jesus died on the cross.

He pursues his case, sometimes in a forensic vein, as for example when he refers to Habermas and Licona as "inexcusable" in their treatment of Tacitus' passing reference to the crucifixion as if it were an independently verified statement (p. 103). Throughout, however, Alter is fulsome in the citation of literature and relentless in pursuing apologetic arguments and their possible refutations. Above all, he keeps his eye on the prize of understanding what we even mean when we say a person has died, and whether our sources would permit us to know at what stage death had occurred in a particular case in the past.

Alter often targets the accounts of the New Testament in particular, showing how they have been differently shaped, and often for demonstrably theological rather than historical interests. But he also lavishes concern on alleged evidence outside the New Testament, and that is a wise decision. Not only apologists for Resurrection "in the same body," but also many popular contributors, have treated sources such as Tacitus superficially, but as if they established the truth of events. In this regard, Tacitus is joined by Josephus, Mara bar Serapion, and the Shroud of Turin. All these are subjected to searching scrutiny in enjoyable and comprehensive discussions that Alter skillfully develops.

Analysis by means of presentation by point and counter-point maintains a focus on the apologetic purpose of many contributors, and also forwards Alter's own agenda of calling attention to the lack of standing for the assertion that Jesus died on the cross (see p. 152), and that it does not "offer a rationale for converting to Christianity" (p. 162). Alternative explanations have been explored since the emergence of Gnostic literature, including the claim that another person was executed in place of Jesus. Muslim interpretation took up this vein of thought, and Alter engages that form of apologetics in some detail. Once the ins and outs of discussion have been explored, the various presentations in the Gospels concerning Jesus burial and tomb then look far less factual than they are often presented in contemporary discussion.

This highly concentrated volume is only the first fruit of a series dedicated to "The Resurrection and Its Apologetics." The care of this initial foray promises future volumes that are relentless in their argumentation, sharp in their polemics, and judicious in their selection of the evidence and the arguments presented.

Bruce D. Chilton
Bernard Iddings Bell Professor of Philosophy and Religion
Executive Director, the Institute of Advanced Theology

Preface

The *Resurrection and Its Apologetics: Jesus' Death and Burial* is a multivolume, in-depth counter-apologetic resource with the stated goal of making a significant contribution to academia and the non-academic world. It seeks to achieve this goal by undertaking a review and analysis of the numerous topics

> Proverb 27:17 instructs us that "Iron sharpens iron, and one man sharpens another" (ESV).

> Aristophanes writes, "Certainly he who was wise who declared: 'Never pronounce until you have heard both sides of the story.'"[1]

> Similarly, Seneca advises, "Who shall decide a question without hearing the other side, even though he decide justly, will not act with justice."[2]

> Lastly, theologian Clement Francis Rogers writes in his book, *The Case for Miracle*, "No question is really settled till you heard both sides. As long as the arguments against a case are ignored you have a lurking feeling of insecurity. You have heard what may be said for it, but you do not quite know what may be said against it, and you fear the arguments on the other side may be stronger than you think."[3]

Achieving its stated goals requires openly engaging with and interacting with leading Christian thinkers. Prominent thinkers include William Lane Craig, Gary R. Habermas, Michael R. Licona, Sean McDowell, Lydia and Tim McGrew, and Peter Williams.

Each issue opens with a quote from a leading Christian apologist arguing for Jesus' bodily resurrection, followed by an in-depth analysis of

---

[1] Aristophanes, *The Wasps*, 725.
[2] Seneca, *Medea*, 198.
[3] Rogers, *The Case for Miracle*, 69.

their reasoning. Afterward, this book presents alternative options to the stated apologetics. The central points of focus are the *rebuttals*. In the interests of intellectual honesty, readers are encouraged to re-examine the *entire* source material of the cited Christian apologists.

This text reviews and analyzes the most salient claims in defense of Jesus' bodily resurrection. The information is from both contemporary and older sources. The arguments forwarded in this text are those made by a representative sample of Christian apologists, mostly conservative evangelicals who have published many books and articles on the *resurrectio Christi*. Their words are clear, concise, and uncompromising. After quoting from their writings, there is the presentation of other defenders who express the same view. The guiding purpose of this format is to provide the reader with an opportunity to examine the arguments put forward by a broad selection of apologists for Jesus' resurrection. The aim is to be as fair and academically honest as possible.

Interestingly, the theological position of Islam is often ignored in academia. There are approximately 1.9 billion Muslims globally, making Islam the second-largest religion behind Christianity. However, members of the Islamic community reject the belief that Jesus died on the cross. Islam also does not accept the thinking that Jesus is the Son of God as espoused in Christian theology. The first Minimal Fact (used by many apologists to argue for Jesus' resurrection) is the belief that Jesus died on the cross by crucifixion. No resurrection could occur if Jesus did not die on the cross. Nevertheless, Islam's theological rationale for challenging Jesus' death and resurrection receives only superficial lip service. Consequently, investigating this topic is relevant to academia and a large portion of the non-academic world.

Reviewing the literature finds a skewed apologetic offering that is often one-sided. In 2020, Michael Alter published *A Thematic Access-Oriented Bibliography of Jesus's Resurrection* (Resource Publications, a Wipf and Stock imprint). One year later, Alter and Darren Slade published the article: "Dataset Examination of Authors of English Texts Written on the Topic of Resurrection: A Statistical Critique of Minimal Facts Apologetics." Alter identified 735 texts written exclusively on the resurrection spanning five centuries. The data revealed: (1) 680 pro-resurrection books by 601 authors; (2) 204 were authored by ministers, 146 by priests, and 249 by people associated with seminaries; (3) 70 were authored by laypeople; and (4) 22 were authored by women. Roughly 7,000 English sources were identified, exclusively from books. They write:

This investigation substantiates assertions that Christians of various denominations write the vast majority of texts published on the subject of Jesus' resurrection. This review determined that virtually all of the pro-resurrection authors were Christian believers. Furthermore, many of these Christians are, in fact of the matter, more than just "believers." A literature review confirms that many are apologists, evangelists, ministers, priests, or administrators/professors in theological seminaries and universities. Consequently, many writers have an a priori view on the topic. Besides, many have a vested interest in the outcome of their research. Since belief in the historicity of the empty tomb is a central tenet of Christian belief (as reflected in the Apostles' and Nicene Creeds), it may infer that most scholars who accept the reality of the empty tomb have an a priori commitment to this tenet – in other words, their belief in the empty tomb is a pre-critical one.[4]

In addition, they state this "means any so-called scholarly consensus on the subject of Jesus' resurrection is wildly inflated due to a biased sample of authors who have a professional and personal interest in the subject matter."[5]

In contrast: (1) the fifty-five contra books were by forty-two authors; (2) twenty-eight of those authors had no relevant degrees; (3) the fifty-five contra books represented only 7.48 percent of the total 735 documented books on Jesus' resurrection; and (4) the forty-two contra authors represented only 6.99 percent of all authors writing on the subject. Significantly, many contra books are old, unscholarly, and do not engage or interact with the leading and cutting-edge topics. Consequently, the relevance of this text.

The Minimal Facts Approach to Jesus' resurrection is associated with its originator, Gary R. Habermas. He identified twelve purportedly known historical facts, extrapolating four that met two requisites. The four Minimal Facts include:

1. Jesus died by crucifixion.
2. Jesus' disciples believed he rose and appeared to them.
3. The church persecutor Paul suddenly changed.
4. The skeptic James, brother of Jesus, was suddenly changed.

During the past several decades, the Minimal Facts approach has been the most frequently employed apologetic in defense of the resurrection. Due

---

[4] Alter and Slade, "Dataset Examination of Authors," 384.
[5] Alter and Slade, "Dataset Examination of Authors," 367.

to its importance, two volumes explore that topic. Lydia McGrew advocates the Maximal Facts strategy. That subject is under review in a later volume.

PART I—Volume 1 exclusively investigates the first Minimal Fact. It comprises four sub-units. **Part I**, Jesus died by crucifixion, consists of twelve chapters. It examines a variety of topics. Select examples include the following:

1. Jesus was not brain-dead while on the cross
2. Problems with the Gospels and Early Non-Gospel Texts Problems with Josephus, Mara bar Serapion, and Tacitus.
3. The Gospel of John and Jesus' Crucifixion
4. Medical Issues
5. The Shroud of Turin
6. Islamic Theology and Jesus' Crucifixion

PART II of Volume I (chapters 13–19) will also examine the reality or not of a tomb burial. Christian apologists advance numerous arguments that are frequently an argument from silence.

1. Was it possible to deny that the tomb was empty since its location was well known and anyone could examine it?
2. Could the disciples preach the resurrection in Jerusalem if the tomb in Jerusalem were not empty?
3. Why was there a lack of controversy or interest in the empty tomb by the Roman leadership, Jewish religious authorities, and Jesus' followers?
4. What were the consequences of an empty tomb?

PART III of Volume 1 (chapters 20–21) explores the topic of the Supernatural. This more speculative part of the text addresses an often-disregarded issue. Noteworthy, this section is neither verifiable nor unfalsifiable. Frequently, Christian apologists do not engage in it. When they do, the interaction is superficial. It analyzes three alternative supernatural explanations for the resurrection.

PART IV is the Conclusion of Volume 1.

PART V—Volume 2 continues investigating the Minimal Facts Approach including. Three of the remaining Minimal Facts include:

Preface xix

1. Jesus' disciples believed he rose and appeared to them (chapters 23–27).
2. The church persecutor Paul suddenly changed (chapters 28–29).
3. The skeptic James, brother of Jesus, was suddenly changed. (chapter 30)

Additionally, the text will discuss:

1. An overview of problems associated with the Minimal Facts Approach (chapter 31)
2. Specific Problems with the Minimal Facts Approach (chapter 32)

PART VI—McCullagh's Arguments to the Best Explanation is employed by apologists to defend the resurrection. C. B. McCullagh, an Australian philosopher of history, identifies and discusses seven criteria he believes provides the Arguments for the Best Explanation. Later, his Best Arguments were adopted in defense of the resurrection. Perhaps, one of its most formidable proponents is William Lane Craig.

PART VII—The Apostles' martyrdom is perhaps one of the most well-known defenses of the resurrection. Christian apologists often claim that Paul, James, the brother of Jesus, and eleven of the twelve original disciples died *martyr's* death for their beliefs. Furthermore, they believe that these followers' willingness to suffer hardships, persecution, and even death for their beliefs made the invention of a resurrection account unlikely. Part VII incorporates an analysis of sources presumed to support the alleged martyrdom. Sean McDowell's *The Fate of the Apostles Examining the Martyrdom Accounts of the Closest Followers of Jesus* (2015) provides a significant foil for this section.

PART VIII—The Messiah and 1 Corinthians 15:3–4 (A Jewish Perspective). The Jewish case against Jesus the Messiah is a significant part of this text. Readers must review this section meticulously and think carefully about the arguments. Christians believe that Jesus is the Messiah and the Savior of the human race, who died for the sins of humanity on the cross (1 Cor. 15:3). Verse 4 adds the essential "that he was buried and raised to life on the third day as the Scriptures say." Judaism and Islam reject this belief for reasons that continue to elude many Christians. Here, readers receive a rational explanation of why Judaism and Islam refuse to accept Jesus as the Son of God. The Jewish case against Jesus consists of four points:

1. Nowhere in the Bible is a prophecy stating that the Messiah will die for our sins and rise to life on the third day.
2. Jesus could not have been the Messiah because he failed to fulfill the biblical prophecies.
3. Jesus cannot possibly be either the Lamb of God or the new Paschal lamb, as Christians claim he is.
4. Jesus' death on the cross could not possibly atone for the sins of humanity.

An additional significant point bears consideration. The Islamic opinion of Jesus as the Messiah differs from Christianity. Similar to Judaism, Islam rejects the thinking that Jesus' death as the Messiah was an altruistic sacrifice to atone for the sins of humanity. Introducing the Christian biblical Messiah to a Muslim via the Islamic portrait appears to be an exercise that constructs a building on a faulty foundation. Thus, an understanding of the material in Part VIII will make another contribution to academia and the non-academic world, regardless of one's faith.

PART IX—The Epilogue brings the body of this text to its logical conclusion.

During the late stage of the peer review process, the author became aware of Bruce Chilton's text, *Resurrection Logic: How Jesus' First Followers Believed God Raised Him from the Dead* (2019). He hit the nail on the head, identifying several crucial concepts:

1. My focus is to understand how those of Jesus' disciples who claimed God had raised him from the dead explained their conviction and related his resurrection to the hope of their own.[6]
2. The variety of the disciples' views of the resurrection presses the issue of not what, but *how*, the disciples believed.[7]
3. Controversy is only exacerbated by questions along the lines of, "What really happened?"[8]
4. Adjusting the question from "What happened?" to "*How* did the disciples believe in the resurrection?" changes the ground of discussion.[9]

---

[6] Chilton, *Resurrection Logic*, xii.
[7] Chilton, *Resurrection Logic*, 3.
[8] Chilton, *Resurrection Logic*, 203.
[9] Chilton, *Resurrection Logic*, 204.

Slightly revised from Chilton, many pages in this text inquire and speculate about the disciples' and apostles' backgrounds during and prior to encountering Jesus. Furthermore, they investigate the invisible elephant in the room: (1) What did the disciples and apologists think they saw? (2) What did they believe (they experienced)? This approach, highlighted in Volume 2, offers a glimpse into overlooked factors. Previously discussed, Islamic Theology and Jesus' Crucifixion—Did Jesus Die on the Cross? is essential. It also engages these topics through the lens of Islam. *A prior*, based on theology, this text explores how and why Muslims "disbelieve" the resurrection. Moreover, in the following volumes, this author intends to further engage with Chilton's poignant question: "How did the disciples believe in the resurrection?"

This book is a scholarly analysis of Christian apologetics. For those readers who may not know what apologetics is, John Frame, writing in the *Evangelical Dictionary of Biblical Theology,* provides a handy definition: "Apologetics is the theological discipline that defends the truth of the Christian message."[10] Apologetics, derived from the Greek word *apologia*, means defense. Apologists, therefore, seek to defend what they believe. Numerous passages in the Christian Scriptures support the concept of Christian apologetics. Perhaps the most often cited passage is 1 Peter 3:15, which states, "But in your hearts honor Christ the Lord as holy; always being prepared to make a defense to anyone who asks you for a reason for the hope that is in you; yet do it with gentleness and respect" (ESV).

The Resurrection and Its Apologetics: Jesus' Death and Burial will critically survey the voluminous writings of leading evangelistic and Christian apologists about Jesus' death and resurrection and analyzes their claims, interpretations, and challenges. People spanning the world, seeking intellectual freedom to question and explore aspects of religion, will learn from this comprehensive critical inquiry. Being a scholarly text, "their religious claims" must be respected and are the object of this investigation, not the abolition of their religious faith.

---

[10] Frame, *Evangelical Dictionary*, 57.

Acknowledgments

Virtually all books are a team project. There is no letter "I" in the word team. *The Resurrection and Its Apologetics: Jesus' Death and Burial* is no different.

This text was made possible through the efforts of many people. Alphabetically, I also wish to recognize the contribution of five external readers:

David Austin was a crucial external reader from Down Under (Australia). He is a rationalist and skeptic about the resurrection of Jesus. David has published several guest essays about the resurrection online at Patheos.com (A Tippling Philosopher). This Aussie made several important contributions. Noteworthy, he contributed ideas and textual matter to the content. In addition, David caught several errors that slipped multiple draft readings.

Professor Evan Fales, author of *Reading Sacred Texts* (GCRR Press), was a delightful surprise contributor to this project. He earned a Ph.D. in Philosophy at Temple University and taught at the University of Iowa before his retirement. His areas of interest include philosophy of religion, modal logic, epistemology, metaphysics, and philosophy of science. Initially, I reached out to Evan, requesting that he write a two-sentence endorsement of this text. No promise was made. He requested to examine the manuscript. To my pleasant surprise, he read the draft, sent me numerous editorial comments and recommendations on improving the final product, and identified some textual errors. Due to his input, the text has a smoother read, and several issues were clarified. Dr. Fales exemplifies the highest ideals of a true educator and professional.

Gerald Sigal is a member of the Orthodox Jewish community and a long-time Jewish counter-missionary. He has published numerous texts that serve as a "vaccination" against proselytizing *Klal Ysrael*. Several of his noteworthy texts include *The Jew and the Christian Missionary: A Jewish Response to Missionary Christianity* (1981); *Trinity Doctrine Error: A Jewish Analysis* (2006); *Isaiah 53: Who is the Servant?* (2007); *The Resurrection Fantasy: Reinventing Jesus* (2012); and *The Jewish Response to Missionary Christianity* (2015). I helped edit several of these works. With his forte in Torah and Jewish counter-missionary work, Gerry made suggestions that further enhanced the usefulness of *The Resurrection: The First Minimal Fact and the Tomb Burial.*

Darren M. Slade (Ph.D. and CEO of the Global Center for Religious Research) assisted in editing a prior stage of this text. He offered critical comments, enhancing the organization and readability of the text. He also co-authored with me "Dataset Examination of Authors of English Texts Written on the Topic of Resurrection: A Statistical Critique of Minimal Facts Apologetics." Darren is a gentleman and a consummate professional.

Vincent J. Torley earned a Ph.D. and MA in philosophy and teaches in Japan. He is also a Catholic who writes about apologetics. Vincent is a consummate, intellectually honest seeker of truth. He has contributed several noteworthy essays to TSZ (The Skeptical Zone). In 2018, he published a 30,000-word objective review of my earlier text, *The Resurrection: A Critical Inquiry* (2015). Vincent is a wordsmith—I am jealous. He smoothed out and added the human touch to my draft that several computer grammar-checks lacked. In effect, he assumed co-ownership of this project, seeking to produce an intellectually honest analysis of the topic. With virtually every email, Vincent sent numerous criticisms and suggestions. Significantly, Vincent assisted in reordering the flow of logic and enhanced the readability and clarity of the text. Therefore, if the text outline appears logical and sequential, it is in great measure due to his input. He often helped me realize that key ideas needed clarification and expansion, and he helped me identify discrepancies in the text to improve the initial manuscript. Additionally, he guided me in making those dreaded "cuts and deletions" to produce a reader-friendly and useful text. I hope his knowledge and insight regarding this topic have been richly rewarded.

Rabbi Moshe Shulman (Executive Director, Judaism's Answer) has been active in Kiruv Rechokim (Jewish Outreach), countering missionaries and teaching Torah and Chassidus worldwide for almost thirty years. He also appears on *Tenak Talk,* "Debunking Missionary Claims." Rabbi Shulman did not work on this project. However, he enormously contributed to the 2015 text, *The Resurrection: A Critical Inquiry*. Many important ideas that he previously suggested are in this text.

Another person who deserves special mention is Anthony Buzzard. Anthony is a prolific biblical Unitarian. In 2003, Anthony challenged me to prove that Jesus was not physically resurrected from the dead. Due to his challenge, I have published three texts on that topic:

The Resurrection: A Critical Inquiry (2015);
A Thematic Access-Oriented Bibliography of Jesus's Resurrection (2020); and now,
The Resurrection: The First Minimal Fact and The Tomb Burial (2024).

Bruce D. Chilton is a scholar of early Christianity and Judaism. He is the Bernard Iddings Bell Professor of Religion at Bard College, former Rector of the Church of St John the Evangelist, and formerly Lillian Claus Professor of New Testament at Yale University. He holds a Ph.D. in New Testament from Cambridge University. Bruce has widely published and founded two academic journals, the *Journal for the Study of the New Testament* and *The Bulletin for Biblical Research*. With his numerous time constraints, I am honored and grateful to have a distinguished scholar of his caliber agreeing to write the foreword to this text.

I also wish to acknowledge the efforts of Kelcey Norris, Christian Farren, and Savanah N. Landerholm for their work in copyediting, typesetting, and proofreading this book, as well as Abdullah Al Mahmud for his cover design and all the other members of the Wipf and Stock staff for their helpfulness throughout the production of this text.

Segue

The Christian mystique spans the entire world, exerting a profound influence even over the lives of people who do not consider themselves Christians. The fundamental tenet of orthodox Christianity is that following Jesus' crucifixion, God raised him from the dead in his original physical body.[1] Christian faith in the resurrection rests on this bedrock belief. Left unstated are some other doctrinal assumptions undergirding this belief:

- God exists as a single God and not a multiplicity of gods (Mark 12:29; 1 Tim. 2:5). Moreover, this single God, the Christian God, exists as a Trinity of three persons: the Father, the Son, and the Holy Spirit (Matt. 28:19; 2 Cor. 13:14; 1 Pet. 1:1–2). Other monotheistic religions, consequently, such as Islam and Judaism, are in error regarding the number of the Godhead.
- Jesus Christ is the only begotten Son of God (John 3:16).
- God the Son preexisted (John 1:1–18; 8:58; Col. 1:17; Rev. 22:13) as a member of a triune deity.
- "For in him [God the Son] all things were created: things in heaven and on earth, visible and invisible, whether thrones or powers or rulers or authorities; all things have been created through him and for him" (Col. 1:16; cf. John 1:3; Rom. 11:36; 1 Cor. 8:6).
- All of the following doctrines are heresies: Adoptionism, Albigensianism, Apollinarianism, Arianism, Docetism, Donatism, Dynamic Monarchianism, Ebionism, Eutychianism, Gnosticism, Kenoticism, Macedonianism, Modalism, Modalistic Monarchianism, Monophysitism, Monotheletism,

---

[1] Yet it was transformed into a living, powerful, and glorious body (cf. 1 Cor. 15:43; Phil. 3:21).

Nestorianism, Patripassianism, Pelagianism, Psilanthropism, Sabellianism, Socinianism, and Tritheism.
- The Christian Scriptures are the sole infallible rule of faith and practice (*sola Scriptura*).
- God's providence is in overall control of events (Rom. 8:28).
- Miracles are real, as are angels, demons, and the Christian concept of Satan.
- Every human has a corrupted nature, both a source of actual sin and somehow sinful in itself. Original sin is the result of a personal act by Adam (Gen. 3).
- Human beings are born depraved and cannot save themselves by their efforts (i.e., an Augustinian/Calvinist doctrine).
- Jesus is simultaneously one hundred percent (fully) God and one hundred percent (fully) human (two natures in one person; the Hypostatic Union).
- Jesus is God incarnate in human flesh.
- While Jesus lived among us, he chose to "conceal under a veil of flesh" his divine attributes (*kenosis*; Phil. 2:7).
- Jesus was conceived by the power of the Holy Spirit and born of the virgin Mary (Matt. 1:20–23; Luke 1:27–35).
- Jesus, who is also fully God, like any person, required food, clothing, and shelter as an infant, child, teenager, and adult.
- Jesus, who is fully God, decided to reveal himself to twelve original disciples, at least four of whom were fishermen, and most of whom were from the area of Galilee (Mark 1:16–20; 2:13–17; 3:13–19; Matt. 3:18–22; 10:1–4; Luke 5:1–11, 27–32; John 1:35–51).
- God the Father sent his only Son, Jesus, to die on the cross to atone for *all* humanity's sins (the redemption).
- Each person can only be saved through the death of Jesus Christ on the cross (which expiated the effects of Adam's sin), through personal repentance from sin and faith in Jesus as humanity's one and only Savior. The believer is made righteous, born again by the Holy Spirit, and is now a child of God. The believer who dies in a state of grace is assured an ultimate destiny in heaven.
- God the Father permitted his Son to be spit upon, assaulted, scourged, and crucified under the rule of Pontius Pilate by pagan

Roman soldiers (the humiliation) (Mark 15:15–24; Matt. 27:26–35; Luke 23:33; John 19:15–18).
- God the Father darkened the world for three hours, rent the temple's veil, and caused an earthquake to occur while Jesus, the Son of God who was fully God, was crucified on the cross (Mark 15:33, 38; Matt. 27:45–51; Luke 23:44–45).
- Jesus, who was fully God, died on the cross.
- Jesus, who was fully God, was buried for three days and three nights (Matt. 12:40; cf. 1 Cor. 15:4).
- After Jesus' death, the bodies of dead saints arose from their graves, walked into Jerusalem, and appeared before many people (Matt. 27:52–53). Afterward, God the Father raised Jesus from the dead (the resurrection and the exaltation) on the third day, according to the Scriptures (1 Cor. 15:4). God the Father then permitted a great earthquake to occur shortly before a group of women arrived at Jesus' tomb while an angelic being descended from heaven, moved a one- to two-ton stone, and frightened into a state of unconsciousness an unknown number of soldiers who were guarding the tomb (Matt. 28:1–15).
- God the Father took Jesus' corpse and transformed it into a living, powerful, and glorious body (cf. 1 Cor. 15).
- Jesus, who is fully God, transported himself through closed doors or walls, appearing and disappearing at will after his resurrection (Luke 24:31, 36; John 20:19, 26).
- Spanning forty days after Jesus' death, he appeared to his disciples, who became convinced that he had appeared to them and that he had risen from the dead, despite not recognizing him on multiple occasions (Acts 1:3; Matt. 28:17; Luke 24:15–31; John 20:15; 21:4).
- Jesus, the Son of God, invited his disciple Thomas to place his hand inside Jesus' flesh (John 20:27).
- Jesus, who was fully God, ascended into heaven (the ascension) and is now seated at the right hand of God the Father (Acts 1:10–11).
- Currently, Jesus is in heaven interceding for all believers (Rom. 8:34).

- God chose to permit Paul's letters, the Gospels, and Acts to appear conflicted and in error, and God also allowed the scribes to make errors while writing out their copies of the Christian Bible.[2]
- Jesus will come again to judge the living and the dead, and his kingdom will have no end.

Most, if not all, of these assertions, are matters of faith. In no way can these claims be proven. Often, these assertions are called a *mystery*. In reality, Christians have faith in a mystery. In the mind of many theists, God exists, and miracles not only can but do happen. This text contends that Jesus' bodily resurrection need not have been one of those miracles.

This text will reveal there are numerous *theistic* rationales that challenge the Christian explanation for Jesus' alleged bodily resurrection. Even if Jesus' body did rise from the dead by some supernatural agency (i.e., something not natural but able to affect nature), this event need not have been a miracle worked by God to vindicate Christian beliefs about Jesus. There also exist conjoined (i.e., containing two or more assumptions) *naturalistic* explanations for Jesus' disciples' faith in the resurrection. These conjoined explanations are: (1) less *ad hoc* (i.e., less contrived as they contain fewer additional suppositions) than the Christian hypothesis that Jesus rose from the dead; (2) more plausible; (3) more probable; (4) greater in their explanatory scope and power than the Christian hypothesis; and (5) disconfirmed by fewer accepted beliefs. Furthermore, this text asserts that there are, in fact, supernatural or conjoined naturalistic explanations that can better explain:

1. Why Jesus' body was missing after the crucifixion?
2. People repeatedly thought they saw him alive despite his earlier public execution.
3. Why numerous people may have come to believe in Jesus even to the point of being willing to suffer persecution and martyrdom.
4. How the early church managed to grow.

---

[2] Alter, *The Resurrection*, 10–12.

Caveat

For the sake of discussion, this text will accept thirteen basic ideas or tenets as a premise. The first three presumed facts relate directly to God. In contrast, the last ten facts are about Jesus specifically:

1. God exists.
2. The Hebrew Bible is God's revealed word.
3. Miracles (i.e., supernatural events) can and occur.
4. Jesus lived during the first century in Roman-occupied land that today is called Israel.
5. Jesus spoke Aramaic and Hebrew.
6. Jesus was a Galilean who preached and healed.
7. Jesus selected disciples, referred to as the Twelve.
8. Jesus confined his activity to Israel.
9. Jesus engaged in a controversy about the Second Temple.
10. Jesus was crucified outside Jerusalem by the Roman authorities.
11. Jesus was crucified and died on the cross during the rule of Pontius Pilate.
12. Jesus' followers continued as an identifiable movement after his death.
13. Some Jews openly resisted parts of the new movement (Gal. 1:13, 22; Phil. 3:6); and this persecution endured, at least, to a time near the end of Paul's career (2 Cor. 11:24; Gal. 5:11; 6:12; cf. Matt. 10:17; 23:34).

Habermas and Licona's First Minimal Fact: Jesus Died by Crucifixion—An Overview

Gary Habermas and Michael Licona's first Minimal Fact is that "Jesus died by crucifixion."[1] Their four-paragraph presentation approximates one full page. The single proof based on the Christian Bible is one sentence: "That Jesus was executed by crucifixion is recorded in all four gospels."[2] That is it! Then, in the following sentence, the authors add, "However, a number of non-Christian sources of the period report the event as well."[3] As their coup de grâce, they quote the highly critical scholar of the Jesus Seminar, John Dominic Crossan: "That he was crucified is as sure as anything historical can ever be."[4] Likewise, Gerd Lüdemann said, "Jesus' death as a consequence of crucifixion is indisputable."[5] Later, in chapter five of their work, they present "crucial medical evidence favoring Jesus' crucifixion" and refute the suggestion that he could have survived his execution (the swoon theory). In another work, Licona identifies three historical facts as part of "the historical bedrock," the first of which is Jesus' death by crucifixion.[6]

For the sake of discussion, this text accepts the assumption that a man named Jesus of Nazareth lived in Roman-occupied Palestine (known today as Israel) in the first century and that Pontius Pilate ordered him crucified. However, several authors challenge this mainstream accepted view, proposing that Jesus of Nazareth never existed. If Jesus did not exist, this crucifixion and subsequent resurrection did not happen. David Mills expresses this view in a humorous rhyme:

---

[1] Habermas and Licona, *Case for the Resurrection*, 48–49.
[2] Habermas and Licona, *Case for the Resurrection*, 49.
[3] Habermas and Licona, *Case for the Resurrection*, 49.
[4] Habermas and Licona, *Case for the Resurrection*, 49.
[5] Habermas and Licona, *Case for the Resurrection*, 50.
[6] Licona, *Resurrection of Jesus*, 468.

> Today some say that Jesus died,
> And still remains quite dead.
> But these who speak have surely lied.
> The real truth is, instead,
> That Jesus Christ, whose blood was spilled,
> Is no corpse, I insist!
> For how could someone have been killed,
> Who never did exist?[7]

The subject of the Christ Myth theory is beyond the scope of this text.[8] Some scholars have suggested that Jesus may have been a composite figure based on several people who existed in history at the time. An alternative option espoused by Muslim scholars is that Jesus was a historical individual, although not crucified. Instead, an individual who looked a lot like him (possibly Simon of Cyrene) volunteered to be crucified in his place. Others speculate that Jesus had a twin brother who suffered crucifixion. Leaving the Christ Myth, "compound character," and "lookalike" theories aside and following Habermas and Licona's lead (except for exploring the traditional Islamic opinion), this text will focus primarily on the Gospel narratives detailing Jesus' crucifixion, the reported death narratives, the removal of Jesus' body from the cross, and the preparation of his body for burial. First, the topic of death requires defining.

---

[7] Mills, *Atheist Universe*, 36.

[8] See Carrier, *On the Historicity of Jesus*; Doherty, *Jesus: Neither God Nor Man*; Lataster, *Questioning the Historicity of Jesus*; *There was No Jesus*; Loftus and Price, *Varieties of Jesus Mythicism*; Price, *The Case Against the Christ*; Price, *The Christ-Myth Theory*; Price, *The Incredible Shrinking Son of Man*; Wells, *Jesus Legend*; *The Jesus Myth*; and Zindler, *The Jesus the Jews Never Knew*.

2

Jesus Was Not Brain-Dead While On the Cross

> For everything there is a season, and a time for every matter under heaven: a time to be born, and a time to die; (Ecclesiastes 3:1–2, ESV)

Brain Death and Clinical Death

Proponents that God raised Jesus from death unequivocally state that Jesus' death is the indispensable prerequisite to his resurrection, the crowning proof that he is both God and the Messiah. Furthermore, proponents of Jesus' resurrection assert that there is overwhelming historical and factual evidence that Jesus died *and died literally on the cross*. In contrast, skeptics and detractors reject the notion that he died on the cross. Either way, without death, there cannot be a resurrection. This chapter is not concerned with the presumption that he died or did not die due to his crucifixion. To the contrary, chapter 2 presents information from the lens of skeptics that there is insufficient evidence that Jesus was brain-dead on the cross *before* the removal of his body or prior to his entombment.

Clinical death is often depicted by the cessation of breathing (chest does not move), cardiac arrest (no heartbeat or pulse), enlargement or lack of change of the pupils, and sometimes the release of the bladder or bowel. Other common signs of death are pallor mortis (paleness) which happens 15–120 minutes after death; livor mortis, a settling of the blood in the lower dependent portion of the body; and algor mortis, the reduction in body temperature. This cooling of the body after death proceeds at a definite rate, influenced by environmental temperature and protection of the body until matching ambient temperature, the temperature in a room, or the temperature surrounding an object, and rigor mortis, the stiffening of the limbs of the corpse (Latin *rigor*) and difficulty in moving or manipulating these limbs. All the Gospels validate Jesus' death on the cross by detailing his cessation of breathing (Mark 15:37–39; Matt. 27:50–54; Luke 23:46–47; and John 19:30–37).

In contrast to clinical death, *Mosby's Medical Dictionary*, ninth edition (2012), states *brain death* is:

> an irreversible form of unconsciousness characterized by a complete loss of brain function while the heart continues to beat. The legal definition of this condition varies from state to state. The usual clinical criteria for brain death include the absence of reflex activity, movements, and spontaneous respiration requiring mechanical ventilation or life support to continue any cardiac function. The pupils are dilated and fixed. Because hypothermia, anesthesia, poisoning, or drug intoxication may cause deep physiologic depression that resembles brain death these parameters must be within normal limits prior to testing. Diagnosis of brain death may require evaluating and demonstrating that electrical activity of the brain is absent on two electroencephalograms performed 12 to 24 hours apart. Brain death can be confirmed with electroencephalograms showing a complete lack of electrical activity (a flat line) or vascular perfusion studies showing a lack of blood flow to the brain.[1]

Consequently, John's record of a spear pierced into Jesus' side is highly significant because it could demonstrate a state of brain death evinced by his unresponsiveness to stimuli or pain. This affirmative demonstration focuses on three assumptions:

1. John's account is historical and not a theological invention.
2. The narrative did not fail to omit significant facts such as a reflex action to the piercing, an argument based from silence.
3. No drug was induced into Jesus while he was on the cross that could cause deep physiologic depression resembling brain death.

A conspiracy theory is that covert drug delivery to Jesus occurs while on the cross. This text rejects the idea of a conspiracy theory.

Given that the piercing episode was an invention, there is no unequivocal proof that Jesus was brain-dead while still on the cross. Furthermore, the Gospels do not report any additional neurological tests that proved Jesus was brain dead:

1. No pupil reaction to light
2. No response of the eyes to caloric (warm or cold) stimulation

---

[1] *Mosby's Medical Dictionary*, 239.

3. No jaw reflex (the jaw will react like the knee if hit with a reflex hammer)
4. No gag reflex (touching the back of the throat induces vomiting)

The existing technology of Jesus' day prohibited verification by an electroencephalogram. Finally, there is no absolute way of knowing whether a drug was induced into Jesus while he was on the cross.

However, as mentioned above, there is another possibility explaining how Jesus did not die while still on the cross. Jesus' body could have been taken down from the cross while he was unconscious, comatose (not perceptibly alive), or clinically dead, and he had not entered into a state of brain death. Later, he entered a state of brain death between removing his body from the cross and preparing the body for burial. In effect, Jesus would not have died on the cross but *after* being taken down. Therefore, his death resulted from his beatings, scourging, and crucifixion.

Richard Carrier's literature review confirms that being mistaken for dead is not impossible. Ancient accounts of misdiagnosed deaths exist. Pliny the Elder, writing in the 60s and 70s CE, collected several examples in his *Natural History* (7.176–79). He reports people thought dead, observed as dead all through their funeral, and on the pyre, ready to be set aflame, but who walked away nonetheless. This fact demonstrates that arguments about Roman soldiers' special skills confirming death are moot if correct. Another presumably fatal account that includes a wound that would seem almost undoubtedly fatal was a cutthroat, 7.176. Carrier adds that Alexander the Great experienced an impaling by a spear, which punctured one of his lungs, yet he recovered.[2]

Indeed, this was more common than imagined before the twentieth century, sometimes causing widespread hysteria. Jan Bondeson's *Buried Alive: The Terrifying History of Our Most Primal Fear* details numerous examples. Even earlier, in 1895, the physician J. C. Ouseley wrote that as many as 2,700 people were buried each year prematurely in England and Wales. However, others estimated the figure to be closer to 800.[3] Furthermore, contemporary accounts of misdiagnosed deaths exist (internet), proving that even medical experts can be in error.

---

[2] Carrier, "How Do We Know He was Dead?"
[3] Carrier, "How Do We Know He was Dead?"

More than fifty years after the neurological determination of death—also known as "brain death"—was admitted as a new criterion of death.[4] Debates still focus on one question: Is brain death a good criterion for determining death?[5] Controversy about determining death is worldwide. For example, one investigation collected and reviewed official national brain death/death neurologic condition (BD/DNC) protocols from 136 contacts worldwide between January 2018 and April 2019. "Conclusions: There is considerable variability in BD/DNC determination protocols around the world."[6] Verheijde et al., writing in the *Journal of Religion and Health,* say, "The conception and the determination of brain death continue to raise scientific, legal, philosophical, and religious controversies."[7] For example, is the separation of the soul from the human body necessitated for the occurrence of brain death?[8] If so:

1. How did the soul of Jesus separate from the body of Jesus?
2. Where did the soul of Jesus go after separating from the body?
3. How can the death of Jesus be substantiated?

Adding to the confusion, Nair-Collins and Miller write, "Several scholars argue that in cases of 'brain death', the body or organism remains alive, but the person (as distinct from the organism) has died due to irreversible unconsciousness."[9] Writing earlier, Mack Drake and colleagues add:

> Although the medical and legal concepts of brain death are generally accepted, establishing the diagnosis is not simple and must be performed accurately. The details of how to diagnose brain death have been codified in guidelines by panels of experts; however, precision in the brain death examination varies, and skepticism has been expressed in the lay literature about the accuracy of brain death determination.[10]

---

[4] Beecher, *"A Definition of Irreversible Coma,"* 337–40.
[5] Pérez, "Brain Death Debates."
[6] Lewis, "Determination of Death by Neurologic Criteria," 299.
[7] Verheijde, et al., "Neuroscience and Brain Death Controversies,"1745.
[8] Verheijde, et al., "Neuroscience and Brain Death Controversies,"1745.
[9] Nair-Collins and Miller, "Do the 'Brain Dead' Merely Appear," 747.
[10] Drake, et al, "Brain Death"; Cf. Geer et al, "Variability of Brain Death," 284–89; Edlow and Kinney, "Defining the Boundary Between Life and Death," 3–5.

Was Jesus Brain Dead on the Cross: A Debate

In the eyes of skeptics, the relevance is that medical-journal articles provide support for the hypothesis that Jesus died on the cross lack evidentiary proof. Table 1 presents a terse analysis of the augments that Jesus was *not* brain dead before his body was removed from the cross or just before its burial preparation. Arguments by proponents of Jesus' death on the cross appear in the left column. This text supports the opinion that Jesus died on the cross as a collective result of his beating, scourging, and crucifixion. Nonetheless, presenting the arguments from both sides of the aisle is essential (see Table 2-1).

Table 2-1: Did Jesus Die While on the Cross?

Pro-Jesus' Death While on the Cross		Con-Jesus' Death While on the Cross	
Jesus' Death Predicted in the Hebrew Bible		*Jesus' Death Was Not Predicted in the Hebrew Bible*	
Ps. 22:16 [AV]	Jesus' hands and feet were "pierced."	Ps 22:16 [AV]	The AV translation "they pierced my hands and feet" is not based on the standard Masoretic Text: The word translated as "pierced" should read "lion." Therefore, the phrase should read as "like a lion [they maul], my hands and feet" (NJPS).
Isa. 53:5–10	**The "Suffering Servant" is Jesus**	Isa. 53:5–10	
		1. The suffering servant is Israel (collectively or a righteous remnant).	

2. In vv. 5–8, the speaker [is the Gentile nations] confesses that they were the cause of the servant's distress and are more deserving of his afflictions than he was.

3. Jesus' actions contradict Isa 53:7. He did *not* remain dumb or silent (Matt. 26:39; 27:46; John 18: 6, 8, 20, 23, 34, 36–37).

4. Isa. 53:8 is contradicted by the Hebrew Bible. There is no indication that Jesus' suffering was to serve as atonement for humanity's sins.

5. Isa. 53:9 is contradicted by Jesus' actions. He acted violently (Mark 11:15–16; Matt. 21:12) and advocated violence (Luke 19:27).

6. Isa. 53:10 is contradicted by Jesus' words. He did not willingly offer himself as a sacrifice (Mark 15:34; Matt. 27:46).

7. Isa. 53:10 is contradicted by Jesus' life. Jesus did not see his seed = *zer'a* (biological children, not spiritual children such as the church) during his life. In Scripture, *zer'a* always means a biological or physical offspring.

Dan. 9:26	The seventy weeks.	Dan. 9:26
		1. The punctuation mark *a'tnach* is ignored in Christian translation.
		2. The AV omits the definite article in Dan. 9:26, "And after *the* three score and two weeks…"
		3. The words *vayn lo* are incorrectly translated in the AV as "but not for himself."
		4. The Christian chronology of Nehemiah is incorrect.
Zech. 12:10	Portrays Jesus.	Zech. 12:10[11]
		1. The predominant perspective on Zechariah 12:10 among Jewish commentators described the mourning over those Jews slain while defending the kingdom of Judah and the city of Jerusalem. Those who fell in the battle were described as having been *thrust through* with the swords and spears of soldiers from the attacking nations. In other words, this verse describes a historical event from the biblical times around which written. Rashi wrote: "And they shall look to Me to complain about those of them whom the nations thrust through and slew during their exile." An alternative explanation is that this text describes a future event.
		2. After Jesus' death, the Jewish leadership still demonstrated no remorse. That is, on Saturday, they went to Pilate, calling Jesus a "deceiver" and worried that his disciples might come and steal his body.

---

[11] See Alter, *The Resurrection*, 188–206.

	3. The Distorted Historical Context of Zechariah 12: Israel is saved.
	4. The Distorted Historical Context of Zechariah 12: Prophetic fulfillment.
	5. The Distorted and Mistranslated Subjects of "I" in Zechariah 12:10.
	6. The Distorted and Mistranslated Subjects of "*him*" in Zechariah 12:10.
	7. The Figurative Subject of "*him*" in Zechariah 12:10.
	8. The Distorted and Understood *pronoun* "*him*" in Zechariah 12:10.
	9. Zechariah 12: Contradictory to the Olivet Discourse.

Jesus' Death by Crucifixion: *Rationale*	*Jesus' Death by Crucifixion:* *Doubted/Rejected*
1. Jesus had no sleep the night before being crucified.	1. The Jewish-Palestinian milieu *refutes* the argument that Jesus had no sleep the night before being crucified.
	a. A night inquest/ trial on the first evening of Passover held by the chief priests and scribes challenges the historicity and veracity of the Gospel accounts.
	b. The conflicting details of the inquest/trial challenges the historicity and veracity of the Gospel accounts.
2. Jesus was beaten, scourged, and whipped.	2. Jesus was *not* beaten, scourged, and whipped *enough* to facilitate his rapid demise on the cross (a la Mel Gibson's *The Passion*).

Jesus Was Not Brain-Dead 11

	a. The degree of scourging is unknown and subject to speculation.
	b. The time of Jesus' scourging is unknown and subject to speculation.
	c. The number of times Jesus is stricken is unknown and subject to speculation.
	d. The specific implements employed on Jesus during his scourging are unknown and subject to speculation.
	e. The specific type and severity of wounds or injuries resulting from the scourging are unknown and subject to speculation.
	f. Perhaps Pilate secretly ordered that he wanted a "mild" scourging because (1) he believed that Jesus was innocent or (2) to incense the chief priests.
3. Jesus collapsed while carrying his cross.	3. Jesus did *not* collapse while carrying his cross.
	a. This presumed episode appears in Mark 15:21 and Matthew 27:32. However, if Matthew's account solely centers on Mark, then there is only one source and no multiple attestation.
	b. Neither Gospel reports that Jesus collapsed while carrying the cross.
	c. No reason is given why the Romans compelled Simon the Cyrene to bear Jesus' cross. Perhaps, Jesus was just walking too slowly for their needs.

4. Jesus bled because "the soldiers platted a crown of thorns, and put it on his head" (John 19:2).	4. Jesus did *not* bleed because of the thorns on his head.
	a. Only John mentioned Jesus' head platted with a crown of thorns. Therefore, this claim does *not* fulfill the criterion of multiple attestations.
	b. There is *no* mention that Jesus' head was bleeding because of a crown of thorns.
	c. *No* facts detail how the thorns were placed on Jesus' head.
	d. There is *no* description of the alleged type of thorns placed on Jesus' head.
5. Jesus was crucified (presumably nailed to a cross by his hands).	5. Jesus was *not* nailed to a cross by his hands.[12]
a. John 20:25 implies the nailing of Jesus' hands. b. John 20:27 implies the nailing of Jesus' hands.	a. It is speculated that "the nailing and spearing were derived by John from Psalm 22:17 (16 AV) and Zechariah 12:10 under the erroneous supposition that those passages were prophetically describing the crucifixion of Jesus and under the further assumption that the crucifixion procedures followed those prophecies meticulously.

---

[12] See also, Slade, "The History and Philosophy of Depicting a Violently Crucified Christ," 117–54.

b. A scholarly opinion exists that Jesus' hands did not get nailed. Instead, he was fastened or tied with a rope. Recently, Gunnar Samuelsson wrote an extensive thesis (University of Gothenburg) and published *Crucifixion in Antiquity*. He investigated the philological aspects of how ancient Greek, Latin, Hebrew, and Aramaic texts, including the New Testament, depicted the practice of punishment by crucifixion. Mohr Siebeck, his publisher, summarized: "The accounts of the death of Jesus are strikingly sparse. Their chief contribution is usage of the unclear terminology in question. Over-interpretation, and probably even pure imagination, have afflicted nearly every dictionary that deals with the terms related to crucifixion as well as scholarly depictions of what happened on Calvary. The immense knowledge of the punishment of crucifixion in general, and the execution of Jesus in particular, cannot be supported by the studied texts."

c. The two pilgrims on the road to Emmaus did not recognize Jesus despite the supposed nail wounds on his hands. This recognition is predictable since Luke 24:30 recorded that Jesus broke bread, blessed it, and handed it to the two travelers.

6. Jesus was crucified (presumably nailed to a cross by his feet).	6. Jesus was *not* nailed to a cross by his feet.
	a. It is speculated that John derived the nailing and spearing from Psalm 22:17 (16 AV) and Zechariah 12:10 under the erroneous supposition that those passages were prophetic.
	b. Mohr Siebeck, the publisher of Gunnar Samuelsson's previously mentioned book, summarizes that "The New Testament is not spared from this terminological ambiguity. The accounts of the death of Jesus are strikingly sparse. Their chief contribution is the usage of the unclear terminology in question. Over-interpretation, and probably even pure imagination, have afflicted nearly every dictionary that deals with the terms related to crucifixion as well as scholarly depictions of what happened on Calvary. The immense knowledge of the punishment of crucifixion in general, and the execution of Jesus in particular, cannot be supported by the studied texts."
	c. Out of the thousands of crucified victims—only one artifact has been discovered; the crucified man from Giv'at ha-Mivtar.[13]
	d. In the Gospel of Matthew (28:8), the women grasped Jesus' feet and worshipped him without mention of his presumed feet wounds.
	e. The two pilgrims on the road to Emmaus did not recognize Jesus despite the supposed nail wounds to his feet.

---

[13] Tzaferis, "Crucifixion," 44–53.

	f. Luke 24:34–43 reports Jesus appearing before the Eleven gathered in Jerusalem. During this encounter, Jesus stated in verse 39: "See my hands and my feet, that it is I myself. Touch me, and see. For a spirit does not have flesh and bones as you see that I have" (ESV). This verse does not necessarily support the idea that Jesus' feet experienced piercing. Perhaps Luke was attempting to substantiate the mere physicality of Jesus' resurrection.
7. Jesus, suspended from the cross from 9:00 a.m. to approximately 3:00 p.m.	7. Jesus, suspended from the cross from 9:00 a.m. (Mark 15:25) to approximately 3:00 p.m., probably would *not* result in his death.
	a. Presumably, Jesus underwent a *typical* crucifixion. However, Jesus' crucifixion lasted approximately six hours, whereas crucifixions lasted three to six days before death. Supposedly this would mean that Jesus had an *excellent* chance of being alive when being removed from the cross.
	b. Pilate was amazed that Jesus died after such a brief period on the cross.
	c. Jesus' "cross mates" were still alive when he supposedly expired.
	d. Being mistaken for dead is possible.
	1) Josephus watched one of the three crucifixion victims survive (*Life of Flavius Josephus* § 420–21).

	2) History provides examples of people temporarily surviving after having the most horrible things happen to their bodies. The Coast Guard WWII hero Douglas Munro was pierced a dozen times by Japanese rifle bullets. Nevertheless, he continued to drive his landing boat, dying only after completing his mission—receiving the Medal of Honor posthumously.
	3) Jan Bondeson's book, *Buried Alive: The Terrifying History of Our Most Primal Fear*, provides numerous details of ancient and contemporary mistakes concerning living people assumed to have been dead.
8. The fact that the Roman soldier did *not* break Jesus' legs, as they did to the other two crucified criminals (John 19:31–33), means that the soldier was sure that Jesus was dead.	8. Jesus' legs were *not* broken because he was presumed dead, whereas the legs of his "cross mates" were.
	a. The Roman soldiers directly violated their orders. Pilate ordered that the Roman soldiers break the legs of the crucified. Nonetheless, these soldiers did *not* execute this specific command in the case of Jesus. It is unreasonable to suppose that the Roman soldiers would disregard their orders and potentially subject themselves to severe punishment for disobedience, punishment dictated by Roman military law. The Roman military did not tolerate insubordination and enforced disciple meticulously and scrupulously.

Jesus Was Not Brain-Dead 17

	b. John reported that a Roman soldier pierced Jesus' side with a spear rather than break his legs on the cross, not to violate the prohibition found in Exodus 12:46 about breaking the bones of the Passover lamb. Therefore, the incorporation of this account for theological reasons.
9. Jesus was pierced with a spear in his side (John 19:36–37).	9. The pierced side was an apologetic and theological invention.
	a. Skeptics demand evidence that Jesus received a stabbing while suspended from the cross.
	b. Only John directly mentioned Jesus received a spearing in the side. Therefore, this text does not fulfill the criterion of multiple attestations or that of God's instructions.
	c. Perhaps John's account of Jesus being speared was written as an apologetic that Jesus died.
	d. Perhaps the piercing episode was incorporated for theological reasons (Isa. 53 or Zech. 12:10): [36] For these things took place that the Scripture might be fulfilled: "Not one of his bones will be broken." [37] And again another Scripture says, "They will look on him whom they have pierced" (John 19: 36–37, ESV).
	e. Perhaps the piercing episode was incorporated for theological reasons. A Roman soldier pierced Jesus' side with a spear rather than break his legs on the cross to not violate the prohibition found in Exodus 12:46 about breaking the bones of the Passover lamb.

	f. Perhaps John's narratives in 20:20 and 20:27 were written to corroborate themselves with details that seemingly created an illusion that the piercing side episode was historical. That is, John attempted to demonstrate that the risen Jesus and the Jesus crucified days earlier were the same (a "designed coincidence").
	g. Given that Jesus received a stabbing, it is unknown with what type of spear.
	h. Given that Jesus received a stabbing, unknown are any details describing the spear's tip.
	i. Given that Jesus receives a stabbing, it cannot be known if the spear was shoved deeply into Jesus' side instead of being a poke to see if he would react to painful stimuli.
10. Blood and water came out of Jesus' side after being pierced.	10. Blood and water coming out of Jesus' side after being pierced was a theological invention and could *not* be confirmed (unverifiable).
	a. Perhaps John wrote the piercing episode in conjunction with the flowing blood and water to serve as a symbol: (1) Spirit, which flowed forth from the dead Jesus, (2) the duality of his actions, his baptism of water and his baptism of blood, (3) a new and higher life passes into humanity, (4) the life-giving water that flowed from Ezekiel's new Temple (Ezek. 47:1–2), (5) the dispensation of the Temple, and (6) *Leviticus Rabbah*, 15 (115c), contains the information that man is made of half water, half of blood: if he is virtuous, the two elements are in equilibrium.

	b. There is no means to prove that the fluid that flowed from Jesus' body was 100 percent water. "The source of the water could have been from pleural fluid (that can look like water), which accumulated in the chest cavity."[14]
	c. How could John know blood and water exited Jesus' body?
	d. Raymond Brown (*The Death of the Messiah*) criticizes often-cited medical analyses of Jesus' death. He concludes: "In my judgement the major defect of most of the studies I have reported on thus far is that they were written by doctors who did not stick to their trade and let a literalist understanding of the Gospel accounts influence their judgements." For example, Luke reported that Jesus' "sweat became like blood." Here, Luke is not describing a real medical condition (hematidrosis); rather he is employing the use of a metaphor.[15]

Jesus was confirmed dead when taken down from the cross.	*Jesus was not confirmed brain dead when taken down from the cross.*
1. The centurion	1. The centurion
	a. Is the centurion's report historical? His final words appear to be embellished over time in the various gospels.

---

[14] Lavoie, *Resurrected*, 164.
[15] Brown, *Death of the Messiah*, 2:1092.

	b. The Gospels admit (see Mark 15:39 and John 19:33) that those attending Jesus' crucifixion assumed that he was dead before they even took him down from the cross and had a chance to examine his body. Consequently, detractors question how Jesus' brain death could be determined by the centurion from a distance of quite possibly a few yards.
	c. The narratives do not explain how the centurion confirmed that Jesus was brain dead.
2. The other Roman soldiers: a. Jesus could not have survived crucifixion. Roman procedures were meticulous in eliminating that possibility. Roman law even laid the death penalty on any soldier who let a capital prisoner escape in any way, including bungling a crucifixion. It was never done.	2. The other Roman soldiers
	a. They admit (see Mark 15:39 and John 19:33) that those attending the crucifixion assumed that Jesus was dead before they even took him down from the cross and had a chance to examine his body. Consequently, detractors question how the Roman soldiers could determine that Jesus was brain dead from a distance of quite possibly a few yards.
b. Professional Roman soldiers crucified Jesus, who performed crucifixions regularly and knew what they were doing. Furthermore, they had more experience with death than the average citizen due to their profession. Consequently, the signs of death would have been readily identifiable.	b. The narratives do *not* explain how the Roman soldiers confirmed that Jesus was brain dead while he hung from the cross.
c. Lastly, if they were unsure, why would they not have broken Jesus' legs as they did to the others crucified alongside him? Indeed, they would have done so if they were even a little uncertain.	c. It cannot be argued that the Roman soldiers thought that Jesus was already dead and, therefore, that breaking his legs was unnecessary. The certainty that Jesus was already dead did not exist in the soldiers' minds except by the centurion mentioned in Mark 15:39 and Luke 23:47.

	d. If the soldiers believed Jesus was dead, why did a soldier pierce his side with a spear? The only conceivable motives for doing so would be an act of brutality and cruelty or to make sure that Jesus was dead. Given that the Roman soldier doubted Jesus' death, the most effective means of guaranteeing his demise was obeying his superior's order and breaking the legs.
	e. Truth is sometimes stranger than fiction. It is a fallacious argument that the Roman soldiers: (1) knew what they were doing and (2) would have known when someone was dead. The Gospels do *not* provide information regarding the soldiers' age, battle experience, participation in previous crucifixions, or the number of dead bodies they had witnessed. Therefore, these soldiers may have been inexperienced or had limited experience with dead bodies.
3. John, an eyewitness, certified that he saw blood and water from Jesus' pierced side (John 19:34–35). This blood and water show that Jesus' lungs had collapsed, and he had died of asphyxiation.	3. There is *no* proof that John saw blood and water exiting Jesus' pierced side (John 19:34–35).
	a. It is dubious that John would be able to see any water oozing from Jesus assuming that he was already covered with blood from his prior scourging.
	b. It is dubious that the Roman soldiers would permit John or anyone else to get close enough to examine the crucified body.
	c. The narratives do *not* explain how John confirmed that Jesus was brain-dead.

4. The witnesses	4. The witnesses provide *no* support that Jesus died on the cross before being taken down.
	a. Luke 23:48 reports that those attending Jesus' crucifixion assumed that he was dead before they even took him down from the cross and had a chance to examine his body. Consequently, detractors question how a man's brain death could be determined from a distance of quite possibly a few yards. Was their interpretation based on the centurion's reactions?
	b. Did Matthew 27:54 imply that "they that were with him," along with the centurion, actually knew that Jesus was truly dead, or were they reacting to the (1) darkness over the land, (2) renting of the Temple's veil, (3) an earthquake, and (4) opening of the graves and the coming out the saints that slept?
	c. The narratives do *not* explain how the witnesses confirmed that Jesus was brain dead while still on the cross.
5. Pilate's inquiry	5. Pilate's inquiry *partially* supports the hypothesis that Jesus did not die on the cross.
	a. Mark 15:44 reported: "Pilate was surprised to hear that he should have already died. And summoning the centurion, he asked him whether he was already dead" (ESV).
	b. Matthew, Luke, and John omit any reference to Pilate's doubt since their agenda requires Jesus' death.

6. Taken down from the cross.
   a. Joseph
   b. Nicodemus
   c. Servants
   d. Roman soldiers?
 	
Jesus was confirmed dead prior to and during his entombment.
	6. Taken down from the cross.

	a. Joseph
	1) It is *unknown* if Joseph of Arimathea lowered Jesus' body from the cross. Perhaps he employed unidentified servants.
	2) It is *unknown* if Joseph of Arimathea could lower Jesus' body from the cross (no age or physical description).
	3) However, Craig suggests that the taking down from the cross of Jesus' body "does not necessitate that Joseph himself ascended the ladder and pulled out the nails. The Romans may have taken down the body for him."[16]
	b. Nicodemus
	1) The historicity and veracity of Nicodemus are *not* multi-attested.
	2) It is *unknown* if Nicodemus helped to lower Jesus from the cross.
	3) It is *unknown* if Nicodemus could physically lower Jesus' body from the cross (no age or physical description).

---

[16] Craig, *Assessing the New Testament Evidence*, 177.

c. Servants

1) It is *unknown* if any of Joseph of Arimathea's servants helped to lower Jesus from the cross. However, Mark 16:6 narrated that a person described as a young man, who was perhaps an angel, stated to the three women who had arrived at the empty tomb: "And he said to them, "Do not be alarmed. You seek Jesus of Nazareth, who was crucified. He has risen; he is not here. See the place where they laid him" (ESV). Thus, Mark's narrative declared that "more" than one person (i.e., they) helped to place Jesus' body in the tomb and possibly assisted in taking it down from the cross.

2) It is *unknown* if Joseph of Arimathea's servants were present while removing Jesus from the cross.

d. Roman soldiers?

1) According to the Gospels, it is *unknown* if any Roman soldiers helped lower Jesus from the cross.

2) According to the Gospels, whether Roman soldiers observed Jesus' body lowered from the cross is unknown.

3) However, Acts 13:27–29 claimed that Jesus' body was taken down from the cross by those who crucified him.

Jesus was brain-dead prior to or during his burial.	*Jesus was not confirmed brain dead prior to or during his burial.*

1. His body was handled/prepared for burial.
    a. Joseph
    b. Nicodemus
    c. Servants
	1. His body was handled/prepared for burial.

	a. Joseph
	1) Perhaps the entire body preparation and burial narrative was an invention (i.e., versus dumping Jesus' body in a ditch) to protect Jesus' honor or provide proof that he was, in fact, dead.
	2) Presumably, if Joseph handled or prepared the body (wrapped the body in a cloth or linen shroud), he would know if Jesus was dead unless he was part of a conspiracy (rejected by this text).
	b. Nicodemus
	1) Perhaps the entire body preparation and burial narrative was an *invention* (i.e., versus Jesus' body dumped in a ditch) to protect Jesus' honor or to provide proof that he was, in fact, dead.
	2) Perhaps Nicodemus is an *invention*. His name is not multi-attested.
	3) If Nicodemus helped Joseph to handle or prepare the body (wrapping the body in a cloth or linen shroud), he would know if Jesus was dead unless he was part of a conspiracy.

	c. Servants
	1) Perhaps the entire body preparation and burial narrative was an *invention* (i.e., dumping Jesus' body in a ditch) to protect Jesus' honor or to provide proof that he was dead.
	2) If any servants helped handle/prepare the body (wrapping it in a cloth or linen shroud), they would know if Jesus was dead unless they were part of a conspiracy.
2. Jesus' body preparation was in a tomb with one hundred pounds of spices.	2. Jesus' burial in a tomb with one hundred pounds of spices was a legendary embellishment/invention.
	a. The historicity and veracity of Nicodemus' purchase of the one hundred pounds of "myrrh and aloes" are *not* multi-attested.
	b. Contrary to John's assertion, packing bodies in spices was *not* a Jewish practice. Instead, this was an Egyptian custom. Perhaps the mention of spices was an invention meant to link the burial of Jesus with that of Israel (Jacob) and Joseph (Gen. 50:2, 26).
	c. The historicity and veracity of Nicodemus' purchase of the one hundred pounds of "myrrh and aloes" sounds like legendary embellishment. C. H. Dodd's comment on the quantity of spices merits consideration: "It seems likely that the somewhat extravagant estimate of the weight of myrrh and aloes provided is a touch introduced by the evangelist, who perhaps is somewhat addicted to numbers, especially large numbers (153 fishes—if the appendix is by the same author)."[17]

---

[17] Dodd, *Historical Tradition*, 139n1.

Jesus Was Not Brain-Dead 27

	d. Perhaps the author of John wrote part or all of his burial account based on Gamaliel the Elder (i.e., a copycat) as an attempt at one-upmanship.
	e. Assuming that John was aware of the tradition of the wise men bringing gifts to the young Jesus, verse 39 was composed as a literary device (illusion) creating the form of a literary bookend.
Jesus had no food or water for approximately twelve hours (since his last meal) between the Last Supper and his crucifixion.	**Presumably, Jesus would n o t have died if he had received no food or water for approximately twelve hours (since his last meal) and after previously having been severely scourged and crucified.**
Jesus had no medical treatment before, during, or after being scourged and crucified.	**Conspiracy theorists postulate that Jesus received medical treatment before, during, or after being beaten, scourged, and crucified.**
	a. Jesus probably would have died if he did not receive adequate medical assistance before, during, or thirty-six hours after having been scourged and crucified.
	b. Those advocating a conspiracy [Rejected by this text] posit that Jesus received some drug on the cross. Specifically, there was a mysterious sponge that contained vinegar which was given to Jesus just before he allegedly "gives up the ghost" (see Mark 15:36; Matt. 27:48; John 19:29).

c. Conspiracy theorists challenge; how could any Gospel writers know the contents of this mysterious sponge? Each writer claimed it was vinegar. Again, how could they know that it was vinegar? Presuming that the Gospel writers witnessed Jesus' crucifixion (and there is a good reason not to accept this position), would they have gone up to the person who put the sponge to Jesus' lips and asked what was in the sponge? Perhaps the sponge was filled with vinegar, but that does not preclude it from being filled with other substances. Conspiracy theorists suggest there was lacing of this mysterious sponge with opium. Opium was available in Judea in those days, and Jesus could very easily have procured it.

Source: Modified from Alter, The Resurrection: A Critical Inquiry, 252–65.

Conclusion

Christian theology is unequivocal: Jesus died on the cross as a cumulative result of the beatings, scourging, and crucifixion. Detractors reject the belief that Jesus died on the cross, and skeptics require convincing evidence. Detractors and skeptics offer arguments supporting their rationale that continue evading Christian comprehension. *Brain death* is a contemporary topic that lacks consensus. This chapter provides readers with partial arguments rejecting the opinion that Jesus experienced brain death on the cross. Readers must determine if they accept those arguments. The following chapters will continue this investigation.

3

Problems with the Gospels and Acts

A host of problems confront the critical reader regarding the events before, during, and immediately following Jesus' execution, as recorded in the Gospel narratives and the Acts of the Apostles.

Problems with the Passion Narratives

1. There exist two different timelines of Jesus' crucifixion: Was it at 9 a.m. or noon?[1]

2. There are differing accounts of what happened at the crucifixion, with several omitting or contradicting crucial details found in other narratives: (1) John overlooked the presence of the chief priests at the cross; (2) the conversation of the thieves on the cross differs between the various Gospels; (3) John 20:17—in which the risen Jesus tells Mary Magdalene that he has not yet ascended to his Father—contradicts Luke 23:43—in which the dying Jesus assures the Good Thief, "Today, you will be with me in Paradise"; (4) there are significant omissions from Luke's narrative when compared to Matthew's such as in Matthew 28:17 is the doubting disciples at a mountain in Galilee; (5) the last words attributed to Jesus, while on the cross, are reported differently by the Evangelists; (6) Jesus dies *after* he uttered his last words? (compare Luke 23:46 and John 19:30 with Mark 15:34, 37 and Matt. 27:46, 50); (7) Jesus' sayings on the cross were most likely ahistorical and appear to have been written to suit a theological agenda;[2] (8) the three hours of darkness are also likely ahistorical, written for a theological purpose and at odds with scientific knowledge about the duration of solar eclipses.

---

[1] Alter, *The Resurrection*, 112–14.
[2] Lüdemann, *Jesus' Resurrection: Fact or Figment?*, 61.

(9) There are many contradictory narratives about the environment, like the tearing of the temple's veil[3]; (10) there are several highly dubious details, especially in Matthew, regarding the first earthquake[4]; (11) the alleged episode of the resurrected saints is found only in Matthew and its problematic timeline (did the saints rise on Friday or Sunday?) raises legitimate doubts about its historicity; (12) the actions of the Roman soldiers at the cross evolve over time in the Gospel narratives; (13) there are differing and contradictory accounts of the actions taken by Jesus' female followers, such as their identities, arrival time at the cross and purpose for showing up;[5] (14) the theological agenda of John regarding "the beloved disciple" (Several scholars discuss the motives of John regarding "the beloved disciple," i.e., he can serve as a prototype of faith and the ideal disciple and witness.[6]); (15) the theological rationale for Jesus' bones not being broken, an event which is recorded only in John; (16) the impossibility of knowing for a fact that none of his bones were broken, up to and during his crucifixion (who checked the wrist bones and rib bones?); (17) the theological rationale for the blood and water flowing from Jesus' side, an episode that likewise only appears in John 19:18.

The crucifixion narratives appear written for theological reasons: Zechariah 12 and Psalm 22:16 [AV] are quoted along with the spearing episode and appear only in John to fulfill Psalm 22, Isaiah 53, and Zechariah 12:10. However, one should not lose sight of the many similarities between the Gospels. This fact should not be surprising since Mark's Gospel was a template for Matthew and Luke, as described below.

There are also problems with the Gospel narratives of the removal of Jesus' body and its preparation:

1. Joseph of Arimathea's request for the body:
   a. There are differing accounts in the Gospels marred by omissions, contradictions, and improbabilities with the timeline for requesting Jesus' body and the logistics of that request.

---

[3] Alter, *The Resurrection*, 160–64.
[4] Alter, *The Resurrection*, 143–46.
[5] Alter, *The Resurrection*, 316–24.
[6] Bauckham, *Jesus and the Eyewitnesses*, 550–59; *The Testimony of the Beloved Disciple*, 73–91; Brown, *The Community of the Beloved Disciple*, 82–86.

Pilate's response to the Jewish leaders' request is historically dubious.

Theological motivations exist for inventing the character of Joseph of Arimathea. He appears to have evolved in the various Gospel narratives. This theological agenda in the Gospel accounts also contains an anti-Jewish motif. What is more, the Gospels do not mention what transpired with the bodies of the thieves.[7]

2. Removal and preparation of the body:
   a. Confusion exists as to who removed Jesus' body (Joseph of Arimathea, Joseph and Nicodemus, servants, or Romans) and when that removal occurs (Wednesday, Thursday, or Friday).
   b. The Gospel accounts of the purchased linen and spices and the preparation of Jesus' body contain many doubtful and improbable details. Were the spices purchased before the start of the Sabbath or at the end of the Sabbath?[8]

Conclusion

Collectively, the issues specified above raise doubts as to whether the Gospel narratives accurately detail the events immediately before, at the moment, and following Jesus' death. Consequently, the Gospel narratives (and Acts 13:28–29) only provide information about the details of Jesus' death which is *low confidence* at best. The Office of the Director of National Intelligence defines the term as follows:

Confidence in the Sources Supporting Judgments: Confidence levels provide assessments of the quality and quantity of the source information that supports judgments.

Low confidence generally means that the information's credibility and/or plausibility is uncertain, that the information is too fragmented or poorly corroborated to make solid analytic inferences, or that reliability of the sources is questionable.[9]

---

[7] Alter, *The Resurrection*, 207–27.
[8] Alter, *The Resurrection*, 228–48.
[9] The Office of the Director of National Intelligence, "Background to 'Assessing Russian Activities,'" 13.

Problems with Josephus

What about the number of early Christian and non-Christian sources that discuss this event? Josephus (ca. 37–100 CE.), a famous Jewish historian, wrote his *Jewish Antiquities* (*AJ*) in the thirteenth year of the reign of the Roman emperor Flavius Domitian, around 93 or 94 CE.[1] It is critical to highlight that he wrote his account almost sixty years after Jesus had died. The value of this passage is only as great as the likelihood of its being authentic—a matter of dispute. Three extant copies of *Jewish Antiquities* come from either Christian or Arabic sources. Those manuscripts contain a *single* passing reference to Jesus being the brother of James and his execution at the hands of Ananus, the High Priest (Book 20.9.1). The paragraph makes no mention of Jesus' crucifixion. A second brief passage in Book 18, the *Testimonium Flavianum* (*TF*), is the focal point of this section. It includes Jesus' crucifixion under the orders of Pilate and the alleged third-day resurrection. Jesus nor Christians appear elsewhere in Josephus' works.

Habermas and Licona, in their text, cite Josephus in a listing "Jesus Died Due to Crucifixion (non-Christian sources)."[2] The authors devote two sentences to this historian in their discussion about Josephus. (1) "The first-century historian Josephus reports that during the fall of Jerusalem in AD 70, the Romans felt such hatred toward the Jews that they crucified a multitude of them in various postures." (2) Josephus writes, "When Pilate, upon hearing him accused by men of the highest standing

---

[1] John Meier describes Josephus as "The first and most important potential "witness" to Jesus' life and activity." [See *A Marginal Jew*, 56] Consequently, this text, like Meier's, will devote a disproportionate space and time to review the controversy revolving around this personality and his writings. Darrell Bock, a Christian apologist, concurs, saying, "The most important extrabiblical evidence for Jesus comes from the Jewish historian Joseph ben Matthias, better known as Flavius Josephus ..." [*Studying the Historical Jesus*, 53]. So too, do Köstenberger, Kellum, and Quarles affirm in *The Cradle, the Cross*," 107, "The testimony of Josephus constitutes the most important early testimony about Jesus of Nazareth outside the Bible."

[2] Habermas and Licona, *Case for the Resurrection of Jesus*, 50.

amongst us, has condemned him to be crucified ..."³ Later, in footnote 42, they devote pages 266–70 to Josephus and the *TF*.

Untold to many readers, the *Testimonium Flavianum* is a paragraph from the *AJ* that the *vast* majority of biblical scholars and historians tend to consider to be at least partially falsified (an interpolation). Norman Geisler wrote in the *Baker Encyclopedia of Christian Apologetics*,

> The genuineness of this passage has been questioned by scholars from all areas of belief because it seems doubtful that a Jew who lived and worked outside the Christian context would have said such things about Jesus. Even the apologist theologian Origen (ca. 185–ca. 254) said that Josephus did not believe Jesus was the Messiah (*Contra Celsum* 1:47).⁴

A minority of writers deny its authenticity altogether. A noteworthy fact to keep in mind is that since Jesus died about 30–33 CE, Josephus was not contemporaneous with him. He was born about four to seven years *after* Jesus' crucifixion. Hence, he cannot independently confirm the Gospel accounts of Jesus' life. For Christian apologists, the weight of Josephus' claims is not that he was an eyewitness to the events, but information about Jesus' death on the cross was widespread and common knowledge at the time (if it is authentic).

Perhaps, the most commonly cited and yet controversial supposed "proof text" cited by defenders of Jesus' crucifixion and resurrection is Josephus' *Testimonium Flavianum*. Paul Hopper says, "If it were authentically the work of Josephus, it would have massive historical importance since it would be the only known non-Christian witness to the life of Jesus to have survived from the first century of the Common Era (CE)."⁵ Similarly, Christopher Price, a Christian apologist writing in *Shattering the Christ Myth*, says, "The most important extra-biblical references to Jesus are found in Josephus' *Antiquities to the Jews*."⁶ As previously mentioned, the extant copies of *Jewish Antiquities* come from either Christian or Arabic sources. Noteworthy, "All [three manuscripts] derive from the same textual family."⁷

---

³ Habermas and Licona, *Case for the Resurrection of Jesus*, 48–49.
⁴ Geisler, *Baker Encyclopedia of Christian Apologetics*, 382. Later, he offers six reasons for accepting the *TF*'s genuineness.
⁵ Hopper, "A Narrative Anomaly in Josephus," 148.
⁶ Price, "Firmly Established by Josephus," 21.
⁷ Olson, "Eusebius and the Testimonium Flavianum," 306.

James Paget, in *The Journal of Theological Studies*, is unequivocal:

> Whatever we make of the above, it remains the case that what evidence we do possess for the reading of Josephus from the second century to the tenth is exclusively Christian and that the works of the Jewish general are known to us only through the endeavours of Christian scribes and theologians.[8]

In the Christian edited versions of the *Jewish Antiquities*, "one" significant section purportedly deals with Jesus' crucifixion as portrayed in the New Testament. That paragraph, a primary focus of this section, is identified as *AJ* 18.63–64 [= XVIII 3, 3 = Book 18, Chapter 3, Paragraph 3]. This noteworthy excerpt is commonly called the *Testimonium Flavianum* (*TF*):

> At that time lived Jesus, a wise man, if he may be called a man; for he performed many wonderful works. He was a teacher of such men as received the truth with pleasure. He drew over to him many Jews and Gentiles. This was the Christ. And when Pilate, at the instigation of the chief men among us, had condemned him to the cross, they who before had conceived an affection for him did not cease to adhere to him. For on the third day he appeared to them alive again, the divine prophets having foretold these and many other wonderful things concerning him. And the sect of Christians, so called from him, subsists to this time.[9]

In other words, the *TF* is "the Flavian Testimony [to Jesus]," the "witness of Flavius [to Jesus]," or "the testimony of Flavius Josephus [to Jesus]."[10] In the opening section of his autobiography, *The Life of Flavius Josephus*, Josephus reports (1) he was born into a distinguished priestly and aristocratic family and (2) at the age of nineteen, he had attached himself to the Pharisees. Josephus, therefore, is a Jewish historian, born into a noble family, and a Pharisee, who is, in effect, testifying to the existence of Jesus and aspects of his life. Christian apologists argue that Josephus' mentioning of the personage of Jesus helps to substantiate and lend credence to his historicity and crucifixion. In the *TF* (*AJ* 18.63–64),

---

[8] Paget, "Some Observations on Josephus and Christianity," 539.
[9] Whiston, *Josephus: Complete Works*, 379.
[10] Doherty, *Jesus: Neither God Nor Man*, 533; Mason, *Josephus and the New Testament*, 225; Meier, *A Marginal Jew*, 59.

a brief passage occurs about Jesus' crucifixion under Pilate, the alleged third-day resurrection, and his appearance on the third day. As previously mentioned, scholars extensively discuss this passage's authenticity. Most agree that it contains interpolations (modifications) by Christian hands, and some writers deny its authenticity altogether. As early as 1592, the Protestant scholar Lucas Osiander (1534–1604) doubted the authenticity of the *TF* passage. Later, other dated sources challenged or questioned its historicity.[11]

Presumably, there are at least four possible perspectives on the authenticity of the *Testimonium*.

1. It is entirely authentic (Josephan): Josephus wrote it.
2. It is entirely a Christian forgery (spurious).
3. "The original word in as a whole has been lost, though some traces of what Josephus wrote may still be found."[12]
4. It contains Christian interpolation (alterations or changes) by one or more people in Josephus' authentic material about Jesus. Furthermore, two or three insertions are easily isolated from the non-Christian core.

Gerd Theissen and Annette Merz, writing in *The Historical Jesus*, say, "The hypothesis of unqualified authenticity is rarely put forward now."[13] Nicholas Peter Legh Allen, in a doctoral dissertation, elaborates. "Now, claims are sometimes made by advocates of partial interpolation that the residual and 'authentic' Josephan text, after the removal of the obvious Christian layers, may be recognized by its lack of what has been termed 'gospel flavour.'"[14] Many Christian scholars discuss and admit the possibility or probability of an interpolation of the *TF* by Christian hands.[15]

The literature about the *TF* is robust. James Carleton Paget's article on the matter runs to eighty-six pages. The paper is closely argued, contains extensively annotated pages, surveys ninety-seven books and articles, and is still not comprehensive.[16] Alice Whealey has written a 231-

---

[11] Louis Cappel (1568–1658), Tanaquilius Faber (1615–1672), Benedikt Miese (1849–1910), and Arthur Drews (1865–1935).

[12] Meier, *A Marginal Jew*, 59.

[13] Theissen and Merz, *The Historical Jesus*, 66.

[14] Allen, *Christian Forgery in Jewish Antiquities*, 125–26; *Clarifying the Scope*, 165.

[15] Licona, *Resurrection of Jesus*; Meier, *A Marginal Jew;* Eddy and Boyd, *The Jesus Legend*; Evans, *Jesus and His Contemporaries*.

[16] Paget, "Some Observations on Josephus," 539–624.

page book on the reception history of the *TF*.[17] Contributing to the literature include Allen's doctoral dissertation and *Christian Forgery in Jewish Antiquities: Josephus Interrupted*.[18]

Table 4-1: Arguments About the Authenticity of the Testimonium Flavianum

Arguments for Authenticity	Arguments against Authenticity
Found in all surviving manuscripts.	Christian content was unlikely from a Jewish writer (esp., "He was the Messiah.").
Quoted in full by Eusebius, ca. 324 CE.	Writers earlier than Eusebius do not cite the passage. Furthermore, Origen states that Josephus did *not* believe Jesus was the Messiah.
A more accepted reference to Jesus in Book 20 indicates that he must have been described earlier in the *Antiquities*, logically in the discussion of Pilate.	The passage breaks the continuity of the narrative concerning Pilate.
Vocabulary and style are generally consistent with that of Josephus	There are stylistic peculiarities not in Josephus, such as using the first person in "the principal men among us."
No other passage in the *Antiquities* has been seriously questioned, so the burden of proof is on the skeptics.	Interpolations in manuscripts of Josephus (e.g., accounts of Jesus in the Slavonic version).

Source: Goldberg, *The Mystery of the Testimonium Flavianum (Josephus.org)*

Detractors and several Christian writers argue that the reference to Jesus being the Messiah ("Christ"), the idea that Josephus would call

---

[17] Whealey, *Josephus on Jesus*.
[18] M.F.A. (RU), M.A. (NMMU), M.Th. (NWU), Ph.D. (NWU), D.Phil. (UKZN), Laur. Tech. F.A. (PET). Professor emeritus, Professor ad hominem. Rated Researcher (C1) with the South African National Research Foundation. He has authored and co-authored numerous academic books and accredited scientific articles on various topics including Art History, New Testament, Cognate and Deuterocanonical Literature, Sindonology and the History of Judaism and Christianity.

Jesus a "wise man" who taught "such men as receive the truth with pleasure" is out of place and does not fit well with the surrounding narrative. Seemingly, a more powerful argument against partial authenticity is an argument from silence. In this section, there is an examination of that argument.

Arguments in Support of the *TF*'s Authenticity

John Meir: *The Marginal Jew*

The late John Meir was an American biblical scholar and Roman Catholic priest. His analysis of the *TF*, one of the most detailed, is frequently cited in the literature. He argues that the *TF* is partially authentic:

> But even if these deletions do uncover an earlier text, is there sufficient reason to claim that it comes from Josephus? The answer is yes; our initial, intuitive hypothesis can be confirmed by further considerations drawn from the text's history, context, language, and thought...
>
> Third, the vocabulary and grammar of the passage (after the clearly Christian material is removed) cohere well with Josephus' style and language; the same cannot be said when the text's vocabulary and grammar are compared with that of the NT. Indeed, many keywords and phrases in the *Testimonium* are either absent from the NT or are used there in an entirely different sense; in contrast, almost every word in the core of the *Testimonium* is found elsewhere in Josephus—in fact, most of the vocabulary turns out to be characteristic of Josephus.[19]

Meier writes that "after the clearly Christian material is removed" assuming that by bracketing or removing the three most overtly Christian statements from the *TF*, an authentic "core" text is achievable.[20] Later, in this section, his hypothesis is examined.

Robert A. Van Voorst: *Jesus Outside the New Testament*

---

[19] Meir, *The Marginal Jew*, 63.
[20] Meir, *The Marginal Jew*, 62–67.

Robert A. Van Voorst, author of *Jesus Outside the New Testament*, presents a different type of apologetic.[21] He proposes adopting a "neutral reconstruction" of the text and devotes several pages to arguing for support of that hypothesis. His analysis of the *TF* is also frequently cited in the literature. Lataster has criticized his methodology:

1. Van Voorst's approach appeal to hypothetical sources.
2. Van Voorst fails to prove that such sources existed and/or that they are reliable.
3. Van Voorst admits that these sources remain hypothetical.[22]

Supporting this evaluation, Van Voorst, in contradiction, concludes, "their [the neutral] cumulative effect makes a convincing case, and shows why recent scholarship tends to favor it."[23]

Van Voorst identifies six arguments from internal evidence that scholars have commonly given in support of the theory that the text of the *Testimonium* has an authentic Josephan core. Ken Olson's guest blog provides a concise and handy summary:

> 1. The passage calls Jesus a "wise man," which while complimentary is not what one might expect a Christian interpolation to say because the label was not at all a common Christian one.
> 2. That Jesus is said to have been a "worker of amazing deeds" (paradoxōn ergōn poiētēs) may be a positive statement, but the wording is not likely to come from a Christian. The phrase "amazing deeds" is itself ambiguous; it can also be translated as "startling/controversial deeds," and the whole sentence can be read to mean simply that Jesus had a reputation as a wonder-worker.
> 3. According to the passage, Jesus was a teacher of people who accept the "truth with pleasure." Christian writers generally avoid a positive use of the word "pleasure" (hēdonē), with its connotation of Hedonism.
> 4. The statement that Jesus won over "both Jews and Greeks" represents a misunderstanding perhaps found among non-Christians like Lucian. However, anyone remotely familiar with the Gospel

---

[21] Doctoral study in religion at Union Theological Seminary in New York City, parish pastor, retired from Western Theological Seminary in Holland, Michigan, where he served for nineteen years as a professor of New Testament.

[22] Lataster, *Questioning the Historicity of Jesus*, 65n129.

[23] Van Voorst, *Jesus Outside the New Testament*, 95.

tradition knows that Jesus did not win over "many Greeks" to his movement, even though "Greeks" here means Gentiles.

5. The sentence "Those who had first loved him did not cease [doing so]" is characteristically Josephan in style and points to the continuance of Christianity after the death of its founder. It implies that the love of Jesus' followers for him, not Jesus' resurrection appearances to them, was the basis for Christianity's continuance

6. Calling Christians a "tribe" (phylon) would also be unusual for a Christian scribe; a follower of a missionizing faith would be uncomfortable with the more narrow particularistic implications of the word. (modified)[24]

Arguments Rejecting the *TF*'s Authenticity

Rebuttal One: Goldberg's Proofs

Gary Goldberg, in 1995, published a thought-provoking article in *The Journal for the Study of the Pseudepigrapha*. The title is "The Coincidences of the Emmaus Narrative of Luke and the Testimonium of Josephus." His investigation provided empirical evidence that the *TF* matches Luke in content, concepts, and sequence. Most of these intersections involve the Emmaus episode. Unknowns include whether

1. Josephus would have had access to the Emmaus narrative in Luke 24,
2. he heard oral stories based on Luke 24,
3. Josephus had access to a "common source,"[25]
4. a forger or redactor added the account into Josephus' text based on Luke 24, sometime during the next 200 years, or the similarity was sheer chance.

The modified Testimonium-Luke Comparison table from Goldberg presents the texts side-by-side. This table demonstrates the consistent presence and order of the themes in the two texts. The exact order of the Greek texts is maintained. The table merely adds line breaks

---

[24] Olson, *"The Testimonium Flavianum,"* directly quoting Van Voorst, *Jesus Outside the New Testament*, 89–90. In the blog, Olsen refutes the six arguments presented by Van Voorst. See below.

[25] Goldberg, "The Coincidences of the Emmaus Narrative," 8, 13.

to clarify the relationship between clauses. Also, correspondences of Greek words with the same root are visible in boldface. Goldberg writes, "The reader should note that, in the quoted text, I have chosen not to include in the Jesus description the verses 24:22–24, a narrative flashback which recapitulates the discovery of the empty tomb by the women."[26]

Regarding the sequence match, Goldberg writes, "One can best experience this sequence by reading the text of Luke, halting at each noun or each verb of action, and then looking to the Josephus text for a corresponding phrase at the same location."[27] He then shows that the nineteen elements in the *TF* are in order as the same nineteen elements in the Emmaus narrative:

> [Jesus] [wise man / prophet-man] [mighty/surprising] [deed(s)] [teacher / word] [truth / (word) before God] [many people] [he was indicted] [by leaders] [of us] [sentenced to a cross] [those who had loved/hoped in him] [spending the third day] [he appeared/spoke to them] [prophets] [these things] [and numerous other things] [about him][28]

Richard Carrier adds two insightful comments. First, a twentieth element exists identifying Jesus as the Christ. Second, Goldberg also overlooks a twenty-first correspondence. Carrier, says, both the matching part of Luke and the Testimonium begin with the same verb in the same position. He adds, "'It comes to pass / it came to pass'" (exact same verb, exact same place, just differing in tense—see Table 4-2).[29]

Table 4-2: Testimonium-Luke Comparison[30]

Josephus, *Jewish Antiquities* 18.3.3 Sec. 63–64	Gospel of Luke 24:18–21, 25–27

---

[26] Goldberg, "The Coincidences of the Emmaus Narrative," 62.
[27] Goldberg, "The Coincidences of the Emmaus Narrative," 64.
[28] Goldberg, "The Coincidences of the Emmaus Narrative," 64.
[29] Carrier, "Josephus on Jesus?" cf. Carrier, *On the Historicity of Jesus*, 333n81.
[30] Goldberg, "Testimonium-Luke Comparison Table." Bold text in this table appear in the original.

Jesus wise man **Iesous** sophos **aner**	Jesus the Nazarene who was a man prophet **Iesou** tou Nazoraiou hos egeneto **aner** profetes
if a man one can call him indeed eige andra auton legein cre	(no match)
for he was of amazing **deeds** a worker en gar paradoxon **ergon** poietes	mighty in **deed** dunatos en **ergoi**
a teacher didaskalos	and word kai logoi
of people who with pleasure the truth received	before God
and many of the Jews and many of the Greeks were won over kai pollous men 'Ioudaious, pollous de kai tou Hellenikou epegageto.	and all the people kai pantos tou laou
The christ [or messiah] he was. ho christos houtos en.	(no match)
and him an indictment kai auton endeixei	how they handed him over hopos te paredokan auton

by the principal men *ton proton andron*	the chief priests and leaders *hoi archiereis kai hoi archontes*
among **us** *par' **hemin***	of **us** ***hemon***
to a **cross** condemned by Pilate ***stauroi** epitetimhkotos Pilatou*	to a judgment of death and **crucified** him. *eis krima thanatou kai **estaurosan** auton.*
did not stop the first followers. *ouk epausanto hoi to proton agapesantes.*	But we were hoping that he would be the one to redeem Israel *hemeis de helpizomen hoti autos estin o mellon lutrousthai ton Israel*
(no match)	but besides with all these things *alla ge syn pasin toutois*
For appearing to them *ephane gar autois*	(no match)
a **third day** having ***triten** echon **hemeran***	this **third day** spending ***triten** tauten **hemeran** agei*

again alive *palin zon*	today since these things happened. [...] And he said to them, "Oh, fools and slow of heart to believe *hemeron aph' ou tauta egeneto.[...]kai autos eipen pros autous, O anoetoi kai bradeis tei kardiai tou pisteuein epi*
the divine **prophets** these **things** *ton theion **propheton tauta***	all that the **prophets** have spoken. Were not these **things** necessary *pasin hois elalesan hoi **prophetai**. ouchi **tauta** edei*
(no match)	to suffer the christ *pathein ton christon*
and thousands other wonders about him foretold. *te kai alla myria **peri autou** thaumasia eirekoton.*	and to enter into his glory. Then beginning with Moses and all the prophets, he interpreted to them the things about himself in all the scriptures. *kai eiselthein eis ten doxan autou; kai arxamenos apo Mouseos kai apo panton ton propheton diermeneusen autois en pasais tais graphais ta **peri eautou**.*
And to now the tribe of the Christians, named after him, has not disappeared. *eis eti te nun ton Christianon apo toude onomasmenon ouk epelipe to phylon.*	(no match)

Source: adapted from Goldberg, Testimonium-Luke Comparison Table

44 The Resurrection and Its Apologetics

Approximately twenty-six years later, Goldberg published a follow-up investigation in *The Journal for the Study of the Historical Jesus*. A phrase-by-phrase study found that *TF* can hypothetically derive from the Emmaus narrative via Josephus' employment of paraphrasing. Goldberg used existing research as well as novel database searches.[31] He numbered (labeled) the correspondences C1, C2, C3 ... Goldberg writes a concise summary: "As will be seen, the study identifies thirty-one shared concepts at analogous positions in the Emmaus narrative and the TF. Those concepts comprise almost the entirety of the TF" (see Table 4-3).[32]

Table 4-3: Thirty-One English Correspondences Identified by Goldberg

Numbered Correspondence	Numbered Correspondence	Numbered Correspondence
(C1) happens	(C12) people/people & Judaeans & Greeks	(C23) third day [accusative case]
(C2) in these days/about this time	(C13) powerful…before all & we were hoping*/won over	(C24) brings/having
(C3) Jesus	(C14) the Christ	(C25) living/alive
(C4) man	(C15) delivered/indictment	(C26) prophets
(C5) prophet/wise	(C16) chief priests and leaders/principal men	(C27) told/told*
(C6) powerful in deed/doer	(C17) our/among us	(C28) these things
(C7) deeds	(C18) judgment of death/sentenced	(C29) all/countless
(C8) before…all the people/surprising	(C19) crucified/cross	(C30) glory*/wonders
(C9) powerful in…word/teacher	(C20) we were hoping that he/those first loving him	(C31) about him
(C10) word before God/truth	(C21) and with all these things & some women among us*/did not cease	
(C11) all/many & many	(C22) said to them*/appeared to them	

---

[31] Goldberg, "Josephus's Paraphrase Style," 3.
[32] Goldberg, "Josephus's Paraphrase Style," 6.

Source: Goldberg, Thirty-One English Correspondences

In summary, Goldberg provides significant data:

1. Of the thirty-one numbered correspondences, twelve shared word roots in the proper context.
2. There are nine vocabulary pairs with paraphrase support for substitution.
3. There are at least eight pairs with indirect support through the usage of association.
4. The remaining two pairs have no explicit parallels for vocabulary replacement.[33]

His research study raises another relevant question. Are the thirty-one paraphrased explanations a coincidence? Goldberg responds to his rhetorical question with a tentative answer: "If coincidence is then excluded, an alternative explanation is that a sophisticated forger deliberately rewrote Luke 24.18–27 using Josephus's vocabulary."[34] Goldberg adds, "I will conclude with some implications of the model. The study shows Josephus closely following a Christian source and treating it with a degree of courtesy and guarded respect."[35] Returning to Goldberg's relevant 1995 article, he says these coincidences can have only two other explanations if not due to a common source. First, they are due to chance. Detractors argue the second point. *Testimonium* is not, in fact, authentic. Instead, it is the composition of a later Christian writer, and this writer was partly influenced by the excerpt, directly or indirectly. Goldberg concludes, "Therefore, these coincidences can have only two other explanations. Either they are due to chance; or the Testimonium is not, in fact, authentic, that it is the composition of a later Christian writer, and that this writer was in part influenced, directly or indirectly, by the excerpt from Luke."[36]

Goldberg's research eliminates the certitude espoused by apologists that the *TF* was *not* dependent upon or derived from the New Testament. Contrary to apologists, the content, concepts, and sequence of the *TF* match Luke. Acceptance of Goldberg's hypothesis creates additional ramifications. First, the *TF* is not independently attested.

---

[33] Goldberg, "Josephus's Paraphrase Style," 29.
[34] Goldberg, "Josephus's Paraphrase Style," 31.
[35] Goldberg, "Josephus's Paraphrase Style," 32.
[36] Goldberg, "The Coincidences of the Emmaus Narrative," 67.

Second, its source of information requires classification as hearsay. Finally, that information is best enumerated second, third, or fourth-hand. Noteworthy, Luke says so much in his Prologue. The reader must judge whether these points of contact are coincidental or deliberate.

Rebuttal 2:
Ken Olson and the un-Josephan Character
of the Language and Phrasing of the TF

Proponents of the *TF* argue that the language in the relevant passages in the *TF* is Josephan. In a dispute, several writers found the style of the *TF* more Eusebian than Josephan. For instance, Ken Olson writes:

> Some of the language used in this section of the *Testimonium* is paralleled in Eusebius' work, but not in Josephus. These include: καὶ ἄλλα μυρία ("and myriads of other things"), which occurs eight times elsewhere in Eusebius' work; τῶν Χριστιανῶν ... τὸ φῦλον ("tribe of Christians"), which occurs twice elsewhere; and εἰς ἔτι τε νῦν ("to this very day"), which occurs six times elsewhere.[37]

In addition, Olson wrote the following words:

> The frequently employed argument that the language is "Josephan," and therefore must either come from Josephus himself or be a masterful forgery, runs into difficulties especially in places where we find parallels in Eusebius but not in Josephus. Such language, of course, could still conceivably have been used by Josephus. It is impossible to prove absolutely that it was not. But it is difficult to see how it can be used as a positive argument for authenticity. And if we adopt the hypothesis that Eusebius is so deeply influenced by the *Testimonium* that he has imitated not only its language but its apparent Christology as well in several of his works, this seems not only improbable but comes near to removing the hypothesis of authenticity from any possibility of falsification. The confidence that many scholars place in the *Testimonium* or its reconstructed core text is misplaced.[38]

Carrier lends support to Olson. He writes that "The vocabulary and phrasing of the *Testimonium* match Eusebius in every peculiar case,

---

[37] Olson, "A Eusebian Reading," 109–10.
[38] Olson, "A Eusebian Reading," 111.

while frequently not matching Josephus."[39] Therefore, the surviving manuscripts contain Eusebian footprints. Then Carrier provides a beneficial list of examples:

1. "teacher of human beings"
2. "worker of amazing deeds"
3. "Christian ... tribe"
4. receiving godly things "with pleasure"
5. "the truth" in the plural to mean the truth of God
6. and the exact phrase "and myriads of other things"
7. and the exact phrase "to this very day"
8. and calling Jesus a "wise man" (verbatim)[40]

Finally, he discusses several points of concern. First, many concepts in the *Testimonium* are peculiar to Eusebius. For example, "the belief that Jesus won over many Jews and Greeks during his ministry, is a peculiar Eusebian trope."[41] Second, Josephus never elsewhere uses or explains the word "Christ."[42] Carrier elaborates on the importance of the word "Christ." He says, "A Christian not only readily would, but would also be the only sort of author likely to forget that the intended readers of the *Antiquities* don't know what calling him that means."[43]

Rebuttal 3:
Paul Hopper's Linguistic Analysis

During the past fifty years, language research has increased the understanding of narrative language. Areas of study include verbal inflections, discourse particles, word order, and word focus. Building on that research, Paul Hopper employed a linguistic (morphological and syntactic) analysis of the *TF* in four episodes relating to Pontius Pilate.[44] The narratives begin in Book 18:55 and finally mention him in 18:89. The third episode narrates Pilate sentencing Jesus for crucifixion. Employing

---

[39] Carrier, "Josephus on Jesus?"
[40] Carrier, "Josephus on Jesus?"
[41] Carrier, "Josephus on Jesus?"
[42] Carrier, "Josephus on Jesus?"
[43] Carrier, "Josephus on Jesus?"
[44] Hopper, PhD, in Linguistics from the University of Texas is the Distinguished Professor of the Humanities Emeritus at Carnegie Mellon University, former editor of the journal *Language Sciences,* a Collitz Professor at the LSA's Linguistics Institute, and has been a Fulbright Fellow and a Guggenheim Fellow.

48   *The Resurrection and Its Apologetics*

a technical analysis of language, Hopper identifies several anomalies and difficulties:

> Emplotment: The *Testimonium* has no such plot. From the point of view of its place in Josephus's *Jewish Antiquities*, it does not qualify as a narrative at all. **The *Testimonium* could not be understood as a story except by someone who could already place it in its "intelligible whole", the context of early Christianity.** The *Testimonium* gains its intelligibility not through its reporting of novel events but by virtue of being a "repetition of the familiar" (Ricoeur 1981:67) – familiarity here meaning familiarity to a third century Christian readership, not to a first century Roman one. **The "intelligible whole" posited by Ricoeur as the indispensable foundation for a story does not lie, as it does for the other events told by Josephus in this part of the *Jewish Antiquities*, in the larger narrative of the interlocking destinies of Rome and Jerusalem, but instead in the Gospel story** of the Christian New Testament, and it is from the Gospels, and the Gospels alone, that the Jesus Christ narrative in the *Testimonium* draws its coherence and its legitimacy as a plot, and perhaps even some of its language. It is not just that the Christian origin of the *Testimonium* is betrayed by its allegiance to the Gospels, as that **without the Gospels the passage is incomprehensible.** Once again to draw on Paul Ricoeur, the *Testimonium* does not so much narrate to first century Romans new events, but rather **reminds third century Christians of events already familiar to them**. (Bold for emphasis)[45]

In section 8.3, Hopper examined genre and compared the *TF* and credal formulas *vis a vis* the historical narrative of Josephus. His comments deserve diligent reading:

> The *Testimonium* is anchored in a radically different discourse community from that of the rest of the *Jewish Antiquities*. **The *Testimonium* reads more like a position paper, a party manifesto, than a narrative.** Unlike the rest of the *Jewish Antiquities,* it has **the same generic ambiguity between myth and history that Kermode (1979) has noted in the Gospels as a whole**....It is, in other words, a political interpolation. **It serves to validate the Christian claim of the crucifixion** of the sect's founder

---

[45] Hopper, "A Narrative Anomaly," 165–66.

during Pilate's administration, and, by positioning its text within that of the genre "history", with its ethos of truth, to warrant the historical authenticity of the Gospels. **But told as a series of new events to a first century Roman audience unfamiliar with it the *Testimonium* would have been a bizarre addition and probably quite unintelligible.**

The *Testimonium Flavianum* qualifies poorly as an example of either history or narrative. Where, then, does it fit generically? **The closest generic match for the *Testimonium* is perhaps the various creeds that began to be formulated in the early fourth century, such as the Nicene Creed (325 CE).** Some credal elements are clearly present...

The Josephus of the *Testimonium* is represented as aligning himself with Christians (versus the Jews) and admitting that the blame for the crucifixion of Jesus the Messiah lies with the Jews; it need hardly be said that such an admission on Josephus's part is inconceivable. (Bold for emphasis)[46]

His article, in its entirety, must be examined.

Feldman agrees that the *TF* contains phrases far more commonly used by Eusebius than Josephus. In his 1999 article, he says, "The principal internal argument against the genuineness of the *Testimonium* is that it says that Jesus was the Christ, whereas Josephus, as a loyal Pharisaic Jew, could hardly have written this."[47] Returning to the 2012 essay, he devotes almost five pages to interacting and engaging with this topic.[48] The entry is required reading.

Rebuttal 4:
Creed Analysis

Commentators write about the relationship between the *TF* and various church creeds. Commentators identify and discuss common points of contact (see Table 4-4, italics for emphasis). For example, the elements found in the Nicene Creed (325 CE) and the Apostles' Creed (c. 5th century) are easily distinguishable when lined up parallel to the *TF*:

---

[46] Hopper, "A Narrative Anomaly," 166–67.
[47] Feldman, "Josephus," 912; cf. "On the Authenticity of the *Testimonium*," 23; Meier, *A Marginal Jews*, 60.
[48] Feldman, "On the Authenticity of the *Testimonium*," 22–27.

1. Jesus was a man
2. Jesus was the Messiah (Christ)
3. Jesus performed miracles.
4. Jesus was crucified during the rule of Pontius Pilate.
5. Jesus was ordered crucified by Pontius Pilate.
6. Jesus came back to life on the third day after his death.
7. The biblical prophets foretold many details of his life.
8. The movement founded by him; the Christian church continues to flourish.

Table 4-4: Common Points of Contact Between the TF, the Nicene Creed, and the Apostles' Creed [49]

Testimonium Flavianum (Whiston translation)	**Nicene Creed**	**Apostles' Creed (Catechism of the Catholic Church)**
Now, there was about this time, Jesus, a wise man, if it be to call him a *man*; for *he was a doer of wonderful works,* –a teacher of such men as receive the truth with pleasure. He drew over to him many of the Jews and many of the Gentiles. He *was [the] Christ;* and when Pilate, at the suggestion of the principal men amongst us, had *condemned him to the cross*, those that loved him at first did not forsake him, f*or on the third day he appeared to them alive again, the third day, as the divine prophets had foretold these and ten thousand other wonderful things concerning him; and the*	We believe in one God, the Father, the Almighty, maker of heaven and earth, of all that is, seen and unseen. We believe in one Lord, *Jesus Christ*, the only Son of God, eternally begotten of the Father, God from God, Light from Light, true God from true God, begotten, not made, of one Being with the Father. *Through him all things were made.* For us men and for our salvation, he came down from heaven: by the power of the Holy Spirit he was *born of the Virgin Mary*, and *became man.* For our sake he was *crucified under Pontius Pilate; he suffered died and was buried. On the third day he rose again in fulfillment of the Scriptures*; he ascended into	I believe in God the Father almighty, creator of heaven and earth. I believe in *Jesus Christ*, his only Son, our Lord. He was conceived by the power of the Holy Spirit and *born of the Virgin Mary Under Pontius Pilate He was crucified, died, and was buried. He descended to the dead. On the third day he rose again.* He ascended into heaven and is seated at the right hand of the Father. He will come again to judge the living and the dead. I believe in the Holy Spirit, *the holy catholic Church*, the communion

---

[49] Italics added for emphasis.

tribe of Christians, so named from him, are not extinct at this day.	heaven and is seated at the right hand of the Father. He will come again in glory to judge the living and the dead, and his kingdom will have no end. We believe in the Holy Spirit, the Lord, the giver of life, who proceeds from the Father and the Son. With the Father and the Son he is worshipped and glorified. *He has spoken through the Prophets. We believe in one holy catholic and apostolic Church.* We acknowledge one baptism for the forgiveness of sins. We look for the resurrection of the dead, and the life of the world to come. Amen.	of saints, the forgiveness of sins, the resurrection of the body, and the life everlasting. Amen.

Source: Whiston, Josephus, *239; Libreria Editrice Vaticana,* Catechism of the Catholic Church

Hopper points out that several credal elements are present. Examples illustrating credal elements are easily recognizable to the observant reader: (1) Jesus was the Messiah, (2) he was crucified under Pontius Pilate (passus sub Pontio Pilato, in the words of the Apostles' Creed), (3) he came back to life on the third day after his death, (4) the movement founded by him that is the Christian church continues to flourish, (5) he performed miracles, and (6) the biblical prophets foretold many details of his life.[50]

Another point of connection that Hopper and others discuss is the measure of creed length by the number of Greek words. The *TF* contains seventy-seven Greek words. By comparison, there are seventy-six words in the Latin Apostles' Creed and ninety-one in the Greek Apostles' Creed.[51] Question: Are these multiple credal connections and similarities mere coincidences?

---

[50] Hopper, "A Narrative Anomaly in Josephus," 160.
[51] Hopper, "A Narrative Anomaly in Josephus," 166; See http://www.creeds.net/ancient/apostles.htm. In contradiction, Allen says the *TF* "contains 89 words in the Greek version." See Allen, *Clarifying the Scope*, 187.

Hopper minces no words in his final analysis. In section 9, Conclusion, he undermines any thought about the authenticity of the *TF*:

> The narrative grammar of the *Testimonium Flavianum* sets it sharply apart from Josephus's other stories of the procuratorship of Pontius Pilate. **The most likely explanation is that the entire passage is interpolated**, presumably by Christians embarrassed at Josephus's manifest ignorance of the life and death of Jesus. The *Jewish Antiquities* would in this respect be consistent with the other chronicler of this age, Josephus's contemporary and rival historian, Justus of Tiberias, who wrote a history of this period that conflicted with Josephus and claimed Josephus's version to be self-serving. Justus's work has not survived, but we know from other sources that he wrote in great detail about the exact period of Tiberius' reign that coincided with Jesus' ministry – and that he did not mention Jesus. **Outside the Gospels, there is no independent contemporary (i.e., first century CE) account of these events**. The silence of other commentators, and the absence of any mention of the *Testimonium* by Christian writers for two full centuries after Josephus, even when engaged in fierce polemic about Jesus, are strong indications that the passage was not present in Josephus's own extraordinarily detailed account of this period. The activities of a religious fanatic who moved around Galilee and Judaea preaching a gospel of peace and salvation, was said to have performed miracles, was followed by crowds of thousands of adoring disciples, and within the space of a few hours invaded the hallowed grounds of the Temple, was hauled up before the Sanhedrin, tried by King Herod, interrogated by Pontius Pilate and crucified, all amid public tumult, made no impression on history-writers of the period. (Bold added)[52]

The entire twenty-three-page article is required reading.

Roger Viklund, an independent Swedish researcher of theology and detractor, offers the following sober words to conclude his lengthy analysis. He starts with a rhetorical question: "It is therefore legitimate to ask whether Josephus could have written the *Testimonium* at all."[53] Next, he identifies reasons for challenging the *TF*'s authenticity. First, he argues, "The presence of Christian beliefs in the *Testimonium* militates against the suggestion that the *Testimonium* in part, or in its entirety, could have been

---

[52] Hopper, "A Narrative Anomaly in Josephus," 167.
[53] Viklund, "The Jesus Passages in Josephus."

written by Josephus."[54] Viklund points out that the *TF* contains a sample of Christian values. However, no evidence exists that he was a Christian. Second, he opines it is preposterous to think that Josephus believed in the "explicit appointment of Jesus as the Messiah."[55] He argues Josephus "would not have written such a thing without a detailed explanation of the concept of the Jewish term Messiah."[56] Expanding on the subject, Viklund says the Jesus in the *TF* is "depicted in a diametrically opposed manner compared to the picture Josephus presents of other Messiah aspirants."[57] Adding to the cumulative argument, he mentions a common fact in the literature: "Not a single Church Father mentions the *Testimonium* before Eusebius in the fourth century reproduces the passage" despite being familiar with Josephus.[58]

Rebuttal 5:
Argumentum ex silentio

The church fathers were quite fond of quoting passages, which supported Christianity, and these early church fathers were familiar with the works of Josephus. However, not one quotes the *TF* passage in defense of Christianity until Eusebius in the fourth century. For example, Louis H. Feldman notes in his 1999 entry on Josephus in *The Cambridge History of Judaism* these facts:

1. The *TF* does not appear in numerous Christian writers - Pseudo-Justin and Theophilus in the second century, Minucius Felix, Irenaeus, Clement of Alexandria, Julius Africanus, Tertullian, Hippolytus, and Origen in the third century, and Methodius and Pseudo-Eustathius in the early fourth century.
2. The first to cite the *Testimonium* is Eusebius (c. 324).
3. Eleven Christian writers cite Josephus but not the *Testimonium*.
4. Not until Jerome in the early fifth century that there is another reference to it.[59]

Feldman, in a later 2012 writing, repeats his *argumentum ex silentio*. He says, "The fact, if it is a fact, that no ante-Nicene Christian is

---

[54] Viklund, "The Jesus Passages in Josephus."
[55] Viklund, "The Jesus Passages in Josephus."
[56] Viklund, "The Jesus Passages in Josephus."
[57] Viklund, "The Jesus Passages in Josephus."
[58] Viklund, "The Jesus Passages in Josephus."
[59] Feldman, "Josephus (CE 37–c. 100)," 911–12.

known to have used Josephus's works in apologies directed to Jews is certainly surprising in view of the charge, as seen in *The Dialogue with Trypho*, that Jesus never lived and in view of the eagerness of Christians to convert Jews."[60] Then, Feldman acknowledges that he is offering an *argumentum ex silentio*. However, in self-defense, he argues, "but when the number of writers is so great and when these are writers who are very much involved with theological questions, especially questions regarding the nature of Jesus, the omission is striking.[61]

Adding to the controversy about the lack of references to Josephus, Feldman points out additional facts for consideration from his 2012 entry. First, he opines that the silence of John Chrysostom is particularly striking. His rationale is that "There is hardly a church father who is more vehement in his attacks on the Jews."[62] Second, Feldman offers contrasting hypotheses. First, "If Josephus had indeed portrayed Jesus in a negative light, it seems likely that he would have cited this to strengthen his tirade against the Jews."[63] Conversely, "Since the *Testimonium* was positive, he might well have cited it to show that the Jews were guilty of the crime of deicide."[64] Finally, he identifies and elaborates on the importance of four writers after Eusebius. He says, "We find four Christian writers in the fifth century who know the works of Josephus but who do not cite the *Testimonium*: Orosius, Philostorgius, Theodore of Mopsuestia, and Augustine. It is not until Isidore of Pelusium and Sozomenus in the fifth century that we find clear citations of the *Testimonium*."[65]

Josephan scholar Steve Mason lends support to the argument that is also an *argumentum ex silentio*: "The strongest evidence that Josephus did not declare Jesus' messiahship is that the passage under discussion does not seem to have been present in the texts of the *Antiquities* known before the fourth century."[66] Mason adds a crucial fact, "We do not possess the original Greek text that Josephus wrote; we have only copies, the earliest of which (known as P and A) date from the ninth and tenth centuries."[67] Finally, he offers an argument from silence. "If the famous, imperially sponsored Jewish historian had declared Jesus to be Messiah, it

---

[60] Feldman, "On the Authenticity of the Testimonium," 15.
[61] Feldman, "On the Authenticity of the Testimonium," 15.
[62] Feldman, "On the Authenticity of the Testimonium," 16.
[63] Feldman, "On the Authenticity of the Testimonium," 16.
[64] Feldman, "On the Authenticity of the Testimonium," 16.
[65] Feldman, "On the Authenticity of the Testimonium," 17.
[66] Mason, *Josephus and the New Testament*, 167.
[67] Mason, *Josephus and the New Testament*, 167.

would presumably have helped their cause to mention the fact, but they do not."[68]

Other writers were concerned that parts of the *TF* were outside the literature before or after Eusebius.[69] What follows is a list of "absent" sources and a summary modified from Godfrey.[70] He writes, "The following chronological overview of the extant references, variations and omissions may tell their own story for those interested in exploring this topic."[71] This blog entry requires reading its entirety (Bold and italics in the original).

93 CE
Josephus: The book *Jewish Antiquities* by Josephus is published in Rome. The surviving manuscripts contain a description of Jesus. However, it requires asking, was this description present in the year 93? "In deference to the sensibilities of his Roman protectors, Josephus seems at pains to avoid any mention of Jewish Messianic hopes. The only reference to a Messiah is in the description of Jesus and Christians, which first appear with Eusebius."[72] That writing occurs in the fourth century.

ca. 140s CE
Justin Martyr writes lengthy polemics against the unbelief of Jews and pagans and arguments for Christianity. His work contains no reference to Josephus. Godfrey inquires, "Had Josephus written about Jesus, positive or negative, could such works have remained unknown to Justin?"[73]

ca. 170s CE
Theophilus, Patriarch of Antioch writes lengthy polemics against pagan refusal to believe in Christianity. Godfrey notes that "No reference to Jesus in Josephus, although he **cites Josephus** in his Apology to Autolycus, Bk 3, chap. 23."[74]

ca. 180s CE

---

[68] Mason, *Josephus and the New Testament*, 229.
[69] Allen, "Clarifying the Scope," 167–68; Carrier, *On the Historicity of Jesus*, 335–36; Doherty, *Jesus: Neither God Nor Man*, 538; Mason, *Josephus and the New Testament*, 229–31.
[70] Godfrey, "The Jesus Reference in Josephus."
[71] Godfrey, "The Jesus Reference in Josephus."
[72] Godfrey, "The Jesus Reference in Josephus."
[73] Godfrey, "The Jesus Reference in Josephus."
[74] Godfrey, "The Jesus Reference in Josephus."

56   *The Resurrection and Its Apologetics*

Irenaeus writes at length against unbelief without any reference to a work by Josephus. "[I]t is clear that Irenaeus was unfamiliar with Book 18 of 'Antiquities' since he wrongly claims that Jesus was executed by Pilate in the reign of Claudius (Dem. ev. ap. 74), while Antiquities 18.89 indicates that Pilate was deposed during the reign of Tiberius, before Claudius" (Wikipedia's citation of Whealey's 'Josephus on Jesus'). Had Josephus discussed Jesus how could Irenaeus have been ignorant of the fact? Surely some knowledge of such a passage in the famous Jewish historian would have reached Irenaeus and others. Fragment XXXII from the lost writings of Irenaeus, however, does **know Josephus**—see 32:53.[75]

ca. 190s CE
Clement of Alexandria was a Christian theologian, philosopher, and apologist. He is regarded as a Church Father and venerated as a saint. Clement wrote extensively in defense of Christianity against pagan hostility. Godfrey writes, "He **knew Josephus' works**—see Stromata Book 1 Chapter 21—no reference to any mention of Jesus by Josephus."[76]

ca. 200s CE
Tertullian has been called "the father of Latin Christianity" and "the founder of Western theology." Furthermore, he was an early **Christian apologist and prolific writer. Noteworthy, he** wrote lengthy apologetics against unbelief and heresy and in justification of Christianity. Yet, no reference to a passage about Jesus by Josephus appears in his works. Nevertheless, he elsewhere **knows Josephus' works** —see Apologeticum ch.19.[77]

ca. 200s CE
Minucius Felix was one of the earliest Latin apologists. He has no references to Jesus from Josephus, although **he knows and cites Josephus**—see chapter 33.[78]

ca. 210s CE
Hippolytus was one of the most important second-third-century Christian apologists. "He wrote volumes of apologetics but appeared to know

---
[75] Godfrey, "The Jesus Reference in Josephus."
[76] Godfrey, "The Jesus Reference in Josephus."
[77] Godfrey, "The Jesus Reference in Josephus."
[78] Godfrey, "The Jesus Reference in Josephus."

Problems with Josephus 57

nothing of a reference to Jesus by Josephus. Fragments of his works—see On Jeremiah and Ezekiel.145—show he **knows Josephus**."[79]

ca. 220s CE
Sextus Julius Africanus was a Christian traveler and historian who is not known to cite Josephus' passage on Jesus, although **he did know of Josephus'** works—see Chapter 17.38 of his Chronography.

ca. 230s CE
Origen was the early Greek church's most important theologian and biblical scholar. Origen **knows Josephus**: Four citations of Josephus are found here, but none reference a Jesus passage in Josephus.

1. Origen cites a passage in Josephus on the death of James "the brother of Jesus" (Book 20 of the Antiquities);
2. States Josephus did not believe in Jesus (Origen in fact notes that Josephus proclaimed the Roman emperor Vespasian as the long-awaited world ruler of biblical prophecy).
3. Summarized what Josephus said about the Baptist in Book 18.
4. Said Josephus attributed the destruction of Jerusalem to the murder of James the Just (something not found in our copies of the works of Josephus)—(Josephus actually implies the destruction of Jerusalem was punishment for the murder of Ananias).
5. Does not cite any reference to Jesus from Josephus.[80]

ca. 240s CE
Cyprian (North Africa): Bishop of Carthage, recognized as a saint, and a prolific apologist with no reference to Jesus in Josephus.

ca. 270s CE
Anatolius was a Syro-Egyptian saint, Bishop of Laodicea, and teacher of Neoplatonic philosophy. "He demonstrates his **knowledge of Josephus** in his Paschal Canon, chapter 3. Nevertheless, he has no reference to Jesus in Josephus."[81]

ca. 290s CE

---

[79] Godfrey, "The Jesus Reference in Josephus."
[80] Godfrey, "The Jesus Reference in Josephus."
[81] Godfrey, "The Jesus Reference in Josephus."

Arnobius (North Africa): Prolific apologist with no reference to Jesus in Josephus.

ca. 300s CE
Methodius was an early Christian bishop, ecclesiastical author, and Church Father. He "opposed Origen and **cites Josephus** (see On the Resurrection—the citation is misplaced at the bottom of the page) but does not reference a Jesus passage in Josephus."[82]

ca. 300s CE
Lactantius (North Africa): "Prolific apologist with no reference to Jesus in Josephus."[83]

Eusebius quotes a reference in Josephus to Jesus that survives today in all manuscripts:

> Now there was about this time Jesus, a wise man, if it be lawful to call him a man; for he was a doer of wonderful works, a teacher of such men as receive the truth with pleasure. He drew over to him both many of the Jews and many of the Gentiles. He was [the] Christ. And when Pilate, at the suggestion of the principal men amongst us, had condemned him to the cross, those that loved him at the first did not forsake him; for he appeared to them alive again the third day; as the divine prophets had foretold these and ten thousand other wonderful things concerning him. And the tribe of Christians, so named from him, are not extinct at this day.

Godfrey says, "Some expressions in the text above are Josephan. However, he opines that it is used in a way contrary to how Josephus uses them elsewhere."[84] Furthermore, he says, "Some expressions are characteristic of those found in other writings of Eusebius."[85] Godfrey continues, "Eusebius in fact cites this passage three times—in three of his works."[86] Therefore, his action asserts reputable Jewish support for the good character of Jesus:

1. *Demonstratio Evangelica*

---

[82] Godfrey, "The Jesus Reference in Josephus."
[83] Godfrey, "The Jesus Reference in Josephus."
[84] Godfrey, "The Jesus Reference in Josephus."
[85] Godfrey, "The Jesus Reference in Josephus."
[86] Godfrey, "The Jesus Reference in Josephus."

Problems with Josephus 59

2. *History of the Church*
3. *Theophany*

ca. 370s CE
Jerome was a Christian priest, theologian, historian, and Saint. He is best known for his translation of the Bible into Latin. Jerome cites Josephus ninety times but cites the *Testimonium* (the Josephan passage about Jesus) only once, and that is in his *Illustrious Men*, 13: "It is likely that Jerome knew of the Testimonium from the copy of Eusebius available to him."[87]

The silence on the *Testimonium* outside *De Viris Illustribus* 13 may well relate to the period prior to his attaining access to the Eusebian text of Josephus.[88]

ca. 380s CE
St John Chrysostom was an early Church Father, biblical interpreter, and archbishop of Constantinople.

1. In his Homily 76 he writes that Jerusalem was destroyed as a punishment for the crucifixion of Jesus.
2. He discusses Josephus, but makes no reference to any passage about Jesus in Josephus.
3. In his Homily 13 he writes that Josephus attributed the destruction of Jerusalem to the death of John the Baptist.[89]

ca. 370s CE
Latin **Pseudo-Hegesippus** and the Hebrew Josippon dependent on Ps-Hegesippus, cite free paraphrases of the Josephan reference to Jesus first cited in Eusebius.[90]

ca. 400s CE
Augustine (North Africa) was a theologian, philosopher, prolific apologist, and writer. He is considered one of the most important Church

---

[87] Godfrey, "The Jesus Reference in Josephus."
[88] Eddy and Boyd, *The Jesus Legend*, 197.
[89] Godfrey, "The Jesus Reference in Josephus."
[90] Godfrey, "The Jesus Reference in Josephus."

Fathers of the Latin Church. He knew nothing of any reference to Jesus by Josephus.

The reader must adjudicate whether the prior discussion of this circumstantial evidence is compelling to accept the hypothesis that *TF* is a forgery and written (in part or whole) about the fourth century.[91]

Rebuttal 6:
The Missing TF from the AF Table of Contents

Josephan manuscripts do not contain a table of contents that identifies the *TF*. Several writers discuss the extant Greek Josephan manuscripts and include a table of contents applicable to each book of the *AJ*.[92] The perception of detractors and skeptics argue that Christians who created a table of contents for *Antiquities* would have included a reference to the *TF* if such a reference existed. This circumstantial argument from silence challenges the total or partial authenticity of the *Testimonium*.

Feldman exemplifies this rationale, expressing the following opinion about this omission:

> The fact that an ancient table of contents, already referred to in the Latin version of the fifth or sixth century, omits mention of the *Testimonium* (though, admittedly, it is selective, one must find it hard to believe that such a remarkable passage would be omitted by anyone, let alone by a Christian, summarizing the work) is further indication that there was no such notice...[93]

In his doctoral dissertation, Allen discusses the significance of this omission:

> What is of extreme importance to this debate is that Book XVIII of the *AJ* boasts a Table of Contents that lists twenty topics dealt with within the book. What must be considered to be the most important issue here is not that Josephus (or his assumed Jewish assistants) failed to

---

[91] Extensive literature refutes the common argument from silence: "There are no contemporary references to Jesus." See Holding, "Refuting 'Remsberg's List,'" 89–94; O'Neill, "Jesus Mythicism 3."

[92] Birdsall, "The Continuing Enigma of Josephus," 618; Doherty, *Jesus Neither God Nor Man*, 547–48; Feldman, *Josephus, Judaism and Christianity: Introduction*, 57; Price, "Firmly Established by Josephus," 43–44; Viklund, "The Jesus Passages; Wells, *The Jesus Legend*, 51; *The Jesus Myth*, 202; Zindler, *The Jesus the Jews Never Knew*, 50–51.

[93] Feldman, *Josephus, Judaism and Christianity*: "Introduction," 57.

mention the *TF* in the table of contents – indeed such a small interlude about a minor Jewish religious leader (if authentic), would hardly warrant such an inclusion.

What is far more telling is the undisputable fact that, as Christianity became more dominant, it is strange that nobody bothered to even embellish this table of contents due to the need to *highlight* Josephus' brief mention of Jesus (of Nazareth) within Book XVIII of the *AJ*? This fact alone should be seen as possibly the most convincing evidence that no one knew of the *TF* before the time of Eusebius.[94]

John Tors writes, "However, inasmuch as this table of contents is 'selective,' not exhaustive, this argument proves nothing."[95] Similarly, Etienne Nodet has shown that all an absence meant is that Josephus did not consider its inclusion important. Christopher Price contributed a chapter in *Shattering the Christ Myth*, which dovetails the thinking of Viklund and Nodet. He argued the following points:

1. The anti-authentic "argument assumes that the table of contents was written by Christians before the Testimonium was interpolated."
2. "There is no evidence that the table of contents was written by Christians."
3. Citing Professor Thackeray, he concluded "that the author of the table of contents was like a Jew and possibly one of Josephus' assistants…Thackeray's conclusion is entitled to substantial respect."[96]

However, as quoted prior, Feldman disputes Thackeray's hypothesis, as does Doherty.[97] Like many arguments from both sides of the aisle, it is an *argumentum ex silentio*.

Price, in a 2009 online essay, adds a defense. He says, "The better explanation is that whoever created the summaries, they were not Christian. Thus, no significance can be gleaned from the fact that the table does not refer to the TF."[98] Readers will be the final judge of whether the absence of a table of contents in the *AF* is significant.

---

[94] Allen, "Clarifying the Scope," 218.
[95] Tors, "The Testimony of Josephus."
[96] Price, "Firmly Established by Josephus," 43. In contrast, Meier, in *A Marginal Jew*, writes, "An intriguing allied question is whence Josephus drew his information. Thackeray leaves open the possibility that in Rome Josephus had met Luke or read his work," 67. Readers are left to evaluate the reality of that possibility.
[97] Doherty, *Jesus: Neither God Nor Man*, 547.
[98] Price, "Did Josephus Refer to Jesus?"

Rebuttal 7:
The Disputed Content

The content matter of the *TF* has been subject to extensive investigation. Proponents of the partial authenticity of the *TF* acknowledged that parts of it are inauthentic and contain Christian glosses that no Jew would have written. For example, the Christian apologist Edwin Yamauchi penned, "Almost everyone agrees that there are a number of phrases in the passage which are so patently Christian that a Jew like Josephus would not have penned them."[99] Several examples of these excerpts are listed below:

1. "He was the Christ [Messiah]"
2. "He appeared to them alive again on the third day"
3. "He won over many of the Jews and many of the Greeks"
4. "For the prophets of God had prophesied these and countless other marvelous things about him"[100]
5. "Tribe of Christians"[101]

Writers from both sides of the aisle present differing views for their respective opinions about the authenticity of the disputed words and phrases. The literature is massive and discussed in many sources identified in this section.[102]

Rebuttal 8:
The Disputed Claim: "He was the Christ [Messiah]"

---

[99] Yamauchi, "Josephus and the Scriptures," 54; cf. Bock, *Studying the Historical Jesus,* 55–56.

[100] An alternative point of view is that the *TF* does *not* claim to be a testimony. What the *TF* says is that you must check out the Hebrew Bible prophecies to see if what it says about Jesus is true. It provides Scriptural proof that Jesus could not be "the Messiah." Later in the section, that topic is investigated.

[101] Allen, *Christian Forgery in Jewish Antiquities,* 203–17; Dunn, *Jesus Remembered,* 1:141; Feldman, "On the Authenticity," 22–27; Goldberg, "The Coincidences of the Emmaus," 59–77; "Josephus's Paraphrase Style," 1–32; Hillar, "Flavius Josephus," 5–6, 9–24; Hopper, "A Narrative Anomaly," 167; Mason, *Josephus and the New Testament,* 229–32; Meier, *A Marginal Jew,* 60–61; Olson, "A Eusebian Reading," 109–10; Yamauchi, "Josephus and the Scriptures," 54–55; Van Voorst, *Jesus Outside the New Testament,* 207–30.

[102] See works by Allen, Carrier, Doherty, Feldman, Goldberg, Hopper, Mason, Meier, Olson, Price, and Van Voorst.

Problems with Josephus   63

The phrase in the *TF* that "He was the Christ [Messiah]" is almost universally rejected by historians and apologists. Josephan scholar Steve Mason devotes approximately four pages containing several explanations and elaborating why the affirmation of Jesus being the Messiah is problematic. Culled from his text are three lines of thought:

1. Christ

First, the word "Christ" (Greek *christos*) would have special meaning only for a Jewish audience. In Greek, it means simply "wetted" or "anointed." Within the Jewish world, this was an extremely significant term because anointing was the means by which the kings and high priests of Israel had been installed. The pouring of oil over their heads represented their assumption of God-given authority (Exod 29:9; 1 Sam 10:1)....

But for someone who did not know Jewish tradition the adjective wetted would sound most peculiar. Why would Josephus say that this man Jesus was "the Wetted"?...

Since Josephus is usually sensitive to his audience and pauses to explain unfamiliar terms or aspects of Jewish life, it is very strange that he would make the bald assertion, without explanation, that Jesus was "Christ." He has not used this term before and will use it again when he calls James the "brother of Jesus, the one called Christ" (*Ant.* 20.200)....

2. "This man was Christ"

A second problem with the statement "This man was Christ" is that its solemn phrasing makes it seem to represent Josephus' confession of faith: he believed Jesus to be Messiah. In addition to that direct statement, the passage says things that only a Christian could have written, it seems, about Jesus' appearances after death, his being more than just a man, and the many ancient prophecies concerning him...But that seems impossible [Josephus must have been a Christian]. As we have seen, he writes as a passionate advocate of Judaism. Everywhere he praises the excellent constitution of the Jews, codified by Moses, and declares its peerless, comprehensive quality. (Yet even Moses, who was as close as possible to God, is never credited with being more than a man.) Josephus rejoices over converts to Judaism. In all of this, there is not the slightest hint of any belief in Jesus....

3. *Ant.* 18.63–64

> The strongest evidence that Josephus did not declare Jesus' messiahship is that the passage under discussion does not seem to have been present in the texts of the Antiquities known before the fourth century....
>
> Most significantly, the renowned Christian teacher Origen (185–254 CE flatly states, in two different contexts, that Josephus did not believe in Jesus' messiahship....
>
> The first author to mention the *Testimonium* is Eusebius, the church historian who wrote in the early 300s.[103]

Other writers confirm his opinion and add to his arguments. Doherty offers several factors to evaluate:

1. Even if some of his readers knew of Jewish Messiah expectation, Josephus' linking of Jesus with the Messiah concept would have been further misleading in that such expectation was in no way fulfilled in Jesus.
2. Could Josephus seriously expect no puzzlement on his readers' part by his attachment of the "Messiah" term to one who had been ignominiously crucified and never came close to becoming king of the Jews, let alone of the nations? His readers may well have wondered how anyone, Jew or gentile, could have come to believe that this executed preacher and miracle worker had been the Messiah of Jewish prophecy, a wonderment that would have extended to their curiosity over why Josephus was presenting them with such an unexplained conundrum.
3. Since Josephus lived and wrote his work in Rome, a member of Roman aristocratic society, he was presumably aware of all this complexity and peril inherent in the subject of the Christos, and of the necessity to explain it in detail. If for no other reason, it is likely he would have avoided the term and subject altogether in any connection with Jesus.[104]

Eddy and Boyd point out several contradictions with the statement that "*He was the Messiah.*" First, "Only a Christian would have said this." Second, they opine that "It seems that Josephus did not even believe that the Messiah would be Jewish."[105] In support of this opinion, they say that

---

[103] Mason, *Josephus and the New Testament*, 165–70.
[104] Doherty, *Jesus: Neither God Nor Man*, 545–47.
[105] Eddy and Boyd, *The Jesus Legend*, 191.

Josephus "seems to have thought that his patron, the Roman general Vespasian, was the Messiah (e.g., see *Jewish War* 6.5.4)."[106]

Remarkably, when examining the Messiah (i.e., Christ) appearance in the *TF*, proponents do not engage scriptural rationales that Josephus would not acknowledge Jesus was the Messiah or could have been the Messiah.[107] Volume 2 investigates this subject. Readers must remember that Josephus was a knowledgeable Pharisee. He knew the Hebrew Bible. How could he even suggest that Jesus was a presumed Messiah, with Scripture refuting any possibility? Presumably, Josephus would add at least one sentence mocking this mistaken belief by the "many Jews" (an argument from silence). The Bible is explicit and uncompromising in identifying the requisites to be "the Messiah."

1. He must be a direct male descendant of King David and King Solomon, his son.
2. Elijah, the prophet, will precede the Messiah and "pave the way" for his arrival.
3. His arrival will herald the commencement of the messianic era.
4. The Bible states that Messiah is to redeem Israel.
5. The ingathering of all Jewish people in Israel.
6. The Messiah will live during the wars of Gog and Magog.
7. The Messiah is supposed to rebuild the Third Temple (Note: The Second Temple was standing when Jesus lived.).
8. The true Messiah is to reign as King of the Jews.
9. The Messiah will be a military king who will rule from sea to sea.
10. The Messiah will restore the Jewish people to the full observance of the Torah.
11. There will be no more hunger or illness.
12. World peace will prevail.
13. All of the dead will rise again.

Lastly, Josephus wrote approximately sixty years after the crucifixion of Jesus and twenty years after the destruction of the Second Temple. With his knowledge of the Bible, how could he imagine Jesus was the Messiah or that the followers were *not* fools and say as much?

Rebuttal 9:
Disproportionate Number of Words

---

[106] Eddy and Boyd, *The Jesus Legend*, 191.
[107] Not a single comment from proponents: Bock, Boyd, Charlesworth, Dunn, Eddy, Habermas, Licona, Meier, Price, Tors, or Van Voorst.

in a Josephan Paragraph

Another speculative hypothesis exemplifying an argument from silence is the number of words (i.e., length) in the *TF*. Price elaborates writing, "This argument asserts that the passage in Josephus is 'unusually short' to match Josephan style."[108] The *TF* contains seventy-seven Greek words. Several writers discuss the measure of the *TF*'s length by the number of Greek words compared to "similar" content in other works. Allen offers that conservative scholars employ two approaches when discussing the *TF*'s length:

> As a result, more conservative scholars will attempt to do one of two things at this juncture. Either they will argue the complete opposite and demonstrate that the very *brevity* of the *TF* points to it being authentic (Josephan), or do a seeming *volte-face* and alternatively claim that when composed, it was *far longer* or more neutral, if not extremely negative in character.
>
> Here a typically conservative argument runs along the following lines. A committed, early Christian apologist would not have been satisfied with such an understated reference. Instead, while using the opportunity to give fraudulent, extra-biblical/scriptural, and pseudo-independent historical support to Jesus being an actual, celebrated, flesh-and-blood personage, they would have insisted on elaborating him as the incarnation of the supreme deity. Thus the *TF* must be authentic since it is so short.[109]

In contrast, Allen provides a condensed rebuttal by skeptics. He argues that for skeptics, "It is the very shortness of length, coupled with its compactness of dogmatic material that gives the TF away as being quite fraudulent."[110] In his opinion, this response does not make any sense.

On this very point, Doherty stated his analysis:

> In fact, the shortness of the passage [*TF*] could be seen as a strike *against* authenticity. If the 'authentic' *Testimonium* is supposed to represent more or less what Josephus wrote, why is it so lacking in detail when compared to that which he gives to his surrounding anecdotes? Such an original passage would pale in comparison to the rich accounts of the crisis over Pilate's attempted introduction into the

---

[108] Price, "Did Josephus Refer to Jesus?"
[109] Allen, "Clarifying the Scope," 187–88.
[110] Allen, "Clarifying the Scope, "189.

city of the effigies on the army standards, or the riots over his use of Temple funds to finance the new aqueducts. The related incidents succeeding the *Testimonium* are also very detailed - two scandals happening "about the same time,'..."[111]

Another argument from silence against the authenticity of the *TF* is that Josephus goes into extended detail about the lives of numerous personages of relatively "modest" import. These include several people who shared the name Jesus, some who were supposed messiah figures, and ordinary people.

- John the Baptist (*Ant*. 18, 5, 2—p. 382, Whiston)
- Jesus, the son of Saphat, the ringleader of the robbers (*J.W.* 3, 9, 7—p. 518, Whiston)
- Jesus ben Ananias (*J.W.* 6.5.3—pp. 582–83, Whiston) Athronges the Shepherd, 4 BCE/death of Herod (*J.W.* 2:60–65 = 2.4.3—p. 473, Whiston)
- Theudus (*Ant*. 20, 5, 1—pp. 418–19, Whiston; *Ant*. 20: 97–98—pp. 418–19, Whiston)
- Paulina (*Ant*. 18:3, 4—pp. 379–80, Whiston).

The *TF* spends about six lines on Jesus. Detractors presume it is inconceivable that Josephus would devote only a few sentences to someone who even remotely resembled the Jesus found in the New Testament. Nevertheless, Josephus writes proportionally more about these "less important" personages who were less significant in contrast. Apologists think otherwise with their rationales.

Eddy and Boyd evaluated the length of material that discussed John the Baptist compared to Jesus. They approached the length discrepancy from a different perspective. They ask why would Josephus have a lengthier discussion about John the Baptist after commenting about Jesus? They present two explanations,

1. If the entire *Testimonium* was the work of a Christian interpolator, it seems he would have followed the Gospel pattern and placed it *after* the discussion on John the Baptist, whom Christians regarded as a forerunner of Jesus.

---

[111] Doherty, *Jesus Neither God Nor Man*, 537.

2. The interpolator would have created an account that at least paralleled the Baptist discussion in terms of length.[112]

In contradiction, Meier interprets this topic from a different lens:

> A final curiosity encompasses not the *Testimonium* taken by itself but the relation of the *Testimonium* to the longer narrative about John the Baptist in *Ant.* 18.5.2 §116–19, a text accepted as authentic by almost all scholars. The two passages are in no way related to each other in Josephus. The earlier, shorter passage about Jesus is placed in the context of Pontius Pilate's governorship of Judea; the later, longer passage about John is placed in a context dealing with Herod Antipas, tetrarch of Galilee-Perea. Separated by time, space, and placement in Book 18, Jesus and the Baptist (in that order!) have absolutely nothing to do with each other in the mind and narrative of Josephus. Such a presentation totally contradicts-indeed, it is the direct opposite of the NT portrait of the Baptist, who is always treated briefly as the forerunner of the main character, Jesus. Viewed as a whole, the treatment of Jesus and John in Book 18 of *The Antiquities* is simply inconceivable as the work of a Christian of any period.[113]

These discussions revolve around a vital question: Who wrote the original and current version of the *TF*, and what did it contain: Josephus or a Christian interpolator? If Josephus did not write the *TF*, the discussion is not relevant. If he wrote the *TF*, the unanswerable question remains why did he write a lengthier discussion of John the Baptist, who was less significant, contradicting his usual literary style?

Rebuttal 10:
Names

A circumstantial factor presumably adds weight to the hypothesis that part (or all) of the *TF* is an interpolation. This hypothesis focuses on the name Jesus appearing in *AJ*. Jesus was a common name during the first century. Harold Leidner, an independent Jewish researcher and advocate of the "Christ Myth," based on the *Loeb* ten-volume edition, reports that there are approximately 1,932 individual names in the *AF, of which* "Jesus"

---

[112] Eddy and Boyd, *The Jesus Legend*, 196–97; cf. Boyd and Eddy, *Lord or Legend?*, 134.
[113] Meier, *A Marginal Jew*, 66.

appears twenty-one times.[114] Allen explains, "The obvious concern is over how Josephus (as the presumed author of the *TF*), refers to Jesus (of Nazareth) when compared to many of the other individuals mentioned in his works, each of which shares the same name."[115] Leidner's list, derived from the Loeb index, is instructive:

1. Jesus son of Naue
2. Jesus son of Saul
3. Jesus, high priest, son of Phineas
4. Jesus son of the high priest Jozadak
5. Jesus son of Joiada
6. Jesus, high priest, son of Simon
7. Jesus, high priest, son of Phabes
8. Jesus, high priest, son of Seë
9. Jesus the Christ
10. Jesus son of Damnaeus, became high priest
11. Jesus son of Gamliel, became high priest
12. Jesus son of Sapphas
13. Jesus, chief priest, probably to be identified with 10 or 11
14. Jesus son of Gamalas, high priest
15. Jesus, brigand chief on the borderland of Ptolemais
16. Jesus son of Sapphias
17. Jesus brother of Chares
18. Jesus a Galilean, perhaps to be identified with 15
19. Jesus in ambuscade, perhaps to be identified with 16
20. Jesus, priest, son of Thebuthi
21. Jesus son of Ananias, rude peasant, prophesies the fall of Jerusalem.

Leidner elaborates that the list unmistakably demonstrates that Josephus follows the Judaic custom of linking the son's name to that of the father: "X son of Y," and Josephus does this throughout his writings. He further argues that Josephus was consistent in hundreds of cases and in the twenty cases identified above, except for several minor figures involved in the turbulent events in Galilee during the war with Rome. Leidner argues that "The text indicates family linkages for all except number fifteen, "Jesus, brigand chief." Analyzing the data, he says, "These minor Jesuses appear in the narrative with every indication of time, place,

---

[114] Leidner, *The Fabrication of the Christ Myth*, 19, 23.
[115] Allen, "*Clarifying the Scope*," 157.

and detail to show that they were authentic figures. This has never been questioned."[116]

In the *TF*, Josephus tells his readers nothing about Jesus (of Nazareth) in terms of his lineal descent, his status in the community, his background (if ignoring the possible import of the *JP* (*James Passage*), or his familial connections. This reality troubled Leidner. He found it puzzling that Jesus, the presumed Christ was not recorded as "Jesus son of Joseph."[117] Leidner elaborates on the relevance of this subject. In his eyes, it is strange that Josephus does not describe or elaborate on that number nine in his list as "Jesus son of Joseph."[118] Leidner opines that Josephus would undoubtedly have known the father's name. Illustrating this point, he asks a hypothetical question. What would be the first question asked "Jesus" by a Jewish court: "Who are you, and what is your name?" He suggests, "There would be little dispute about the passage if the name Joseph were included."[119] Leidner points out that the "Jesus-passage" in the *TF* begins: "About this time there lived Jesus, a wise man if indeed one ought to call him a man."[120]

Leidner points out that other passage versions also omit the father's name. Sarcastically, he inquires, "Could Josephus, Temple priest, and historian, have written this way?"[121] He argues, "The plain inference is that this crucial line was written by a Christian for Christian readers, for whom only one Jesus existed in all history, and that one without human paternity."[122] Leidner continues the line of attack, offering that pronouncing the name "Jesus" would "immediately summon up the majesty of Christ to the Christian reader." There would be no need to mention a father presuming these Christian readers knew that Jesus was the Son of God.

Consequently, the name of a human father was omitted. It requires asking, would Josephus have ever thought in those terms? Leidner and others argue he never wrote that opening line. Therefore, if Josephus did not write it, then it would be difficult to salvage the rest of the passage. Leidner further says, "It could not exist without that line.[123]

Based on the known data, Leidner argues that Jesus was a myth. "The prior material indicates that the person of 'Jesus of Nazareth' could

---

[116] Leidner, *The Fabrication of the Christ Myth*, 19–21.
[117] Leidner, *The Fabrication of the Christ Myth*, 21.
[118] Leidner, *The Fabrication of the Christ Myth*, 21.
[119] Leidner, *The Fabrication of the Christ Myth*, 21.
[120] Leidner, *The Fabrication of the Christ Myth*, 21.
[121] Leidner, *The Fabrication of the Christ Myth*, 21.
[122] Leidner, *The Fabrication of the Christ Myth*, 21.
[123] Leidner, *The Fabrication of the Christ Myth*, 21.

be constructed out of Judaic sources without the need for a historical figure. Thus the gospel story comes under doubt at the very outset of our inquiry."[124] Leidner's line of reasoning and Allen's overview need examination.[125] The reader will judge whether this line of circumstantial evidence weakens the claimed authenticity of the *TF*.

Rebuttal 11:
Context, Flow, and Meier's
Reconstruction Hypothesis

The burden of proof rests on the proponents to prove that *TF* or portions of it are authentic. A topic of scholarly debate is "context and flow." Detractors argue that the context of the *TF* passage comes in the middle of a collection of stories about calamities that happened to the Jewish people. Additionally, the crucifixion of Jesus would not have been a Jewish calamity since thousands met their demise similarly. This passage in the *TF* interrupts the normal flow of the text. Alternatively, proponents of this section of the *Antiquities* could claim it is about events leading up to the outbreak of the war with Rome and the destruction of the temple. Christians argue that Jesus' death was (perhaps?) the event leading to the destruction of the Second Temple. Fittingly, the *TF* mentioned the death of Jesus. Therefore, the *TF* fits this section of *Antiquities*. However, it requires asking if Josephus thought that the crucifixion and death of Jesus were (perhaps?) the cause of the temple's destruction; why did he not say so? Consequently, critics also argue that with this expunged paragraph, the end of the section before it and the beginning after it blends perfectly. The literature is diverse.

Robert Stein, retired Chair of New Testament at The Southern Baptist Theological Seminary in Louisville, Kentucky, writes, "The authenticity of this passage is that it breaks the continuity of Josephus's argument."[126] Noteworthy, the preceding narrative ends with the words, "Thus ended the uprising."[127] However, the following passage begins "about the same time another outrage threw the Jews into an uproar." Stein concludes, "Thus, whereas omission of the Testimonium permits the

---

[124] Leidner, *The Fabrication of the Christ Myth*, 25.
[125] Allen, *"Clarifying the Scope,"* 157–61; cf. See Leidner, *The Fabrication of the Christ Myth*, 19–27.
[126] Stein, *Jesus the Messiah*, 30.
[127] Charlesworth, *Jesus Within Judaism*, 93.

passage to read smoothly, its presence breaks the continuity and makes one wonder if the testimony is a foreign insertion."[128]

Princeton Theological Seminary's George L. Collord Professor of New Testament Language and Literature James H. Charlesworth wrote that the passage breaks the continuity of the narrative, which tells of a series of riots. Specifically, §65 seems to belong directly after §62. First, "Once the clearly Christian sections are removed, the rest makes good grammatical and historical sense."[129] Second, he opines, "The peculiarly Christian words are parenthetically connected to the narrative; hence they are grammatically free and could easily have been inserted by a Christian."[130] Charlesworth concludes his analysis with these instructive words. "These sections also are disruptive, and when they are removed, the flow of thought is improved and smoother."[131]

Lending support to this evaluation, Meier writes in *A Marginal Jew* the following analysis of the *TF* passage. "In short, the first impression of what is Christian interpolation may well be the correct impression. A second glance confirms this first impression."[132] Then Meier repeats a frequently made claim that "Precisely these three Christian passages are the clauses that interrupt the flow of what is otherwise a concise text."[133]

Six pages later, Meier offers his hypothesis: the *TF* flows after expunging three "Christian" extracts (i.e., objectionable material) from the text:

> In contrast, I have simply bracketed then clearly Christian statements. What is remarkable is that the text that remains—without the slightest alteration—flows smoothly, coheres with Josephus' vocabulary and style, and makes perfect sense in his mouth. A basic rule of method is that, all things being equal, the simplest explanation that also covers the largest amount of data is to be preferred. Hence I submit that the most probable explanation of the *Testimonium* is that, short of the three obviously Christian affirmations, it is what Josephus wrote.[134]

---

[128] Stein, *Jesus the Messiah*, 30.
[129] Stein, *Jesus the Messiah*, 30.
[130] Charlesworth, Jesus Within Judaism, 93.
[131] Charlesworth, *Jesus Within Judaism*, 93–94.
[132] Meier, *A Marginal Jew*, 61.
[133] Meier, *A Marginal Jew*, 61.
[134] Meier, *A Marginal Jew*, 67.

Problems with Josephus 73

Darrell Bock, another Christian apologist, engages in the *TF* reconstruction controversy. Bock presumes Josephus wrote something about Jesus. However, his certitude is unverifiable. After reviewing several hypotheses, he says, "Nor can we be positive which of the above suggestions is closest to Josephus's original text."[135]

Renowned Christian apologist and theologian F.F. Bruce engaged in the reconstruction hypothesis. His analysis is insightful and requires diligent contemplation:

> This attempt to reconstruct what Josephus originally wrote amounts simply to the extrusion of those words which are felt to be Christian interpolations. But if in fact the original text was tampered with, it is possible that the tampering was not restricted to interpolation; it may have included the removal or modification of expressions felt to be offensive.[136]

Josephan researcher Steve Mason also devotes space in his book to this controversy:

> So, what is the problem? (a) To begin with, the most obvious point: the passage does not fit well with its context in Ant. 18. Like the tourist negotiating a bustling, raucous Middle-Eastern market who accidently walks through the door of a monastery, suffused with light and peace, the reader of Josephus is struck by this sublime portrait. Josephus is speaking of upheavals, but there is no upheaval here. He is pointing out the folly of Jewish rebels, governors, and troublemakers in general, but this passage is completely supportive of both Jesus and his followers. Logically, what should appear in this context ought to imply some criticism of the Jewish leaders and/or Pilate, but Josephus does not make any such criticism explicit. He says only that those who denounced Jesus were "the leading men among us." So, unlike the other episodes, this one has no moral, no lesson. Although Josephus begins the next paragraph by speaking of "another outrage" that caused an uproar among the Jews at the same time (18.65), there is nothing in this paragraph that depicts any sort of outrage.[137]

Similarly, Peter Kirby discusses difficulties with the *TF*.[138]

---

[135] Bock, *Studying the Historical Jesus*, 57. See his discussion spanning 55 to 57.
[136] Bruce, *Jesus and Christian Origins*, 39.
[137] Mason, *Josephus and the New Testament*, 227.
[138] Kirby, "Josephus and Jesus: The Testimonium Flavianum Question."

Goldberg has critiqued Meier's bracketing hypothesis without the benefit of new research. He comments, "But the evidence for selecting these three phrases to delete is not, in Meier's terminology, probative: it is a plausible idea, but not a necessarily true one."[139] Later, Goldberg adds, "Meier's is a reconstruction that rests only on its plausibility, not on its necessity. It is only one of many other plausible suggestions."[140] Following a detailed analysis (available online), he concludes Meier's "argument for the particular [his] reconstruction is not very solid" and "the reasons for deleting the resurrection passage in the Testimonium are weaker than those for including it."[141]

Detractors might posit that Meier's hypothesis is subject to dispute, written in 1991 and without the benefit of advances contributed by Carrier, Feldman, Goldberg, Hopper, and Olson.[142] For example, Olson criticizes Meier's presumptions:

> Meier's linguistic analysis is premised on the assumption that an early Christian writer would have followed the language of the New Testament when writing about Jesus. I was certain that Eusebius does not do this and don't know of any early Christian authors who did. Meier, in fact, does not claim that his linguistic analysis consistently finds Josephan language in the "core text" and New Testament language in the "Christian interpolations." He acknowledges that some examples go the other way, and that his main argument is from content (see the end of note 83.n.42)[143]

Olson also says, "The text does not divide easily into Christian and non-Christian sections on the basis of either language or content."[144]

Continuing with his analysis of Meier's hypothesis, Olson responds to an important question Meier asks:

> In the course of defending his proposition that this summary description of Jesus is not conceivable in the mouth of an ancient Christian, Meier asks: "What would be the point of a Christian interpolation that would make Josephus the Jew affirm such an imperfect estimation of the God-man? What would a Christian scribe

---

[139] Goldberg, "Critique of the Argument of Meier."
[140] Goldberg, "Critique of the Argument of Meier."
[141] Goldberg, "Critique of the Argument of Meier."
[142] Carrier, "Josephus on Jesus? 2014"; "Jesus among the Historians."
[143] Olson, "The Testimonium Flavianum."
[144] Olson, "A Eusebian Reading," 100.

intend to gain by such an assertion?" [Meier 1991: 64] This is an excellent question and one that deserves an answer. The question itself reveals a key assumption made by Meier and other scholars who have examined the issue. They assume that the interpolation (or interpolations) in the text of *Antiquities* 18 was composed by the scribes engaged in copying the manuscripts of Josephus and first appeared in its present context between Antiquities 18.62 and 18.65. This is possible, but there is a more likely alternative. The passage fits much better into the larger literary context it occupies in Eusebius' work. Eusebius uses the passage as part of an extended argument that he makes in the *Demonstration* and later reproduces in the *Theophany*. In this context, the *Testimonium* sounds very different from the way it sounds when Meier and other scholars read it as the work of Josephus. The theory of Josephan authorship controls their interpretation of the text.[145]

Returning to Carrier, he writes that "The TF doesn't fit the context of *JA* 18.62 and 65 (e.g., it does not describe "a disaster befalling the Jews" nor explain the rising tensions between Jews and Romans leading to war).[146] In his text, Carrier elaborates on why the *TF* does not fit the context of *JA* 18.62 and 18:65. First, the next paragraph begins by saying, "About the same time also another terrible thing threw the Jews into disorder" (*Ant*. 18.65). However, Josephus had just ended with the sedition resulting in a public massacre (described in *Ant*. 18.60–62). Carrier continues with his analysis. In brief, "The *original* text obviously went directly from the massacre to the following scandal, with no digression in between."[147] This reality leaves no logical place for the unrelated digression on Jesus and the Christians (in *Ant*. 18.63–64).

Second, Carrier correctly points out that the next story in Josephus' work is also about a religious controversy. The controversy involving Judaism and the Isis cult is told at great and elaborate length. For instance, in *Antiquities* 18.65–80, the narrative appears eight times longer than the *TF*. However, it dealt with a more "trivial affair." In Carrier's opinion, "The latter demonstrates that Josephus would have written a great deal more about the Jesus affair if he had written anything about it at all."[148] In contrast, a forger would have been limited by the remaining space available on a standard scroll for volume 18 (or by the

---

[145] Olson, "A Eusebian Reading," 100–1.
[146] Carrier, "Josephus on Jesus? Why You Can't Cite Opinions Before 2014."
[147] Carrier, *On the Historicity of Jesus*, 336.
[148] Carrier, *On the Historicity of Jesus*, 336.

space available in the margin, if that is where the passage began its life). Hypothetically, this presumption could explain its bizarre brevity, in comparison with the preceding and following narratives, and it is astonishing content. Carrier elaborates that this reality "would require several explanations and digressions which are curiously absent."[149]

Rebuttal 12:
Are the Partial Authenticity Hypothesis,
the Reconstruction Hypothesis, and the
Neutral Hypothesis an Illusion?

Proponents of "the partial authenticity," "the reconstruction hypothesis," and "the neutral hypothesis" beg the question: they presume Josephus knew about Jesus from sources unknown, wrote about Jesus in his *TF*, and the original material (or ideas it contained) that he wrote are recoverable. Due to the amount of space and time devoted to this presumption by its proponents and its significance, several quoted responses are essential. Allen engages Meier's partial authenticity hypothesis writing in his doctoral dissertation.

He argues that most conservative scholars accept Meier's "partial authenticity thesis. The rationale is that it still leaves those scholars with enough material to claim an historical reference to Jesus of Nazareth. Allen charges that the vast majority of these scholars never mention "the problem that if even they can see something fallacious about this out of place passage due to its overt Christian glosses why should any of it be authentic?"[150] He continues criticizing the thinking of these scholars. "The Christian glosses are the very indication that the entire text is suspect."[151] Then Allen confronts the topic of bracketing: "To simply remove the bits that one does not like and artificially reconstruct something intelligible with those words that can be regarded as devoid of Christian content makes absolutely no sense."[152] Readers must judge the validity of Allen's argument.

Michael Licona, a Christian apologist, in the *Resurrection of Jesus: A New Historiographical Approach,* leaves readers with words to ponder:

---

[149] Carrier, *On the Historicity of Jesus*, 336.
[150] Allen, "Clarifying the Scope," 231.
[151] Allen, "Clarifying the Scope, "231.
[152] Allen, "Clarifying the Scope," 231.

Unless and until an early manuscript of *Antiquities of the Jews* 18 is discovered, uncertainty will have a valid presence in discussions pertaining to whether Josephus mentioned Jesus in 18.63 and, if so, what precisely he said. Scholars will continue to debate reconstructions that differ in plausibility. Accordingly any use of Josephus in our investigation will be done with great caution. I assign this text a rating of *possible*. (Italics in the original)[153]

Readers must answer a vital question: Did Licona's writing the word "possible" reassure your confidence that the *TF* is trustworthy?

Rabbi Moshe Shulman critically analyzed the opinions of proponents supporting a reconstruction hypothesis. Without mincing words, he says, "The bottom line is that we can have no idea what was really 'original' since the text has been tampered with."[154] Then he adds, "Any of the wordings could be Christian, and any of the additions that we see below (including mine) are purely speculative and may exist only in our imagination."[155] Shulman concludes by writing, "It is fun to try to make a reconstruction, but we cannot seriously lay claim to having discovered anything that we can call 'the original version.'"[156]

Octavio da Cunha Botelho, somewhat with sarcasm, concludes his essay about the *TF*:

An Endless Ocean of Speculation

> Due to the extent of the controversy, the study above used only the most influential works today, that is, the hypotheses most cited and analyzed by scholars, as addressing all opinions, an attempt that at the moment, with the endless increase in the number of speculation on the subject is a difficult task. Thus, the *Testimonium Flavianum* remains, with no forecast of completion, like a growing ocean of hypotheses. As mentioned at the beginning of this study, certainty about the knowledge of the original text, as well as whether or not the passage existed in the work The Antiquity of the Jews, will only be possible with the discovery of Josephus' autograph manuscript, until then, the multiplication of speculations and conjecture will continue to happen, because whatever is proposed, it will simply be hypothesis ...

---

[153] Licona, *Resurrection of Jesus*, 242.
[154] Shulman, "Josephus and Jesus."
[155] Shulman, "Josephus and Jesus."
[156] Shulman, "Josephus and Jesus."

The *Testimonium Flavianum* has already been so stirred and stirred that if Josephus could be hearing what they have already speculated about his text, and if each speculation caused a contortion, he would be so contorted in his grave, that his skeleton would be irretrievably damaged. Anyway, the maximum credibility that can be found in the results of research and analysis in studies on the *Testimonium*, except for a very small number of confirmations, is that some hypotheses are more likely and others less likely. Therefore, until Josephus' autograph manuscript is found, the words "I think that", "may be", "probably", "it's possible", "likely", "perhaps", "I have the impression" and other terms that express uncertainty will continue to multiply in studies on the subject.[157]

Roger Viklund, a detractor, is blunt in his analysis of the methodology of proponents of the *TF*:

A subjective method. The method of removing everything which seems alien to Josephus' conceptions, and thus think that by this you have re-created a text that lies close to the genuine text, is essentially subjective, unscientific, deceptive, and therefore reprehensible. This is not a valid method, since by using it you can create a "genuine" text from whatever faked text you like. If you confine yourself to the method of eliminating everything which on the surface appears to be spurious, you could easily create seemingly authentic texts from texts forged throughout. You can simply remove and remove until you have eliminated everything that can be criticized, and at once you have created what you originally sought. Such an approach cannot be called serious

These kinds of methods are all about creating what you originally are looking for and what you want to be the truth; that is, to find ways to interpret the text of the Testimonium in order to defend the opinion that Josephus has written the paragraph. There is no real support for these interpretations in the form of preserved material. Of course one cannot dispute the possibility of such interpretations, that is, the proposed hypotheses are not falsifiable... (Bold in the original)[158]

---

[157] Botelho, "The Endless Dubiety," 19.
[158] Viklund, "The Jesus Passages in Josephus."

Similarly, over fifty years ago, Shlomo Pines summed up the situation. He wrote, "In other words, the reconstructions had, by and large, only a subjective validity."[159] Apparently, nothing is new under the sun.

Theissen and Merz add an often-ignored consequence of the partial and reconstruction hypothesis. They write that "The method of reconstruction depends on the prior decision that the basis is a report with negative colouring."[160] However, Theissen and Merz add a caveat that requires consideration: "It is assumed that the Christian reviser primarily replaced hostile expressions with positive or neutral ones."[161] If correct, readers must ponder, what were the negative words in the report?

Rebuttal 13:
Eusebius Forged the TF Hypothesis

Several writers propose the hypothesis that Eusebius or Pamphilus was responsible for the forgery found in the *TF*. Lataster, a detractor, offers his opinion on the subject focusing on Eusebius being the first person to mention the *TF*: "It is no wonder why some scholars would not only suspect that the passage is entirely fraudulent, but that it was Eusebius himself who fabricated it."[162]

Alice Whealey elaborates on this hypothesis.

1. Eusebius is the first person to have quoted the *Testimonium* in his works.
2. Eusebius quotes it three times.
3. Eusebius was also the first writer who used Josephus' works extensively.
4. Eusebius is the only person who could plausibly have forged *ex nihilo* or substantially rewritten the textus receptus *Testimonium* if it was forged or rewritten.

Whealey concludes, "No other ancient writer knew Josephus' works anywhere near well enough to have crafted something so similar to

---

[159] Pines, *An Arabic Version*, 21; cf. Mason, *Josephus and the New Testament*," 236.
[160] Theissen and Merz, *The Historical Jesus*, 70.
[161] Theissen and Merz, *The Historical Jesus*, 70.
[162] Lataster, *There Was No Jesus*.

Josephus' style."¹⁶³ The unknown remains are whether Eusebius forged or redacted the *TF*.

Olson is another investigator who makes a strong case that Eusebius is the forger of the *TF*. Concluding his *Catholic Biblical Quarterly* article, he wrote:

> When we turn to the question whether Eusebius wrote the passage, the situation is very different. No author cites the *Testimonium* before Eusebius, nor does any author cite it for nearly a century after Eusebius. Eusebius himself cites it three times, always to refute pagan attacks on Jesus' character, and we know from other examples that Eusebius incorrectly attributes to Josephus views that support his own. The passage is made up of vocabulary and concepts paralleled in Eusebius' works *Contra Hieroclem*, *Demonstratio evangelica*, and *Historia ecclesiastica*. Complete certainty is unattainable, but we have very good reasons to suppose that Eusebius wrote the *Testimonium*.¹⁶⁴

He has penned several works that require examining.¹⁶⁵

Finally, Carrier also supports the position that all manuscripts of *JA* are descendants of the Eusebian text. In a review of the literature, he and others previously cited offer multiple conjoining points for consideration:

1. Eusebius is the first one to cite the *Testimonium*, which he does first in the *Demonstratio*, then in the *Historia ecclesiastica*, and finally in *Theophania*.
2. It was not cited for at least a hundred years after Eusebius.
3. The style (of writing) of the *TF* is more Eusebian than Josephan.¹⁶⁶
4. The narrative structure of the *TF* is not Josephan (time, story, emplotment, apologetic).¹⁶⁷
5. All surviving manuscripts of the *Antiquities* derive from the last manuscript of it produced at the Christian library of Caesarea between 220 and 320 AD.
6. Both references to Jesus were probably added after their first custodian, Origen (who had no knowledge of them), but by the

---

¹⁶³ Whealey, "Josephus, Eusebius of Caesarea," 74.
¹⁶⁴ Olson, "Eusebius and the *Testimonium Flavianum*," 322.
¹⁶⁵ Olson, "A Eusebian Reading," 97–114 and "The Testimonium."
¹⁶⁶ Olson, "A Eusebian Reading," 97–114.
¹⁶⁷ Hopper, "A Narrative Anomaly," 147–68; Whealey, "Josephus, Eusebius of Caesarea," 74.

time of their last custodian, Eusebius (who is the first to find them there). The long one deliberately; the short one accidentally.
7. The additions may have been made by, or at the direction or under the supervision of, Eusebius, or his predecessor at the library, Origen's successor, Pamphilus.
8. Apart from all manuscripts of *JA* descent, there is no evidence the *JA* ever contained the *TF* in any form.[168]

Rebuttal 14:
Van Voorst's Six Claims Refuted

Six arguments, earlier made by Van Voorst, were cited. Allen's concise and detailed response, culled from Olson's lengthy analysis, refutes each argument.[169] Allen concludes this section by saying the following words:

> Scholarship is not based on some form of democracy or majority opinion but rather on providing substantiated evidence to support an argument. Even if one were to reject the overall conclusion that it was most likely Eusebius who wrote the *TF*, it would not change the fact that Van Voorst's six arguments are based on false premises about what a Christian writer would or would not have written. Arguments about what a generic Christian writer is likely to have done always need to be checked against the actual practice of real Christian authors.[170]

Conclusion

Since the 16th century, liberal and conservative scholars have regarded the *TF* as either entirely interpolated or drastically altered by a later generation of believers. At least three fundamental problems exist concerning Jesus in the *TF*:

1. Authenticity: Does the *TF* come from Josephus or some later Christian writer/s?
2. Independence: Even if the *TF* is authentic, is it an independent witness, or did Josephus get his information from other Christians or the Gospels?

---

[168] Allen, "Clarifying the Scope," 233–42; Carrier, "Jesus among the Historians."
[169] Allen, "Clarifying the Scope," 277–82; Olson, "The Testimonium Flavianum."
[170] Allen, "Clarifying the Scope," 281–82.

3. Core: Can a reconstructed version (core?) be identified if the *TF* is not original?

Advocates of the *Testimonium* claim that it is factual. Given the general definition of "fact" as "a thing that is known or proved to be true," can the *TF* be accepted as a "fact"? The *Testimonium* narrative is not a given fact. Identifying a proposition as a "fact," despite scholars considering the passage edited, redacted, or an interpolation raises factors for readers to judge.

Problems with Mara bar Serapion

Mara bar Serapion wrote a letter to his son (also called Serapion) while in Roman captivity. In that letter, he possibly referred to Jesus' crucifixion. It is important to note that he does not explicitly mention Jesus by name or the source of his information. The unique sentence from his works that may refer to Jesus reads, "But Socrates is not dead, because of Plato; neither is Pythagoras, because of the statue of Juno; nor is the wise king, because of the new laws he laid down."[1] That is it! Oddly, the historical philosophers Pythagoras and Socrates are specifically named, unlike the unknown, "wise king."

Problems exist with the letter's content not included by Habermas and Licona:

1. Jesus was never a king in the secular sense.
2. Serapion's letter clearly states that the Jews were removed from their land the very moment their "Wise King" was murdered (i.e., "from that very time"). However, the crucifixion of Jesus took place about 30–33 CE In contrast, the Second Temple was destroyed in 70 CE, a difference of over three decades.

Van Voorst's analysis includes reasons for questioning the usefulness of the letter:[2]

1. If Mara has Jesus in mind, why does he not use his name? That Mara does not use "Jesus" or "Christ" is particularly striking because he implicitly appeals to the fame of the wise king's teaching. This king and his laws are on a level with Socrates and Pythagoras, who were "household names" in the ancient world. (p. 55)
2. A date in the second century is indeed the most likely. (p. 56)

---

[1] Van Voorst, *Jesus Outside the New Testament*, 54.
[2] Van Voorst, *Jesus Outside the New Testament*, 55–57.

3. Where did Mara obtain his information on Jesus? Like many ancient authors, he does not name his sources, so we are left to puzzle them out. (p. 57)
4. The results of the study of the historical Jesus are slim. Mara's letter is not an independent witness to Jesus for two main reasons. First, it links the life of "the wise king" with his movement and its teachings, making it possible that Mara learned about the wise king from Christians. Second, its assertion that the Jews killed Jesus is dubious at best. By his logic, for Mara to implicate the Romana would go against his main point, that people who persecute and kill their wise men do so at their peril. In sum, Mara's letter says more about Christianity than about Christ. (p. 57)
5. Nevertheless, the balance of the evidence favors a Christian origin [of his information]. (p. 57)[3]

Eddy and Boyd came to similar conclusions:

1. Sometime between the late first century and the third century, a man named Mara bar Serapion wrote a letter to his son from prison." (p. 173)
2. The letter may be as late as the third century, by which time aspects of the Christian tradition had widely circulated throughout the Roman Empire. Thus, many "argue that this passage cannot be treated as an independent attestation of Jesus' existence or of his death." (p. 174)
3. So, while we cannot rule out the possibility that Serapion is dependent on Christian teachings for his information, we have no reason to assume that he was. (pp. 174–75)[4]

Craig Evans, writing in *Jesus and His Contemporaries: Comparative Studies*, briefly comments about Serapion, saying,

> There are other sources which may be of minimal value, though various uncertainties usually accompany them....One Mara bar Serapion, in a letter of this missive cannot be established with certainty. Proposed dates range from the first to the third centuries.[5]

---

[3] Van Voorst, *"Jesus Outside the New Testament,"* 55–57.
[4] Eddy and Boyd, *The Jesus Legend*, 173–75.
[5] Evans, *Jesus and His Contemporaries*, 41.

Lastly, Earl Doherty accurately questions the likelihood that a pagan writer such as Mara ben Serapion would place the seemingly insignificant Jesus on the same level as "household names" such as Socrates and Pythagoras.[6]

---

[6] Doherty, *Jesus: Neither God Nor Man*, 655.

Problems with Tacitus

Habermas and Licona cite Tacitus (56–117 CE) in support of Jesus' resurrection. Discussing the crucifixion, they quote two sentences from Tacitus' *Annals* (Book 15, sec. 44):

> Nero fastened the guilt [of the burning of Rome] and inflicted the most exquisite tortures on a class hated for their abominations, called Christians by the populace. Christus, from whom the name had its origin, suffered the extreme penalty during the reign of Tiberius at the hands of one of our procurators, Pontius Pilate.[1]

The actual name of this work is *Ab excess divi Augusti* ("From the death of the divine Augustus").[2] Tacitus' excerpt requires careful, critical, and assiduous analysis from those on both sides of the religious aisle.

In these crucial sentences, presumably, Tacitus is providing information about Jesus. It requires answering why the Tacitus text is vital. Robert Bowman, a well-known Christian apologist, elaborates why Tacitus' excerpt is noteworthy:

> Tacitus does not tell his readership very much about Christ. However, what he tells his readers agrees with the New Testament without being dependent on it. From his brief comments, we learn the following facts about Christ:
>
> 1. He was known as Christus.
> 2. His followers, who were named for him, were known as Chrestians (i.e., Christians).
> 3. The movement he founded began in Judea.
> 4. He was executed during the reign of the Roman emperor Tiberius (AD 14–37).

---

[1] Habermas and Licona, *Case for the Resurrection*, 49.
[2] Van Voorst, *Jesus Outside the New Testament*, 39.

5. He was executed by the order of the Roman procurator Pontius Pilate (AD 26–36).
6. The religion he founded was regarded by cultured Romans as a loathed "superstition."[3]

Upon careful reading, proponents argue that Tacitus tells his reader more than the fact that Jesus suffered crucifixion. He gives his readers specific information about this person — he was executed by the command of Pilate. This person was equivalent to the ruling "governor," the execution occurred during the reign of Tiberius, and the "statement that the movement began in Judea is correct if one understands Christianity to begin with the reports of Jesus' resurrection (even though Jesus began his ministry in Galilee, something most Christians would know but one would not expect Tacitus to know)."[4] Consequently, readers have a time, place, and person.

The Academic Debate about *Annals* 15:44

The academic debate surrounding this passage has mainly concerned two issues. First, what were the sources of Tacitus' information? Second, questions exist about its authorship. Some detractors argue that 15:44 is an interpolation. Consequently, they question its reliability.

Where did Tacitus obtain his information? The author did not identify his source material. Darrell Bock is blunt, "We do not know the source of Tacitus's information."[5] O'Neill points out, "Unlike modern historians, ancient ones did not footnote their sources or even consistently or regularly note where they received their information.[6] Birgit van der Lans and Jan N. Bremmer also acknowledge the difficulties confronted by researchers: "His contribution illustrates the challenges posed to the (ancient) historian faced with a differentiated body of authors whose interpretations depend on individual rhetorical considerations, and whose sources of information are more often than not irretrievable."[7]

---

[3] Bowman, "Tacitus, Suetonius, and the Historical Jesus"; O'Neill, "Jesus Mythicism 1"; Meier, *A Marginal Jew*, 1:90.

[4] Bowman, "Tacitus, Suetonius, and the Historical Jesus."

[5] Bock, *Studying the Historical Jesus*, 52.

[6] O'Neill, "Jesus Mythicism 1."

[7] van der Lans and Bremmer, "Tacitus and the Persecution of the Christians," 300.

A review of the literature from both sides of the religious aisle offers speculations based on the absence of evidence. Proponents and detractors argue from silence that Tacitus' information was hearsay. If that hypothesis is correct, it was from a secondary source. The sources of his information include several working postulations:

1. Tacitus repeated what Christians at the time were saying.
2. He obtained the information from official documents.
3. Tacitus learned the information from another historian he trusted (e.g., Josephus or Pliny the Younger).
4. Tacitus' information "is probably based on the police interrogation of Christians."[8]

John P. Meier, in *A Marginal Jew*, offers the following input:

> An important question is the source of Tacitus' information. Some scholars, highlighting similarities to the *Testimonium*, suggest that Tacitus had read Josephus. While that is possible, one must recognize that many differences as well as similarities in the two texts. It could be instead, that Tacitus is simply repeating what was common knowledge about Christians at the beginning of the 2nd century. Tacitus had been the governor of the province of Asia (i.e., the western third of Asia Minor) ca. AD 112, and might have had judicial contacts with Christians similar to those reported by Pliny the Younger. In addition, Pliny was a close friend of Tacitus and might have conveyed to him the knowledge he had gained about Christians. Nor can we exclude the possibility that Tacitus used Roman archives. However, if he did so, his mistake in calling Pilate a procurator instead of a prefect shows that he is not directly citing any official record. In any case, while Tacitus at the best supplies us with another early non-Christian witness to the existence, temporal and geographical location, death, and continued historical impact of Jesus, he tells nothing that Josephus had not already said.[9]

Readers must be cognizant that Meier couches and hedges his comments with loaded words and phrases such as "It could be instead," "And might have had," "And might have conveyed," and "Nor can we exclude the possibility that."

---

[8] Duhling and Perrin, *The New Testament Proclamation and Parenesis, Myth and History*, 7.

[9] Meier, *A Marginal Jew*, 91.

1. Tacitus Repeated What Christians at the Time were Saying.

Many writers discuss the hypothesis that Tacitus was possibly repeating common knowledge.[10] James Charlesworth believes that "Most likely, Tacitus was not working from official documents."[11] He offers two additional hypotheses. First, he probably obtained information about Jesus from conversations with others at locales unknown. Second, perhaps he obtained information "during the time he was governor of the western portion of Asia Minor about 112 CE"[12]

Robert Van Voorst remarks in *Jesus Outside the New Testament: An Introduction to the Ancient Evidence*, "The most likely source of Tacitus's information about Christ is Tacitus's own dealings with Christians, directly or indirectly."[13] Almost 100 years prior, Arthur Drews, an advocate of the Christ Myth, penned similar words relevant to this topic and bear repeating despite being a dated source. "Tacitus might have derived his information about Jesus, if not directly from the gospels, at all events indirectly from them by means of oral tradition."[14]

Dan Barker, a former evangelical and ordained minister, wrote a refutation of the usefulness of that claim via a comparison. "A modern parallel would be a 20th century historian reporting that Mormons believe that Joseph Smith was visited by the angel Moroni, which would hardly make it historical proof, even though it is as close as a century away."[15] Repeating what was common knowledge proves nothing. In addition, it is worth noting that Tacitus wrote his work about 115 CE. "That would be about 85 years or so after the crucifixion of Jesus."[16] By that time, no person would still be living, old enough to have witnessed the event and to be able to testify about it. Additionally, unknown would be the year that Tacitus presumably obtained this information.

---

[10] Allen Clarifying the Scope, 1, 267; Charlesworth, *The Historical Jesus*, 33–34; Mason, *Josephus, Judea, and Christian Origins*, 113n62; "Sources that Mention Jesus," 8; Meier, *A Marginal Jew*, 91; Prchlík, "*Auctor nominis*," 108; Van Voorst, *Jesus Outside the New Testament*, 52; Zindler, *The Jesus the Jews Never Knew*, 14.

[11] Charlesworth, *The Historical Jesus*, 34.

[12] Charlesworth, *The Historical Jesus*, 33–34.

[13] Van Voorst, *Jesus Outside the New Testament*, 52.

[14] Drews, *The Witnesses to the Historicity of Jesus*, 22. Although a dated source, his thirty-page analysis (20–56) contains significant literature, reviewing from those on both sides of the aisle. His text is available online and is a beneficial consultation.

[15] Barker, *Godless*, x.

[16] Bowman, "Tacitus, Suetonius, and the Historical Jesus."

Tim O'Neill adds a fundamental reality:

> The fact remains, however, that wherever Tacitus got his information, the Mythicist assumption [or anyone else's assumption] that he was "only repeating what Christians claimed" has no solid foundation and is severely undermined by much of what we know about Tacitus' use of his sources.[17]

Notably, "if" Tacitus was only repeating what others claimed or said, this information does not meet the requirements of being classified as independent evidence. It is hearsay. The bottom line is that nobody knows when, how, or where he obtained his information.

2. He Obtained the Information from Official Documents or Written Records.

Could Tacitus have obtained his information from official documents or written records? Some proponents suggest that Tacitus consulted "official" sources. Robert Van Voorst, an apologist, points out that there were two types of records in Rome, the *Commentarii Principis* and the *Acta Senatus*. The former "contained records like military campaigns, edicts, rescripts, and other legal actions by the emperors."[18] Tacitus' report that it was "secret and closed, so he could not consult it" is noteworthy.[19] The latter, the *Acta Senatus*, contained the Senate's archives of its actions and activities. These were open, and Tacitus reports that he used them. Next, Van Voorst expresses his opinion:

> But a report about Jesus would probably not belong there. It would not be a report from Pilate or, for that matter, any Roman official in Judea, because Judea was an imperial, not senatorial, province, and so its governors would not ordinarily have reported to the Senate. The Senate *could* have investigated the fire of 64 and made some comments for explanation about Christ that ended up in its archive. But this remains a supposition, since we have no reference to it from any surviving source.[20]

---

[17] O'Neill, "Jesus Mythicism 1."
[18] Van Voorst, *Jesus Outside the New Testament*, 50.
[19] Van Voorst, *Jesus Outside the New Testament*, 50.
[20] Van Voorst, *Jesus Outside the New Testament*, 50.

Anglican bishop and ancient historian Paul Barnett speculates about where Tacitus obtained his information: "As a former consul in Rome, Tacitus would have had access to official archives and may have seen Pilate's report to Tiberius about the execution of Jesus and others in Judea in 33."[21] According to Maurice Goguel (1880–1955), Dean of the Protestant Faculty of Theology in Paris, "But one fact is certain, and that is, Tacitus knew of a document, which was neither Jewish nor Christian, which connected Christianity with the Christ crucified by Pontius Pilate."[22] Similarly, Peter Kirby, from *Early Christian Writings*, opines, "The present writer believes that the most persuasive case is made by those who maintain that Tacitus made use of a first century Roman document concerning the nature and status of the Christian religion."[23] Additionally, some advocates claim he accessed the Roman archives. This argument centers on the opinion that Tacitus was a meticulous researcher, frequently consulting written documents and multiple sources.

O'Neill supports the argument and provides several grounds that bolster the opinion that Tacitus was a meticulous researcher. For example, he quotes C.W. Mendell, who highlighted how Tacitus handled his sources with due care:

> In the Histories there are sixty-eight instances in which Tacitus indicates either a recorded statement or a belief on someone's part with regard to something which he himself is unwilling to assert as a fact; in other words, he cites divergent authority for some fact or motive … [These] would seem to indicate a writer who had not only read what was written by historians….but had also talked with eye witnesses and considered with some care the probable truth where doubt or uncertainty existed….Tacitus assumes the responsibility of the historian to get at the truth and present it. His guarantee was his own reputation. To make this narrative colorful and dramatic, he felt justified in introducing facts and motives which he might refute on logical grounds or leave uncontested but for which he did not personally vouch. There is no indication that he followed blindly the account of any predecessor."[24]

O'Neill continues by saying, "Mendell goes on to note 30 separate instances in the *Annals* where Tacitus is careful to substantiate a statement

---

[21] Barnett, *Gospel Truth*, 39.
[22] Goguel, *Jesus the Nazarene*, 43.
[23] Kirby, "Information on Cornelius Tacitus."
[24] Mendell, *Tacitus*, 201–4.

or distance himself from a claim or report about which he was less than certain."[25]

Why do detractors and skeptics challenge this hypothesis? First, detractors dispute the argument that Tacitus was a "meticulous researcher." The phrase "meticulous researcher" is subjective. It requires quantification and a mutually acceptable understanding. How can this descriptive characteristic be evaluated and judged if it is unaccepted what is meant by the phrase "meticulous research"?

Second, even if Tacitus was a "meticulous researcher," that presumption does not negate the probability that his research was deficient or made errors here or elsewhere. Jens Schröter writes, "In analyzing historical material scholars would usually ask for their origin and character, their tendencies in delineating events from the past, evaluate their principal credibility ..."[26] Proponents of the historicity of *Annals* 15 argue that Tacitus was a "meticulous researcher." They base their argument on a legal technicality: "character evidence" and "habit evidence." These concepts are discussed extensively in books, journals, and legal proceedings:

> The definition is also tricky because you have to distinguish "fixed" behavior from a "tendency" to behave in certain ways. Fixed patterns of behavior are called habits which fall under [Federal] Rule [of Evidence] 406 and are admissible ... Character evidence under rule 404 is evidence of a general tendency to behave in certain ways, which is not usually admissible.[27]

Habit Evidence is under Rule 406 of the Legal Code. Culled from the literature, readers must consider the following information when determining whether Tacitus meets the criteria of a "meticulous researcher."

1. What is a habit? Habit evidence involves "systematic conduct" of doing something with "invariable regularity"; where there is a "regular response to a repeated specific situation."[28]

    a. Difference in habit of doing something (admissible) vs. habit of being something (usually not admissible).

---

[25] O'Neill, "Jesus Mythicism 1." See Mendell, *Tacitus*, 205.
[26] Schröter, "The Criteria of Authenticity," 52.
[27] Tanford, "Rule 406, Habit."
[28] Tanford, "Rule 406, Habit."

b. It is harder to prove a "negative" habit (a habit of not doing something) than a positive habit (a habit of doing something).
c. Habit can be proved in two different ways:

   1) The opinion of eyewitnesses to habit behavior
   2) Specific instances of conduct.

2. FACTORS in determining habit:

   a. Similarity of instances
   b. Number of instances
   c. Regularity of instances
   d. Reliability of the evidence[29]

Ronald Mellor, a distinguished professor of history at the University of California, Los Angeles, whose area of research has been ancient religion and Roman historiography, in *Tacitus*, says regarding his "meticulous research," the following opinion:

1. Tacitus relayed unverifiable rumors.
2. Tacitus occasionally reported a rumor or report that he knew was false ("He alludes to a rumor that the emperor was killed by his wife Livia, to prevent Agrippa's reinstatement.).[30]

Jeffrey Jay Lowder, a skeptic, reviewed research about *Annals*. He cites Michael Grant, an English classicist (Litt.D. Cambridge), author of *Greek & Roman Historians: Information and Misinformation,* and says the following with supporting information: "Tacitus was only skeptical 'on occasion,' that he 'persistent[ly] and lamentabl[y]' accepted many rumors, and that he "conducted extremely little independent research, quite often [he] quotes the sources that were available to him" [Grant 1995, 39–40]. If this opinion is correct, it is consistent with the hypothesis that Tacitus simply repeated what he learned from Christian sources.

Grant quotes the following excerpt from Goodyear:

> One feature very damaging to Tacitus's credit is the manner in which he employs rumors. Of course, a historian may properly report the state of public opinion at particular times, or use the views of

---

[29] Tanford, "Rule 406. Habit; Routine Practice."
[30] Mellor, *Tacitus*, 44.

contemporaries on major historical figures as a form of 'indirect characterisation' of them. But Tacitus often goes far beyond this.

He implants grave suspicions which he neither substantiates nor refutes. Their cumulative effect can be damning and distorting ... Time and again Tacitus is ready with an unpleasant motive, susceptible neither of proof nor of disproof.[31]

Lowder concludes by writing, "Again, we simply do not have enough data to justify the claim that Tacitus probably had independent sources for his information about Jesus."[32]

Third, presuming the Romans were meticulous in their records, it requires asking, does it seem probable, not possible, that the crucifixion record of an obscure person living in Jerusalem would go back nearly eighty years (the *Annals* were written c. 115 CE) had existed and were located for examination? Moreover, what would these records about Jesus, a carpenter, be doing in the records of the Roman Senate? Is it credible that records about an obscure crucifixion were sent over 1400 miles (2300 km) to Rome? Plausibly Tacitus consulted "sources" during his writing, yet, there is no means to prove or disprove (unfalsifiable and unverifiable) that he consulted any records or reports detailing the crucifixion of Jesus. This apologetic presumes that:

1. Roman archives had records of the crucifixion,
2. Tacitus had access to official records, and
3. He would have had a motive for investigating the historicity of Jesus.

In reality, (1) nobody knows whether official records (now lost) said anything about Jesus. (2) Researchers need to determine whether Tacitus would have access to the presumed records. (3) If records existed, there is the question of accuracy. Their worth is thus questionable. (4) Nobody knows whether Tacitus would have been motivated to research the archives.

Paul Rhodes Eddy and Gregory A. Boyd, two apologists, elaborate on this topic in their text:

Fourth, some argue that it is unlikely that the trial of a minor insurrectionist would have been recorded in Roman records. And even

---

[31] Goodyear, *Tacitus*, 31. Quoted in Grant, *Greek & Roman Historians: Information and Misinformation*, 41.
[32] Lowder, "Jury Chapter 5."

if it had, it is unlikely that Tacitus would have had access to these archives. Not only this, but even if Tacitus had such access, there is no reason to suppose he would have been motivated to investigate the Christian claim about Jesus' execution under Pilate. Hence, some conclude, we have compelling reasons to suppose that this passage in *Annals* is based on nothing more than early second-century Christian hearsay.[33]

Expanding on the analysis, Doherty asks would Tacitus "have *chosen* to make such a search in regard to the claims of a minor and disreputable sect."[34] This question is unanswerable.

Carrier questioned the possibility or probability that Tacitus examined official records:

> If we instead assume the passage has not been tampered with, then where would Tacitus have learned of this? Not likely from government records. His report contains no distinctive information that one would expect from such a source, and Tacitus would not have wasted countless hours of his life hunting through obscure archives just to verify a single embarrassing anecdote the Christians themselves were already admitting to. Moreover, it is very unlikely any such records would have survived in Rome for Tacitus to consult, the capitol's libraries having burned to the ground at least twice in the interim, once under Nero, and again under Titus.[35]

Earl Doherty is a Canadian detractor and advocates the hypothesis that Jesus originated as a myth. He concludes in *Jesus Neither God Nor Man*, with the following insight:

> Archives or Hearsay?
> The latter question involves the issue of whether any report of the crucifixion of Jesus would have been sent from Judea (presumably by Pontius Pilate) to Rome and there lodged in an archive, still to be recoverable some eighty years later. The Romans executed thousands upon thousands of people during their history, and it is surely unreasonable to assume that every one of them was scrupulously recorded, with such a record carefully maintained. One would think that the required storage space alone would have been phenomenal.

---

[33] Eddy and Boyd, *The Jesus Legend*, 180.
[34] Doherty, *Jesus Neither God Nor Man*, 590.
[35] Carrier, *On the Historicity of Jesus*, 344.

We have no evidence of such extreme a mania for record-keeping, covering one aspect of the administration of an empire which included the lands of the entire Mediterranean basin and beyond. How many hours would Tacitus have been forced to spend searching out the confirmation of a Christian tradition about their reputed founder, and would he have felt that it would have justified the effort? Where exactly would he have looked? Did those archives not only collect and preserve, but also compile detailed indexes to executed criminals? Would such eight-decades-old records have been readily accessible? Would any particular item of information have been further buried in a long scroll, a report to the Home Office covering several months of administrative accounts by Pilate and his officials, or are we to think that Pilate thought Jesus was important enough to deserve a separate missive back to the emperor, as later Christian forgers of such things naively presumed?[36]

3. Tacitus' Information from Josephus or Pliny the Younger

The hypothesis that Tacitus learned his information from other historians like Josephus or Pliny the Younger is unverifiable. If Tacitus was present at an interrogation, there exists no proof that he carried out independent fact-checking.[37] Holding, a Christian apologist doubts this possibility. He says, "Suggestions have also been made that Tacitus got his information from Josephus, but this is rejected by Tacitean scholars: Mendell, for example, says that Tacitus 'clearly knew nothing' about Josephus [Mende.Tac, 217 - see also Hada.FJos, 223]."[38] O'Neill opines that Tacitus consulting Pliny for information is "too conjectural to be judged likely."[39] The reader must evaluate this speculation based on silence.

4. Information from Interrogated Christian Prisoners.

Neither can it be verified that Tacitus obtained his information from interrogated Christian prisoners. Even apologist Van Voorst says, "A more likely source, but still not demonstratable, is a police or magistrate's report made during investigations of the fire [discussed next], which may have mentioned the genesis of Christianity."[40] Notice that he couched his

---

[36] Doughty, *Jesus Neither God Nor Man,* 589–90; cf. *The End of an Illusion.*
[37] Carrier, *On the Historicity of Jesus,* 344.
[38] Holding, "Tacitus on Jesus."
[39] O'Neill, "Jesus Mythicism 1."
[40] Van Voorst, *Jesus Outside the New Testament,* 50.

defense with the phrase, "which may have mentioned." Somewhat related, Lawrence Mykytiuk writes that when Tacitus was Proconsul of Asia, "He likely supervised trials, questioned people accused of being Christians and judged and punished those whom he found guilty." Therefore, Mykytiuk argues, "Tacitus stood a very good chance of becoming aware of information that he characteristically would have wanted to verify before accepting it as true."[41]

Once again, readers must note how Mykytiuk hedges his words, "He likely supervised" and "Tacitus stood a very good chance." In the eyes of detractors, this argument is an appeal from silence and nothing less than grasping at straws.

Returning to the topic of motivation, presumably, proponents argue there would be no reason for Tacitus not to take the basic Christian story at face value if that is where he obtained his information. In contrast, detractors could object, arguing that a meticulous investigator should be dubious of his sources, especially in this case, from believing Christians.

Proponents of the authenticity of the *Annals* face confrontation by the "Accounts of the Fire in Rome" detailed in 15:44–47. This challenge exists despite attestation by three writers: Tacitus, Cassius Dio, and Suetonius. Accompanying this challenge are presumed factoids about the reported persecution of Christians associated with the "Great Fire in Rome." (See 1–10 below) If the details of the fire are "imprecise," that potential reality contributes to reasons why detractors and skeptics doubt its authenticity or reliability. Briefly, Tacitus, in chapters 38 through 45, provides details about the "Great Fire of Rome" and its aftermath occurring in July of the year 64. Readers are encouraged to examine the text available online. Investigators point out a variety of difficulties with the texts. Those lengthy discussions are outside the scope of this text. However, cumulatively, detractors argue that they challenge the reliability and aspects of the historicity of the reported events.

Interpolation

Over the years, detractors and skeptics have doubted, questioned, or denied the authenticity of the *Annals* 15:44 because they consider these sentences to be an interpolation.[42] Questions arise concerning these and related passages. The most controversial is: Did Tacitus write 15:44, or is this material a later Christian interpolation? A variety of arguments consist

---

[41] Mykytiuk, "Did Jesus Exist," 2.
[42] Carrier, *On the Historicity of Jesus*, 264–83; Doherty, *Jesus: Neither God Nor Man*, 587–630; Lataster, *There was No Jesus,* 142.

of points listed below. Van Voorst, an apologist, and others ask numerous questions:

1. Tacitus anachronistically identifies Pilate as a procurator when the proper title would have been prefect. (48, 51)
2. Tacitus refers to the founder of the name as 'Christus,' while written records would presumably have used the name, Jesus. (43)
3. Did Tacitus employ *Christus* as a personal name for Jesus? (45–46)
4. Why did Tacitus fail to use the personal name "Jesus"? (46)
5. Tacitus' usage of the word "Christians." (43)
6. Did Tacitus write the word *Chrisiano* (Christians) or "*Chrestians*? (44)
7. Did Tacitus initially write the word *Chrestianoi* or *Christianoi*? (44)
8. Is Tacitus correct in linking the fire and the Neronian persecution of Christians? (44)
9. Did Nero order the fire, was its cause accidental or did Christians set the fire? (44)
10. "Under what legal authority or judicial findings were Christians persecuted." (44)
11. Why did not Tacitus explicitly trace any "shameful acts" of the Christians that he reports to Christ? (49)[43]

Doherty says, "What witness outside Tacitus do we have to the persecution of Christians by Nero in association with the fire? There is none, as we have seen, from Christian sources—until the late 4th century."[44] Why would this Nero-Great Fire-Christian persecution text have been developed, and what are their connections? This topic is open to speculation. Doherty presents an interesting hypothesis:

> Other influences on the Christian impulse to build up Nero as the great persecutor would have been Peter and Paul's association with that emperor and the legends of their martyrdom in Rome during his time. As well, Nero was seen as the Antichrist, due to arrive at the apocalyptic End-time, the future enemy of the Messiah; thus, in a balance between future and past, it was natural for him to become the great enemy of Christianity at its beginning ('the first to express hostility to the faith,' a thought encountered in more than one writer).

---

[43] Van Voorst, *Jesus Outside the New Testament*, 43–51.
[44] Doherty, *Jesus Neither God Nor Man*, 624.

Drews also suggests (*op. cit.*, p.46) "the political interest of the Christians in representing themselves as Nero's victims, in order to win the favor and protection of his successors on that account."

Indeed, we could consider, for those reasons just outlined, that the gradual development of a Christian conception of Nero as the first great persecutor could have occurred without *any* particular event, minor or otherwise, being at the root of it, other than growing legends about the martyrdoms of Peter and Paul. This option, however, would probably require that the passage in Suetonius about 'punishment of the Christians' be judged an interpolation, and thus we return to it for a second look.[45]

Meier believes the passage is genuine. "Not only is it witnessed in all the manuscripts of the *Annals* the very anti-Christian tone of the text makes Christian origin almost impossible."[46] Notably, Meier adds a caveat, "almost." Lataster presents a reason for challenging this apologetic: "For example, it is interesting that the name 'Jesus,' 'Jesus, son of Joseph' or 'Jesus of Nazareth' is never used, and that this is Tacitus' only reference to Jesus."[47] However, naming Jesus, although desirable, was not necessary.

The literature contains multiple reasons for questionings the authenticity of *Annals* 15:44. The following is a list gathered from writers on both sides of the religious aisle who discuss this topic:

1. The early Christian fathers Tertullian, Clement of Alexandria, and Origen did not cite Tacitus' work. Neither do other Christian writers acquainted with Tacitus, such as Jerome, Sidonius, Apollinaris, Sulpicius, Severus, and Cassiodorus.

Detractors argue it is highly notable that no other ancient source associates Christians with setting the "Great Fire" and the burning of Rome (ca. 64 CE) until the fourth-century writer Sulpicius Severus (*Chronicle* i.e., *Sacred History*, 2.29–30). Carrier writes: "But no one seems to have ever known Christians were in any way connected with it, until late in the fourth century. *The Letters of Seneca and Paul* (a late 4th century forgery), epistle 12, is the first mention of the event in such a connection, claiming....'Oh! Christians and Jews have even been executed as contrivers of the fire, like

---

[45] Doherty, *Jesus Neither God Nor Man,* 616.
[46] Meier, *A Marginal Jew,* 91.
[47] Lataster, Questioning the Historical Existence, 203.

usual!'"[48] However, Jeffrey Jay Lowder, a detractor, counters that the (1) argument is irrelevant and (2) the fact that a later author expanded the passage in no way makes it probable that the original passage was interpolated.[49]

2. No historical evidence exists that Nero persecuted Christians. However, he did persecute Jews, so perhaps Tacitus was confused.[50]

3. Tacitus claims that around 64 CE, a "huge or vast multitude" of Christians were discovered and executed. This information undermines the extract's reliability since it is evident that a "huge or vast multitude" of Christians in Rome at this time did not exist, as there was not even a multitude of them in Judea. Significantly, Tacitus did not define the term "multitude."

4. Tacitus has in no other part of his writings alluded to Christ or Christians.

5. Raphael Lataster, in *Questioning the Historicity of Jesus*, identifies a curiosity:

Also of interest is that this supposed reference to the death of Jesus is made in Book 15 (covering 62–65 CE), rather than in Book 5 (covering 29–31 CE). Though Tacitus supposedly claims the death of Christ happened during the reign of Tiberius, Tacitus makes no mention of Jesus in the books he wrote covering the reign of Tiberius; he only makes this one comment among the books covering the reign of Nero.[51]

Expanding on this oddity, Lataster elaborates why this reference by Tacitus is dubious:

Furthermore, most of Book 5 and the beginning of Book 6 (covering CE 32–37) is lost. The *Annals* is suspiciously missing information

---

[48] Carrier, "The Prospect," 276.
[49] Lowder, "Josh McDowell's "Evidence" for Jesus."
[50] Moss, *The Myth of Persecution*, 139; Shaw, "The Myth of the Neronian Persecution," 73–100.
[51] Lataster, *Questioning the Historicity of Jesus*, 204; cf. *There Was No Jesus*, 142–43.

Problems with Tacitus 101

from 29 CE to 32 CE, a highly relevant timeframe for those that believe (historically or religiously) in Jesus. It is equally suspicious that the only section missing in the space dedicated to Tiberius' rule happens to coincide with what many Christians would consider to be the most historically noteworthy event(s) to occur during Tiberius' reign. Professor of Classics Robert Drews theorised that the only plausible explanation for this gap is "pious fraud"; that the embarrassment of Tacitus making no mention of Jesus' crucifixion (or associated events such as the darkness covering the world or the appearances of resurrected saints) led to Christian scribes destroying this portion of the text (and perhaps later fabricating the Book 15 reference).[52]

Meier counters by writing, "Unfortunately for us, one of the gaps in the *Annals* occurs during the treatment of AD 29, with the narrative resuming in AD 32. Hence, the most likely year for the trial and death of Jesus (AD 30) is not covered in our present manuscripts of the *Annals*."[53]

6. No original manuscripts of *Annals* exist. The surviving copies of Tacitus' works derive from two principal manuscripts: the Medicean manuscripts. These works, written in Latin, are in the Laurentian Library in Florence, Italy. The earliest known extant manuscript dates about the eleventh century, nearly 1,000 years after the publication of *Annals* (Medicean Tacitus, Flor. Laur. 68.2). That manuscript is in the monastery of Monte, 80 miles southeast of Rome.[54]

Another common argument refuting the authenticity of *Annals* 15:44 is that the excerpt is not referred to or quoted in other works, especially Christian, until the fourth century (mentioned previously). For example, Richard Carrier writes the following:

In the final analysis, given the immensity of the persecution Tacitus describes, its scale in terms of the number of victims, its barbarity, and the injustice of it being based on a false accusation of arson to cover up Nero's own crimes, what are the odds that no Christian would ever

---

[52] Lataster, *Questioning the Historicity of Jesus*, 204. Lataster cites Robert Drews' 1984 article, "The Lacuna in Tacitus."
[53] Meier, *A Marginal Jew*, 89.
[54] Newton, *The Scriptorium*, 96; Zara, "The Chrestianos Issue."

have heard of it or made use of it or any reference to it for over three hundred years?"[55]

This argument is nothing more than opinion.

O'Neill counters Carrier, offering two possible explanations for this situation:

1. It is actually hard to know how well-known his histories were.
2. Even if the *Annals* and the passage were known to early Christian writers, it is not hard to see why a passage that links their sect to arson and which calls it "a most mischievous superstition....evil....hideous and shameful....[and with a] hatred against mankind" would not be one they would highlight.[56]

Tim O'Neill also presents a host of robust rebuttals to the arguments listed above that challenge the authenticity of *Annals* 15:44. Readers are encouraged to consider his well-written response. Returning to the topic of an "independent source," the late conservative New Testament scholar R. T. France, in his *The Evidence for Jesus,* adds an insightful opinion:

> Tacitus' reference to 'Christus' is evidence only for what was believed about Christian origins at the time he wrote ... by itself it cannot prove that events happened as Tacitus had been informed, and certainly it cannot carry alone the weight of the role of 'independent testimony' with which it has often been invested.[57]

Doherty (and other detractors would concur) offers an opinion. His rationale is that the fundamental accuracy or authenticity of its central feature, the persecution of the Roman Christians for the fire, is discredited and unsustainable. Hence, the reliability of 15:44 is unsalvageable. Consequently, there is no way to salvage its accompanying feature, referencing "*Christus*" as executed by Pontius Pilate.[58] Of course, proponents of *Annals* 15:44 beg to differ.

Lastly, Steve Mason, in a 2017 essay, offers his conclusion:

> Tacitus' account of Nero and the Christians adds nothing material to our information about Jesus. If he drew his statement about Jesus from

---

[55] Carrier, "The Prospect," 282–83.
[56] O'Neill, "Jesus Mythicism 1."
[57] France, *The Evidence for Jesus*, 23.
[58] Doherty, *Jesus: Neither God Nor Man*, 622.

Christian oral reports, that brief notice would have roughly the same evidentiary value as gospel statements, with the difference that a critical non-Christian finds it credible.[59]

The end of the matter is that nobody knows with certitude the source of Tacitus' presumed information. Noteworthy, it is unverified that Tacitus wrote the paragraph. Consequently, *Annals* is not an independent source that provides evidence that Jesus suffered crucifixion. Finally, presuming Tacitus received his information about eighty years after the time and people told it to others, it is irrelevant whether or not the passage is genuine.

Conclusion

Habermas and Licona's two-sentence quotation from *Annals*, without acknowledging that the extract from Tacitus is a matter of "dispute," is inexcusable. By itself, the unqualified material from *Annals* gives its readers the impression that, although unspecified controversy concerning the passage exists, it is more than credible and certitude. However, skepticism concerning the authenticity of *Annals* 15:44 is well-known by Christian apologists, detractors, and academics knowledgeable about Tacitus. Habermas and Licona do a disservice to their "predominantly" Christian audience by not admitting and openly informing and engaging this reality.[60] In conclusion, these lines of evidence, considered cumulatively, make it apparent that the passage is not independently attested and at least plausible that the Jesus reference is a later Christian interpolation, even if many modern scholars reject this view.

---

[59] Mason, "*Sources that Mention Jesus,*" 7.
[60] Habermas and Licona, *Case of the Resurrection*, 273 n53. They write one sentence: "It should be noted that most scholars accept this passage in Tacitus as authentic, but a very few question it."

Additional Problems with the Gospels

Any reference to the four Gospels being independent, objective, contemporaneous eyewitness accounts of the resurrection is, at best disingenuous or deliberately misleading at worst. The scholarly consensus (although conservative Christian apologists would beg to differ) is that Mark wrote his Gospel around 65 to 70 CE. or thirty-five years after Jesus' alleged resurrection. Matthew wrote about 80 to 85 CE., and Luke/Acts, approximately 85 to 90 CE. In contrast, Richard Pervo advocates about 115 CE. based on Luke's use of both Josephus' *Antiquities* and some of Paul's letters.[1] The Synoptic Gospels, consequently, were written forty to fifty years after the events they narrate. The Fourth Gospel, John, was written about 90 to 95 CE, or sixty to sixty-five years later than the resurrection, and is significantly different from the Synoptic Gospels in its content. In addition to being questionably reliable, the Gospel authors are anonymous.[2] The sources of their information are not only problematic but also unknown.

The Oxford Annotated Bible states, "Neither the evangelists nor their first readers engaged in historical analysis. They aimed to confirm Christian faith (Luke 1.4; John 20.31). Scholars generally agree that the Gospels were written forty to sixty years after the death of Jesus. They thus do not present eyewitness or contemporary accounts of Jesus' life and teachings."[3] Additionally, these works are *not* independently attested.

Biblical scholars generally agree that Matthew and Luke copied and edited Mark. Understandably, copies and re-edited works tend to focus on the same people and events as the original works. Robert Stein makes the following observation in his book, *Studying the Synoptic Gospels Origin and Interpretation*: "Of the 11,025 words found in Mark, only 304 have no parallel in Matthew and 1,282 have no parallel in Luke. This data means that 97.2 percent of the words in Mark have a parallel in Matthew

---

[1] Pervo, *Acts: A Commentary*, 5; Pervo, *Dating Acts*; cf. O'Neill, *The Theology of Acts*, 17–21.

[2] Alter, *The Resurrection*, 5–12.

[3] Coogan, *The Oxford Annotated Bible,* 1,778.

and 88.4 percent have a parallel in Luke."[4] William Barclay confirms this observation in *Barclay's Guide to the New Testament*: "Mark has 661 verses; Matthew has 1,068 verses; Luke has 1,149 verses. Matthew reproduces no fewer than 606 of Mark's verses, and Luke reproduces 320. Of the 55 verses of Mark which Matthew does not reproduce, Luke reproduces 31; so there are only 24 verses in the whole of Mark which are not reproduced somewhere in Matthew or Luke."[5]

Would Matthew, an alleged eyewitness and "presumably" an independent writer, need to borrow as much as 80 percent of the material in the Gospel of Mark, a non-eyewitness? If Matthew copied Mark, how could he corroborate Mark's claims? It is absurd to think that Matthew, writing independently some years after Mark and employing only purported eyewitnesses, would have penned almost word-for-word 11,025 words found in Mark, while there are only 304 words in Matthew without parallel. Beyond that, how can it be claimed that Luke is independent of Mark and Matthew if he penned almost word-for-word an identical text? These similarities are explainable if Luke is copying and editing their works. In effect, there is only one source: the anonymous author of Mark. Unfortunately, his sources of information are unknown.

Examining the four Gospels in their chronological sequence is necessary to evaluate specific arguments that presumably lend credence to the idea that Jesus died because of crucifixion. Mark 15:37, Matthew 27:50, Luke 23:46, and John 19:30 report that Jesus cried out and then "breathed his last" and "gave up his spirit." The sources of these descriptions are anonymous. Most significantly, these words cannot confirm that Jesus was brain dead (The permanent, irreversible, and complete loss of *brain* function, which may include cessation of involuntary activity necessary to sustain life.) If historical, the most they could establish is that he was *either* in a coma *or* clinically dead. Detractors offer additional options that exist, rejected by this text, including (1) the swoon theory or (2) the conspiracy theory.

---

[4] Stein, *Studying the Synoptic Gospels*, 52.
[5] Barclay, *Barclay's Guide to the New Testament*, 2.

What, then, about the centurion's declaration reported in the Gospels?

Mark 15:39 And when the centurion, who stood facing him, saw that this way he breathed his last, he said, "Truly this man was the Son of God!"

Matt. 27:54 When the centurion and those who were with him, keeping watch over Jesus, saw the earthquake and what took place, they were filled with awe and said, "Truly this was the Son of God!"

Luke 23:47 Now when the centurion saw what had taken place, he praised God saying, "Certainly this man was innocent!"

The words Mark puts on the lips of the centurion provide no evidence that Jesus was alive or dead while still on the cross. Crucially, detractors think these words have the hallmarks of legend and embellishment. Also, it requires asking how the centurion, presumably standing a few yards away, knew that Jesus was dead. Did people usually survive crucifixion? No, they did not. However, J. Duncan M. Derrett writes, "Meanwhile it is a fact that crucified victims may be taken down alive." For evidentiary proof, he cites:

Herodotus 7.194; Josephus *Life* 420–421, *Josephus: The Life; Against Apion*, vol. 1, trans H. St. Thackeray (Cambridge, MA: Harvard University Press, 1926). Loeb Classical Library, p. 155. Mishnah *Yev.* 16:3; Tosefta, *Yev.* 14.4c; Palestinian Talmud 5, p. 15 c; Iamblichus, *Babyloniaca* 2 and 21. R. Hercher, *Erotici Scriptores Graeci* (Leipzig, 185), 1.221, 229. (405, note 6)[6]

Therefore, evidentiary proof exists that people could survive crucifixion. Finally, and most oddly, John's Gospel omits any reference to the centurion.

After removal from the cross, not one of the Gospels provides indisputable evidence that Jesus was brain dead. One episode is detailed by Josephus when someone survived a crucifixion *(Life* §420–421). Romans were expert executioners. In reality, people did not survive crucifixion. Some detractors believe that up to this point in the New Testament, Jesus could have been alive. Richard Carrier, a detractor,

---

[6] Derrett, "Financial Aspects of the Resurrection," 394.

states, "Being mistaken for dead is not impossible."[7] A review of the footnote literature provides evidence, past (Pliny, Plato, Aulus Cornelius Celsus) and present (Jan Bondeson's *Buried Alive: The Terrifying History of Our Most Primal Fear*, 2001), lending credence to the hypothesis that Jesus could have survived a crucifixion (disputed by this text). He concludes, "All these considerations make it clear that no one can argue that the odds of misdiagnosis were less than 0.6% (0.00599), making the odds of survival-plus-misdiagnosis 0.2% (0.0019767)."[8] Hence, for detractors, the first "minimal fact" is an "assumption," not a "fact."

---

[7] Carrier, "Why I Don't Buy the Resurrection Story."
[8] Carrier, "Why I Don't Buy the Resurrection Story."

Problems with the Gospel of John and Jesus' Crucifixion

Christian apologist Michael Licona's first bedrock historical fact is that a man named Jesus, who lived in first-century Palestine, was crucified and died.[1] He also writes, "In addition, no evidence exists that Jesus was removed while alive..."[2] Therefore, Jesus must have been dead before his body's removal. If Jesus were alive at this stage but died a day later in the tomb of exposure to cold, then Licona's first bedrock historical fact is *false*. Consequently, it is crucial to ascertain whether Jesus was dead when taken down from the cross. The account in John's Gospel of Jesus' pierced side is highly relevant here, as some apologists have claimed that it proves Jesus was already dead. This text will defend a contrary view.

After Jesus' supposed death on the cross, John reported breaking his legs. The Jewish leadership visited Pilate and requested an order for the three to have their legs broken to hasten their death. Permission was approved, and the soldiers shattered the legs of the two thieves. Nevertheless, when they came to Jesus, John reported that he was already dead. It is inexplicable how the soldiers knew this. Significantly, this episode only appears in John's Gospel. Hence, it is uncorroborated and, therefore, lacks multiple attestations. Compounding matters, this entire episode appears written to support John's goals. These were to disseminate Christian propaganda and to fulfill a theological agenda.

Proponents of Jesus' resurrection assert that professional Roman soldiers, who performed crucifixions regularly, would have known what they were doing. Furthermore, they had more experience with death than the average citizen due to their profession. However, as discussed, skeptics of the resurrection account question these claims. Truth is sometimes stranger than fiction.

Why would John have invented the breaking of the legs incident? The evangelist himself provides the answer. John 19:36 states, "For these

---

[1] Licona, *Resurrection of Jesus*, 468.
[2] Licona, *Resurrection of Jesus*, 311.

things took place that the Scripture might be fulfilled: 'Not one of his bones will be broken.'" The NIV cross-references this verse to Exodus 12:46, Numbers 9:12, and Psalm 34:20.

Throughout John's Gospel, the author endeavors to reinforce his theological point that Jesus is "the Lamb of God who takes away the sins of the world."[3]

1. John is the only Gospel that identifies Jesus as "the Lamb of God who takes away the sins of the world." From the very start of John's Gospel, John the Baptist, Jesus' forerunner, declares that Jesus was "the Lamb of God"[4]:

John 1:29—The next day he saw Jesus coming toward him, and said, "Behold, the Lamb of God, who takes away the sin of the world!
John 1:36—and he looked at Jesus as he walked by said, "Behold, the Lamb of God!"

However, the most frequent allusion to Jesus as a lamb in any New Testament writings occurs in the book of Revelation, where Jesus has that title twenty-eight times.

2. Jesus' death, which represents the salvation of God, is purportedly similar to sacrificing the lamb, which symbolizes salvation for the ancient Israelites during the Passover exodus. John's Gospel is the *only* Gospel in which Jesus dies on the same day as the Passover lamb, the day of preparation. This concept appears in 1 Peter 1:19. The verse states, "but with the precious blood of Christ, like that of a lamb without blemish or spot" (ESV).

3. John's Gospel is the only Gospel in which Jesus dies at the same hour as the Passover lamb, in the afternoon, to demonstrate that Jesus is the Lamb of God.

4. Jesus dies in Jerusalem, the same place as the Passover lambs.

5. Jesus dies at the hands of the same people as the Passover lambs, allegedly the Jewish leaders, especially the priests. However, others may argue that the most proximate agent of Jesus' death sentence is Pilate.

---

[3] Alter, *The Resurrection*, 76.
[4] Alter, *The Resurrection*, 76.

6. John 19:31–37 is the only verse in the Gospel in which a Roman soldier pierces Jesus' side with a spear rather than breaking his legs on the cross not to violate the prohibition in Exodus 12:46 of breaking the bones of the Passover lamb.

The month of Nisan has the sign of the lamb. It also corresponds to the zodiac sign of Aries the Lamb. It was the age of the lamb. Coincidentally, during the first century, Passover occurred during the spring equinox. On March 21, the sun rose in the sign of the lamb. Coincidentally, lambs are born in spring, coinciding with the resurrection accounts.[5]

Consequently, the piercing episode is noteworthy because it is understood (explicitly in John) being direct evidence that Jesus came in fulfillment of Scripture. Exodus 12:46, which John *misinterprets* as indicating that the Messiah is the Lamb of God who will be slain (even though the original text of Exodus 12:46 is not a prediction about the Messiah and does not speak about a person who can take away the sins of the world). Second, it shows Jesus to be, literally, the salvation of God, just as the sacrifice of the lambs represented salvation for the ancient Israelites during the Passover exodus.

It is hard to imagine that the three Synoptic Gospels (Mark, Matthew, and Luke), and the supposed, three earlier sources ("Q"–a common source of Matthew and Luke, "M"–material unique to Matthew, and "L"–material unique to Luke) would have omitted this most crucial saying of John the Baptist, where he explicitly claimed that Jesus was the "Lamb of God," who takes away the sins of the world. It is vital to point out that *all* six sources came to the same conclusion. Why did these six sources decide this monumental idea was unimportant and not significant enough to record?

This teaching is a theological point that John wishes to stress. Its value for him and his readers is not as history per se; this teaching is pure theology, a belief that he wants to "prove." This teaching is rooted in belief, not in history. That agenda necessarily makes it suspect–not theologically, but historically. In closing, John attempts to reinforce the theological point that Jesus is "the Lamb of God, who takes away the sin of the world" (John 1:29, ESV).

Later in his narrative, John reported that, instead of breaking Jesus' legs, a soldier pierced his side with a spear. This event raises an important question: If the soldiers believed that Jesus was dead, why did

---

[5] Alter, *The Resurrection*, 76–77.

one soldier pierce his side with a spear? The only conceivable motives for doing so would be either as an act of gratuitous brutality and cruelty or to make sure that Jesus was dead. Supposing that the Roman soldier had even the slightest doubt about Jesus' death, the most effective means of guaranteeing his death would have been obeying the orders of his superior and breaking the legs.

Roman military discipline is another reason for rejecting its alleged historicity. Pilate ordered that the Roman soldiers break the legs of the three men. However, according to John, these soldiers did not execute Pilate's direct order in Jesus' case. It is unreasonable to suppose that Roman soldiers would have disregarded their orders and potentially subjected themselves to severe punishments for disobedience inflicted by Roman military law. Military insubordination was subject to meticulous and scrupulous retribution. It may also be significant that if Jesus' cross were between the other two crosses, the soldiers would have to have passed Jesus' cross to reach the third cross after breaking the first thief's legs. It would have been simple for the soldiers to break Jesus' legs as they passed him, and that would have saved them from possible disciplinary action for ignoring a direct order.

Subsequently, John reports that after Jesus' piercing, there was a sudden flow of blood and water from his side. Christian apologists assert that the wound was on the same side as his heart. It is noteworthy that John does not identify the stabbed side.

Ian Wilson, writing in *The Shroud: Fresh Light on the 2000-Year-Old Mystery*, advocates a right-side piercing:

> The other feature of the chest wound, it may be remembered, was its location on the right side, where we might have expected the soldier to have aimed his lance at Jesus' left side in order to make sure the blow was a fatal one, straight to the heart. Yet, again, however, we find that what we may not expect turns out to be correct after all. As part of their drill training Roman legionaries were specifically taught to aim their lances *sub alas*, 'below the armpit', just as indicated on the Shroud [of Turin]. They were also taught to aim at the right side of the opponent's body, because in any combat with a right-handed enemy carrying a shield it was a logical target.[6]

The Shroud Center of Colorado provides a clear photograph (Fig. 3). Their comment says, "Blood flow from [a] wound to the chest is on the **right**

---

[6] Wilson, *The Shroud*, 81.

side of the actual body wrapped in the Shroud." (Bold in original)[7] If authentic, the Shroud of Turin provides evidence that the piercing did not strike the heart.

Some detractors believe that the piercing was a mere poking. Neither is any description provided of the spear or its tip. John's record that a spear pierced Jesus' side is significant because it could demonstrate a state of brain death evinced by his unresponsiveness to stimuli or pain. Hence, this incident was the surest proof that Jesus was dead.[8]

On the contrary, this text asserts that the entire piercing episode is a total invention for at least two reasons. First, as already discussed, it could have served as an apologetic and thereby refuted the claim (made by the Docetists and some Gnostics) that Jesus was not truly dead or that he did not die a human being as a result of his crucifixion. Second, it served John's theological agenda. John 19:37 reads, "And again another Scripture says, 'They will look on him whom they have pierced'" (ESV). Footnotes in Christian Bibles point out that the verse cited here is Zechariah 12:10.

The piercing event is also historically unconvincing because John 19:35 records that "He who saw it has borne witness—his testimony is true, and he knows that he is telling the truth—that you also may believe" (ESV). First, there is no evidence to confirm that John, or anyone else, saw or could have been close enough to witness blood and water exiting Jesus' pierced side. Second, there is the issue of sunlight. If Jesus were suspended from the cross several feet off the ground and stabbed late in the afternoon after the three hours of darkness had ended, the witnesses would have been looking directly into the sun as it was setting on the western horizon. Thus, looking into the sun could have impeded their vision.

Third, it is dubious that witnesses would have been able to see any water oozing from Jesus' side. Presumably, blood already covered the body from his prior scourging. Fourth, this text rejects the suggestion that the Roman soldiers would have allowed John, or anyone else, to get close enough to examine the crucified body of Jesus. He was condemned and executed for claiming to be "king of the Jews." Leniency would not occur. This text asserts that the "blood and water" was not literal but based on symbolism.[9] Craig Keener says, "The theological significance of the water from Jesus' side is clear enough in the context of the entire Gospel. Given John's water motif (1:31, 33; 2:6; 3:5; 4:14; 5:2; 9:7; 13:5) and is

---

[7] The Shroud Center of Colorado, "The Shroud of Turin," 5. Examine the photograph.

[8] Loke, *Investigating the Resurrection,* 118.

[9] Alter, *The Resurrection,* 186–87. D.A. Carson, in *The Gospel According to John* (see 19:35), discusses and rejects symbolism.

especially its primary theological exposition (7:37–39), the water has immense symbolic value."[10] Licona, writing in *Paul Meets Muhammad*, puts the following argument into the mouth of a hypothetical Muhammad who is attempting to refute the historicity of the piercing episode:

> Moreover, many theologians agree that the blood and water are theological terms that are used elsewhere in the New Testament and were used by John for theological rather than historical purposes. For example, in 1 John 5:6 and 8, John says about Jesus, "This is the one who came by water and blood, Jesus Christ; not with the water only, but with the water and with the blood" and "the Spirit and the water and the blood; and these three are one." Notice it is the same author, John, who is writing these.[11]

Later, Licona counters his hypothetical Muhammad by writing: "John appears to have been more attentive to detail than the others.... Even if John had a theological motif in mind in mentioning the blood and water, this does not mean that he invented the blood and water flowing from Jesus."[12] However, Licona's opinion is an argument based on silence. On the contrary, the author of John's Gospel declares that he wrote for theological reasons:

> but these are written so that you believe that Jesus is the Christ, the Son of God, and that by believing you may have eternal life in his name (John 20:31, ESV).

Fifth, curiously, the Gospel of Luke, whose author claims that he has examined many sources, omits the piercing episode. Luke's omission strongly suggests that John invented the piercing event after Luke had finished writing his narrative. Alternatively, Luke verified from Mark and Matthew that no such event occurred. If there was no piercing, perhaps the clearest apologetic that Jesus died is refuted.

Sixth, in medicine, Christian apologists cite doctors claiming the blood and water episode proves Jesus died. Contradicting these claims, some detractors argue that the piercing incident proved that Jesus was still alive. The detail that blood and water flowed from the wound after the lancing stroke, as John declares in his Gospel, demonstrates without a doubt, in their opinion, that there was still blood circulating. The reason is

---

[10] Keener, *The Gospel of John*, 1153–4.
[11] Licona, *Paul Meets Muhammad*, 43.
[12] Licona, *Paul Meets Muhammad*, 56–58.

that blood cannot flow from a dead body without a heartbeat and blood pressure. Why not? Amongst other reasons, blood exists in a vacuum and begins to pool in the center of the body after the heart has stopped beating. Anyone can test this by holding a glass straw, placing it in water, and closing their finger over the upper end. Next, pull the straw from the water with its lower part in the air. No water flows out but remains in the straw. Adopting a contrary view, some Christian apologists assert that blood and water could have flowed or leaked out from the body of a dead person.

Seventh, some Christian apologists point to the Shroud of Turin as evidence of Jesus' historicity and crucifixion. Conversely, the Shroud is employed to refute the claim that Jesus survived the crucifixion. In any case, this Christian counterargument rests on the assumption that the Shroud is the authentic burial cloth of Jesus. The linen cloth measures about 4.4m long by 1.1m wide. On the Shroud are the front and back images of a man, whom many presume to be Jesus. He appears naked, longhaired, and bearded, with elongated arms, legs, and thumbs tucked under his fingers. Blood is still dripping from his body.

The Shroud of Turin

Sindonology is the "scientific" study of the Shroud of Turin (or the Turin Shroud). Over fifty official centers and organizations exist around the world, according to the Shroud of Turin website. Most of this "science" directly tries to prove that the Shroud is the actual burial cloth of Jesus Christ. At the opposite end of the spectrum, Flavia Manservigi, in *Sindon*, writes, "There are also sites and blogs specifically dedicated to 'unmasking' the Shroud-deception,[1] but above all sindone.weebly.com, defined by the authors a reference point to provide verifiable dates and data on many little-known aspects of this fascinating 'impossible object.'"[2]

There exist numerous books, articles, and essays on this topic. Several select texts published since 2000 include:

Eric Folds, *The Shroud of Turin and What It Means About the Purpose of Your Life*, Xulon Press, 2021.
Gerard M. Verschuuren, *A Catholic Scientist Champions the Shroud of Turin*, Manchester, NH: Sophia Institute Press, 2021.
Andrea Nicolotti, *The Shroud of Turin: The History and Legends of the World's Most Famous Relic*, Waco, TX: Baylor University Press, 2020.
Giulio Fanti and Pierandrea Malfi, *The Shroud of Turin: First Century After Christ!* 2nd ed. Singapore, Jenny Stanford, 2020.
Mark Antonacci, *Test the Shroud at the Atomic and Molecular Levels*, Chesterfield, MO: LE Press, 2015.
Robert Wilcox, *The Truth About the Shroud of Turn: Solving the Mystery*, Washington, DC: Regnery Press, 2019.
Ian Wilson, *The Shroud*, London: Bantam Press, 2010.

---

[1] Such as the following two websites: shroudturinfake.yolasite.com and shroudofturinwithoutallthehype.wordpress.com.

[2] Manservigi, "Pseudo-Neutral," 22.

The following is a partial list of sources that discuss why some people think the Shroud is *not* authentic. This information comes from numerous sources, with pros and cons.[3]

One:
Radiocarbon Dating

In 1988, the British Museum coordinated an investigation conducted independently by three internationally-recognized research laboratories. That investigation examined a sample taken from a corner of the Shroud. Scientists subjected samples of the Shroud to radiocarbon dating. In the official report published by *Nature*, Damon et al. wrote, "The results of radiocarbon measurements at Arizona, Oxford, and Zurich yield a calibrated calendar age range with at least 95 percent confidence for the linen of the Shroud of Turin of CE 1260–1390 (rounded down/up to nearest ten years). These results, therefore, provide conclusive evidence that the linen of the Shroud of Turin is mediaeval."[4]

Since the 1989 publication in *Nature*, devout religious believers (sometimes called authenticists or shroudies) in the Shroud have disputed the carbon dating results. Papers and studies have reported problems with the 1988 investigation of Di Lazzaro and colleagues.[5] Advocates for the authenticity of the Shroud argue that the accuracy of dating is in dispute. Further testing is needed.

Shroud proponents argue that these results are invalid due to several factors. These factors include the following points:

1. Not followed were the agreed testing protocols.
2. Radiocarbon dates are often wrong.
3. Contamination of the samples.
4. The parts of the Shroud that were tested were all taken from a peripheral area that nuns repaired in the sixteenth century and were not representative of the whole cloth.

---

[3] Farey, "The Medieval Shroud 2"; Joseph, "The Shroud and the Historical Jesus"; O'Neill, "Is There Evidence Supporting"; Rimmer, "Shroud of Turin"; The Shroud of Turin website; *Sindon: The Magazine of the International Center of Shroud Studies* 2020.

[4] Damon et al., "Radiocarbon Dating of the Shroud of Turin," 614.

[5] Di Lazzaro, et al. "Statistical and Proactive Analysis," 926; Casabianca et al. "Radiocarbon Dating," 1223–231; Marinelli, "The Question of Pollen Grains"; Walsh and Schwalbe, "An Instructive Inter-Laboratory Comparison."

5. The material was deliberately switched and did not come from the Shroud.
6. The laboratories deliberately falsified the results. Other investigators dispute these allegations.

Excuse One: The Agreed Testing
Protocols were Not Followed

Hugh Farey provides an overview of the controversy.[6] The 1983 British Society for the Turin Shroud Newsletter accurately predicted the laboratories used.[7] Initially, twenty-three out of thirty-eight laboratories failed to meet three essential criteria for adequate performance. Afterward, the number of laboratories involved in testing was reduced from seven to three, thereby minimizing damage to the relic. Damon et al. report,

> Following this intercomparison, a meeting was held in Turin in September-October 1986 at which seven radiocarbon laboratories (five AMS and two small gas-counter) recommended a protocol for dating the shroud. In October 1987, the offers from three AMS laboratories (Arizona, Oxford and Zurich) were selected by the Archbishop of Turin, Pontifical Custodian of the shroud, acting on instructions from the Holy See, owner of the shroud. At the same time, the British Museum was invited to help in the certification of the samples provided and in the statistical analysis of the results. The procedures for taking the samples and treating the results were discussed by representatives of the three chosen laboratories at a meeting at the British Museum in January 1988 and their recommendations were subsequently approved by the Archbishop [Cardinal Anastasio Ballestrero] of Turin.[8]

Harry Gove (1922–2009) was a nuclear physicist and contributor to the development of accelerator-based dating techniques. Moreover, he developed the method of radiocarbon dating used to date the Shroud of Turin. However, his Rochester laboratory was one of the four *not* selected

---

[6] Farey, "The Medieval Shroud 2," 5.

[7] Newsletter of the British Society for the Turin Shroud (No. 5, pp. 3–4). The article, "Radiocarbon Dating," says, "As most BSTS members are aware, any decision on carbon dating the Shroud awaits optimum technical advances in the new, small-sample dating techniques. Three laboratories have been tipped as most likely jointly to carry out the dating when the technical difficulties have been overcome."

[8] Damon et al., "Radiocarbon Dating of the Shroud of Turin," 611.

by the Vatican. In 1988, he wrote a letter to the journal *Nature* and identified seven changes to the agreed protocols. These modifications have led many to believe a conspiracy transpired:

1. The involvement of seven laboratories has been reduced to three. This eliminates the possibility of detecting a mistake made in the measurement by one or more of the three laboratories. As Tite knows, such mistakes are not unusual.
2. The use of both decay counting and accelerator mass spectrometry (AMS) has been changed to AMS only. The two methods are distinct and independent.
3. The amount of cloth each AMS laboratory receives has been increased by almost a factor of two. With this much material, several more laboratories could have been included.
4. Representatives of the three laboratories will not be permitted to observe the sample removal from the shroud. Tite will at this operation.
5. The shroud and control samples will not be unravelled and thus, despite Tite's comments to the contrary, the shroud sample will be much more easily identifiable.
6. The scientific body connected with the Roman Catholic church which has a high reputation in the world of science, the Pontifical Academy of Sciences, has unaccountably been excluded from official participation in any aspect of this important and controversial radiocarbon measurement.
7. The acknowledged textile expert selected at the Turin Workshop to remove the shroud sample has been replaced by some unnamed person.[9]

Gove concluded his public correspondence letter with a telling accusation. The innuendo in the last sentence is unmistakable:

All these unnecessary and unexplained changes unilaterally dictated by the Archbishop of Turin will produce an age for the Turin Shroud which will be vastly less credible than that which could have been obtained if the original Turin Workshop protocol had been followed. Perhaps that is just what the Turin authorities intend.[10]

---

[9] Gove, "Radiocarbon-dating the Shroud," 110.
[10] Gove, "Radiocarbon-dating the Shroud," 110.

One year later, in a 1990 paper published in *Radiocarbon*, Gove conceded that the "arguments often raised, ... that radiocarbon measurements on the shroud should be performed blind seem to the author to be lacking in merit; ... lack of blindness in the measurements is a rather insubstantial reason for disbelieving the result."[11]

Excuse Two: Radiocarbon Dates
are Often Wrong

Specific tests conducted on the Shroud are likely to be correct. Farey writes, "In general, when a radiocarbon date is 'wrong' the problem usually boils down to contamination with other material of the 'wrong' period."[12] Additionally, the sample cuts should not directly affect the radiocarbon tests. Farey also writes:

> Other reasons for an incorrect date are related to the exact procedures, regarding the physical measurements of the C_{14}, and the calibration of those measurements C_{14} against background radiation and standard 'blanks'. These are peculiar to each laboratory, and sometimes to each test. The fact that all three laboratories testing the Shroud produced a medieval date speaks strongly against serious 'laboratory error' by any of them.[13]

In opposition, research published in the journal *Radiocarbon* refutes allegations by authenticists.[14] They write:

> We conclude from our observations and the history of our sample, that our sample was taken from the main part of the shroud. There is no evidence to the contrary. We find no evidence to support the contention that the 14C samples actually used for measurements are dyed, treated, or otherwise manipulated. Hence, we find no reason to dispute the original 14C measurements, since our sample is a fragment cut on the arrival of the Arizona 14C sample in Tucson on 24 April 1988 by coauthor Jull, and has been in his custody continuously.[15]

---

[11] Gove, "Dating the Turin Shroud – An Assessment," 87–92.
[12] Farey, "The Medieval Shroud 2," 6.
[13] Farey, "The Medieval Shroud 2," 6.
[14] The literature challenging the radiocarbon findings is extensive. Shroud newsletters, journals, and websites extensively engage this controversy. Prominent writers include Tristin Casabianca, Giulio Fanti, Paola Di Lazzaro, Emanuela Marinelli, Joe Marino, and Robert Rucker.
[15] Freer-Waters and Jull, "Investigating a Dated Piece," 1521–527.

Excuse Three: Conspiracy to Engage in Forgery and Falsification

Again, Farey refutes this allegation:

> Finally, all else having been discredited, there are the deliberate fakery hypotheses of Bruno Bonnet-Eymard, a recusant monk, and Stephen Jones, an Australian physics teacher. The first relies on the Shroud samples being replaced by fourteenth century duplicates from the Victoria and Albert Museum, and the second on the manipulation of the programs of the computers in all three laboratories producing the results by agents of the KGB. As with most such conspiracy theories, a few details which in isolation appear corroborative are clearly refuted when seen in their wider context.[16]

Farey, the former editor of The Newsletter of the British Society for the Turin Shroud, elaborates on other disputes and rebuttals.[17]

Two: Historical Records or Documentary Evidence

There are no definitive historical records of the Shroud's existence before the 14th century.

The first reference to the "Shroud" dates to 1390, when the Bishop of Troyes, Bishop Pierre d'Arcis, wrote a letter to the Pope in Avignon, Clement VII, telling him that a noble family in his diocese was displaying a relic for veneration that was, in fact, a fake. The Bishop informed Clement that the De Charny family had also displayed this supposed "Shroud" about thirty-five years earlier. Furthermore, it had been investigated by the then Bishop of Troyes, Henri de Poitiers. He was suspicious of how such a significant relic could suddenly appear in the hands of a French family. Furthermore, he was skeptical that there would be no mention of a miraculous image on the burial cloths of Jesus in the gospels or any other Christian writing of the previous millennium.[18]

D'Arcis informed the Pope that Bishop Henri inquired as to the origin of this remarkable artifact and quickly discovered it was a fake:

---

[16] Farey, "The Medieval Shroud 2," 6.
[17] Farey, "The Medieval Shroud 2," 7–10.
[18] O'Neill, "Is There Evidence Supporting"; cf. Farey," The Medieval Shroud 2," 36–44.

Eventually, after diligent inquiry and examination, he discovered how the said cloth had been cunningly painted, the truth being attested by the artist who had painted it, to wit, that it was a work of human skill and not miraculously wrought or bestowed.[19]

As it happens, Pope Clement VII (who was actually one of two rival claimants to the papacy at that time, the other being Pope Urban VI in Rome) was a relative of the De Charny family and so would be inclined to defend them against this charge of faking the "Shroud" if it had no basis. Clearly, it did have a basis, however, so Clement instead ordered the De Charny to stop declaring the "Shroud" to be the genuine article and to display it as a "representation" of the shroud of Jesus only. But he also granted indulgences to any pilgrims who went to see this "representation," so his cash-strapped relatives still got the pilgrims and money they were seeking in the first place, via their scam.

So the very first mention of the "Shroud" is a declaration by the local bishop that it had been proven a fake and that the artist who had faked it had admitted doing so. And this was upheld by the Pope, despite an incentive not to do so.[20]

An English translation from Pierre d'Arcis' actual Latin letter appears in Rev. Herbert Thurston's "The Holy Shroud and The Verdict of History" in *The Month*:

The case, Holy Father, stands thus. Some time since in this diocese of Troyes the Dean of a certain collegiate church, to wit, that of Lirey, falsely and deceitfully, being consumed with the passion of avarice, and not from any motive of devotion but only of gain, procured for his church a certain cloth cunningly painted, upon which by a clever sleight of hand was depicted the twofold image of one man, that is to say, the back and front, he falsely declaring and pretending that this was the actual shroud in which our Saviour Jesus Christ was enfolded in the tomb, and upon which the whole likeness of the Saviour had remained thus impressed together with the wounds which He bore. This story was put about not only in the kingdom of France, but, so to speak, throughout the world, so that from all parts people came together to view it. And further to attract the multitude so that money might cunningly be wrung from them, pretended miracles were worked, certain men being hired to represent themselves as healed at the moment of the exhibition of the shroud, which all believed to the

---

[19] Thurston, "The Holy Shroud," 17.
[20] O'Neill, "Is There Evidence Supporting."

shroud of our Lord. The Lord Henry of Poitiers, of pious memory, then Bishop of Troyes, becoming aware of this, and urged by many prudent persons to take action, as indeed was his duty in the exercise of his ordinary jurisdiction, set himself earnestly to work to fathom the truth of this matter ... For many theologians and other wise persons declared that this could not be the real shroud of our Lord having the Saviour's likeness thus imprinted upon it, since the holy Gospel made no mention of any such imprint, while, if it had been true, it was quite unlikely that the holy Evangelists would have omitted to record it, or that the fact should have remained hidden until the present time. Eventually, after diligent inquiry and examination, he discovered the fraud and how the said cloth had been cunningly painted, the truth being attested by the artist who had painted it, to wit, that it was a work of human skill and not miraculously wrought or bestowed ... Accordingly, after taking mature counsel with wise theologians and men of the law, seeing that he neither ought nor could allow the matter to pass, he began to institute formal proceedings against the said Dean and his accomplices in order to root out this false persuasion. They, seeing their wickedness discovered, hid away the said cloth so that the Ordinary could not find it, and they kept it hidden afterwards for thirty-four years or thereabouts down to the present year.[21]

Proponents of the Shroud argue that the 1389 Bishop d'Arcis Letter does not refute its authenticity. They offer a multifaceted defense. Specifically, authenticists argue specific points. Authenticists challenge skeptics who claim that in 1389, Bishop Pierre d'Arcis wrote to Pope Clement VII at Avignon that his predecessor Bishop Henri of Poitiers, had maintained that an artist confessed to having painted the cloth:

1. The paper was perhaps just a draft.
2. Nobody is sure that d'Arcis sent this letter. It is an unsigned paper.
3. D'Arcis gives no evidence of an investigation or the alleged confession supposedly given to his predecessor thirty years earlier.
4. On its face, the d'Arcis letter misstates the facts. It says that the Shroud was "painted," but that is not true.
5. The de Charney family owned the Shroud and successfully challenged d'Arcis' authority in the diocese. D'Arcis' motivation may have been to undercut the authority of de Charney.

---

[21] Thurston, "The Holy Shroud," 21–22.

6. The bishops were corrupt, and their animosity for devotion was jealousy.

Detractors refute these and other charges:

1. The six arguments are pure speculation.
2. The d'Arcis Memorandum is the name of this document.
3. Contrary to proponents, there was an investigation. D'Arcis writes that the previous bishop investigated the controversy, "Eventually after diligent inquiry and examination, he discovered the fraud and how the said cloth had been cunningly painted, the truth being attested by the artist who had painted it, to wit, that it was a work of human skill and not miraculously wrought or bestowed."
4. The fact that the pope did not ban the devotion but regulated it does nothing to prove the bishops wrong.
5. Contrary to authenticists, d'Arcis' motivation may have been sincere. He saw the veneration of the Shroud as a scam to fool pilgrims and get their money.
6. Because the Catholic Church found the origin of the Shroud fraudulent at that time (1389), today's proponents must seek a way to refute this historical evidence since it supports the carbon dating results.[22]
7. There is no concrete evidence that the Shroud existed before the mid-1350s.

Harry Gove clarifies a crucial issue, the character of the Shroud's original owner:

The person who created the image must have been known to the person believed to be the shroud's original owner, Geoffry I de Charny, the French knight who allegedly first announced its existence ca 1353. He died in battle ca 1356 without revealing how and from whom he had obtained it. According to RW Kaeuper (pers comun Aug 29, 1989), de Charny was the exemplar of a medieval knight. He was a literate man and a rigid believer in chivalry. He is the author of the only book on chivalry up to that time ever written by a layman.[23]

Last, Thurston concisely details four arguments for rejecting the authenticity of the Shroud:

---

[22] Gormley, "Objections to the Bishops," *Testreligion.com*
[23] Gove, "Dating the Turin Shroud," 91.

1. "We possess nearly a score of documents which have some direct or indirect bearing on the facts reported in the Bishop's memorial ..."
2. "A more important confirmation is to be found in the fact that whereas Pierre d'Arcis describes the shroud as fabricated in the time of his predecessor, it curiously happens that the history of the supposed relic for thirteen hundred years down to that precise date remains an absolute blank....the more inexplicable does it become that neither the Evangelists, the Fathers, the Oriental travelers, nor any of the apocryphal writings, speak of it before the fourteenth century ..."
3. "The Pope's decision was that when the cloth was shown there was to be no elaborate ceremonial, no vestments, or lights or other observances customary of veneration of relics ..."
4. "But the most damning and conclusive piece of evidence, one to which Canon Chevalier himself, it seems to me, has hardly given sufficient prominence, is the undoubted fact that Geoffrey de Charny and the canons had never ventured to maintain to the Pope that their shroud was an authentic relic ..."[24]

The Pray Manuscript Controversy

The National Library of Budapest houses a document titled the Pray Manuscript (PM) or Pray Codex (PC) (available online). It is named after the discoverer Gyorgy Pray (1723–1801), a Hungarian Jesuit historian. This manuscript has been dated to 1192–1195 CE, seventy years earlier than the oldest carbon-14 dating of the Shroud of Turin (1260–1390 CE). The Pray Manuscript contains several pages of text and four panels of illustrations. These panels include five paintings, with the third panel in two parts. Striking, the top panel depicts the burial/entombment of Jesus (the "before" the resurrection). The image shows "Jesus lying dead on one half of a shroud, the rest being held by two disciples while another pours a jar of ointment onto his chest."[25] The image of Jesus in the Pray Manuscript (top panel) depicts preparation for burial in a shroud in basically the same pose as the "shroud man" in the Shroud of Turin (TS). Less conspicuous, the lower section illustrates the arrival of the holy women on Easter morning, who find an angel at the empty tomb.

---

[24] Thurston, "The Holy Shroud," 26–28.
[25] Farey, "The Prayer Codex," 19.

Ian Wilson, an author of historical and religious books and former Chairman of the British Society for the Turin Shroud, wrote some points of interest in this illustration reminiscent of the Shroud of Turin. The main ones were the depiction of Jesus:

1. He is entirely naked, like the body image of the Shroud of Turin.
2. His wrists crossed over his groin and pelvis, identical to the Shroud.
3. His hands only have four fingers with the thumbs presumably retracted, matching the detail on the Turin Shroud.
4. The fabric shows a herringbone pattern, similar to the weaving pattern of the Shroud of Turin.
5. The PM bears a configuration of four tiny circles on the lower image, which appear to form a letter L, "perfectly reproducing four apparent "poker holes" on the Turin Shroud," which also appear to form a letter L.[26]

Hence, for over six hundred years, nobody (medievalists, art historians, textile experts, theologians, amateurs) knew about and put forward the idea that the Shroud of Turin was reminiscent of the Pray Manuscript. Uniquely, only after Wilson published his book did writers discuss a hypothesis that the PM was an indirect product of the Shroud of Turin.

Authenticists argue that the presumed contact points correlate with the image in the Shroud. The presumption is that the illustrator of the Pray Manuscript incorporated the Shroud of Turin as a partial template. Specifically, the anonymous artist of the Pray Codex "used the Turin Shroud to incorporate details into his illustrations."[27] Therefore, the Shroud of Turin was already in existence before 1195.[28] If correct, this reality undermines the 1988 published carbon-14 dating test results of the *ST* in a calibrated year span of 1260–1390 (discussed below). **Tristin Casabianca prepared an informative table: "Qualitative survey of the characteristics of the folio XXVIIIr of the Pray Codex mentioned by Turin Shroud scholars (2008–2020)."**[29] He listed eleven points of contact mentioned by at least one author:

---

[26] Wilson, *The Shroud*, 243.
[27] Marino, "Does the Hungarian Pray Manuscript."
[28] Jones, "The Pray Manuscript (or Codex)."
[29] Casabianca, "The Ongoing Historical Debate," 3.

1. Poker holes
2. Decorative holes
3. Crossed arms
4. Total nudity
5. Bloody stain
6. Herringbone weave
7. Long fingers
8. No thumbs
9. No sign of violence
10. No image on the sheet
11. Psalter of Ingeborg

Collin Berry adds a caveat to ponder in an online discussion: "There's an axiom that appears at the fuzzy boundary line between science and statistics: 'Correlation does not imply causation!'"[30] Detractors dispute the arguments offered by authenticists.

Culled from several sources is their refutation:

1. In four locations, an "L"-shaped set of burns appears on the Shroud. The cause of these holes is subject to academic debate. One hypothesis is that they resulted from damage before the first known fire of 1532. These burns are often called poker holes. They resemble holes in the ST. (a) The L-shaped arrangement of the poker holes seen in the Pray tomb illustration has "almost certainly nothing whatsoever to do with the Shroud and the L-shaped poker holes and EVERYTHING to do with simple laws of randomness and probability.[31] (b) Farey wrote:

> I believe it was a Dominican priest and theologian André-Marie Dubarle who first interpreted the illustration above as a representation of the Shroud, and what probably first struck him were the little groups of circles (marked A and B above) one of which resembles a pattern of holes on the Shroud, apparently created by hot charcoal or incense falling from a thurible while the cloth was folded in four, as the pattern repeats four times, the holes getting smaller each time. Indeed, the group of holes at A does not seem to serve any other purpose, functional or decorative, but as it is clearly on the lid of the sarcophagus (marked green) and not on the cloth folded up on top (blue), it is difficult to believe it is related to the Shroud.[32]

(c) Any resemblance between the Codex and the Shroud is purely coincidental. (d) Subjective. Groups of five or eight holes exist, and

---

[30] See the comment section of McDaniel, "The Shroud of Turin Is Definitely a Hoax."
[31] Berry, "A Masterly Demolition."
[32] Farey, "The Pray Codex," 22.

viewers can bring them together. (e) Berry writes the following opinion in a website discussion:

> So you have to ask whether any significance can be attached to the groupings of 4 little circles In the tomb scene (largely obscured by the zig zag pattern on the alleged "shroud" that some, but by no means all interpret as a herringbone weave).
>
> It's a simple matter to show that if you place four little circles ("points") at random on a sheet of parchment or paper, then the most probable pattern where the letters of the alphabet are concerned is an L. Why?
>
> Any letter with a curve can straightaway be eliminated – 4 points are simply not sufficient to define a curve in 11 letters of the alphabet, i.e., B, C, D, G, J, O, P, Q, R, S, U. That leaves just 15 straight-sided letters. But 9 of those (A, E, F, H, I (with bars to distinguish from the number 1), K, M, W, and X need 5 or more points. That leaves just 6 that might be feasible, i.e., L, N, T, V, Y, and Z.
>
> N and Z are highly improbable – needing four defining points at the corners of a rectangle with its 4 right angles. Y and T are also rather improbable, requiring the lowest point to be precisely positioned relative to the other three (with T especially improbable since the top 3 points need to be in a straight line).
>
> That leaves just L and V. But one cannot make a symmetrical V with 4 points (3 as distinct from 4 being needed).
>
> That means there is one letter that is uniquely most probable if one places our points at random on paper – the letter L.[33]

(f) For over six hundred years, nobody knew and put forward the idea that the Shroud of Turin resembles the Pray Manuscript.

2. Decorative holes: (a) The alleged holes are possibly decorative elements, as seen on the angel's wing and various clothing items. (See above) (b) Only the artist knows the reason for drawing these holes. (c) Proponents and detractors can only offer their best opinion.
3. The crossed arms with the right over the left: (a) If a body is buried flat on its backside, there are three probable positionings. They (the hands) will be (1) placed at the sides by the hips, (2) crossed over with the hands of each arm contacting the opposing shoulder

---

[33] Berry, "A Masterly Demolition."

area, or (3) crossed over the genitals. The probability, therefore, is thirty-three percent that they are crossing the pelvic area. (b) Humans have two arms. Thus, the odds are fifty-fifty that the right arm would cross the left. (c) Traditionally, the right arm or hand is considered a sign of favoritism, righteousness, and strength. Scripture frequently mentions the right hand.[34] (d) Broussard points out, "In Scripture, those on Jesus' right are the ones to be saved (Matt. 25:32–33) and they are saved by the blood that he shed for them (Matt. 26:28)."[35] (e) Out of modesty, if you are going to depict a naked corpse, that is what you will do with the hands. The only alternative is to cover the private parts with the shroud. (f) It is a regular position in an entombment representation in the case of Jesus or others. (g) Freeman writes, "The laying out of Christ with his hands crossed over the pelvic area also appears in western art at much the same time as the *epitaphioi* [an embroidered cloth displayed on Good Friday and Holy Saturday], as, for instance, in an enamel of the laying out from the altar in Klosterneuburg (Austria) of 1181 and in the so-called Pray Codex of c.1192–5 from Hungary. It also appears in sculpture."[36]

4. Total nudity: (a) Jesus is naked, uniquely in the medieval era, is a false and deceptive argument.[37] (b) Examples of a naked Jesus exist in medieval iconography.[38] (c) Unexplained, paradoxically, the naked body in the PB is not scourged or wounded. Despite being naked, it does not match the Shroud of Turin. (d) The Shroud figure is naked, which would have been repugnant and unacceptable for a medieval artist depicting Christ as a deceptive apologetic. Jesus is naked, but his genitalia is not visible. It requires asking, are paintings of a naked Jesus on a cross except a covering of his genital area repugnant and unacceptable? Artists had no problem drawing or sculpting his "partial" nudity.

---

[34] Exod. 15:6; Ps 44:3; 110:1; Isa. 41:10; Mark 16:19; Matt. 22:44; 26:54; Luke 22:69; Acts 2:33; 7:55–56; Rom. 8:34; 1 Pet. 3:22; Heb. 1:3; 8:1; 10:12; 12:2; Col. 3:1.

[35] Broussard, "Which Side of Jesus Was Pierced?"

[36] Freeman, "The Origins of the Shroud of Turin."

[37] See "Book of Hours Southern Netherlands" (Brabant?), C. 1375-1400: The entombment of Christ. Books of hours were the most popular books for laypeople in the late Middle Ages and Renaissance. They contained sets of prayers to be performed throughout the hours of the day and night and illuminated with miniature paintings.

[38] First, Lübeck, Schleswig-Holstein, Dom, altar, 13th Century; second, "Book of Hours Southern Netherlands" (Brabant?), C. 1375–1400: The entombment of Christ; and a third example is The Cloisters, 13th century.

5. Bloody stain: (a) Why no blood? Witnesses who described the Shroud of Turin emphasized the marks of blood. (b) The PM shows no signs of being scourged.
6. Herringbone weave: (a) There is no representation of herringbone weave in the top Pray Manuscript picture. (b) The herringbone weave is in the bottom Pray image. (c) Detractors argue these are gravestone ornaments. (d) Readers can find similar ornaments on other gravestone medieval representations.
7. Long fingers: (a) This was the standard representation of the hands of icons of that time. (b) Artistic license. (c) Only three of eleven Turin Shroud scholars spanning 2008–2020) mentioned this characteristic.
8. Four fingers on each hand and with no visible thumbs: (a) It is a standard position in medieval imagery when the hands are crossing, (b) artistic license, and (c) the thumb could have been left out by mistake. (d) Whenever Christ has crossed hands, the probability is greater that his thumbs will be either absent or barely visible, as a simple search for images ancient and modern of "Man of Sorrows" shows. Nyet [Sergey Romano] provides thirteen examples.[39] (e) It is more or less natural for an artist to "hide" the thumbs. (f) The omission of the thumb could have been by mistake. (g) Casabianca, in a review of De Wesselow's text, comments that "he [De Wesselow] is aware that some Byzantine artists do not often represent them, ["omitted thumbs"] even when they should do so according to our current common Western perception.[40] (h) Only the artist knows the reason for omitting the thumb.

Differences

The Codex Manuscript is consistent and inconsistent with other images found in the art world. Noteworthily, and pointed out by authenticists, the Shroud of Turin and Pray Manuscript share several features. Nonetheless, believers in the Shroud fail to point out that differences exist between the two. Additionally, in many ways, the Pray Codex does not match the Shroud of Turin. Moreover, several of these differences are more significant than the publicized similarities. David Mo, a skeptic blogger, wrote the following argument:

---

[39] Nyet [Sergey Romano], "The Shroud of Turin and the Pray Codex."
[40] Casabianca, "The Ongoing Historical," 5.

For the Codex Pray: The "sindonists" do not consider the important differences between the codex and the image of the Turin cloth. Only similarities. Bad method.

Then, the "sindonists" [do] not consider that the characteristics they define as unique can be found easily in medieval art. The artist painted Codex Pray according to usual conventions of his time. He could take the position of the arms, the absence of thumbs, etc., from other paintings of the time. Even the nude. The assumption that [he] only did it from the Shroud of Turin is unnecessary and unlikely.

You can group arbitrarily a number of features of a work of art that does not exist in another and pretend it is unique. In the same way you can arbitrarily group two sets of characteristics of two works of art and say that they alone possess them. Especially if your knowledge of medieval art is not very deep. This can be done even with two works of different periods. It is an arbitrary procedure that proves nothing. Bad method.[41]

Several examples of differences include the following list:

1. The TS has blood on the head (presumably from the crown of thorns), but the PM does not.
2. The TS has facial abrasions and bruises, but the PM does not.
3. The TS has telltale signs of a swollen face, but the PM does not.
4. The TS has Jesus with a full beard, but the PM does not (Jesus has a sparse beard).
5. The TS has approximately 120 scourge (whip) marks, but the PM does not.
6. The PM has two disciples holding the Shroud, but the TS does not.
7. The PM has Jesus anointed at the burial, but the TS does not.
8. The PM has Jesus lying dead on half of a Shroud, but the TS does not (Jesus lies flat).
9. The PM has creases on Jesus' buttocks on the crease, but the TS does not.
10. The PM has a cross on the bottom of the image, but the TS does not.
11. The PM has a "halo" under Jesus' head (in Christian iconography, "the Christ Pantocrator," but the TS does not.[42]

---

[41] Mo, "A Masterly Demolition."

[42] See the Christ Pantocrator mosaic from the dome of the Church of the Holy Sepulchre in Jerusalem and the oldest known icon of Christ Pantocrator, encaustic on panel (Saint Catherine's Monastery).

12. The TS has a wound on the side, but the PM does not.
13. The TS has the right palm over the base of the left hand, but the PM does not (It has the arms intersect above the wrists.)
14. The TS has nail wounds on the feet, but the PM does not.
15. The PM omits a direct representation of the Shroud with an imprint of Christ, as one would expect a medieval illustration would represent it.
16. The PM has a shroud ending at the shoulders.
17. The PM has an angel walking on the Shroud.

In numerous ways, the Codex Manuscript is "inconsistent" with the Shroud of Turin. That is, believers can arbitrarily group features that interest them and forget another they have no interest. Alternatively, it requires understanding that "there is no way of definitively proving that Shroud man was Jesus Christ." In short, the alleged identity between the image of Turin and the Codex Pray is false or subjective.

Faking Holy Relics was
Widespread During the Middle Ages

Richard Housley, quoted by Richard Corfield, acknowledges, "Around that general time (the 14th century) there was a big market for religious icons and relics simply because they would pull in lots of pilgrims and generate a lot of local income. Religious centres such as cathedrals liked to have relics and reliquaries on site for this reason alone."[43]

In contradiction, literature abounds, purportedly tracing the history of the Shroud.[44] Readers must examine the purported history and separate facts from non-facts. Critical questions must be asked and answered by those on both sides of the aisle.

Three:
Ancient Fabric

In the year 2000, fragments of a first-century CE burial shroud were discovered in a tomb near Jerusalem, believed to have belonged to a Jewish high priest or member of the aristocracy. Based upon this

---

[43] Corfield, "Chemistry in the Face of Belief." Cf. Freeman, "The Origins of the Shroud." cf. Freeman, "The Origins of the Shroud."

[44] Nicolotti, *The Shroud of Turin*; Marino, "Possible Post-Biblical and Pre-1350s References"; Markwardt, "Modern Scholarship and the History," Turin Shroud Center of Colorado, "Section 1: Historical Evidence," 7–46.

discovery, the researchers stated that the Turin Shroud did not originate from Jesus-era Jerusalem. The Shroud was composed of a simple two-way weave, unlike the complex herringbone twill of the Turin Shroud.

The Shroud's fabric is linen woven in a three-to-one herringbone twill. It is a weave common in France in the fourteenth century and the style of linen most common in medieval Western Europe. Linen from the first century Middle East, however, was almost always plain or tabby woven linen. Farey provides the following analysis:

> Weaving a 3/1 twill requires that four different sets of warp threads be successively lifted clear of the rest to make four different "sheds" through which the weft shuttle is passed. If the warp threads be numbered 1-2-3-4-1-2-3-4-1-2-3-4 and so on, then all the 1s must be lifted first, then all the 2s, 3s and 4s in succession, before returning to the 1s. In order to do this all the threads in each set must be attached to a single bar, and the four bars lifted in succession. Looms capable of this are unknown to history, archaeology or literature before about the twelfth century. Ancient looms from the middle east capable of very wide or long pieces of material are known, but nothing with the crucial four-bar lifting technology.[45]

Four:
Dirt Particles

One source frequently appealed to by Shroud proponents is the 1986 article, "New Evidence May Explain Image on Shroud of Turin: Chemical Tests Link Shroud to Jerusalem," in *Biblical Archaeological Review*, by American crystallographer Joseph A. Kohlbeck and Eugenia L. Nitowski, who later joined the Carmelite order and took the religious name of Sister Damian. They discuss a calcium sample of the Shroud from an area known as the "bloody foot." They mention that the limestone sample was primarily travertine aragonite with small quantities of iron and strontium but no lead. Later, in 2002, American scientists Kohlbeck and Richard Levi-Setti examined some dirt particles from the Shroud's surface. The dirt was travertine aragonite limestone. Kohlbeck and Levi-Setti compared the spectra of samples taken from the Shroud with limestone samples from ancient Jerusalem tombs using a high-resolution microprobe. The chemical signatures of the shroud samples and the tomb limestone "was an unusually close match."[46]

---

[45] Farey, "The Medieval Shroud 2," 20.
[46] Turin Shroud Center of Colorado, *The Shroud of Turin*, 63.

Often, a key paragraph from the 1986 paper is missing in articles on the Shroud. Kohlbeck said in the 1986 *BAR* article:

> Of course, this doesn't prove the aragonite on the shroud came from Jerusalem, but this could be a reasonable explanation. Nevertheless, aragonite with these traces can no doubt be found elsewhere in the world as well as in Jerusalem. On the other hand, those who claim the shroud is a 14th-century forgery need to explain how the aragonite got there.
>
> Scientists continue to compare the chemical composition of shroud limestone and Jerusalem limestone. Their hope is that they will detect rare trace elements on both samples that will clearly distinguish them from aragonite samples elsewhere in the world. To date [1986]—no such "marker" has been found.[47]

Five:
Blood Stains

In 1978, American chemist Walter McCrone identified the reddish-brown stains on the shroud as containing iron oxide and concluded that its presence was likely due to simple pigment materials (red ochre and vermilion tempera paint) used in medieval times, which can produce images with unusual transparent features. A follow-up report appears in *Accounts of Chemical Research*. In that paper, McCrone wrote:

> The Shroud artist used a style of painting and painting material common in Europe during the 14th century. A chapter entitled "Practice of Painting Generally During the Fourteenth Century" in an 1847 book by Sir Charles Locke Eastlake entitled *Methods and Materials of Painting of the Great Schools and Masters* covers precisely the Shroud-like images. He refers to the process as the English or German mode of painting faint images ("grisaille," a light monochrome image). As Eastlake writes: "... After the linen is painted, its thinness is no more obscured that if it had not been painted at all, as the colours have no body." "The peculiarity of the English method appears to have been its absolute transparency. "A manuscript of the time contains directions for the preparation of transparent colours for painting on cloth." Eastlake continues: "The Anglo-German method appears, from the description, to have been in all

---

[47] Kohlbeck and Nitowski, "New Evidence May Explain," 24.

respects like modern water-colour painting—except that fine cloth, duly prepared, was used instead of paper."[48]

Shroud proponents' respond: "McCrone's critics admit that both iron oxide and mercury have been found, but the problem is that they are not found in sufficient quantities to form a visible image. On the other hand, iron oxide is also a component of blood and the only place where iron oxide is found on the Shroud is in the areas where blood is present."[49] Furthermore, the iron may have originated from dust fragments where the Shroud was stored, or they could have come from a fire that damaged the Shroud in 1532.

Nitowski identified several problems with McCrone's iron oxide finger-painting theory:

1. Through the microscope, the iron oxide particles as viewed on McCrone's slides "showed no directional patterns across fibers."
2. If red paint can be found, there are two possible explanations: during the time of Christ, aside from infrequent use of frescos and quite often an inscription concerning the dead was written in red paint above the nich or kokh, where the body was to be laid various colors of paint were used at the time of interment or the traditional reburial of skeletal remains ... A possibility for paint contamination on the Shroud could result from the action of a member of the burial party whose haste to finish before the Sabbath, dripped paint down onto the shrouded body on the bench. It has also been found by Don Luigi Fossati that medieval copies of the Shroud were laid on top of the Shroud to produce "touch relics" and could have been a source of some types of paint contamination.[50]

Di Lazzaro criticized McCrone's hypothesis saying, "There is a *non sequitur* and fallacious argument that is explained by an example." He elaborates on the error:

Imagine eating pasta with meat sauce. If one performs a microscopic analysis of a speck that fell on your shirt, you find sauce particles. From this analysis on a square millimeter of fabric, you cannot assume that the whole shirt is stained with sauce, it would be a meaningless

---

[48] McCrone, "The Shroud of Turin," 77–83.
[49] Joseph, "The Shroud and the Historical Jesus," 5.
[50] Nitowski, *The Field and Laboratory Report*, 14–15.

extrapolation. However, McCrone made a similar extrapolation, concluding that a few particles with a diameter of a thousandth of a millimeter on a few linen fibers were proof that the double image on the Shroud -a total area of about 2 square meters- was painted.[51]

Matteo Borrini and Luigi Garlaschelli, writing in the *Journal of Forensic Science*, arranged for forensic scientists to use Bloodstains Pattern Analysis techniques (BPA) to investigate the arm and body positions necessary to yield the pattern seen on the Shroud. Using a living volunteer and a mannequin for modeling several body positions, researchers determined that the patterns were consistent with multiple poses, which contradicts the theory that Jesus was buried in the cloth lying down.[52] In an interview with Charles Q. Choi on LiveScience, Borrini says, "… these cannot be real bloodstains from a person who was crucified and then put into a grave, but [are] actually handmade by the artist that created the shroud."[53]

Choi illustrates this with a telling example. Two short rivulets of the blood on the back of the left hand of the shroud are only consistent with a person standing with their arms held at a 45-degree angle. However, in direct contrast, "The forearm bloodstains found on the shroud match a person standing with their arms held nearly vertically."[54] Choi elaborates, "person couldn't be in these two positions at once."[55]

There are also claims of "bloodstains" on the cloth, but Jewish law dictated the cleansing of the corpse before wrapping, and bodies do not bleed after death. Moreover, the logistics of

1. Jesus' death on the cross,
2. the subsequent notification of Joseph of Arimathea of Jesus' death,
3. Joseph is traveling to Pilate's headquarters to meet with him,
4. The waiting time before Joseph was finally granted an audience with Pilate,
5. Pilate sent a centurion to confirm Jesus' death, followed by the centurion's return to Pilate with a report,
6. Pilate's granting permission to take the body of Jesus,
7. Joseph's obtaining material to prepare the body for burial,

---

[51] Di Lazzaro, "Let No One Who Is Not a Mathematician," 4.
[52] Borrini and Garlaschelli, "A BPA Approach," 1.
[53] Borrini and Garlaschelli, "A BPA Approach," 1.
[54] Choi, "Shroud of Turin Is a Fake."
[55] Choi, "Shroud of Turin Is a Fake."

8. Joseph's traveling to Golgotha (where Jesus hung on the cross), and
9. Joseph's removing the body and transporting it to the tomb he had prepared for Jesus would have required considerable time: not minutes, but hours.

Would a body still be capable of bleeding after all that time elapsed?[56]

Six:
Flowers and Pollen

Max Frei-Sulzer, a Swiss criminologist, was invited to conduct a palynological survey. Palynology studies observing and identifying minute botanical traces, such as pollens and fungal spores. "Frei-Sulzer's preferred method of obtaining evidence was to push little strips of sticky tape as firmly as he could onto a piece of fabric, then pull them off, restick them onto glass slides, and examine them under a microscope."[57] Later, he went to Israel and Turkey on several pollen-collecting expeditions. Afterward, he published his findings, lending credence to authenticating the Shroud. Papers about the controversy surrounding Frei-Sulzer's work are in several publications.[58] Farey highlights five inconsistencies with the findings and assertions of Frei-Sulzer:

1. He identified too many plants from too few samples. Although Frei-Sulzer himself did not quantify his results, subsequent investigators found that about half of it came from only two plants, such that, if his identifications were correct, all the other plants must have been present as only one or two grains.
2. His identifications were far too precise. In 1998, Uri Baruch, a palynologist with the Israel Antiquities Authority, examined thirty-four of Frei-Sulzer's pollens and could only confirm three at the species level. Even today, many genera have such similar pollen that they are almost impossible to split into individual species. As genera, their geographical distribution is much wider than that of individual species, so claims restricting their source to Jerusalem, or even to the Middle East in general, are seriously weakened.

---

[56] Alter, *The Resurrection*, 208–10, 228–38, 265–66.
[57] Farey, "The Medieval Shroud 2," 11.
[58] Ciccone, "La Truffa Dei Pollini"; Farey, "Problems with Pollen," 12; Marinelli, "The Question of Pollen Grains."

3. His range of pollen was unrealistic. A large proportion of his pollen is from entomophilous (insect-fertilized) plants, which could not have been naturally deposited on the cloth, and several of them flower in the second half of the year after the date of the crucifixion. To suggest that the entomophilous pollen all arrived from flowers placed around the body in the tomb implies that some twenty different species of flowers were collected in the afternoon of Good Friday, some of which are only found on the shores of the Dead Sea. Furthermore, many are unattractive scrub plants with thorny stems and spiky leaves, hardly appropriate for decorating an entombment.
4. His range of pollen does not match a typical pollen assemblage. Fabrics in the open air collect much more tree and grass pollen than anything else and fewer from flowering bushes. Frei-Sulzer's collection shows the opposite, reflecting the subjective way he gathered his reference spectra rather than the actual distribution of plants in an area.
5. He published no photographs for independent verification. His published articles are illustrated with large-scale and very detailed photographs of clusters of pollen under a Scanning Electron Microscope, unattributed and captioned only with a species name … and all his photographs are from his own or others' reference specimens. Even so, none of them are clear matches of the images of the pollen of the named species in PalDat, "the world's largest database for palynological data," and many have been re-identified by subsequent investigators. Baruch, for example, found that about a quarter of the collection was from plants that did not correspond to any of Frei's identifications, at the species or genus level.[59]

Dr. Alan Whanger first noticed the image of pressed flowers on the Shroud in 1985. He was co-founder of the Council for Study of the Shroud of Turin (CSST), where he served as the Chairman. In 1997 Israeli botanist Avinoam Danin reported that he had identified several species, including *Chrysanthemum coronarium*, or garland chrysanthemum, a species native to the Mediterranean. Shroud proponents, therefore, suggest that the Shroud must have been in Jerusalem at least once. Shroud proponents also assert that pollen samples from the Shroud may contain

---

[59] Farey, "The Medieval Shroud 2," 12–13.

Judean pollen. Later, Danin writes that he was "sorry to state that we cannot use the pollen for any geographical indication."[60]

American investigator Joe Nickell also refutes the usefulness of Frei's pollen samples. He writes that an independent review of the pollen strands shows that one out of the twenty-six provided contains significantly more pollen than the others, perhaps pointing to deliberate contamination.[61] Farey suggests that the pollen found on the Shroud could have been placed there out of devotion during religious rituals.[62] In contrast, Marzia Boi, writing in *Archaeometry*, provides partial support for the Shroud's authenticity.[63]

Paolo Di Lazzaro, research manager of the Aeneas of Frascati and Vice Director of the International Centre of Sindonology, and Daniele Murra presented a joint paper, "A Ray of Light on the Shroud of Turin," at the Proceedings of the Conference "FIAT LUX – Let there be Light." In section 3.1, Pollen on the Shroud, they wrote: "Despite [the fact that] the pollen investigation was one of the first scientific studies made on the ST in 1973, we were not able to find any peer reviewed papers on this topic. Most papers are published in conference proceedings, books, journals without peer review and websites, and only few of them are authored by scholars qualified in palynology."[64]

Seven:
Anatomy

Another tool in the arsenal of authenticists is anatomical accuracy. To advance their credibility, they appeal to the authority of pathologists who have examined the Shroud. Mark Antonacci, the author of *The Resurrection of the Shroud* (2000), lists twenty-four of the "most notable medical scientists" who think the Shroud is authentic. However, a literature review confirms a lack of consensus among the experts.

In 2010, Gregory S. Paul, an American researcher in paleontology, published an article stating that the proportions of the image are not realistic, as the forehead is too small, the arms are too long and of different lengths, and the distance from the eyebrows to the top of the head is non-representative. His analysis found that the rear view of the shroud "shows

---

[60] Quoted by Farey, "The Medieval Shroud 2," 13. See also, Danin, "Pressed Flowers."
[61] Nickell, *Inquest on the Shroud of Turin,* 113–14.
[62] Farey, "Problems with Pollen," 49.
[63] Boi, "Pollen on the Shroud of Turin," 316–30.
[64] Di Lazzaro, "A Ray of Light," 9.

both the top of the head and the heels, and provides a height a little over 1860 mm (6 ft 1 in)."[65]

Farey offers the following critical comments on Paul's claims. Upfront, he remarks that the analysis does not make sense.

1. It seems to derive the man's height in the ventral image from the length of the upper leg, and assumed ratios between that length the length of the lower leg, and the height of the body.
2. Without an accurate assessment of the length of the upper leg and an authoritative table of ratios, the ventral height (not significantly under 1830 mm) is no more than a guess.
3. The rear view does not show the top of the head.
4. The rear view shows one heel. It is pronated, so, a precise height is little more than a guess.
5. Paul goes on to estimate brain size from head measurements. Notably, the article's subtitle reads, "If it's Real the Brain of Jesus was the Size of a Protohuman's!" Farey concludes, "The imprecision of the images that the data for this cannot be more than a guess, and the conclusion derived from it unjustified."[66]

Giulio Fanti and colleagues write, "Although anatomical details are generally in close agreement with standard human-body measurements, some measurements made on the Shroud image, **such as hands, calves and torso, do not agree with anthropological standards** (Ercoline 1982; Simionato 1998/99; Fanti and Faraon 2000; Fanti and Marinelli 2001)."[67] (Bold in original) Paul concludes that the features are explainable if the Shroud is the work of a late medieval Gothic artist. Skeptics add that the fingers of the figure are too long and thin to be natural. However, they, too, align with the way figures were portrayed in Gothic art. Compounding matters, the arms are of different lengths, with the right forearm noticeably longer than the left forearm. Finally, "The front side of the figure on the shroud doesn't match the *back* side of the figure. In fact, the two figures aren't even the same length; the front side of the figure on the shroud is 1.95 meters long, but the figure on the back of the shroud is 2.02 meters long!"[68]

Aleteia, an Italian magazine, reports in an interview with Giulio Fanti, based on the Shroud of Turin, that he created a 3D "carbon copy"

---

[65] Paul, "The Shroud of Turin."
[66] Farey, "The Medieval Shroud 2," 26.
[67] Fanti et al. "Evidences for Testing Hypotheses about the Body Image," 6.
[68] McDaniel, "The Shroud of Turin."

of Jesus. Fanti says, "According to our studies, Jesus was a man of extraordinary beauty. Long-limbed, but very robust, he was nearly 5 feet 11 inches tall, whereas the average height at the time was around 5 feet 5 inches. And he had a regal and majestic expression."[69] Gregory Paul suggests the man in the Shroud was "a little over 1860 mm (6 ft 1 in)."[70] In a computerized anthropometric analysis, Fanti and Marinelli write, "The height obtained is 174 ± 2.5 cm."[71]

In contrast, a 1979 work by Dorothy Crispino points out that the height of the man in the image ranges from 162 cm to 187 cm.[72] Therefore, although not impossible, the man's height in the image raises doubts about its authenticity. Fanti and colleagues explain how the potential height discrepancy raises questions regarding the credibility of the Gospel narratives: "The authors who believe the Shroud is a false claim that the Man of the Shroud, about 1.80 m height, was a giant compared to his contemporaries and therefore it wouldn't have been necessary for Judas to give him the famous kiss to point him out in the group."[73]

Eight:
Artistic Evidence

O'Neill writes:

> The man depicted on the "Shroud" strikes many people as being Jesus because it "looks like Jesus." That's because it "looks like" traditional representations of Jesus that have dominated western art for centuries: a man with flowing, shoulder-length hair and a neat, short beard. Closer examination of the face on the "Shroud" image shows that it does not just "look like" the traditional western artistic depiction of Jesus, but it actually looks exactly like late thirteenth/early fourteenth century depictions of Jesus: the hair flows in slightly stylized locks and the beard is fashionably forked in the style of that time. This is not just a traditional depiction of Jesus, it's a traditional late Medieval depiction of him, exact down to every detail of the iconography of the time.
>
> All depictions of Jesus in the period in which the "Shroud" first appeared had the same iconographical elements: flowing, shoulder-

---

[69] Massaro, "This 3D 'Carbon Copy.'"
[70] Paul, "The Shroud of Turin."
[71] Fanti and Marinelli, "Computerized Anthropometric Analysis."
[72] Crispino, "The Height of Christ," 5–6.
[73] Fanti, Marinelli, and Cagnazzo, "Computerized Anthropometric Analysis," 2.

length hair, moustache, and a small, forked beard. And we find all of these elements on the so-called "Shroud", which first appeared in this very period.

But this is nothing like what we know about how a devout Jew of Jesus' time would have looked. First Century Jews kept their hair and beards short, since longer hairstyles were considered too "Hellenic" - associated with the practices and pagan lifestyle of the Greeks who were influencing Jewish culture since Alexander's conquest of Palestine. A devout Jew like Jesus would not have had long hair or a fashionable beard at all, but would have kept both trimmed to avoid association with paganism.[74]

Nine:
Coins Placed on the Eyes

Another claim made to support the Shroud's authenticity is the alleged imprint of a small Roman coin lying on the right eyelid of the man in the image.[75] Once again, Farey provides an insightful review. In the early 1970s, John Jackson and Eric Jumper observed small bumps on the eyes of the 3D image of the face on the Shroud. They obtained the image by using a VP-8 Image Analyzer. Jackson and Jumper speculated that they might be coins. In 1979, Father Francis Filas, a Jesuit Professor of Theology at the Loyola University of Chicago thought he saw the letters ECAI in approximately the right place. Later, he was assisted by a professional numismatist, Michael Marx.

Filas claims he found an appropriate coin for the period could be a lepton minted in the time of Pontius Pilate. Coincidentally, the exact year is indicated on the coin. On one side there was the design of a lituus (a ceremonial staff in the shape of a long-tailed question mark), and the inscription TIBERIUS CAESAR. Farey elaborates that in Greek letters this appears as TIBEPIOY KAICAPOC. He also adds "Filas' original ECAI was now understood as the Y at the end of one word (for some reason he always wrote it as U) and the CAI as an unusual variation of the beginning of the next. The curve of a lituus was also observed."[76]

---

[74] O'Neill, "Is There Evidence Supporting the Validity."

[75] Filas, *The Dating of the Shroud of Turin From Coins*; Hamon, "Does the Shroud of Turin," Marino, "Evaluation of the Proposed Existence of Lepton Coins"; Nitowski, *The Field and Laboratory Report*, 108–15; Whanger and Whanger, "Polarized Image Overlay Technique, 766–72.

[76] Farey, "The Medieval Shroud 2," 17.

142 *The Resurrection and Its Apologetics*

Filas soon discovered a coin with the aberrant spelling of CAICAPOS. That finding confirmed this identification. Since 1980, claims of several more have been announced. It requires asking, were these findings the figurative "smoking gun" in support of the Shroud's authenticity? Farey, refutes the claim. "Neither the actual marks on the Shroud, nor the coins, nor any of the archaeological evidence of Jewish burials, are at all definitive."[77] Farey concludes:

1. The letters on the Shroud can clearly be seen to be artefacts of the threads.
2. The misrepresentation of the letter K as a C is clearly exaggerated, and although a few excavated tombs have been found with coins scattered about.
3. A few ossuaries have been found with coins inside, including a few with coins in the upturned bowls of broken skulls.
4. The placing of coins on the eyes of corpses was at best extremely unusual (discussed later).[78]

In addition, in 1978, NASA researchers detected the impressions of coins placed on both eyes of the image. Having distinguished what seemed to be four letters "UCAI" near the arch of the eyebrows, Italian coin expert Mario Moroni identifies these as being part of the inscription on a lepton coin. According to Moroni, they were minted in 29 AD during Pontius Pilate's governorship of Judea. "UCAI" was part of "TIBEPIOU CAICAPOC." However, Antonio Lombatti, writing in the *British Society for the Turin Shroud Newsletter*, rejects this assertion. He says there is no archaeological evidence that there was a first-century Judaic custom of putting coins on the eyelids of the dead. In an exchange with the proponent, Dr. Alan Whanger, Lombatti quotes the testimony of an expert who is one of the foremost specialists in this field, Professor Levy Yitzhak Rahmani, Chief Curator of the Israel Department of Antiquities and Museums, who is also a specialist in Judaic cemeteries:

> No coins of the period 50 BC to 70 AD were found in any tomb. In the first century Jewish Palestine the placing of the coins was looked upon as idolatry; there was only a Greco-Roman custom according to which a coin was placed in the mouth of the deceased, so that he could pay Charon for conveying his shades across the Styx. Prof. N. Avigad of the Hebrew University, who excavated a great many of tombs of the

---

[77] Farey, "The Medieval Shroud 2," 17.
[78] Farey, "The Medieval Shroud 2," 17.

period in question, in and around Jerusalem, and Mr. A. Kloner, District Archeologist, who has lately had a great practical experience in this field, confirmed to me this scarcity of even one coin in such tombs. If at all encountered inside a tomb, such a stray coin has been found in the debris and not even in the tomb's loculi. It may be added that no coins have been reported from inside a Jewish ossuary nor does such a custom exist at the time at all. No archeological or literary evidence exists from the 1st century AD for a custom of covering the eyes of the deceased with coins, then the existence of such a custom from the same period must be denied.[79]

Furthermore, there is no confirmation of a coin placed on the left eyelid. Archaeologists have discussed the presence of coins in first-century Jewish burials, including Hachlili 2005; Hachlili and Killebrew 1983; Rahmani 1994.[80] Nitowski argues against the claim that there is no confirmation of a coin placed on the eyelid. She writes, "It does not seem to be a matter of how prevalent, but that the custom did exist, and apparently in two forms, coins on the eyes and a coin in the mouth."[81] Then she adds, "Where two silver denarii of Hadrian (ca. AD 133) were found placed over the eye orbits with a coin of the Bar-Kokhba Revolt nearby."[82] Nitowski continues quoting Hachlili and Killebrew that "It is highly doubtful that the interred at ʿEn Boqeq was a Jew," without evidence.[83]

Dr. L Y. Rahmani adds another wrinkle to the coin placement over the eye controversy. He discusses the Jewish revulsion of anything Roman:

> Is it plausible that two strictly observant and pious Jews, both members of the Sanhedrin - Joseph of Arimathea and the Pharisee Nicodemus together with Christ's own relatives and disciples, would include in a pious burial, undertaken 'in the manner of the Jews' an obscure foreign practice? ... *would those good Jews cover the eyes of a Jew who had just been put to death by the Romans in a most cruel manner with coins minted by the Roman procurator who had ordered this execution, coins carrying the name of the emperor ... ?*[84]

---

[79] Lombatti, "Doubts Concerning the Coins," 35–37.
[80] Hachlili, *Jewish Funerary Customs;* Hachlili and Killebrew, "Was the Coin-on-Eye Custom," 147–53; Rahmani, *A Catalogue of Jewish Ossuaries.*
[81] Nitowski, *The Field and Laboratory Report,* 108.
[82] Nitowski, *The Field and Laboratory Report,* 108.
[83] Nitowski, *The Field and Laboratory Report,* 108.
[84] Italics for emphasis.

Nitowski replies, "In a time of severe grief and in great haste, would they have bothered to look at the coins or care? What other coins would they use?"[85] However, she seems to forget that Joseph of Arimathea and Nicodemus assumed responsibility for the burial. Joseph was a member of the council (Sanhedrin). Nicodemus was a Pharisee who brought a mixture of myrrh and aloes—about a hundred pounds for the preparation. Presumably, one of them would be aware of the coinage, presuming usage.

A lengthy, multi-part correspondence about this controversy is online. More forcefully, Antonio Lombatti writes, "In short: to call into question the coin(s) to support the authenticity of the Shroud seems to me anti-historical and scientifically unorthodox."[86] Interestingly, in that written exchange, Whanger states for the record (August 29, 1997), "Returning to the main issue of the coins on the eyes, may I state clearly and emphatically that I did not and do not think that putting coins on the eyes of the dead was a Jewish custom. It certainly was not."[87]

Ten:
Writing on the Cloth

In 1979 Italian scientist Piero Ugolotti claimed to have found Greek and Hebrew letters on the Shroud written near the face of the image. These were further studied in 1997 by Professor André Marion and Anne-Laure Courage, whose digital analysis reportedly revealed other writings, including INNECEM (a shortened form of Latin "in necem ibis"— you will go to death"), NNAZAPE(N)NUS (Nazarene), IHSOY (Jesus) and IC (Iesus Chrestus). The uncertain letters IBE(R?) conjectured, "Tiberius." Not to be outdone, in 2009, Barbara Frale, a paleographer in the Vatican Secret Archives, stated that it is possible to read on the image the burial certificate of Jesus of Nazareth, imprinted in fragments of Greek, Hebrew, and Latin writing. She also stated that the text on the Shroud reads, "In the year 16 of the reign of the Emperor Tiberius Jesus the Nazarene, taken down in the early evening after having been condemned to death by a Roman judge because he was found guilty by a Hebrew authority, is hereby sent for burial with the obligation of being consigned to his family only after one full year."[88] Since Tiberius became emperor after the death

---

[85] Nitowski, *The Field and Laboratory Report*, 112.
[86] Lombatti, "Doubts Concerning the Coins."
[87] Whanger, "Whanger, Alan. "A Reply To Professor Antonio Lombatti About The Coins And Other Shroud Issues," August 29, 1997.
[88] Owen, "Death Certificate Is Imprinted."

of Octavian Augustus in AD 14, the sixteenth year of his reign would be between AD 30 to 31.

In opposition, in the *Journal of Conservation Science in Cultural Heritage*, Salvatore Lorusso writes, "It should be noted that these analyses are based entirely on the observation of a number of negative images taken by Giuseppe Enrie, the official photographer during the exposition of 1931."[89] Moreover, there exist additional challenges:

1. Enrie used orthochromatic film with a minimum image resolution of half a centimeter, which according to the skeptics, makes it impossible to identify the writing on the coins.
2. Some skeptics believe that these signs are due to irregularities on the plates and, therefore, not present on the Shroud.

Consequently, Lorusso says it is logical that the various details discovered at different times limit the definition of the Shroud image, as they are read diversely by different scholars with contrasting interpretations.[90]

Frale's methodology has been criticized because the writings are too faint to see. Similarly, linguist Mark Guscin (*British Society for the Turin Shroud Newsletter*, 1999; *The Oviedo Cloth*, 1998), a member of the Spanish Shroud Centre, disputes the work of Marion, stating that the inscriptions make little grammatical or historical sense. Likewise, Barrie Schwortz, arguably one of today's leading authorities on the Shroud, does not support the view of images of coins present on the Shroud. Arif Khan contacted Schwortz in a personal email about the coins. He writes:

> I have not changed my position and do not believe we can read the tiny inscription on a small coin via the Shroud. As the late Don Lynn (STURP [Shroud of Turin Research Project] team member and NASA imaging scientist at the Jet Propulsion Laboratory) said, you cannot visually resolve an inscription smaller than the weave of the fabric itself. Also, it is my opinion that the Disciples of Jesus would not have put a pagan coin on the face of the man that they believed to be the prophesied Messiah. Although Lombatti is a rather vocal anti-Shroud skeptic, I have to agree with him in this case. There are still many pro-Shroud scholars who like the coin inscription theory and continue to promote it in their lectures. Unfortunately, none of the STURP imaging scientists or photographers ever agreed with it.[91]

---

[89] Lorusso, "The Shroud of Turin," 120.
[90] Lorusso, "The Shroud of Turin," 120.
[91] Khan, "The Oviedo Cloth."

Eleven:
Problematic Issues

Even if the Shroud dated from that time, that would *not* mean that it was necessarily the Shroud of Jesus, or even, for that matter, it was a shroud. The cloth seems to have a human impression, perhaps like a man crucified. However, it is widely accepted that crucifixion was the most common way to execute people during the first century CE.

Twelve:
The New Catholic Encyclopedia

R. A. Wild, writing in *The New Catholic Encyclopedia, Second Edition*, concludes his entry on the "Shroud of Turin" by saying:

> In short, while many unanswered questions still remain, not least that of how the images came to appear on the cloth in the first place, it is most unlikely that this object is the authentic burial shroud of Jesus. Instead, while possibly a forgery deliberately intended to deceive the faithful, it could very well have been produced to serve as a devotional object, a pious reminder of how Jesus gave up even his own life for the salvation of humanity.[92]

Conclusion

In conclusion to this review of the Shroud of Turin, the words of Paolo Di Lazzaro, Vice Director of the International Centre of Sindonology, are food for thought:

> Taking into consideration the whole of the results of scientific analyses, at the moment, the scholars have more questions than answers on the origin of the Shroud of Turin. We have to admit that we still do not have sufficient data to determine whether this is an authentic relic or if it is a fake, and to be content with probabilities. Anyone who claims that they are certain that the Shroud is a medieval artifact, or that the Shroud is the authentic funerary cloth of Jesus from Nazareth, adds a substantial dose of faith to the available data.[93]

---

[92] Wild, "Shroud of Turin," 97.
[93] Di Lazzaro, "Let No One Who Is Not a Mathematician," 10.

Consequently, based on the cumulative evidence, detractors and skeptics argue that the Shroud of Turin does not provide evidence that Jesus died on the cross.

Medical Issues Continued

Having provided an overview of the Shroud of Turin controversy, this section continues exploring medical issues relating to the crucifixion and its consequences. Significantly, do the Gospel narratives confirm that Jesus died? There exists a lack of consensus on this vital topic.

Licona, in an imaginary dialogue between Muhammad and St. Paul, points out a challenge that Muhammad could easily offer to the medical argument that Jesus died of crucifixion. It runs as follows:

1. Scholars have also pointed out that the very medical studies Paul appealed to are horribly unreliable.
2. Medical studies assume the description of Jesus' crucifixion in the New Testament is accurate.
3. These medical doctors have misinterpreted descriptions meant solely for theological purposes as though they actually occurred.[1]

For example, Licona references the Gospel of John's report that Jesus was stabbed with a spear that caused blood and water to flow from his body, thus ensuring he was dead.[2]

If there was, in fact, no piercing episode, then many of the medical arguments employed to support Jesus' death via crucifixion are automatically rendered irrelevant.

However, some apologists assert that confirmation of Jesus' death occurred during the removal of his body. This argument postulates that Jesus' body was removed from the cross before the Sabbath for burial. Interestingly, Acts 13:27–29 claims that Jesus' body was removed from the cross by those who crucified him. Those involved in removing Jesus' body could have included some or all of the following people or groups: Joseph of Arimathea, Nicodemus, servants, and the Roman soldiers. Regardless, presumably, it would have been apparent that Jesus was dead

---

[1] Licona, *Paul Meets Muhammad*, 42.
[2] Licona, *Paul Meets Muhammad*, 42.

or alive if there had been contact with his body unless there was a conspiracy.

The counterarguments include the following points. (1) The narratives of Jesus' removal from the cross are contradictory and contain numerous omissions, (2) it is unknown who removed Jesus from the cross, (3) the existence of Nicodemus is not multiple attested, and (4) it is unknown whether Joseph or Nicodemus would have had the physical strength to lower Jesus from the cross. However, why would proponents of the resurrection have invented this scenario recorded in the Gospels? Perhaps, Jesus was buried in a ditch, and the entire body removal episode was an *invention* written to protect Jesus' honor or to provide proof that he was, in fact, dead.

The final argument is that favoring Jesus' death on the cross centers on the accounts recorded in the Gospels of the preparation for his burial. Again, given the handling of Jesus, it would have presumably been apparent whether he was dead or alive unless there was a conspiracy. The handling would have included washing the corpse and wrapping it in a linen shroud.

Skeptics offer an opinion that given a crucifixion, Jesus would be left on the cross for the birds, consumed by dogs, buried in a lime pit, or thrown in a mass grave for the condemned.[3] Proponents refute this argument.[4] In reply, skeptics point out that historical records from that time strongly suggest that it would not have been the Roman practice to permit a decent burial of any enemy of the state. The accounts of Jesus' removal from the cross, the body, and burial in a tomb are likely myths. Moreover, as mentioned earlier, critics point out that Nicodemus is not multiple attested: his existence is recorded only in John's Gospel.

C. H. Dodd's comment about the quantity of spices purchased merits consideration: "It seems likely that the somewhat extravagant estimate of the weight of myrrh and aloes provided is a touch introduced by the evangelist, who perhaps is somewhat addicted to numbers, especially large numbers (153 fishes—if the appendix is by the same author)."[5] John's account of Nicodemus' purchase of seventy-five pounds of "myrrh and aloes" bears all the hallmarks of legendary embellishment. Contrary to John's assertion, packing bodies in spices was *not* a Jewish practice. In fact, this practice was a custom in Egypt. The mention of

---

[3] Casey, *Jesus of Nazareth,* 497; Crossan, *The Cross That Spoke,* 541–45; *Who Killed Jesus?,* 154; Ehrman, *How Jesus Became God,* 161; Hengel, *Crucifixion,* 87–88.

[4] Cook, "Crucifixion and Burial," 213; Wright, *The Resurrection of the Son of God,* 710.

[5] Dodd, *Historical Tradition in the Fourth Gospel,* 139n1.

spices, conceivably, was an invention meant to link the burial of Jesus with that of Israel, once called Jacob and Joseph (Gen. 50:2, 26). Another option is that John may have been a copycat who based part or all of his account of Jesus' burial on contemporary reports of burying Rabbi Gamaliel, the Elder, and then beefed up the details in an attempt at one-upmanship.[6] Possibly the author of John was aware of Matthew's tradition of the wise men bringing gifts to the young Jesus and wrote verse 39 implementing a literary device called allusion, crafting a bookend to the story of Jesus' life. There also exists a question of how the women purchased spices during a religious festival like Passover when most businesses would have been closed.[7] Without the body's preparation for burial, there were no means to confirm that Jesus was dead.

The Gospel reports of Jesus' early death on the cross also raise doubts. Pilate was amazed at how soon Jesus died (Mark 15:44). He died after merely a few hours on the cross, whereas contemporary records detail that those crucified would sometimes survive for days on the cross. The purpose of crucifixion was to set an example, especially for insurrectionists. Noteworthy, the process was public, torturous, drawn out, degrading, and as humiliating as possible. Of course, crucified victims lasted different lengths of time while on the cross, depending on their state of health, the severity of the pre-crucifixion torture, and the means of crucifixion. It is significant that:

1. The crucifixion did not target vital organs or arteries,
2. The severity of Jesus' scourging is not described, and
3. It is unknown how many lashes he received.

One explanation of why Jesus' contemporaries may have been so surprised at how quickly he died relates to his physical build. Examining the evidence of Mark 6:3 and Matthew 13:55, John Meier presumes that Jesus, like his father, was a carpenter or, more precisely, "a woodworker" (*tektōn*).[8] Donald Capps, consequently, argues that Jesus would have been more robust than a typical Palestinian: "The airy weakling often presented to us in pious paintings and Hollywood movies would hardly have survived the rigors of being Nazareth's *tektōn* from his youth to his early thirties."[9] If Jesus was a carpenter, his rapid death on the cross becomes much more puzzling.

---

[6] Rejected by Loke, *Investigating the Resurrection*, 125.
[7] Alter, *The Resurrection*, 302–4.
[8] Meier, *A Marginal Jew*, 280–85.
[9] Capps, *Jesus: A Psychological Biography*, 14.

Time Component

Another reason for thinking that Jesus did not die on the cross is his self-testimony. In Matthew 12:40, Jesus declares that he will show his detractors one sign, the sign of Jonah: "For just as Jonah was three days and three nights in the belly of the great fish, so will the Son of Man be three days and three nights in the heart of the earth." The prophecy of Jonah contains two key components that do not match what happened to Jesus: the prophet's physical condition and the time factor.

If Jesus died on the cross and afterward buried in a tomb, his situation would be completely different from that of the prophet Jonah. Jesus did not duplicate Jonah's feat: Jonah went inside a great fish's belly *alive*, stayed *alive* in the fish's belly for three days and three nights, and was later spit out *alive* from inside the fish's belly. In contrast, Jesus went into the tomb *dead*, stayed *dead* for one day and two nights, and came out of it *alive*.

Insofar as the components of time are concerned, Christian apologists counter in Jewish tradition that part of a day counts as a whole day. Hence, Jesus fulfilled the three-day prophecy. On two grounds, this defense is lacking. First, the onus is on the apologists to unequivocally prove that concerning this specific prophecy, Jesus meant that part of a day would count as a whole day. Numerous Christian Bible commentators advocating a Wednesday or Thursday crucifixion deny the hypothesis that part of a day counts as an entire day. Second, regardless of the previous apologetic, Christian apologists could not prove that Jesus was resurrected on the third day because there were *no* witnesses. On Easter Sunday, visitors to the tomb found a missing corpse. The fact that the Gospels reported many events relating to Jesus' resurrection occurring on or after Easter Sunday is irrelevant. Presumably, even *if* there was a resurrection, it could have happened *before* Easter Sunday.

Licona also offers the following apologetic:

> Analogies need not match in every point and rarely do. The Sign of Jonah certainly does not, since, unlike Jonah, Jesus was not placed out of commission as a result of disobedience to God. Moreover, a responsible hermeneutic interprets questionable texts in light of numerous clear ones. When this is done, it is clear that Jesus' death is implied in the Sign of Jonah. Matthew, who reports the Sign of Jonah, has Jesus predicting his death at least on four other occasions (16:21; 17:23; 20:19; 26:61). Moreover, clear predictions of Jesus' death are reported five times by Mark (8:31; 9:31; 10:33–34; 12:7–8; 14:8), all

of which are reported by Matthew and all but one are reported by Luke.[10]

Licona's apologetic argument is unconvincing:

1. There is the question, should this prophecy be literally or metaphorically interpreted? Presumably, many of the sermons and commentaries on Matthew 12:40 interpret this prophecy literally and use it as a proof text for Jesus' messiahship.
2. The explanation that Jesus predicted his death on multiple occasions in Mark, Matthew, and Luke fails to consider that they wrote these alleged predictions almost thirty-five to fifty years after Jesus died (as most scholars agree on dating the Gospels).
3. If Matthew and Luke copied Mark, which they did, then, in effect, there is only one Gospel source for those predictions: Mark. (A possible non-Gospel source could be 1 Corinthians 15 if it is not an interpolation.)
4. Mark may have invented these predictions and incorporated them into his Gospel for theological reasons (the number "three" is very auspicious in the Hebrew Bible.[11]

Conclusion

The pertinent question relates to the evidence of Jesus' death by crucifixion, as recorded in the Christian Scriptures. Is the evidence overwhelmingly conclusive to any honest and objective seeker of the truth? These chapters show that this is not correct. Contrary to Habermas and Licona, there is good reason to doubt the first minimal fact: Jesus died because of crucifixion while on the cross. Yes, Jesus has been dead for nearly two thousand years. However, the precise *time* he died (before or after his burial) is unknown and subject to speculation.

Finally, the Christian Bible presents differing and contradictory reports, accounts incapable of harmonization, and growing embellishments of the storyline. Besides, there exists the literary or theological agenda of each Gospel author and the author of Acts. It is worth noting that the Gospels were written about thirty-five to seventy years after the events they claimed to report. The Gospel narratives provide readers with very little concrete evidence, although they may have some historical core. However, the credibility and plausibility of the New

---

[10] Licona, "Using the Death of Jesus to Defeat Islam," 99–100.
[11] See Alter, *The Resurrection*, 421–27; 622–26.

Testament are uncertain, the information is fragmented or too poorly corroborated to make solid analytic inferences, and the reliability of the sources is dubious. Therefore, it is *false* to assert that Jesus' death as a result of crucifixion is one of the best-established facts of history.

Islamic Theology and Jesus' Crucifixion—Did Jesus Die on the Cross?

This section is for readers who may be curious why Muslims reject the Gospel accounts of Jesus' crucifixion and what they believe happened instead. The reasons Muslims put forward for denying Jesus' crucifixion are primarily theological. Consequently, many Christian apologists argue that their views should be *excluded* automatically from the scholarly consensus regarding the details of Jesus' death, burial, and alleged resurrection. Nevertheless, it could be countered that the views of Christian evangelical scholars regarding Jesus' alleged burial in Joseph of Arimathea's new tomb should be excluded *for the same reason*, as many secular scholars are skeptical of the details recorded in the Gospel narratives regarding this episode. The readers are left to decide whether these arguments carry any weight. Here is a summary of Muslim views on Jesus' crucifixion.

There are numerous theological reasons why Jesus could not have died because of crucifixion. Almost two billion Muslims reject the notion that Jesus died in this way. Three widely held Muslim opinions include the following: (1) Jesus ascended to heaven without being nailed to the cross, (2) God transformed another person to make him look like Jesus, who was then crucified instead of Jesus (the substitution theory), and (3) Jesus swooned on the cross—that is, he merely *seemed* to die and was revived after being removed from the cross.

Unfortunately, many of these beliefs come from early commentaries on the Qur'an that contradict and are incompatible. One primary reason for this situation is that the relevant passages in the Qur'an are unclear and ambiguous. The pertinent verses from the Qur'an (*sūra Nisa*) read:

> 4:155 And [We cursed them] for their breaking of the covenant and their disbelief in the signs of Allah and their killing of the prophets without right and their saying, "Our hearts are wrapped." Rather,

Allah has sealed them because of their disbelief, so they believe not, except for a few.
4:156 And [We cursed them] for their disbelief and their saying against Mary a great slander,
4:157 And [for] their saying, "Indeed, we have killed the Messiah, Jesus, the son of Mary, the messenger of Allah." And they did not kill him, nor did they crucify him; but [another] was made to resemble him to them. And indeed, those who differ over it are in doubt about it. They have no knowledge of it except the following of assumptions. And they did not kill him, for certain.
4:158 Rather, Allah raised him to Himself. And ever is Allah Exalted in Might and Wise.
4:159 And there is none from the People of the Scripture but that he will surely believe in Jesus before his death. And on the Day of Resurrection he will be against them a witness.

Islam rejects the notion that Jesus is the Son of God, denies the Trinity, repudiates the hypostatic union (that Jesus is both fully God and fully human in one hypostasis, i.e., the union of two natures in one person), and denies Jesus' crucifixion and death on the cross for the salvation of all humanity. However, if you remove the Trinity, the incarnation, the cross, the resurrection, and the Bible from the Christian faith, you have removed everything Christians consider essential to salvation. In effect, Christianity would not exist.

What happened to Jesus? Muslims have a wide range of views. The commentary of Fakhr al-Din al-Razi (d. 606 / 1210) identifies no less than five different versions of the substitution theory of which he was aware:

1. The Jews deliberately crucified another person, then lied about it.
2. A Jew, Titanus, was sent by "Judas, the chief of the Jews" to kill Jesus. However, God caused him to look like Jesus and suffer crucifixion in his place.
3. The man charged with guarding Jesus was made to look like Jesus and was crucified in his place.
4. Jesus asked his twelve disciples for a volunteer, and one man volunteered who was made to look like Jesus and crucified in his place.

5. A hypocritical disciple, who proposed to betray Jesus, was made to look like him and was crucified in his place.¹

Additional substitutes discussed in the literature include:
    a. Simon of Cyrene,
    b. Judas Iscariot,
    c. An anonymous bystander or passer-by, or
    d. Satan.²

A partial list of interpretations, which Joseph Cumming found in the major commentaries on the Qur'an, includes the following: (1) the substitution theory, (2) the sleep theory (that Jesus lost consciousness while on the cross), (3) *wafāt* ("'Death' [*wafāt*] here is the act of seizing [*qabad*]." The meaning is: "I am seizing you to myself."), (4) this verse contains a non-chronological arrangement, with eschatological death and resurrection, (5) God simply "brought an end to Jesus' earthly lifespan," (6) God "took Jesus totally, in body and soul," (7) agnosticism as to when and how Jesus' dying and rising takes place, (8) the Ṣūfī vision of death to self and carnal desires, (9) "like the martyrs, Jesus died a real death, but is alive with God," and (10) real, literal death and resurrection.³

Twelve Theological Reasons Why Many Muslims Challenge that Jesus Died of Crucifixion

The following material is a compilation of evidence taken from the Qur'an and primarily, but not exclusively, from Muslim writers. It outlines twelve *theological* reasons why many Muslims challenge the Christian belief that Jesus died of crucifixion:

1. The Islamic interpretation of God is correct; Christianity is in error:
    a. God is neither a body nor the essential form of a body; His presence within and unification with the human body are not metaphysically possible. Therefore, Jesus could not have been God and died because of crucifixion.

---

[1] Cumming, "Did Jesus Die on the Cross? The History," 40.
[2] Cumming, "Did Jesus Die on the Cross? The History," 40.
[3] Cumming, "Did Jesus Die on the Cross? The History," 31; Cumming "Did Jesus Die on the Cross: Reflections," 47.

Islamic Theology 157

- b. According to Christians, Jesus claimed to be God (i.e., the second member of the Trinity). If this is correct, then he could not have died on the cross because "God is immune to death," and therefore, "You cannot kill God" (Isa. 40:28; 44:6; Jer. 10:10; 1 Tim. 1:17).
- c. If Jesus was indeed God (i.e., the second member of the Trinity), he could not have died on the cross because God cannot be human (Num. 23:19; 1 Sam. 15:29; Hos. 11:9; Job 33:12).

2. The Islamic view of sin is correct:
   a. Although the notion that Jesus died on the cross and redeemed all of the sins of humankind is the basis of all Christian doctrine, the Muslim contra position is consistent with the mentioned Scriptures. In essence, Muslims do not find it necessary for "God" to come down as a man and get murdered, nor sacrifice for anyone to enter heaven. The Muslim position on salvation rests upon God's infinite mercy. Therefore, this is why God, through His prophets, taught repentance for sins committed. Human beings, unlike other creatures, are endowed with free will and have the choice to accept or reject faith. Thus, sin is the byproduct of being human. Sin also enables humans to recognize their imperfections and their need for God, who is the embodiment of perfection. Through repentance, humans are coming to God, asking for His forgiveness. That is why repentance is the key to salvation. In the Old Testament, repentance and forgiveness appear hundreds of times, while in the New Testament, these two words appear fifty-two times.[4]
   b. According to the Christian doctrine, Jesus died on the cross as a sacrifice for our sins. Every human is born with sins, or all humans will eventually sin, and therefore, someone as pure as Jesus needed to suffer crucifixion to nullify these sins. At this point, the question arises: why does anyone have to die for our sins when God, the all-merciful, could as effortlessly grant us forgiveness if we asked for it? Why does He have to make someone suffer for our or someone else's sins? Isn't that unjust of Him? According to the Bible, the way to redemption is obtainable without the need for sacrifice).[5]

---

[4] Imran, *Christ Jesus, the Son of Mary*, 246–47.
[5] Qasem, *A Closer Look at Christianity*.

      c. Jesus could not have died on the cross for *another* person's sin(s) (Ezek. 18:20). Scripture states that the soul who sins is the one who will die. The son will not share the father's guilt, nor will the father share the son's guilt. The righteousness of the righteous man shall be upon him, and the wickedness of the wicked shall be upon him.

      d. The Christian claim that without the death of Jesus and shedding his blood, there is no redemption and remission of sin (Heb. 9:22) is a false doctrine.

      e. The claim that the death of Jesus was for the atonement of our sins is a Christian theological belief. This theological claim––relating to sin—is merely an interpretation of an alleged historical event, Jesus' death.

      f. Nowhere in the four Gospels did Jesus state explicitly that he would die to save humankind from sin. When approached by a man who asked what he could do to gain eternal life, Jesus told him to keep the commandments (Matt. 19:16, 17); in other words, it was sufficient to obey God's Law.

3. Justice:
   a. The death of an innocent and righteous person can neither wipe away a person's sins nor redeem another from their sins. For an innocent person to die in the place of a guilty person is an outrageous injustice.[6]
   b. "But is this just?" That is the question that our Muslim friends ask when they hear that Jesus died in place of sinners. It is not good news because they think it is not just for an innocent man to die in place of the guilty.[7]

4. Allah's Goodness and Mercy:
   a. Since God can forgive, there is absolutely no need for the 'sacrifice' of which Christianity speaks. God is almighty and pardons all people of their sins, only requiring that they repent or even merely remain constant in their faith as Muslims. God is kind; He is not an unmerciful judge.
   b. Allah is almighty—He can do what He likes. Allah is merciful—He forgives whom He wills.
   c. Proverb 10:27 The fear of the LORD prolongs life, but the years of the wicked will be short. (Unless we realize that Jesus

---

[6] Troll, *Muslims Ask, Christians Answer*, 19.
[7] Anyabwile, *The Gospel for Muslims*, 74.

did not die on the cross, we cannot have a literal interpretation of this prophecy.)
d. Proverb 15:29 The LORD is far from the wicked, but he hears the prayer of the righteous. (If this biblical verse is true, God listened to Jesus' cries and delivered Jesus from the grip of an accursed death on the tree.)
e. Psalm 20:6 Now I know that the LORD saves his anointed; he will answer him from his holy heaven with the saving might of his right hand.
f. Psalm 28:8 The LORD is the strength of his people; he is the saving refuge of his anointed.
g. Psalm 41:2 The LORD protects him and keeps him alive; he is called blessed in the land; you do not give him up to the will of his enemies.

5. Deuteronomy 21:23 stipulates that if a man is killed for a capital offense, "his body shall not remain all night on the tree, but you shall bury him the same day, for a hanged man is cursed by God. You shall not defile your land that the LORD your God is giving you for an inheritance" (ESV):
   a. If Jesus was crucified, he was cursed because the Bible says that God curses those who are hanged from a tree.
   b. The logical conclusion of this passage in Scripture is that Jesus is accursed.

6. For many reasons, Allah would not permit crucifixion:
   a. It would be wrong for Allah to allow one of His prophets to die in shame and humiliation.
   b. If Jesus suffered and died, it must be understood that God deserted him, making him disowned.
   c. How could God have abandoned to His enemies so great a prophet as Jesus? How can the Father sacrifice His Son on the cross? This action is simply blasphemy.[8]

7. In two respects, Jesus failed to fulfill the prophecy he gave in Matthew 12:40: "For just as Jonah was three days and three nights in the belly of a giant fish, so will the Son of Man be three days and three nights in the heart of the earth" (ESV):

---

[8] Troll, *Muslims Ask, Christians Answer*, 19.

      a. Jesus was not in the tomb for three "full" days and three "full" nights. (*the time component*)
      b. Jonah was swallowed *alive*, stayed in the fish *alive*, and later spit out *alive*. In contrast, Jesus died, was buried, remained in the tomb while dead, and was resurrected alive. (*the condition/state component*)
      c. Based on this prophecy, Jesus could not have died because of crucifixion.

8. Muslims view the cross as a symbol of defeat, not a proclamation of divine love (i.e., John 3:16). They seek to exalt God and not denigrate Him to such ignominy as suffering and death. For Muslims, the cross is a place of disgrace, not majesty. It is an offense both to God and the prophet of Islam.[9]

9. Muhammad:
      a. Why would God need to send Muhammad if the Son of God himself had lived on earth, had died as the final sacrifice, and had risen again to show his power over death?[10]
      b. Muhammad, as Seal of all the Prophets, has superseded Christ.

10. Deuteronomy 18:15–18 "The LORD your God will raise up for you a prophet like me from among you, from your brothers—it is to him you shall listen— 16 just as you desired of the LORD your God at Horeb on the day of the assembly, when you said, 'Let me not hear again the voice of the LORD my God or see this great fire any more, lest I die.' 17 And the LORD said to me, 'They are right in what they have spoken. 18 I will raise up for them a prophet like you from among their brothers. And I will put my words in his mouth, and he shall speak to them all that I command him'" (ESV). In other words, readers must ask who is more like Moses: Jesus or Muhammad?
      a. Muhammad, like Moses, had a natural death; the Gospels report Jesus had a violent death by crucifixion.
      b. Muhammad, like Moses, died at an old age, whereas Jesus died at about age thirty-three.
      c. Muhammad, like Moses, died married and with children, whereas Jesus died unwed and childless.

---

[9] van Gorder, *No God but God*, 134.
[10] Greear, *Breaking the Islam Code*, 116.

d. Muhammad, like Moses, died a leader of his people, whereas Jesus died rejected by his people.
   e. Muhammad's body, like Moses', lies buried in the earth, whereas Jesus' body rests in heaven.
   f. Muhammad, like Moses, died, and none considered him a God, whereas Jesus was considered a god by some of his followers.

11. The Jewish people
    a. The Jews, who claim to have killed Jesus in *sūrat al-nisā'* (4) 157, are twice in error. They both schemed against the Messenger of God and arrogated to themselves God's power over life and death.
    b. "Humans can no more take a human life than they can create one....God creates life, and He takes life away....No one can die except by God's permission" [*sūrat al 'Imran* (13) 145].

12. The Qur'an
    a. The Qur'an, God's word, declared that Jesus did not die (*sūrat* 4:157).
    b. The Qur'an supersedes the Christian Bible.

In conclusion, Muslim theologians have different answers to the following question: What happened to Jesus before, during, and after the crucifixion? Muslims do *not* support the Christian doctrine that Jesus died by crucifixion, especially not for the remission of sin. The Muslim belief, relating to the remission of sin, is that the sinner only needs to express sincere contrition and be faithful to Muslim laws. Obtaining salvation, no doubt, an innocent person does *not* have to die to eliminate the sin of another.

Conclusion

The first Minimal Fact is that Jesus died by crucifixion. Detractors argue that the New Testament needs to provide adequate information to confirm that hypothesis. The crucifixion/passion narratives contain differing accounts of what happened at the crucifixion, with several omitting or contradicting crucial details found in other Gospels and appearing written for theological reasons: Zechariah 12 and Psalm 22:16 [AV]. It is noteworthy that the piercing event in John 19 is dubious and unconvincing.

Post-New Testament writing does not lend credence to the belief that Jesus died resulting from crucifixion. These works (Josephus and Tacitus) are dated, and the source of the author's information remains unknown. Christian apologists admit that the Josephus text is problematic, suffering from select editing and possible interpolation. The Shroud of Turin is controversial. Voluminous papers, journal articles, and books exist about this topic. Admittedly, researchers still do not have sufficient data to determine whether this is an authentic relic or if the Shroud is a fake. Islam rejects the belief that Jesus died on the cross. Their arguments are primarily theological. The Book of Jonah, literally quoted by Matthew (Matt. 12:39–40), weakens seriously the claim that Jesus died by crucifixion. Given all these unknowns, detractors, doubters, and skeptics argue that the literature provides questionable support for believing that Jesus died on the cross, nor should that purported event offer a rationale for converting to Christianity.

Is Joseph of Arimathea Historical?

Joseph of Arimathea's name appears in all four Gospel accounts. William Lane Craig argues that the person of Joseph of Arimathea is probably historical and therefore serves as evidence supporting the empty tomb.[1] Craig argues, "It seems very unlikely that Christian tradition could invent Joseph of Arimathea, give him a name, place him on the Sanhedrin, and say he was responsible for Jesus' burial if this was not true."[2] Extending this apologetic, the Christian Worldview Press offers that "Considering that all four gospels were written during the first century it would be very difficult to name someone this important while there were still people alive who could check out this claim."[3] David Margolis states that "Listing the man's name, his hometown (a small town at that), and his membership on the ruling council of Jews would have made Joseph's identity easily identifiable and falsifiable. It's quite far-fetched to believe that the gospel writers would have fabricated a prominent figure whom anyone could check out for themselves."[4] Craig believes, "Moreover, his association with Arimathea, an obscure town with no theological or historical significance, further lends historical credibility to the figure of Joseph."[5]

Deconstructing the previous discussion, the collective arguments in rebuttal of the historicity of Joseph of Arimathea include the following:

---

[1] Craig, *Reasonable Faith*, 364; "Reply to Evan Fales,' 72; "Closing Responses [in *Fact or Figment*]," 168; "The Empty Tomb of Jesus," 250; "Did Jesus Rise From the Dead?," 147–48; "On Doubts about the Resurrection," 55; *Assessing the New Testament Evidence*, 175–76; *Apologetics: An Introduction*, 186; cf. Lyons, "On the Life and Death of Joseph of Arimathea," 29–53; O'Collins and Kendall, "Did Joseph of Arimathea Exist?," 235–41.

[2] Craig, *Apologetics: An Introduction*, 186.

[3] Christian Worldview Press, "Was Joseph of Arimathea a Myth?"

[4] Margolis, "The Resurrection of Jesus Christ."

[5] "Closing Responses [in *Fact or Figment*]," 168.

1. Joseph of Arimathea is multiply attested and mentioned in all four Gospels.
2. The burial of Jesus in a private tomb (later found empty) is unlikely to have been an invention.
3. Since there is no reason why anyone would invent the name Joseph for the man who buried Jesus, we should assume it was the name of a historical individual.
4. Arimathea was a real place.
5. Joseph comes from a small town with no historical or theological significance, lending credibility to the story.
6. It is unlikely that the early Christian believers would place a fictional character on the historical council of the Sanhedrin.

In this chapter, there is a presentation of responses to each argument.

Joseph of Arimathea is Multiply Attested

The earliest Gospel (Mark) nowhere implies that Jesus' tomb belonged to Joseph of Arimathea.

Christian apologists assert that Joseph of Arimathea buried Jesus in his family tomb since that event is multiply attested (i.e., appears in two or more independent sources). Specifically, it appears in the four Gospels. This Christian apologetic is false on two accounts. First, two Gospel narratives provide information that suggests that the tomb did not belong to Joseph of Arimathea.

Mark 15:46 is the earliest description, and this source is the core and foundational Synoptic record. Notice Mark's words, "And Joseph bought a linen shroud, and taking him down, wrapped him in the linen shroud, *and laid him in a tomb* that had been cut out of the rock. And he rolled a stone against the entrance of the tomb" (ESV). There is no mention of Joseph of Arimathea placing Jesus' body in his family tomb. On the contrary, Mark, the earliest Gospel narrative, reports the burial in an anonymous tomb.

The Gospel of John also fails to support the idea that the burial was in Joseph of Arimathea's family tomb. John 19:41–42 reads, "Now in the place where he was crucified there was a garden, and in the garden a new tomb in which no one had yet been laid. So because of the Jewish day of Preparation, since the tomb was close at hand, they laid Jesus there"

(ESV). James Tabor elaborates on this hypothesis, arguing that the burial of Jesus was not in Joseph's tomb:

> So, as I often tell my students, "thank God for Mark and John." Mark does not elaborate the choice of the tomb but John makes it clear that this initial burial of Jesus by Joseph of Arimathea is a *temporary and emergency burial of opportunity*. That the tomb is new and unused meant that it could be used for a few hours, until the Sabbath and Passover holiday were past. This particular tomb is chosen because it just happened to be near, as John plainly explains. The idea that this tomb *belonged* to Joseph of Arimathea makes no sense at all. What are the chances that he would just happen to have his own new family tomb conveniently located near the Place of the Skull, or Golgotha, where the Romans regularly crucified their victims? It is ludicrous even to imagine, but neither Mark nor John say anything of the sort.
>
> Everyone has *assumed* Jesus is placed in Joseph's own tomb because of two words added by Matthew in his editing of Mark, namely "He laid it [the body] in *his own* new tomb" (Matthew 27:60). Luke does not have this. And Mark and John are crystal clear as to why this tomb was chosen. This is an obvious interpolation by Matthew and it makes no sense in the context. A tomb that happened to be near the place of crucifixion, just outside the city gates, would not have belonged to Joseph. Matthew adds this phrase, as he often does, to try and make the action of Joseph a "fulfillment" of prophecy. This is one of the major characteristics of Matthew's gospel, something he regularly does (see Matthew 1:22; 2:15; 8:17, etc.). So the idea that this temporary tomb *belonged* to Joseph was most likely added by Matthew for theological reasons. Matthew believes that the text in Isaiah 53 about the "Suffering Servant," refers to Jesus (see Matthew 8:17 where he explicitly notes this). One of the details of that prophecy is that the slain "Servant" makes his grave "with a rich man" (Isaiah 53:9). Matthew seizes on this and suggests that the tomb must have belonged to Joseph of Arimathea—a "rich man."
>
> Taking then what the reader learns from Mark and John, they are in a position to make some clear sense of the core tradition. Jesus is hastily buried just before the Passover Sabbath. After all, what does one do with a corpse a few hours before the Passover Seder, and how can it best be protected from predators? The new tomb, unused, and possibly incomplete, that happened to be nearby, was a perfect temporary solution. The idea was that after the festival the full and

proper rites of Jewish burial could be carried out and Jesus could be placed in a second tomb, as a permanent resting place.[6]

Matthew Ferguson is another detractor who challenges the notion that multiple-attested information supports the existence of Joseph of Arimathea. A significant deficiency is no **clear independent attestation** of Joseph of Arimathea. Ferguson points out, "Perhaps if Joseph's empty tomb were corroborated independently, then there might be evidence that the author of Mark did not invent it."[7] He then adds a caveat, "When a claim is independently attested by multiple sources, that only means that they all go back to an earlier source. It does not entail that they go back to an actual historical event."[8] Examining the Gospels provides evidence that the Synoptics are "substantially influenced by the Markan narrative (80% of Mark's verses are reproduced in Matthew, 65% in Luke."[9]

It is noteworthy that the tomb or burial by Joseph of Arimathea does not appear in any literature from the first century except in the Gospels. In contrast, although John does not follow the ipsissima verba of the earliest Gospel, "there are still clear parallels and adaptations between the texts."[10] He adds, "All of the post-Markan references to the empty tomb can be shown to derive from Mark and are thus not independently attested."[11] In contrast, Ferguson points out that the Apocryphon of James contains "traditions" independent of the canonical Gospels (e.g., Jesus was dishonorably buried in a sand pit.) Ferguson concludes, "If so, this may suggest that when a text was independent of Gospel sources, it was unaware of the tomb of Joseph of Arimathea since this story could have been invented solely by these sources."[12]

The four Gospels are not independent sources, as Matthew and Luke (and possibly John) borrowed from Mark's Gospel.

It is not difficult to explain why Joseph of Arimathea appears in all the Synoptic Gospels. Matthew and Luke were copying Mark; copies can focus on the same people and events as the original. Robert Stein includes this information in his *Studying the Synoptic Gospels:* "Of the 11,025

---

[6] Tabor, "Reading Mark and John."
[7] Ferguson, "Knocking Out the Pillars."
[8] Ferguson, "Knocking Out the Pillars."
[9] Ferguson, "Knocking Out the Pillars."
[10] Ferguson, "Knocking Out the Pillars."
[11] Ferguson, "Knocking Out the Pillars."
[12] Ferguson, "Knocking Out the Pillars."

words found in Mark, only 304 have no parallel in Matthew and 1,282 have no parallel in Luke. This means that 97.2 percent of the words in Mark have a parallel in Matthew and 88.4 percent have a parallel in Luke."[13]

William Barclay, writing in his *Barclay's Guide to the New Testament,* writes about the same subject. He identifies statistical oddities:

1. Mark can be divided into 105 sections.
2. Ninety-three occur in Matthew and eighty-one in Luke.
3. Of Mark's 105 sections, *there are only four that do not occur either in Matthew or Luke.*
4. Mark has 661 verses; Matthew has 1,068 verses; Luke has 1,149 verses.
5. Matthew reproduces no fewer than 606 of Mark's verses, and Luke reproduces 320.
6. Of the fifty-five verses of Mark which Matthew does not reproduce, Luke reproduces thirty-one. Consequently, there are only twenty-four verses in the whole of Mark that are not reproduced somewhere in Matthew or Luke.[14]

Michael Grant includes the following caveat in *Jesus: An Historian's Review of the Gospels*: "Although a story may appear in several different literary forms their multiplicity does not corroborate its genuineness since they can still all be traceable back to a single source" (see Table 12-1).[15] Consequently, the argument that the name Joseph of Arimathea is multiply attested provides no support for its historicity.

Table 12-1: Varying Details about Joseph of Arimathea

	Paul	Mark	Matthew	Luke	Acts	John
Joseph is named	NO	YES	YES	YES	NO	YES
From Arimathea	NO	YES	YES	YES	NO	YES
Counselor	NO	YES [prominent]	NO	YES [no description]	NO	NO
Good Man	NO	NO	NO	YES	NO	NO
Regular Man	NO	NO	NO	YES	NO	NO
Rich Man	NO	NO	YES	NO	NO	NO

---

[13] Stein, *Studying the Synoptic Gospels*, 52.
[14] Barclay, *Barclay's Guide to the New Testament*, 2.
[15] Grant, *Jesus: An Historian's Review*, 201.

	Paul	Mark	Matthew	Luke	Acts	John
Jesus' Disciple	NO	NO	YES	NO	NO	YES
Feared the Jews	NO	NO	NO	NO	NO	YES
Waited for God's Kingdom	NO	YES	NO	YES	NO	NO
Asked for Body	NO	YES	YES [not boldly]	YES [not boldly]	NO	YES [not boldly]
Bought Linen	NO	YES	NO	NO	NO	NO
Removed Body from Cross	NO	YES	NO	YES	NO	NO
Possessed the Body	NO	YES [Implied]	YES	YES [Implied]	NO	YES
Wrapped the Body	NO	NO	YES [with linen]	YES	NO	YES [with Nicodemus's assistance]
Placed Body in Unknown Tomb	NO	YES	NO	YES	NO	YES
Placed Body in His Tomb	NO	NO	YES	NO	NO	NO
Cut Tomb Out of Rock	NO	NO	YES	NO	NO	NO
Rolled Stone at Entrance	NO	YES	YES	NO	NO	NO

Empty Tomb is an Unlikely Invention

Mark had good theological reasons for inventing the story of the empty burial tomb.

Bart Ehrman presents a rational explanation for the empty tomb. In a 2014 blog, Ehrman discusses with his readers an example of changing his mind. He cites the example of "changing his mind about the idea that Jesus' tomb was discovered empty three days after his death."[16] Ehrman states, "It is

---

[16] Ehrman, "Women at the Tomb."

conceivable that any Christian story-tellers would invent the tradition that women found the tomb empty."[17]

1. Christian apologists argue women were widely thought of as untrustworthy and, in fact, their testimony could not be allowed in courts of law. However, no one is talking about a Jewish court of law in which witnesses are being called to testify.
2. Female storytellers perhaps told stories that women were the first to believe, after finding that his tomb was empty.
3. Women finding an empty tomb makes the best sense of the realities of history. Preparing bodies for burial was commonly the work of women, not men.
4. If women were the ones who went to the tomb to anoint the body, naturally they would be the ones who found the tomb empty.
5. Mark 14:50 reports the male disciples fled the scene when Jesus was arrested. Therefore, they were not present for Jesus' crucifixion. If the men had scattered, or returned home, who was left in the tradition to go to the tomb? Women.
6. Mark could have invented the story from a literary perspective:
    a) Mark makes a special point throughout his narrative that the male disciples never do understand who Jesus is.
    b) Despite all of Jesus' miracles, despite all his teachings, despite everything they see him do and say, they never do get it.
    c) Next, fast-forward to the end of the Gospel. Ehrman asks his readers, "Who learns that Jesus has not stayed dead but has been raised?"[18] The answer is the women learned Jesus has been raised, not the male disciples. Yet, the women never tell anyone (Mark 16:8).[19]
    d) Consequently, the male disciples never do come to understand that Jesus had been raised. "That is all consistent with Mark's view."[20]

Ehrman concludes his blog by saying, "In the end, we simply cannot say that there would be "no reason" for someone to invent the story of women discovering the empty tomb."[21]

---

[17] Ehrman, "Women at the Tomb."
[18] Ehrman, "Women at the Tomb."
[19] Ehrman, "Women at the Tomb."
[20] Ehrman, "Women at the Tomb."
[21] Ehrman, "Women at the Tomb."

The lack of multiple attestations.

Joseph of Arimathea possessing a tomb in Jerusalem is a unique detail in Matthew. However, for reasons unknown, the ownership of a burial place is omitted by Paul, Mark, Luke, and John. Hence, the claim that Joseph owns the tomb lacks multiple attestations. In the eyes of skeptics, the author exhibits a habit of making up details (the guards at the tomb, the bribing of the soldiers, and zombies parading through Jerusalem). Hence, Joseph owning a tomb in Jerusalem is doubtful. Readers must decide whether they believe Joseph owned a tomb that was the burial place of Jesus or that Joseph ever existed.

The empty tomb would bolster Christian faith in Jesus' resurrection.

If Joseph of Arimathea was an invented personality, so was his private tomb. Maurice Casey asks an intriguing question: Why should Mark write a story of an empty tomb? Casey offers two speculations as to why the author of Mark came up with his empty tomb story, even though the first disciples of Jesus felt no need to include it in their preaching of Jesus' resurrection. He writes that there are at least two main points to consider. During the first century, various Jewish beliefs about the resurrection existed. How could the first disciples believe God had raised Jesus from the dead, leaving his body in a common criminal's tomb? Casey points out that "It is important that God could raise the dead to his heavenly throne with quite new spiritual bodies" and Jesus "had predicted his own resurrection."[22] Passages such as Daniel 12:1–3 also support the belief that the dead and an empty tomb would rise from the earth. Casey continues, if this view of bodily resurrection were "applied to Jesus, it could easily be taken to mean that his tomb was left empty, provided that he was assumed to have been raised in the same way that other people will be raised at the last day."[23]

Secondly, Casey mentions an apparent reality that not everyone was sympathetic to the teaching of Jesus. Moreover, the opponents of the early Christian movement did not believe that Jesus had risen from the dead. The critical point conjoined the empty tomb and the angel's message declaring, "He has risen; he is not here" (Mark 16.6, ESV). It reassures believers that Jesus had risen from the dead.[24]

---

[22] Casey, *Jesus of Nazareth*, 470, 473.
[23] Casey, *Jesus of Nazareth*, 477.
[24] Casey, *Jesus of Nazareth*, 476.

The silence of the women in Mark proves that the story of the empty tomb is an invention.

Michael Goulder speculated that the empty tomb was a necessary creation of Mark. His rationale is to provide a framework for a physical, bodily resurrection. Goulder inquires what motive underlies Mark's creation of the Empty Tomb story. Its composition was about seventy, or forty years after the crucifixion of Jesus. Paul, the earliest writer, never mentions an empty tomb. However, in 1 Corinthians 15:4, he mentions the record of a tradition, "He was buried." Goulder posits, "Mark may have felt that that was suggestive."[25] He accepts that tradition was in existence that Joseph of Arimathea had buried Jesus, "and that Mary Magdalene and other women had meant to anoint the body, but had not been able to."[26] Goulder advocates that Mark's story supplies "the exact need of a Pauline church which believed in a physical resurrection."[27]

Mark narrates that the women came with their spices and were met by an angel. He says, "You seek Jesus of Nazareth, the crucified one; he is risen, he is not here—behold the place where they laid him" (Mark 16:6). Goulder summarizes, "So Mark has solved the problem of how to make clear in narrative (and so, memorable) form the error of the spiritual resurrection theory: the women saw the place where he had been laid, now without the body— so he had been raised physically."[28]

Goulder proceeded to prove that the empty tomb was the creation of the Markan community:

> The view of the Empty Tomb story as the creation of the Markan church is not just the speculation of a sceptic; there is a contradiction built into the story which gives it away. Mark says the angel told the women to give the message to Peter and the others to go to Galilee, where they would see Jesus; so the congregation is led to think that all is smooth— the disciples got the message, they suppose, and went to Galilee, where the resurrection appearances took place. But now Mark thinks of a difficulty. What are people going to say who hear this story for the first time in 70— especially Jewish-Christians holding the opposition view in 1 Corinthians 15:12, who will be deeply skeptical of physical resurrection stories? Will not they say, "I've been a

---

[25] Goulder, "The Baseless Fabric of a Vision," 57.
[26] Goulder, "The Baseless Fabric of a Vision," 57.
[27] Goulder, "The Baseless Fabric of a Vision," 57.
[28] Goulder, "The Baseless Fabric of a Vision," 57; cf. "Jesus' Resurrection and Christian Origins," 192; cf. "Did Jesus of Nazareth Rise from the Dead?," 64–65.

Christian for forty years, and it is the first time I have heard such a tale? Why have I never heard this before? It is a pack of lies.' So Mark thinks of an answer to this problem. He ends the tale, 'And [the women] went out and fled from the tomb, for trembling and astonishment seized them; and they said nothing to anyone, for they were afraid' (16:8). You know what women are like, brethren: they were seized with panic and hysteria, and kept the whole thing quiet. That is why people have not heard all this before.[29]

Did Jesus' disciples lose track of where they had buried him?

A. J. M. Wedderburn suggests a lost body and that the inability to find the body led to the empty tomb tradition in the Gospels and the account of the manner of Jesus' burial.[30] Wedderburn concludes that the fruitless search for the body of Jesus led to a belief that he rose from the dead.[31] He is unconvinced that the disciples would have known where to look for the body of Jesus. In contradiction to Craig, there exist practical reasons to reject the belief that there lived a Joseph of Arimathea who buried Jesus in his tomb.

No Reason to Invent Joseph's Name

The construction of Joseph of Arimathea's name was from the biblical account of Joseph, son of Jacob.

If the author of Mark invented the character of Joseph, there had to be a reason that he selected that name. Christian commentators have addressed this dilemma. I. H. Marshall, a Christian apologist, discusses the possibility that the name "is intended to be based on the type of Joseph who was responsible for the burial of Jacob (Gen. 50:1–14)."[32] Goulder also believed that a Joseph is in the book of Genesis: "But besides the three witnesses (Deut. 19.15), someone must have buried Jesus in a cave: Gen 50 again supplies his name as Joseph."[33]

---

[29] Goulder, "The Baseless Fabric of a Vision," 57–58. Goulder goes on to remark, "Mark's Gospel finished at 16:8, and the women's silence was a scandal. Both Matthew (28:8) and Luke (24:9) have the women go forthwith to tell the disciples; and an early 'editor' added a spurious ending to Mark (16:9–20) to cover the difficulty" (58n28).
[30] Wedderburn, *Beyond Resurrection*, 62–63.
[31] Wedderburn, *Beyond Resurrection*, 62–63.
[32] Marshall, "The Resurrection of Jesus in Luke," 76.
[33] Goulder, "The Empty Tomb," 212.

Writing along similar lines, Ingo Broer offers that the remembering of Joseph's name was because "The Patriarch Joseph was extremely interested in burials (Gen. 50:14), and indeed Joseph's own burial was a known item on the agenda at the First Redemption, viz. from Egypt, the Exodus (Gen 50:25–26; Exod 13:19; Josh 24:32; Sir 49:15; Heb 11:22; Acts 7:15–16)."[34]

Maybe Joseph of Arimathea was a historical individual, but he had nothing to do with Jesus' burial.

Theissen and Merz discuss the possibility that a Joseph of Arimathea existed, yet he had nothing to do with the entombment. Matthew, instead, incorporated his name because Jesus' burial tomb belonged to Joseph. They elaborate on this explanation that those who dispute the tradition of the empty tomb, as a rule, also tend to put in question the burial by Joseph of Arimathea. Theissen and Merz point out that a rival burial tradition to the Gospels is in Acts 13:29. That crucial verse reads, "And when they had carried out all that was written of him, they took him down from the tree and laid him in a tomb" (ESV). Therefore, "the people in Jerusalem" (in the plural) took Jesus down from the cross and buried him. In John 19:31, it was "the Jews" who asked Pilate to take those who had been crucified down from the cross in good time because of the Sabbath that was dawning. "Since it was the day of Preparation, and so that the bodies would not remain on the cross on the Sabbath (for that Sabbath was a high day), the Jews asked Pilate that their legs might be broken and that they might be taken away" (ESV).

Theissen and Merz acknowledge that "Possibly Jesus was buried anonymously along with the two criminals who were crucified with him."[35] Therefore, no one knew his actual grave. This presumption explains why the burial story would have come into being. They elaborate, "Because the first Christians *could not bear the thought that Jesus had not had an honorable burial.* Here they could have associated this burial with an unused tomb of a Joseph of Arimathea which was *in the neighborhood of the place of execution.*" (Italics for emphasis) [36]

However, at least one problem exists with Theissen and Merz's suggestion. It presupposes that Mark wanted to portray Jesus' burial as honorable. In contrast, Byron McCane pointed out in his article, "'Where No One Had Yet Been Laid': The Shame of Jesus' Burial" in

---

[34] Broer, *Die Urgemeinde Und Das Grab Jesu.*
[35] Theissen and Merz, *The Historical Jesus,* 501.
[36] Theissen and Merz, *The Historical Jesus,* 501.

Authenticating the Activities of Jesus, 1998, all four Gospels portray Jesus' burial as a *dishonorable* one, with no family members and no mourners present.[37]

Lastly, there exists yet another possible explanation for this speculated person. Joseph could have been a historical person whose name was utilized without anyone's consent since he was already dead. (Personal communication with Gerald Sigal.)

Perhaps the name of Joseph of Arimathea was modeled on Joseph, the husband of Mary (Jesus' Mother).

I. H. Marshall presents an alternative hypothesis by choosing Joseph's name. He suggests Joseph maybe because the "husband of Mary, who figures at the beginning of the Gospel, thus achieving some correspondence between beginning and end."[38] Modifying Marshall's supposition, Richard Spencer, in a debate with David Margolis, proposes: "This character is probably named Joseph to match the name of Jesus' father, thus demonstrating the failure of Jesus' family."[39]

The name Joseph was an invention for reasons we are no longer aware of.

Maurice Casey, writing in *Jesus of Nazareth*, presented a critique of noteworthy Christian defenses of the literal historicity of stories found in the Christian Scriptures. Although he did not directly address William Lane Craig or the resurrection accounts, his comment bears consideration. Adopting Casey's words to a different context, Craig's argument is "Nothing more than an illustration of the conservative assumption that if we do not know why a particular Gospel character is named, the story must be literally true."[40]

Joseph was a common Jewish name.

The selection of the name Joseph by the author of Mark was perhaps for a simpler reason. It was a common Jewish name during the first century. Tal Ilan's *Lexicon of Jewish Names in Late Antiquity: Part 1: Palestine 330 BCE–200 CE* (2002) found that Joseph/Joses was the second most

---

[37] McCane, "Where No One had Yet Been Laid," 448.
[38] Marshall, "The Resurrection of Jesus in Luke," 76.
[39] Margolis, "The Resurrection of Jesus Christ."
[40] Casey, *Jesus of Nazareth*, 485.

common male name.[41] Hence, despite Craig's proclamations, there are plausible explanations for why the author, Mark, invented Joseph's name.

Arimathea was a Real Place

Arimathea has still not been identified.

Numerous writers acknowledge the fact that the location of Arimathea is unknown. In addition, it is noteworthy that Ramathaim is but one of three historical locations suggested for the town. In contrast, archaeologists know the location of other biblical cities like Bethlehem, Nazareth, Jerusalem, Capernaum, and Damascus. This absence of proof lends credence to detractors who believe that Arimathea is a literary invention.

The name of Arimathea may have been based on the site of Moses' death and burial.

The location and name of Arimathea have been subject to intense debate, discussion, and speculation. An implied argument raised by Craig relates to the name of the city Arimathea where Joseph is assumed to have resided. Craig believes it is unlikely that early believers would give him a city of origin. In support of the position that Joseph originated from Arimathea, he cites Raymond Brown. Brown accepts that Joseph of Arimathea did the burial is very probable. Brown adds, "While high probability is not certitude, there is nothing in the basic pre-Gospel account of Jesus's burial by Joseph that could not plausibly be deemed historical."[42] He argues that since a Christian fictional creation from a member of the Sanhedrin who does what is right is almost inexplicable, granted the hostility in early Christian writings toward the Jewish authorities responsible for the death of Jesus.[43]

One interesting speculation is by Roger David Aus, an ordained pastor (now retired) of the Evangelical Lutheran Church of America. He studied theology at Harvard Divinity School and Luther Seminary in St. Paul, Minnesota. He is a member of the Society of Biblical Literature, the Society of New Testament Studies, and the Gesellschaft für Wissenschaftliche Theologie. Aus speculates that the name Arimathea comes from the site of Moses's death and burial. Deuteronomy 34:5–6 states that Moses died in the land of Moab, opposite Beth-peor. According

---

[41] Ilan, *Lexicon of Jewish Names*.
[42] Brown, *The Death of the Messiah*, 2:1240–41.
[43] Brown, *The Death of the Messiah*, 2:1240.

to tradition, that locale is the same site as Mount Nebo, "the top of Pisgah." The Hebrew word "Pisgah," which may mean the "cleft" in a mountain, occurs eight times in the Hebrew Bible. Four times it refers to the slopes of Pisgah: Deuteronomy 3:17; 4:49; and Joshua 3:23; 13:20. "The top of Pisgah" also occurs four times, Numbers 21:20; 23:14; and Deuteronomy 3:27; 34:1.

> Targums *Onqelos*, *Pseudo-Jonathan*, and the *Fragment Targum* where available always have רמתא [[Ramatha]] for פסגה [[Pisgah]] in the above passages. *Targum Neofiti 1* has the variant רמתה [[Ramatha]], with an *he* [[ה]] instead of an *aleph* [[א]] as the final letter....
>
> The Aramaic noun רמא [[Rama]] in the singular means "height"....
>
> In light of the above evidence I suggest that the early, Aramaic-speaking, Palestinian Jewish Christian who first formulated the narrative of Jesus' burial borrowed the term (Joseph of) "Arimathea" from Judaic tradition available to him on the site of the death and burial of Israel's first redeemer, Moses. It was the top of "Pisgah," in Aramaic the plural רמתא , "Ramatha," "the heights." It was also the same form employed for the top of "Pisgah" at the end of the Song of the Well in Num 21:20. As noted above, early Judaic tradition maintained that the well followed the Israelites to the site of Moses' death and burial, that is, the Pisgah of Deut 34:1 (with v 6). The author of Jesus' burial probably himself added an initial aleph, often done to place names, as shown in section A. above, n. 2. The Aramaic ארמתא was then basically correctly translated into the Greek as Αριμαθαια.[44]

In Aramaic, the word's added letter *aleph* at the end was the definite article "the."[45]

---

[44] Aus, *The Death, Burial, and Resurrection of Jesus*, 162–65.
[45] Personal communication with Gerald Sigal.

The Lack of Arimathea's Historical or Theological Significance Lends Credibility to the Story

Maybe Arimathea was remembered because it was related to Ramathaim.

Craig asserts that Joseph's association and presumed origin from an obscure town with *no* theological or historical significance further lend historical credibility to his existence. On the contrary, the city attached to Joseph's name makes perfect sense if it is understood to serve as a historical metaphor or reminder. Craig and Karel Hanhart point out that "The epithet 'of Arimathea' is a place name referring to Ramathaim (LXX, *Harmathaim*), a town just north of Jerusalem, famous in Hebrew lore as the birthplace of Samuel, who anointed King David (1 Sam. 1:1; 16:1)."[46]

There are various propositions, but Ramathaim is one of three historical locations suggested for the town, and it still needs to be determined. Ingo Broer similarly offers the memory of Joseph's name because it was related to Ramathaim. "Arimathæa is otherwise called Armatha, Ramatha. '*arimā*, '*arîm*, and '*ārûm* mean 'prudent'; '*armûta* means 'premeditation' and 'subtlety'; and the Aramaic '*arimutā* means wisdom. Joseph certainly showed himself shrewd on this occasion."[47]

Citing Eusebius, he points out that the burial place, spelled Armathaim in the LXX (1 Sam 1:1), was the home of Elkanah ('God has possessed'), father of the divinely-promised prophet of the Kingdom, Samuel. In addition, this was Samuel's birthplace, residence, and burial place, therefore, the place of pilgrimage to Samuel's tomb. Eusebius said (*Onom.* 225, 11 ff), regarding this locale, "It was highly proper that a man from thence should play kinsman to the prophet of the New Testament, the New Covenant, who was also born, as Luke made clear, by the promise of God (*the Magnificat*, Luke 1:46ff., should be compared with 1 Sam, 1–2)." Contrary to Craig's opinion, the selection of Arimathea serves a theological agenda. Furthermore, this presumed "obscure town" possessed historical significance.

---

[46] Craig, *Assessing the New Testament Evidence*, 173; cf. Hanhart, *The Open Tomb*, 420.

[47] Broer, *Die Urgemeinde Und Das Grab Jesu*.

Early Christians Would Not Invent a Fictional Sanhedrin Member

There are two points that convinced John Dominic Crossan that Joseph of Arimathea was a character invented by Mark.

Christian apologists propose that during the composition of the Gospels of Mark and Matthew, likely, Joseph and many members of the Sanhedrin were still alive. These apologists assert that many people who knew these facts could verify the historicity of Joseph. Craig also proposes that it would be unlikely that the early believers would place this fictional character on the historical council of the Sanhedrin. As a member of this high council, which as a whole condemned Jesus (Mark 14:55, 64; 15:1), Joseph would unlikely be a Christian invention: "The sermons in Acts, for example, go so far as to say that the Jewish leaders crucified Jesus (Acts 2:23, 36, 4:10)! Given his status as a Sanhedrist—all of whom, Mark reported, voted to condemn Jesus— Joseph is the last person one would expect to care properly for Jesus."[48] Matt Lefebvre also writes: "From a Christian point of view, this man was a member of the Council that condemned Jesus to death. Why have him take care of Jesus' body, while having Jesus' disciples cower in fear behind locked doors? This would be both an embarrassment and an insult at the same time."[49]

The late John Dominic Crossan, a former Catholic priest, biblical scholar, and member of the Jesus Seminar, is uncompromising. He considers "Joseph of Arimathea to be a total Markan creation in name, in place, and function."[50] He argues that Mark had a problem: those with power were against Jesus, and those for him had no power. The latter had no power to request, beg, or even bribe. Crossan concludes, "What is needed is an in-between character, one somehow on the side of power and somehow on the side of Jesus. What is needed, in fact, is a never-never person. So in 15:43, Joseph is both."[51]

Crossan contends that two points convinced him that Joseph was an invention of Mark (Mark 15:42–47): (1) who Joseph was and (2) what Joseph did. First, Mark's Joseph is deliberately ambiguous. He was among those who judged Jesus (what council he belonged to) and those who

---

[48] Craig, *Reasonable Faith*, 364.
[49] Lefebvre, "Arguments for God's Existence."
[50] Crossan, *Who Killed Jesus?*, 172–73; *Revolutionary Biography*, 154.
[51] Crossan, *Who Killed Jesus?*, 172.

followed Jesus. Second, what did Joseph do with Jesus' body and the bodies of those crucified with him?[52]

Crossan suggests that Mark's story presents the tradition with double dilemmas.

1. If Joseph was in the council, he was against Jesus. If he was for Jesus, he was not in the council.
2. If Joseph buried Jesus from piety or duty, he would have done the same for the two other crucified criminals.[53]

If he buried the two other criminals in his tomb, there could be no empty tomb sequence. Crossan writes collectively, "They persuade me that Mark created that burial by Joseph of Arimathea in 15:42–47. It contains no data from pre-Markan tradition but several problems for post-Markan tradition."[54]

Matthew and Luke were stuck with Mark's account: All they could do was build on it.

Matti Myllykoski challenges the belief that Joseph was a member of the Sanhedrin. His argument centers on the Gospel of Mark. Mark's narrative implies that Joseph or his trusted men followed the final demise of Jesus in order to take care of the burial immediately after his death. If correct, this action makes Joseph look like a particular sympathizer of the cause of Jesus. However, the story itself is very reticent in this respect. Myllykoski asks, "if he [Joseph] was commonly known as such a notably exceptional member of the Sanhedrin—to say the least—why is his sympathy expressed only in a very general and obscure way, i.e., by mentioning that he was looking for the kingdom of God?"[55] Myllykoski does not think "that Joseph originally was known as a member of the council who took pains to bury only and exclusively the body of Jesus. As the tradition was passed on, this well-respected outsider became in the imagination of the early Christians first someone who was looking for the kingdom of God—whatever that meant—and finally a disciple." With time, the tradition grew."[56]

---

[52] Crossan, "Historical Jesus as Risen Lord," 21–22.
[53] Crossan, "Historical Jesus as Risen Lord," 22.
[54] Crossan, "Historical Jesus as Risen Lord," 22.
[55] Myllykoski, "What Happened to the Body of Jesus," 73.
[56] Myllykoski, "What Happened to the Body of Jesus," 73.

About a decade later, the author of Matthew was stuck with Mark's account of Joseph, which he could not delete. He could, however, embellish Mark's narrative. So, Luke was "trapped" by the two prior Gospels, as was John constricted by the three earlier Gospels and the known oral traditions. Consequently, they could not delete the remembered traditions, but they could enhance the earlier Gospels.

By the time of Mark's Gospel, people would have mostly forgotten who was on the Sanhedrin at the time of Jesus' death.

Peter Kirby proposes a rationale as to why the historicity of Josephus is dubious. First, consider there were a number of Palestinian Jews with strong traditional ties. It requires asking, does it seem probable that their memory would be so strong that they would be able to remember the names of those on the Sanhedrin? Moreover, does it seem plausible that they would be able to argue for the exclusion of any fictional name? There were about seventy people who served on the Sanhedrin. Forty years later most of them would have died and been replaced at one point or another. Compounding matters, most people at the time that Jesus died would have also died. "This reality makes it nearly inconceivable that the average Jew knew all the names of the Sanhedrin c. 30 well enough to spot a name that doesn't belong. At the very least, the assumption cannot be granted that there were a considerable number of such sagacious people that would pose a threat to gospel writers."[57]

Kirby presents an analogy, although not perfect. He offers the comparison of expecting the average American to be able to recall the names of the senators in 1960. He says, "Perhaps a few of the most memorable ones stuck in the general consciousness."[58] This scenario raises two questions:

1. Did the author of Mark fear that someone would have been able to produce a list of all the Sanhedrin members c. 30?
2. Did the author of Mark fear that someone would have been able to argue that there never was a Joseph of Arimathea on the Sanhedrin?[59]

Kirby offers a challenge related to Joseph. He argues that describing Joseph as "distinguished: or "prominent" is inadequate, for who is to say

---

[57] Kirby, "Peter Kirby Tomb Rebuttal1."
[58] Kirby, "Peter Kirby Tomb Rebuttal1."
[59] Kirby, "Peter Kirby Tomb Rebuttal1."

that any person on the Sanhedrin is not distinguished or influential? "If it can be argued that people may not have remembered the names of all the members, how much more so may people not have remembered the entire life and times of each member!"[60] Kirby follows up with a supposition, "It cannot be simply supposed that the actual activities of a certain Sanhedrin member on a certain day would be common knowledge." Basing himself on the cumulative analysis, he writes, "Thus, this is not good evidence that Joseph of Arimathea laid Jesus in a tomb."[61]

By 70 CE, most of Jesus' contemporaries were dead.

By the year 70, most of the people who were alive at Jesus' death would have died naturally.[62] Others would have perished during the war or were sold into slavery following the temple's destruction. Few would have survived and remembered who was on the Sanhedrin.

However, estimations by Paul Rhodes Eddy dispute this thinking. He writes, *"Conservative estimates reveal that of the approximately 60,000 eyewitnesses of Jesus's ministry, death, or resurrection who were aged 15 years or older, at least 20,000 would likely have been alive 30 years later, and over 1,000 up to 60 years later."* (Italics added).[63] The speculated data spans the length of Jesus' ministry. According to John, that is about three years. The question is, how many of those potential witnesses residing in Jerusalem would know *and* remember the seventy members of the council of the Sanhedrin? For a comparison, how many people in the United States would remember who served on their District Court or Supreme Court thirty years later?

The readers must judge whether it was probable that neither Joseph nor other members of the Sanhedrin were alive. Contrary to the thinking of Christian apologists, it is probable that neither Joseph nor other members of the Sanhedrin were alive. Neither was it credible that many witnesses knew these facts and were still living and capable of verifying Joseph's historicity.

---

[60] Kirby, "Peter Kirby Tomb Rebuttal1."
[61] Kirby, "Peter Kirby Tomb Rebuttal1."
[62] Blenkinsopp, "Life Expectancy in Ancient Palestine," 52–53; Coale and Demeny, *Regional Model Life Tables*; Frier, "Roman Life Expectancy: The Pannonian Evidence," 328–44; "Roman Life Expectancy: Ulpian's Evidence," 213–51.
[63] Eddy, "The Historicity of the Early Oral Jesus Tradition," 138.

The Embarrassing Nature of the Story Demonstrates Its Authenticity

Contrary to what Christian apologists state, having a member of the Sanhedrin bury Jesus would not have been an embarrassment.

Craig argues that it would be counter-productive for Christians to have a member of the Sanhedrin bury Jesus. Contrary to Craig, reasons exist as to why a believer would need to place this fictional character on the historical council of the Sanhedrin. Joseph's status as a Sanhedrist [member of the Sanhedrin] would undoubtedly have helped him to obtain Jesus' body from the Roman authorities. Perhaps, the early Christian writers reasoned that only a member of the Sanhedrin would have the authority to secure an honorable burial.[64] Keith Parsons elaborates, "The early Christians' embarrassment at the failure of the disciples to care for Jesus' body could easily have led to the invention of a secret friend on the Sanhedrin who would do the proper honours."[65] Finally, Mark's rationale was that a burial by a member of the Sanhedrin would ensure that no hoax was perpetrated by the disciples to produce the discovery of an empty tomb, as alleged in Matthew's early Jewish polemic (Matt. 28:13). Consequently, contrary to Craig, having a member of the Sanhedrin bury Jesus would not be an embarrassment.

Was "Member of the Sanhedrin" a literary device?

A literary device is a tool writers use to hint at more significant themes, ideas, and meaning in a story or writing. An alternate explanation for Mark employing the title "member of the council (Sanhedrin)" was to serve as a literary device. If Joseph's status were as a member of the Sanhedrin, all of whom voted to condemn Jesus, according to Mark, *no* member of the Sanhedrin would be willing to bury Jesus.

Conclusion

Contrary to Craig and others, Mark could have invented Joseph of Arimathea, given him a name, created a place of origin, suggested that he was on the Sanhedrin without being an embarrassment, and said that he was responsible for Jesus' burial. Scripture further refutes the assertion

---

[64] Craig, *Assessing New Testament Evidence*, 173n19.
[65] Parsons, "The Universe is Improbable,"121; cf. Lüdemann, *What Really Happened to Jesus*, 21.

that Arimathea was a town without theological or historical significance. Lastly, it is false to claim that during the composition of the Gospels of Mark and Matthew, it was likely that Joseph or members of the Sanhedrin were still alive to corroborate his existence if it existed.

Proponents of a historical Joseph of Arimathea put forth in their apologetic that Joseph is not the kind of person the Gospel writers would have invented: (1) Every one of the Gospels is hostile toward the Sanhedrin, blaming them at least in part for Jesus' death (Mark 15:1; Matt. 26:59; Luke 23:51; John 11:47–50). (2) If the Gospel writers wanted to invent an honorable disciple of Jesus, they would have never made him a member of the council they hated. (3) Listing the man's name, his hometown (a small town), and his membership on the ruling council of Jews would have made Joseph's identity easily identifiable and falsifiable. Therefore, it is pretty farfetched to believe that the Gospel writers would have fabricated a prominent figure whom anyone could check out for themselves. In a debate, Richard Spencer provides a concise refutation: "Joseph is exactly the type of person Mark could have invented for all the reasons David [his debate opponent] says he wouldn't: it was an intentional irony!"[66]

---

[66] Spencer, "Rebuttal to David Margolis's Reframing Resurrection."

Was the Tomb Really Accessible?

Jesus was publicly executed in Jerusalem. His post-mortem appearances and empty tomb were first publicly proclaimed there. It would have been impossible for Christianity to get off the ground in Jerusalem if the body had still been in the tomb. His enemies in the Jewish leadership and Roman government would only have had to exhume the corpse and publicly display it for the hoax to be shattered. Not only are Jewish, Roman, and all other writings absent of such an account, but there is total silence from Christianity's critics who would have jumped at evidence of this sort. As we will see momentarily, this is not an argument from silence.[1]

Christian apologists argue that no one could deny or refute the claim that the tomb was empty because its location was well-known. Anyone in first-century Palestine (post-crucifixion) could examine it for themselves.[2] The pertinent question is: What does the evidence reveal?

Rebuttal 1:
Arguments Against the Hypothesis that the Tomb was an Undeniable Fact

There are numerous rebuttals to the hypothesis that in first-century Palestine, a tomb or empty tomb was an undeniable fact since the location was publicly known and accessible to everyone. This apologetic presumes the existence of a tomb. Without a tomb, there could not be an "empty tomb." Among these rebuttals are the following:

---

[1] Habermas and Licona, *Case for the Resurrection of Jesus*, 70.
[2] Bock and Wallace. *Dethroning Jesus*, 201; Craig, *Reasonable Faith*, 361; *Apologetics: An Introduction*, 177; Fernandes, *The Atheist Delusion*, 149; Pannenberg, *Jesus, God and Man*, 100; "Did Jesus Really Rise from the Dead?," 134; Perry, *The Easter Enigma*, 96–97; Ramm, *Protestant Christian Evidences*, 193; Stein, *Jesus the Messiah*, 265; Zukeran, "The Resurrection: Fact or Fiction?," 176.

1. This Christian apologetic is an argument based on an assumption, not a fact; the Gospels are *not* historically accurate in *everything* they say. Thorwald Lorenzen, for example, states, "Contemporary New Testament scholars can argue "that Mk [Mark] created the tradition of the empty tomb, or that the church before Mark created the empty tomb narrative in order to explicate and/or define their faith in Jesus Christ."[3]
2. There is no mention in the Christian Scriptures that Paul visited the tomb of Jesus, nor is there even an explicit statement in Paul's letters. These omissions *could* imply that Paul did not know the whereabouts of Jesus' tomb because (1) Jesus was *not* buried but left on the cross to rot; (2) his body was buried in a ditch, common grave, or an unmarked grave with other criminals; or (3) he was reburied later, elsewhere. Resurrection apologists respond that an absence of written records did *not* necessarily mean that Paul did not visit the tomb. They also can counter that this information was just *not* recorded. These two replies are arguments from silence.
3. If there was a reburial of Jesus in a mass grave or some other unmarked site, or possibly stolen by another third party or misplaced in some other way, there is no reason why the Jewish authorities would have known its location.[4]
4. Paul wrote thirteen epistles (six are disputed by New Testament scholars[5]). Not once did he provide an unambiguous and unequivocal statement about Jesus' burial in a tomb.
5. The Christian apologetic that Paul did not have to mention Jesus' empty tomb is an argument based on silence. Komarnitsky counters with the following rationale: if the tomb burial were actual, there would be no reason for Paul to mention any of the basic creed (1 Cor. 15:3–4). Additionally, there would be no reason for the list of appearances (1 Cor. 15:5–7), nor an appearance to Paul (1 Cor 15:8), nor the consequences if Jesus did not resurrect (1 Cor. 15:14–19). His rationale is that "all of these too must have been well known to the Corinthians."[6]

---

[3] Lorenzen, *Resurrection and Discipleship*, 167–68.

[4] Ydit, writing in *Encyclopedia Judaica* states, "Where a grave is in danger of water seepage or if it is not safe against robbers, etc., transfer is permitted."

[5] Carson and Moo, *Introduction to the New Testament*, 48; DeSilva, *Introduction to the New Testament*, 475n1, 734; Porter, "Pauline Authorship and the Pastoral Epistles,"105–23.

[6] Komarnitsky, *Doubting Jesus' Resurrection*, 13.

6. G. W. H. Lampe, an Ely Professor of Divinity at Cambridge University and Canon of Ely Cathedral, also rejects the argument of silence. He writes that "The reference in the ancient tradition to the fact that Jesus had been buried (1 Cor 15.4) does not necessarily imply a belief in a bodily resurrection." Lampe argues, "Since there is no mention here of the empty tomb, it probably does not."[7] He offers two opinions:
   a. It indicates the reality and finality of Jesus' death (he had actually been dead and buried).
   b. It possibly hints that the prophecy of Isaiah 53:9 had been fulfilled in his burial.[8]

However, Lampe continues writing and says:

> But in this case I think that the argument from silence has unusual force. For the situation in which Paul wrote 1 Corinthians 15 was that some of the Corinthians were denying that there is a resurrection of the dead (1 Cor 15.12). In answer to them, Paul marshals every possible argument, and in particular, he adduces the known fact that Jesus was raised from the dead as the foundation for belief in the future resurrection of Christian people. If Jesus' resurrection is denied, he says, the bottom drops out of the Christian gospel. And the evidence that he was raised consists in the appearances to himself and others. Had he known the tomb was found empty it seems inconceivable that he should not have adduced this here as a telling piece of objective evidence.[9]

7. There are no references (inside or outside the Christian Bible) of anyone, except Peter and "the other disciple," visiting the tomb after the women.
8. The identification of the tomb is a contentious issue. Its location by Queen Helena did not occur until 326 CE, almost 300 years after Jesus' death. Kathleen Corley comments, "This strongly suggests that the location of Jesus' tomb was simply unknown."[10]
9. Even if the empty tomb had been examined and verified empty, it would not prove Jesus' resurrection. It would *only* prove that the tomb was empty for reasons unknown.

---

[7] Lampe, "Easter: A Statement," 42.
[8] Lampe, "Easter: A Statement," 42.
[9] Lampe, "Easter: A Statement," 42–43.
[10] Corley, "Women and Crucifixion and Burial of Jesus," 207.

Rebuttal 2:
Independent and Multiple Attestation is a False Argument

Proponents of the empty tomb claim it is independently, multiple attested, and thus reliable. This claim is a false assertion. (1) The allegedly independent, multiple attestations of the empty tomb by the Gospels' authors may be based on Mark, the author of the earliest Gospel. If this is the case, then only one witness existed. (2) Something independently and multiply attested can still be false. (3) The alleged multiple-attested Gospels were written approximately thirty-five to seventy years after the events. (4) Having anonymous writers attesting to each other is irrelevant.

Rebuttal 3:
Criterion of Environmental Contradiction

A modified "Criterion of Environmental Contradiction" lends credence that there was no burial of Jesus in a tomb. It argues, "If a saying or motif in the gospel materials presupposes a situation in the life of Jesus which was impossible, then the saying or motif must be inauthentic."[11] Several motifs are associated with a tomb burial. However, would a tomb burial be probable? Proponents assert that a tomb burial is plausible as well as probable. Craig Evans argues that Roman law permitted the burial of Jesus. In the *Digesta*, compiled by Roman emperor Justinian in the sixth century (530–533 CE) but comprising a great deal of law from the first and second centuries, readers find important and relevant material in chapter 24 of book 48. For example, he says, "Roman law regarding the burial of the executed is far more nuanced —and lenient — than many suppose."[12] In three of the paragraphs that make up chapter 24, the final chapter entitled *De cadaveribus punitorum* ("On the bodies of the punished"), he evaluates "helpful." Paragraphs §1 and §3, both of which directly bear on the question of the burial of the executed, are relevant here:

> §1 Ulpian, *Duties of Proconsul*, book 9: The bodies of those who are condemned to death should not be refused their relatives; and the Divine Augustus, in the Tenth Book of his *Life*, said that this rule had been observed. At present, the bodies of those who have been punished are only buried when this has been requested and permission granted; and sometimes it is not permitted, especially where persons

---

[11] Stein, "The Criteria for Authenticity," 248–49.
[12] Evans, "The Resurrection of Jesus in the Light of Jewish Burial Practices."

have been convicted of high treason. Even the bodies of those who have been sentenced to be burned can be claimed, in order that their bones and ashes, after having been collected, may be buried.

§3 Paulus, *Views*, book 1: The bodies of persons who have been punished should be given to whoever requests them for the purpose of burial.

According to Evans, more than forty percent of Justinian's *Digesta* originates from the writings of the jurist Ulpian (c. 170–223 CE).[13] He reports that one of his frequently cited works is his *officio proconsulis (Duties of Proconsul)*. In the first paragraph of chapter 24, the *Digesta* quotes a noteworthy opinion from the ninth book of *officio proconsulis*: "The bodies of those who are condemned to death should not be refused their relatives." Evans continues, saying Ulpian supports his opinion by appealing to the precedent of the great emperor Augustus who ruled from 31 BCE –14 CE.[14] This opinion finds support in his autobiography, written near the end of his life. Ulpian says, "The bodies of those who have been punished are only buried when this has been requested and permission granted." Evans cites a statement in the *lex Puteolana* (at II.13) that gives the impression that Romans, as did Jews in Israel, had burial pits reserved for criminals and others buried without honor. Evans opines:

1. Presumably, Ulpian's legal opinion and practice were observed during Augustus' rule.
2. Directly relevant to the juridical process concerning Jesus we see in the Gospels. Burial of the bodies of the executed was allowed in the Roman Empire at the approximate time of Jesus.[15]

Evans goes on to say that it was the Augustan administration's practice and the opinion of Ulpian, who lived two centuries later. He further comments that in paragraph §3, it was also the opinion of Paulus, a younger contemporary of Ulpian. Evans concludes, "The Gospel narratives are fully consistent with Roman practice and legal opinion."[16]

Later, Evans discusses and quotes Josephus. Josephus complains about the rebels' crimes during the great Jewish revolt (66–73). He finds

---

[13] Evans, "The Resurrection of Jesus in the Light of Jewish Burial Practices."
[14] Evans, "The Resurrection of Jesus in the Light of Jewish Burial Practices."
[15] Evans, "The Resurrection of Jesus in the Light of Jewish Burial Practices."
[16] Evans, "The Resurrection of Jesus in the Light of Jewish Burial Practices."

their treatment of the ruling priests, whom they murdered particularly heinous. Josephus writes: "They actually went so far in their impiety as to cast out the corpses without burial, though the Jews are so careful about funeral rites that even malefactors who have been sentenced to crucifixion are taken down and buried before sunset."[17] Evans' online article must be examined.

Proponents of a tomb burial also discuss the probability of Roman deference to local Jewish custom and the upcoming Passover festival. Timothy Paul Jones writes, "Other than mass crucifixions during times of war or revolt, it was only when a Roman citizen was executed for high treason that burial was forbidden—a category that the crucifixion of Jesus certainly didn't fit. Jesus of Nazareth was not a Roman citizen."[18] John Granger Cook, writing in *New Testament Studies*, elaborates: "Since Jesus was a *peregrinus* (not a Roman citizen), it is difficult to see that a formal charge like *maiaestas* (or *perduellio* [high treason] would be relevant. I have not found any records of Roman trials in which a *peregrinus* was explicitly accused of *maiestas* by a magistrate."[19]

Cook continues while interacting with Raymond Brown. Afterward, Cook adds, "Probably Pilate classified Jesus' alleged *crimen* (crime) as *seditio* or troublemaking (*se turbulente gessere*), because of the political nature of all (or the majority of?) the crucifixions in first-century Palestine."[20] Cook's conclusion is noteworthy: "But once he identified Jesus as a political criminal guilty of fomenting sedition, it is doubtful that he felt the need to consult juristic texts to justify execution."[21]

Detractors counter that Evans (and others) are disingenuous. The Gospels are abundantly clear about the reason for the execution of Jesus. Jesus was not a criminal, thief, or murderer who committed an act of treason or even an act of high treason. He was an "enemy of the state," committing sedition against the state and threatening insurrection or violent opposition to Roman rule. Pilate ordered the crucifixion on the threat that Jesus was planning to supplant the Roman governorship of Judea to set himself up as king.

> Mark 15:26 And the inscription of the charge against him read, "The King of the Jews."

---

[17] *J.W.* 4.317
[18] Jones, "Apologetics: Is It Possible That Jesus' Body Was Left on the Cross?"
[19] Cook, "Crucifixion and Burial," 199–200.
[20] Cook, "Crucifixion and Burial," 202.
[21] Cook, "Crucifixion and Burial," 202.

Matt. 27:37 And over his head they put the charge against him, which reads, "This is Jesus, the King of the Jews" (ESV).

The *titulus* (placard) on the cross, "King of the Jews," supports this view. The action taken by Jesus was above and beyond "high treason." This reality requires asking a question from silence, does anyone expect an exception for Jesus, even for a potential bribe by Joseph?

Another factor is Pilate. Several pieces of writing provide literary evidence for Pilate. Three secular sources include Tacitus, Josephus, and Philo. The Tacitus reference is one sentence stating that Christus was sentenced to death by the procurator Pilate. Josephus narrates three different events in his life. They reveal various possible characterizations: provocatory, indecisive, stubbornness, and will to give in. In one episode (*Antiquities*, 18.3.2), he uses temple money to fund the building of an aqueduct. When the people demonstrate, he orders soldiers to beat them, which resulted in several deaths. In a third episode, an impostor promised to show the buried sacred treasures of Moses and gathered an armed crowd of Samaritans on Mt. Gerizim. Pilate slaughtered many and captured and executed the leaders. (*Antiquities*, 18.4.1)

In rhetorical language, Philo's Embassy to Gaius (*Legatio ad Caium*, xxxviii, paragraphs 299 to 304) speaks of Pilate in the severest condemnation. Philo calls him a man of most ferocious passions, speaking of his corruption, his insolence, his rapine, his habit of insulting people, his cruelty, his continual murders of people untried and not condemned, and his never-ending and most grievous inhumanity. According to him, Pilate was a man of a very inflexible disposition, very merciless and obstinate. Philo reports an incident when Pilate orders the installation of gold shields in the praetorium.

The earliest literary reference to Pilate can be found in Philo's work *Embassy to Gaius* (*Legatio ad Gaium*) in paragraphs 299 through 303. The part that is of interest follows:

> (**299**) I [*sc*. Agrippa I] can also tell you of something on which he prided himself, although I experienced countless sufferings during his lifetime. But you love and respect the truth. Pilate was an official who had been appointed procurator of Judaea. With the intention of annoying the Jews rather than of honouring Tiberius, he set up gilded shields in Herod's palace in the Holy City. They bore no figure and nothing else that was forbidden, but only the briefest possible inscription, which stated two things—the name of the dedicator and that of the person in whose honour the dedication was made. (**300**) But

when the Jews at large learnt of his action, which was indeed already widely known, they chose as their spokesmen the king's four sons, who enjoyed prestige and rank equal to that of kings, his other descendants, and their own officials, and besought Pilate to undo his innovation in the shape of the shields, and not to violate their native customs, which had hitherto been invariably preserved inviolate by kings and emperors alike. (**301**) When Pilate, who was a man of inflexible, stubborn and cruel disposition, obstinately refused, they shouted, 'Do not cause a revolt! Do not cause a war! Do not break the peace! Disrespect done to our ancient Laws brings no honor to the Emperor. Do not make Tiberius an excuse for insulting our nation. He does not want any of our traditions done away with. If you say that he does, show us some decree or letter or something of the sort, so that we may cease troubling you and appeal to our master by means of an embassy.' (**302**) This last remark exasperated Pilate most of all, for he was afraid that if they really sent an embassy, they would bring accusations against the rest of his administration as well, specifying in detail his venality, his violence, his thefts, his assaults, his abusive behavior, his frequent executions of untried prisoners, and his endless savage ferocity. (**303**) So, as he was a spiteful and angry person, he was in a serious dilemma; for he had neither the courage to remove what he had once set up, nor the desire to do anything which would please his subjects, but at the same time he was well aware of Tiberius' firmness on these matters. When the Jewish officials saw this, and realized that Pilate was regretting what he had done, although he did not wish to show it, they wrote a letter to Tiberius, pleading their case as forcibly as they could.[22]

Does Pilate seem like someone who would grant an honorable burial to someone who insulted him during a trial (Mark 15:5; Matt. 26:14; John 19:11) and commits sedition directly against his rule? Readers will need to be the final arbitrators.

Ehrman refutes any possibility that Jesus would be permitted an honorable burial:

> To sum it up, not only during war but also in times of (relative) peace the Romans publicly humiliated and tortured to death enemies of state precisely in order to keep the peace. Jesus was condemned not for blasphemy, not for cleansing the temple, not for irritating the

---

[22] *Philonis Alexandrini Legatio Ad Gaium*, 128–30.

Sadducees, not for bad-mouthing the Pharisees, not for … well, not for anything but one thing. He was crucified for calling himself the King of the Jews. Only Romans could appoint the King. If Jesus thought he himself was going to be the King, for the Romans this would have been a declaration of war (since he would have to usurp their power and authority to have himself installed as king) (I'm talking about how Romans would have interpreted Jesus' claim to be king, not what he himself may have meant by it). They may have found it astounding, if not pathetic, that this unknown peasant from the rural hinterlands would be imagining that he could overthrow Roman rule in Judea. But Romans didn't much care if someone was a megalomaniac, a feasible charismatic preacher, or a bona-fide soldier in arms. If the person declared "war" on Rome — which a claim to being the King amounted to — the Romans knew how to deal with him. He would be publicly tortured and humiliated, left to rot on a cross so everyone could see what happens to someone who thinks he can cross the power of Rome. There was no mercy and no reprieve. And there was no decent burial, precisely because there was no mercy or reprieve in cases such as this. After the point was made – after time, the elements, and the scavengers had done their work – the body could be dumped into some kind of pit or common grave. But not until the humiliation and the punishment were complete. Yes, it's true that in Jesus' day, the country was not in armed rebellion against Rome. There was a general peace. But this is the very reason *why* there was peace. Would-be offenders – insurrectionists, political enemies, guerilla warriors, rival kings, enemies of the state – were brought face to face with the power of Rome in a very gruesome way, and most people, who for as a rule preferred very much not to be food for the birds and dogs, stayed in line as a result.[23]

Therefore, the likelihood of releasing Jesus' body to a family member or friend seems highly improbable. Proponents will point out the caveat that releasing a body is possible. If the Romans executed Jesus for being a threat to their rule, as the leader, the King of the Jews, charged above his head, why would Pilate turn around and allow his body a dignified burial in a rich man's tomb? Moreover, why would he permit the body to be buried in a known location, which could quickly become a future shrine for Jewish nationalism and independence? Raymond Brown notes, "There was in this period an increasing Jewish veneration of the

---

[23] Ehrman, "Could Jews Bury Crucified Victims?"

tombs of the martyrs and prophets."[24] Peter Kirby inquires, "If Pilate considered the historical Jesus to be an enemy of the state, how much more would Pilate have to fear not only making him a martyr but also establishing a shrine to Jesus right in Jerusalem?"[25] In his opinion, and those of other detractors, "It is in Pilate's best interest to make certain that Jesus would have been buried without honor and in obscurity."[26] The cumulative evidence suggests a tomb burial would be unlikely, although not impossible.

Rebuttal 4:
The Location was Not Well-Known
and Could Not be Examined

The Christian apologetic that it "Was it Impossible to Deny That the Tomb was Empty Since Its Location Was Well-known and Any Person Could Examine It Out for Himself" is based on an assertion. The apologetic contains at least three points of dispute, (1) Jesus had a burial in a tomb, (2) its location was well-known, and (3) any person could examine it. Can this apologetic withstand analysis?

Scholars and theologians are not in agreement. Habermas does not include the empty tomb as a Minimal Fact because about seventy percent of his surveyed research support that it existed. By these words, about twenty-five percent of his data does not accept the empty tomb. Second, many writers suggest that the body was buried in an unmarked and mass grave. Consequently, its location may not have been well-known if that hypothesis is correct. This reality would prevent an examination of the tomb's content. Additionally, if the body of Jesus received a burial in an unmarked grave with other executed criminals, no one could prove that Jesus had not risen from the dead.

Rebuttal 5:
Reburial

Contrary to apologists, Joseph of Arimathea may have decided to rebury Jesus, making an examination impossible. At least seven reasons could explain this reality:

---

[24] Brown, *The Death of the Messiah*, 1280; cf. Craig, *Assessing the New Testament Evidence*, 176.
[25] Kirby, "Case Against the Empty Tomb," 190.
[26] Kirby, "Peter Kirby Tomb Rebuttal1."

1. It is easily possible that he later regretted his involvement with Jesus and wanted to distance himself from such a controversial and radical movement as the early Christians.
2. Perhaps he had a change of heart and lost his faith following Jesus' death.
3. Perhaps the pressure was placed on him by his family, friends, the council, or others, to keep quiet about the whole matter afterward.
4. Perhaps he did speak openly about it, telling people that he had moved the body, but for whatever reason, he was ignored, or his message was not widely heard,
5. Perhaps he died very shortly after the reburial.
6. Perhaps he moved away after the reburial.
7. Perhaps he lost contact with the early Christian movement since he was unknown to the disciples.[27]

Rebuttal 6:
Circular Reasoning

This apologetic fails because the guard episode appears only in Matthew. Proponents argue the empty tomb has enemy attestation as a result of the guards' testimony. However, claiming that the testimony of Roman guards qualifies as enemy attestation is circular in nature because it presupposes the historicity of Matthew's burial tomb details, which is precisely what is being contested in the first place. Further weakening this defense, F. David Farnell quotes William Lane Craig in a 2001 interview with John Ankerberg that most scholars do not accept the guard story: "Well now this is a question that I think is probably best left out of the program, because the vast, vast majority of New Testament scholars would regard Matthew's tomb story, or guard story as 'unhistorical.'"[28]

Conclusion

In conclusion, one can easily deny the assertion of Jesus' burial in a tomb and the claim that if there was a tomb, its location was well-known. However, there is no proof that the burial was well-known to the public. Because his purported burial site was unknown or a late invention, it could *not* be subject to inspection.

---

[27] Fodor, *Unreasonable Faith*, 243–46.
[28] Farnell, "Contemporary 21st Century Evangelical NT Criticism," 2211–222.

Could the Disciples Preach an Empty Tomb in Jerusalem?

Christian apologists believe it would have been impossible to preach that Jesus had been resurrected in Jerusalem if the tomb was not empty.[1] Habermas and Licona refer to this apologetic as the *Jerusalem factor*.[2] Going beyond these assumptions, P.B. Fitzwater, a dated source, inquired: "If the resurrection were not real, why should the apostles have made it the very cornerstone of their preaching?"[3]

This text first counters that first-century Jews may not have regarded an empty tomb as a prerequisite for being raised from the dead. If this was the case, it means that the discovery of Jesus in his tomb would not have destroyed the faith of the early Christians. Next, this issue will argue that the first apostolic preaching of Jesus' resurrection from the dead dates about *seven weeks after* the alleged event. By then, his body may have decayed so severely that it was unrecognizable. (According to Jewish tradition, the *third day* after death was the point beyond which the ravages of decay render the faces of corpses incapable of being legally identified *with certainty* in a court of law.) Parading it around Jerusalem proved nothing if his body was critically decayed and would have had little impact on his disciples' faith. Readers only know what later Christians claimed years later. Finally, there is no record of Jesus' tomb veneration by the early Christians until the fourth century. This reality suggests that even if Jesus had a tomb burial (which some scholars doubt), its location was unknown to the general public. Consequently, it is incorrect to assert that

---

[1] Craig, *Reasonable Faith*, 361; "Did Jesus Rise From the Dead?," 151; "The Historicity of the Empty Tomb of Jesus," 59; *Apologetics: An Introduction*, 190; *The Son Rises*, 82; Flood, *The Resurrection*, 45; Groothuis, *Christian Apologetics*, 544–45; Habermas, *The Resurrection of Jesus*, 34; Habermas and Licona, *Case for the Resurrection of Jesus*, 70–71; Keener, *The Historical Jesus of the Gospels*, 704; Morrow, *Welcome to College*, 139–40; O'Collins, "Resurrection and New Creation," 17; Pannenberg, *Jesus, God and Man*, 106; Stein, *Jesus the Messiah*, 264.

[2] Habermas and Licona, *Case for the Resurrection of Jesus*, 7.

[3] Fitzwater, *Christian Theology*, 160.

preaching the resurrection could not have been possible had the tomb still contained his corpse.

Rebuttal 1:
The Catechism of the Catholic Church

The Catholic Church directly discusses the empty tomb in its *Catechism of the Catholic Church* 2nd edition, 2003. In the relevant portion of section 640, the catechism reads as follows:

> "Why do you seek the living among the dead? He is not here, but has risen." (Lk. 24:5–6) The first element we encounter in the framework of the Easter events is the empty tomb. In itself it is not a direct proof of Resurrection; the absence of Christ's body from the tomb could be explained otherwise (cf. Jn 20:13; Mt 28:11–15). Nonetheless the empty tomb was still an essential sign for all…[4]

Rebuttal 2:
The Message was Conceivable Without an Empty Tomb

Theissen and Merz write that the success of the Easter message in Jerusalem was conceivable *without* an empty tomb because the Resurrection faith is compatible with the knowledge of an unopened tomb. They cite as evidence, Mark 6:14 reports Herod Antipas believed that Jesus was John the Baptist was 'raised from the dead,' although John had been buried by his disciples (6:29). They point out this event was a 'return' to earthly life (not a resurrection to eternal life). Consequently, Theissen and Merz write, "In this case it would have been very natural to ask whether the tomb was empty. We hear no such question."[5] Compounding matters, Mark 12:18 reports that Jesus expressed the belief that the patriarchs of Israel—Abraham, Isaac, and Jacob— are risen and with God.[6] They conclude, "Already in the time of Jesus, however, the tombs of the patriarchs were being venerated without people assuming they were empty (cf. the tomb of Abraham in Herod, which was enclosed within a wall by Herod the Great)."[7]

---

[4] *Catechism of the Catholic Church,* Paragraph 2, #638.
[5] Theissen and Merz, *The Historical Jesus*, 499.
[6] Theissen and Merz, *The Historical Jesus*, 499.
[7] Theissen and Merz, *The Historical Jesus*, 499.

Rebuttal 3:
Burial and Isaiah 53:9

> And they made his grave with the wicked
>   and with a rich man in his death,
> although he had done no violence,
>   and there was no deceit in his mouth (Isa. 53:9, ESV).

Detractors and believers disagree about the meaning of "buried" and "grave." Isaiah 53: 9 states that the servant was buried in a grave. (1) The term grave does not necessitate the burial of a person in a tomb. However, burial in a grave does not exclude a tomb burial. Partially similar to 1 Corinthians 15:3, Paul does not describe a burial of Jesus. He reports that he was buried.

Returning to verse 9, it requires asking what the verse means when it says the servant (1) made his grave with the wicked and (2) with a rich man in his death. Matthew is the exclusive Gospel reporting Joseph of Arimathea with the description of being "rich" and the body of Jesus placed in his tomb. In contrast, Mark and Luke describe Joseph as being a member of the Council (Mark 15:43; Luke 23:50). Proponents ("believers") posit that Matthew deliberately identifies that Joseph was a "rich man." Gerald Sigal presents his analysis.

Matthew has a propensity for adding biblical allusion to his narrative. Therefore, it is not surprising that he alone adds that Joseph was rich and placed Jesus' corpse in his private tomb, thereby supposedly fulfilling: "And his grave was set ... with the rich ..." Furthermore, the character of Josephus of Arimathea was introduced into Matthew's Gospel narrative as a rich man. This description was necessary to fulfill Isaiah 53:9. That verse says that God's servant will be buried "with the rich." This action is one of the numerous examples of Matthew attempting to introduce supposed biblical 'fulfillment of prophecy" into his narrative. The material peculiar to Matthew is a creation of his narrative. "The material peculiar to Matthew is a creation of its author's own imagination."[8] Detractors point out, "It should be emphasized that despite the claim that Jesus was buried in a rich man's tomb he was not buried 'with the rich.'"[9] On the contrary, the Gospels make a point of stating that Jesus alone was buried in the tomb (Luke 23:53; John 19:41). Thus, Sigal concludes, "If Jesus was buried in the new tomb of Joseph, then he was

---

[8] Sigal, *The Jewish Response*, 134.
[9] Sigal, *The Jewish Response*, 134.

buried with neither the wicked nor rich, but alone. Not only was Jesus not buried with the wicked and the rich he was also not the servant."[10]

Another subject is the meaning of the word "rich." Hanhart suggests that the epithet "a rich man" was, in reality, a derogatory sneer based on the LXX Isaiah 22:16.[11] Dated sources suggest the word "rich" could also have properly meant "of good standing."[12]

Several writers offer naturalistic hypotheses for Matthew's inclusion of Joseph's characterization as rich. Daniel Patte, a French-American biblical scholar and Professor Emeritus of Religious Studies, New Testament, and Christianity at Vanderbilt University, writes: "But the mention that he is rich is necessary to explain why he owns a tomb."[13] Benedict Viviano, OP, and a New Testament scholar suggest that "rich" is "to explain the enhanced status of the tomb."[14] John Paul Heil adds: "Nevertheless, Joseph's status as a 'rich' disciple enables him to request and receive the body of Jesus from Pilate (27:58), which neither the other male disciples who have fled (26:56) nor their substitutes, the women who are helplessly passive (27:55–56), are in a position to do."[15] In contrast, Robert Price offered the following hypothesis. First, Joseph is rich and buries Jesus in his private tomb. Second, this background information provides the narrative motivation for tomb robbers. They seek rich funerary tokens they assume have been buried with the deceased. Consequently, the tomb is presumably opulent.[16]

The reader must decide if Joseph's characterization is historical or not. Was it written to fulfill prophecy, explain how, being affluent, Joseph could meet with Pilate, provide credence to an honorable and opulent burial, or provide a rationalization for potential tomb robbers? Of course, additional rationales are possible. Alternatively, it bears repeating that if Jesus experienced a burial in the new tomb of Joseph, then he was buried with *neither* the wicked nor rich, but alone. Then too, several of these rationales could be conjoined.

---

[10] Sigal, *The Jewish Response*, 134–35.
[11] Hanhart, *The Open Tomb*, 182.
[12] Lake, *The Historical Evidence*, 50; Montefiore, *The Synoptic Gospels*, 1:379;
[13] Patte, *The Gospel According to Matthew*, 391.
[14] Viviano, *The Gospel According to Matthew*, 672–73.
[15] Heil, *The Death and Resurrection*, 93.
[16] Price, *The Incredible Shrinking Son*, 327.

Rebuttal 4:
Burial in a Mass Grave

Those who argue that there was no empty tomb often assert that it was a later legend made up by Mark or his sources. Moreover, Jesus might have had a burial instead in a nonidentifiable mass grave for criminals. If this were the case, the early opponents of Christianity would not have had any empty tomb claim to refute. Years later (about 70 CE), by the time of the sacking of Jerusalem, the evidence that would be needed to disprove the claim would have become inaccessible. Jerusalem was destroyed, and its inhabitants were murdered, enslaved, and sent into exile.

Rebuttal 5:
If the Tomb was Not Empty

Maurice Casey challenges the belief that Jesus' resurrection would have been impossible to preach in Jerusalem since the tomb was not empty. He contends that even an identifiable body would not have silenced Jesus' followers. Casey writes that an identifiable body would not have silenced his followers because their faith that Jesus had risen was not dependent on the missing remains of Jesus' body. His argument centers on two excerpts taken from the Hebrew Bible.

How is this view sustainable? He argues that Jesus' followers "would have continued to preach the good news that God had raised Jesus from the dead in accordance with Psalm 16, and he now sits at the right hand of God in accordance with Psalm 110."[17] Therefore, he continues, "that producing Jesus' remains would only impress three groups:

1. Those who did not believe in the resurrection,
2. those who believed God never took anyone to heaven,
3. and those who believed that Jesus was a seditious criminal."[18]

In an online article, "Resurrection redux I," Vincent Torley argued for, and against Jesus' resurrection and an empty tomb.[19] His essay incorporates Maurice Casey's text, *Jesus of Nazareth*. Casey discusses the parable of the rich man and Lazarus, where the rich man is suffering the torments of Hell (Luke 16:19–31). The rich man asks father Abraham if he could at least send Lazarus to warn his five brothers of the suffering

---

[17] Casey, *Jesus of Nazareth*, 497.
[18] Casey, *Jesus of Nazareth*, 497.
[19] Torley, "Resurrection redux I," t.

that awaits them in the place of torment. However, Luke reports that Abraham rebuffs his request: "If they do not hear Moses and the Prophets, neither will they be convinced if someone should rise from the dead" (Luke 16:31, ESV). Torley mentions that Casey's comment is a telling one: "Thus Jesus envisages in story mode a person going to heaven after death without leaving his tomb empty, being sent to five people, and this being described as 'rising from the dead.'"[20]

Second, Torley presents Casey drawing upon the biblical examples of Enoch and Elijah. Both were taken up to Heaven without dying. Therefore, for some Jews living in the first century of the common era, "believing that God had taken someone straight to his throne after their death did not entail that an empty tomb was left behind on earth."[21] Some Jewish rabbis also believed that Moses did not die but went straight up to Heaven and continued to minister there.[22] Finally, he notes that Jesus remarked that when people rise from the dead, they are "like angels in heaven" (Mark 12:25, ESV). For Casey, that suggests that "there is no particular need to imagine that their tombs would be empty."[23]

Interestingly, Casey is prepared to grant that Jesus predicted his resurrection. He conjectures that the original prediction was a saying in which he says that he would rise again after three days. However, Casey observes that the Aramaic word for "rise" in this saying would have been a general term "which could refer to what we might call either resurrection or immortality."[24]

Casey's best illustrations of resurrection without an empty grave were Enoch and Elijah. However, N.T. Wright has pointed out in response that neither of these men died:

The whole point of resurrection, by contrast, is that someone first dies and is then given new life ... The tradition quoted in 1 Cor. 15.4 is precisely about someone who was well and truly dead and who, on the third day, was well and truly alive again. As far as Paul was concerned, this did indeed mean . . . that 'resurrection' had split into two: Jesus first, others later. **Had anyone been able to come back at Paul and say 'but Paul, you know there are three or four people**

---

[20] Casey, *Jesus of Nazareth*, 468–470.
[21] Casey, *Jesus of Nazareth*, 468–470.
[22] See, Siphre on Deuteronomy, Piska 357; Deut. R. XI, 10.
[23] Casey, *Jesus of Nazareth*, 468.
[24] Casey, *Jesus of Nazareth*, 471.

at least who are already resurrected', I do not think he would have written 1 Corinthians 15 in the way he did.[25]

Rebuttal 6:
No Relationship Exists Between
an Empty Tomb and Preaching

When did the disciples start to preach Jesus' resurrection? The first recorded preaching appears in Acts 2:24, on the day of Pentecost: "God raised him up, loosing the pangs of death, because it was not possible for him to be held it" (ESV). Therefore, the apostles did not start preaching Jesus' resurrection until ten days after his supposed ascension that occurred forty days after his resurrection: "He presented himself alive to them after his suffering by many proofs, appearing to them during forty days and speaking about the kingdom of God" (Acts 1:3, ESV).

Therefore, *no* record of the disciples preaching Jesus' resurrection exists until fifty days after Easter Sunday. Why did it take the disciples so long to start preaching Jesus' resurrection if the tomb was supposedly empty since he had made so many appearances? One can only speculate. The message is clear; *no* relationship exists between an empty tomb and the preaching of Jesus' resurrection for the first forty-nine days.

Rebuttal 7:
Decomposition of the Body

If the location of Jesus' body were possible, it would not have been until fifty days after his crucifixion. During that time, it would have decomposed, making its identification impossible. Craig counters that it was, in fact, possible that Jesus' body would still have been identifiable:

1. Jerusalem is approximately 700 meters above sea level and has cool temperatures in April.
2. The body would have had the telltale signs of having been crucified, including holes in his hands, a spear mark in the side, and unbroken legs.[26]

Gerd Lüdemann counters Craig's argument with the following observation: **"At seventy or more degrees, decomposition** will soon

---

[25] Wright, "Resurrecting Old Arguments," 215–16.
[26] Craig, *Assessing the New Testament Evidence,* 204 and a private correspondence between Craig and Lowder, June 27, 2000.

make a face unrecognizable and thwart the surest ways to identify a dead person."[27] During the first century, fingerprints, and dental records, were unavailable. Therefore, Lüdemann writes, "No easy way existed for the Jewish opponents to confront the young Jesus movement with counterevidence. Given the religious enthusiasm of the early community, I doubt whether it would have made any impact on them anyway."[28]

Jeffrey Jay Lowder offers another rebuttal that after seven weeks, "the corpse would not have been easily demonstrated to be the body of Jesus. The time-lag would have made the production of the body a futile exercise, even if its production could have proved anything of significance."[29] In October 1989, Lowder contacted John Nernoff III, a retired pathologist, and asked him about the decomposition of a body at 65 degrees Fahrenheit. According to Nernoff, a face will become nearly unrecognizable after several days at 65 degrees Fahrenheit. However, the temperature inside Jesus' tomb may have been much colder than 65 degrees Fahrenheit. In support of this view, William Lane Craig points out, "Jerusalem, being 700 meters above sea level, can be quite cool in April."[30] Lowder comments, "Given the lack of meteorological records from the time, one can only speculate on what the temperature would have been inside Jesus' tomb. But even if it were cold inside the tomb, Jesus' corpse still would have been unrecognizable after seven weeks of decomposition."[31] Therefore, Lowder again contacted Nernoff, "but this time he asked him to suppose that the average temperature was 45 degrees Fahrenheit." Nernoff stated:

1. Even that temperature could not entirely prevent the decomposition of the body;
2. molds and some bacteria grow at that temperature.
3. furthermore, additional changes in appearance would be caused by desiccation (drying), rigor and its relaxation, and settling of blood in the dependent tissues.[32]

---

[27] Lüdemann, *Fact or Figment*, 153.
[28] Lüdemann, *Fact or Figment*, 153.
[29] Lowder, "Historical Evidence and the Empty Tomb Story," 288–89.
[30] Craig, *Assessing the New Testament Evidence*, 204.
[31] Lowder, "Historical Evidence and the Empty Tomb Story," 289.
[32] Lowder, "Historical Evidence and the Empty Tomb Story," 289.

Lowder concludes, "So even if we assume that Jesus' corpse had been kept cool, seven weeks is still plenty of time for the corpse to become decomposed and disfigured."[33]

Everyday experience demonstrates that people can believe things despite overwhelming evidence to the contrary (e.g., COVID-19 does not kill, COVID-19 vaccination is dangerous, or Trump did not lose the 2020 election). As such, if the followers of Jesus believed that the corpse they saw was that of Jesus, it is not at all implausible that they would have found some way to rationalize this away. Even if someone could find the body, the disciples or other followers could have denied it was Jesus or come up with another means to explain it away (cognitive dissonance). Consequently, the event was not recorded and removed from the Christian narrative.

Furthermore, the temperature in Jerusalem from Friday evening through Easter Sunday is unknown and only subject to speculation.[34] Potentially, in fact of the matter, the weather could have been warm. Under this scenario, the body would rapidly deteriorate.

John 19:34–37 is the only text reporting the spearing of Jesus in the side and his legs not broken. Their historicity is a matter of doubt regarding the telltale signs on Jesus' body. John incorporated these observations for theological reasons: "For these things took place that the Scripture might be fulfilled: "Not one of his bones will be broken." And, again another Scripture says: "They will look on him whom they have pierced" (John 19:36–37, ESV). Another factor to consider is whether or not it was possible to identify the remains that belonged to criminals buried in the graveyard of the condemned. This opinion centers on Dale Allison's *Resurrecting Jesus: The Earliest Christian Tradition and Its Interpreters*, in which he writes the following:

> On the one hand, if Jesus was, as the Gospels have it, buried alone, then all that would have mattered was the place. One could have checked the cave for its one corpse no matter what the condition of that corpse. On the other hand, if Jesus was buried with others, *m. Sanh.* 6:5–6 is evidence that his body would still have been identifiable. The rabbinic text presupposes that, even if a criminal had been buried dishonorably, it was yet possible for relatives to claim the skeleton after some time had passed: "When the flesh had wasted away they gathered together the bones and buried them in their own

---

[33] Lowder, "Historical Evidence and the Empty Tomb Story," 288–89.
[34] Mark 14:54 mentions the guards warmed themselves by a fire after Jesus was arrested.

place." If relatives could collect the bones of an executed criminal after the flesh had fallen off, then those bones were not in a humbled pile of corpses, but must have been deposited in such a way as to allow for later identification . . . Even if it were sometimes otherwise, in the case of Jesus probably "all that would have been necessary would have been for Joseph [of Arimathea] or his assistants to say, 'We put the body there, and a body is still there.'"[35]

However, there are at least two approaches that dispute Allison's argument. Catholic biblical scholar Fr. Raymond Brown (1928–1998) does not think the women were present at Jesus' burial, as he puts it in his magnum opus, *The Death of the Messiah*. He opines, "It is more difficult to argue for an early common tradition involving their presence at the burial."[36]

1. One negative sign is that the women are absent in John.
2. In Mark (the basic Synoptic account), they have no active participation in the burial.

Brown elaborates "that they observe the burial in the tomb so that they can come back to the tomb on Easter and make up for what was lacking in the burial."[37] He says, "The thesis of back-formation, then, is very attractive: namely, that from the role of Mary Magdalene and companions in the empty-tomb tradition and from the early tradition of the presence of three Galilean women at the crucifixion, it was logically assumed that they were at the burial."[38] Why, then, were the women included in Mark's story? Brown concludes by saying, "They were included in the Marcan story of the burial (followed by Matt and Luke) in order to make the burial story more clearly a connective between the crucifixion and the resurrection."[39]

One final rabbinic point about identifying a body (discussed further in Chapter 17) requires consideration:

> Mishnah (*Yevamot* 16:3): They must not give evidence [of identity in respect of a dead man] except on [proof afforded by] the full face with the nose, even though there were also marks on its body or on its clothing. No evidence [of a man's death] must be given before his soul

---

[35] Allison, *Resurrecting Jesus*, 318.
[36] Brown, *The Death of the Messiah*, 2:1276.
[37] Brown, *The Death of the Messiah*, 2:1276.
[38] Brown, *The Death of the Messiah*, 2:1276.
[39] Brown, *The Death of the Messiah*, 2:1276.

has departed, even though they saw him with his arteries cut or crucified or being devoured by a wild beast. They must give evidence [of identification] only during the first three days [after the death. After this period the decay of the corpse makes identification impossible or uncertain.].

Rebuttal 8:
The Condition of the Body is Irrelevant

Habermas and Licona assert that it would have been beneficial for Jesus' enemies to produce an even barely recognizable body because that action "could have dissuaded some believers, possibly weakening and ultimately toppling the entire movement."[40] This apologetic is a rationale based on silence and speculation. It centers on the belief that the events recorded in the Christian Bible are, in fact, historical. Numerous theists and nontheists reject many of those purported events.

Rebuttal 9:
Veneration of the Tomb

Suppose Jesus' "tomb" had existed. In that case, it seems almost certain that there would have been veneration by early Christians (i.e., the actual site of Jesus' miraculous resurrection), and thus its location would have been well known. Jesus alludes to the practice of venerating the tombs of Jewish teachers and prophets. In Matthew 23:29, he says, "Woe to you, scribes and Pharisees, hypocrites! For you build the tombs of the prophets and decorate the monuments of the righteous" (ESV). However, there is no record of such veneration, and it would appear that the actual location was *not* well known. If this is the case, it seems unlikely that Jesus had a burial in a tomb.

    A counterargument focuses on the words of two men, presumably angels. They ask the women at the tomb two important questions in Luke 24:5–7: "Why do you seek the living among the dead? ⁶ He is not here, but has risen. Remember how he told you, while he was still in Galilee, ⁷ that the Son of Man must be delivered into the hands of sinful men and be crucified and on the third day rise" (ESV). Therefore, why should the tomb experience veneration if Jesus was alive? Why venerate a tomb that housed a once-deceased body and was void of bones?

---

[40] Habermas and Licona, *Case for the Resurrection of Jesus*, 70.

James D. G. Dunn, writing in *The Evidence for Jesus: The Impact of Scholarship on our Understanding of How Christianity Began*, states:

> Christians today of course regard the site of Jesus' tomb with similar veneration, and that practice goes back at least to the fourth century. But for the period covered by the New Testament and other earliest Christian writings there is no evidence whatsoever for Christians regarding the place where Jesus had been buried as having any special significance. No practice of tomb veneration, or even of meeting for worship at Jesus' tomb is attested for the first Christians. Had such been the practice of the first Christians, with all the significance which the very practice itself presupposes, it is hard to believe that our records of Jerusalem Christianity and of Christian visits thereto would not have mentioned or alluded to it in some way or at some point.[41]

Jonathan M.S. Pearce concludes that the only real conclusion one can draw is that the early Christians simply did not know the site of the tomb. This reality leaves the reader with the following further conclusions must follow:

1. The later Gospel writers made up such claims, thus the place did not really exist, and the resurrection accounts should be wholly doubted as accurate.
2. Jesus did die but was actually buried in an unknown grave (a shallow grave) as is accustomed for a dishonorable burial.
3. Jesus did not exist. Similar to 1, but that the whole gamut of Gospel claims is false.[42]

Nevertheless, another alternative exists. Jesus received a dishonorable burial. The characterization of an honorable burial includes (1) burial in a family tomb and (2) ritual mourning. The Gospel narratives do not report a burial in his family tomb or ritual mourning. Therefore, he received a dishonorable burial and no tomb veneration.

Presuming this hypothesis is correct, there would not have been any tomb veneration, even with the occupation of a body. Moreover, for some time, it was a place of shame. Afterward, locating the tomb was a viable possibility. The foundation of this hypothesis is that the tomb (rejected by this text) belongs to a wealthy member of the Sanhedrin (Mark 15:43; Matt. 27:57; Luke 23:50–51). Finding the family tomb of a wealthy

---

[41] Dunn, *The Evidence for Jesus*, 67–68.
[42] Pearce, "Why Was Jesus' Tomb Not Venerated?"

member of the Sanhedrin should have been practical, especially if he had a surviving family.

Rebuttal 10:
No Interest in a Tomb

Christian apologists offer no evidence supporting the notion that anyone cared about a tomb, including the followers of Jesus. A possible apologetic is that although the silence of the early Church is considerable, it is ultimately just that, an argument from silence. However, this reality is directly contrary to the Gospels. They

1. Depict massive crowds coming to Jesus and cheering him on as he triumphantly entered Jerusalem riding a donkey,
2. The great wonders witnessed by thousands of people, and
3. Two great earthquakes, an eclipse at midday, and many resurrected saints that nobody else noticed walking into the city and appearing to many people.

Additionally, the apologetic that it would have been impossible to preach in Jerusalem that Jesus had experienced a resurrection if the tomb was not empty presupposes that the opponents of Christianity (e.g., the Jewish and Roman leadership) were interested in deeply investigating its claims.

Rebuttal 11:
No Tomb

Finally, it requires asking, what would be the consequences if no tomb existed? If no tomb or even an identifiable one existed, there would have been no corpse to exhume. In this situation, nobody could falsify the claim that Jesus was dead and buried elsewhere or risen from death by God.

Conclusion

Controversy abounds about the burial or not of Jesus in Joseph's tomb in the Gospels. Several scenarios are possible, although others may exist:

1. Jesus was not buried.
2. The whereabouts of Jesus' body were unknown, and Christians invented a narrative using the Scriptures (Isaiah 53).

3. The body of Jesus was dishonorably buried in a mass grave, and Christians kept the tradition (along with the shame of crucifixion) in accordance with Scriptural motifs.
4. The body of Jesus received a dishonorable burial, and Christians invented an honorable burial to hide the shame of such embarrassment.

To sum up, it would *not* have been impossible to preach in Jerusalem that Jesus had been resurrected from the dead even *if* there was a tomb burial, and it had not been empty.

15

Why a Lack of Controversy Over the Tomb by the Public?

Why did the public lack interest in questioning whether Jesus' tomb was empty? Numerous Christian apologists claim that the lack of controversy over and interest in the tomb substantiates its historicity.[1] This belief focuses on the idea that the silencing of Jesus' disciples would have been forever if the tomb were *not* empty or if the Jewish or Roman leadership could have produced Jesus' body.

Rebuttal 1:
Argument from Silence

Christian apologists claim that the tomb's lack of controversy and interest substantiates its historicity. Since the Roman and Jewish officials did not demand an investigation of the tomb, they reasoned that their inaction demonstrated that it was empty. Apologists use a tactic they criticize skeptics for using: an argument from silence.

Rebuttal 2:
The Onus of Proof Rests on Christian Apologists

The general principle regarding the burden of proof stems from the maxim *onus probandi actori incumbit*, namely, *"he who asserts must prove."* Christian apologists are tasked with proving that Jesus' resurrection was first preached by the disciples in Jerusalem, as claimed in the Christian Scriptures. There are good reasons to suspect that a myth or legend about Jesus' empty tomb developed over time and was later put into a specific time frame by the writers of the Gospels and Acts. Given

---

[1] Barclay, "The Resurrection in Contemporary New Testament Scholarship," 22; Cranfield, "The Resurrection of Jesus Christ," 170; DeLong, *Resurrection: Myth or Fact?*, 19; Fitzwater, *Christian Theology*, 160; Habermas and Licona, *Case for the Resurrection of Jesus*, 70; McDowell, *The Resurrection Factor*, 90; Samples, *Without a Doubt*, 138; Smith, *Therefore Stand*, 375–76.

this speculation to be correct, it is simple to understand why there was a lack of controversy and interest in the empty tomb. Since preaching Jesus' resurrection did *not* occur when apologists allege, there was nothing for anyone to oppose.

Rebuttal 3: Documents Refuting the Empty Tomb Were Lost and Destroyed by the Church or State

"Books could get lost, they could be censored or banned, and they could also be burnt or destroyed."[2] The reality of lost records is in the Hebrew Bible and New Testament. The Hebrew Bible refers to some twenty works that no longer exist. Smith and Bass, staff writers for Apologetics Press, list over twenty works (see Table 15-1).

Table 15-1: Selected Names of "Lost Books"

Lost Books	Biblical References
The Book of the Wars of Yahweh	Numbers 21:14
The Book of Jashar	Joshua 10:12–13; 2 Sam. 1:19–27
The Acts of Solomon	1 Kgs. 11:41
Acts of Gad the Seer	1 Chr. 29:29
Acts of Nathan the Prophet	2 Chr. 9:29
Visions of Iddo the Seer	2 Chr. 9:29
Laments of Josiah	2 Chr. 35:25
Chronicles of King David	1 Chr. 27:24

Source: R&R 23 #12, 2003

Two epistles of Paul are referred to in the New Testament that some consider "lost books": Paul's Letter to the Laodiceans (Col. 4:16) and

---

[2] Rohmann, *Christianity, Book-Burning and Censorship in Late Antiquity*, 1.

Paul's previous Corinthian letter (1 Cor. 5:9). Scholars offer different opinions about these works. The unknown is whether writings refuting the resurrection were lost.

History confirms ordering the destruction of works. The Diocletian Edict (302 CE) ordered leading Manichaeans to be burned alive with their Scriptures. Following the Council of Nicaea (325 CE), the books of Arius and his followers were burned for heresy by Roman emperors. Later, in 364 CE, the Roman Catholic Emperor Jovian ordered the entire Library of Antioch to be burnt. Although unsubstantiated, Elaine Pagels claims that in 367 CE, Athanasius ordered monks in the Coptic Orthodox Church of Alexandria to destroy all "unacceptable writings" in Egypt.

An opposing and less dramatic hypothesis bears consideration as a conjoined factor. Rival texts did not survive because ancient texts needed copyists. If those conflicting points of view could not recruit sufficient support for their ideas, they would not survive. Banned or censored texts, needed a readership willing to purchase the works, and financial supporters to cover the cost of copying disappeared.

The appeal from Rebuttal 2 is an argument from silence. Joseph Butler, an Anglican philosopher and theologian, in *The Analogy of Religion*, writes, "Probable Evidence is essentially distinguished from demonstrative by this, that it admits of Degrees; and of all Variety of them, from the highest moral Certainty, to the very lowest Presumption."[3] Do twenty "lost books" and the history of "bannings" and "burnings" give a high or low degree of certainty that possible writings challenging the empty tomb were lost, partially lost, banned, or destroyed? Readers must be the final arbitrators. Presumably, since there was no preservation of records, there are no means for detractors to refute the claim of Christian apologists. Additionally, apologists know there is no means to prove their claims. Consequently, the Christian apologetic, "The disciples of Jesus would have been silenced forever if the tomb was not empty," is nothing more than a smokescreen that presents an argument from silence.

Rebuttal 4:
The Women Said So, the Public Knew Nothing

Edward Babinski offers an alternative explanation for the lack of controversy over the empty tomb. He put forward the following rationalization. According to most modern biblical scholars, the earliest Gospel that researchers possess is the "Gospel of Mark." The earliest

---

[3] Butler, *The Analogy of Religion*, i.

copies end with the words, "And they went out and fled from the [empty] tomb, for trembling and astonishment had seized them, and they said nothing to anyone, for they were afraid" (16:8, ESV). Therefore, Babinski writes, "So, the very first tale of an 'empty tomb' was combined with these words, 'they said nothing to anyone,' or, in other translations, 'they told no one.'"[4] In plain language, he says, "In other words the 'empty tomb' tale was 'told [to] no one.'"[5] As a result, from early, no one knew about such a tale. Babinski concludes with a critical analysis that bears consideration. "For all anyone knows, an 'empty tomb' story could have arisen up to forty years later, when the first Gospel (Mark) was completed. So what is 'missing' is uncontested evidence that the 'empty tomb' tale was being 'told' early on."[6]

In conjunction with the prior discussion, Edward Lynn Bode, a Catholic priest, raises the possibility that the silence of the women may explain why the legend of the empty tomb was for so long unknown. If the women's visits to the tomb were long unknown, there would have been no reason for the public to raise concerns about the whereabouts of Jesus' body.[7] Bode also points out that others are best known for holding this point of view.[8]

Rebuttal 5:
Paul Didn't Think the Empty Tomb was Very Important

Thorwald Lorenzen, Professor of Systematic Theology and Social Ethics at the International Baptist Theological Seminary in Zurich, Switzerland, explains the lack of controversy about or interest in the empty tomb. The fact that Paul speaks of the "bodily" resurrection of Christ without reference to the empty tomb makes it at least possible that when there was the proclamation of the Easter message in Jerusalem, there may have been no necessity for a reference to the empty tomb. He argues that could also explain why the opponents showed little interest in the empty tomb: "If it was possible to proclaim the Easter message without an explicit reference to the empty tomb (Paul!), then it is equally possible that the opponents did not immediately infer such a connection."[9]

---

[4] Babinski, "What Is 'Missing' From Conservative Christian Apologetics?"
[5] Babinski, "What Is 'Missing' From Conservative Christian Apologetics?"
[6] Babinski, "What Is 'Missing' From Conservative Christian Apologetics?"
[7] Bode, *The First Easter Morning*, 39.
[8] Bousset, *Kyrios Christos*," 65, Creed, "The Conclusion of the Gospel According to St. Mark," 180; Riedl, "Wirklich Der Herr," 99; Wellhausen, *Das Evangelium Marci*, 136.
[9] Lorenzen, *Resurrection and Discipleship*, 172.

Rebuttal 6:
Did the Voices of Objectors Get Drowned Out

Another issue relates to other eyewitnesses' lack of interest in the empty tomb. James Keller offers several rationales for such a lack of controversy or concern. First, it requires asking, what is the relation that some element of tradition has come down to us today with no indication of a challenge in the New Testament community? Keller responds:

1. We can conclude that no eyewitness objected to it effectively being known in the community.
2. His not doing this need not imply that he agreed with the tradition.
3. The tradition may have yet to come to his attention.[10]

Keller elaborates that "this possibility must be kept in mind, given the spread of the New Testament church and difficulties in reproducing and transmitting documents."[11]

However, what happens if the objections do not come to his attention? He replies that "the discrepancies may not have seemed to him to be of sufficient importance to say anything."[12] Furthermore, there is another factor to consider: "Even if he did say something, his criticism may not have been picked up by later writers."[13] Keller concludes, "Unless we have reason to rule out these possibilities in relation to a particular element of tradition, we cannot use the fact that it includes statements which an eyewitness could have refuted as a basis for confidence in the historical reliability of the statements."[14]

Rebuttal 7:
Jewish Authorities Paid No Attention

James Fodor provides a cumulative argument that there is sound reason to doubt officials were interested in an empty tomb or attempting to display a dead body. He argues that Christian apologists present an argument built on highly dubious premises:

---

[10] Keller, "Response to Davis," 113.
[11] Keller, "Response to Davis," 113.
[12] Keller, "Response to Davis," 113.
[13] Keller, "Response to Davis," 113.
[14] Keller, "Response to Davis," 113.

1. The Jewish authorities objected to the early Christians making claims they regarded as blasphemous, stirring up trouble among the people and building up a rival religious power structure.
2. Officials did not attempt to persuade or present counter-evidence to the Christian claims, as they had no interest in engaging in reasoned discourse with the Christian movement.
3. Exhuming Jesus' corpse and displaying it publicly would have required the approval of the Roman authorities.
4. Given the disinterest of the Roman authorities, and their desire to maintain public order and not incite further upheavals, it is unlikely the Roman authorities would have permitted the Jewish authorities to do anything as drastic as publicly display an exhumed body.
5. There is no evidence that the Jewish authorities continued to take an interest in the early Christian movement immediately following Jesus' death. None of his other disciples or followers was arrested, nor is there any indication of efforts to purge the synagogues of those sympathetic to his teachings.
6. Saul's persecution of the early Christian movement occurred several years after Jesus' crucifixion.[15]

Conclusion

Chapter 15 provides seven reasons to believe the conclusion deserves acceptance. Those seven reasons, and perhaps others, explain the lack of controversy regarding Jesus' empty tomb among the general public. In addition, they provide no support for Jesus' resurrection.

---

[15] Fodor, *Unreasonable Faith*, 251–53.

16

Why a Lack of Interest in the Tomb by Roman Leadership?

Christian apologists argue that if belief in Jesus' resurrection was a delusion, lie, or outright conspiracy as proposed by some detractors, why then was it not exposed at that time by the Roman authorities? This apologetic is the so-called *discredited argument*. Christian apologists ask why the Roman authorities failed to produce Jesus' corpse when the rumor spread that he had risen from the dead or why they did not simply open the tomb. The inference is that if the Roman authorities had exposed the empty tomb as a falsehood, it would have ended the Christian movement then and there.

Rebuttal 1:
The Argument Assumes Jesus was in a Separate Tomb

Numerous challenges exist that reject this seemingly common-sense argument offered by Christian apologists. These challenges include the following points:

1. Accepting the historicity of Jesus' crucifixion does not guarantee his burial in a tomb or the discovery of an empty tomb. If there were no burial in a tomb or an empty tomb itself, Roman authorities could not investigate these circumstances or produce Jesus' corpse. His burial and the empty tomb may have been the invention of men or the outcome of legend. That being the case, the event never occurred.
2. There is also conjecture that the Roman authorities could not or did not expose the empty tomb because the burial of Jesus' body might have been a common grave for criminals. Paul, the earliest writer of the Christian Bible, declared in 1 Corinthians 15:4 that Jesus was "buried." The late Michael J. Cook elaborates: "Accordingly, because 'buried' requires no disproportionate attention, we are wrong to dwell on it unduly unless the Greek for

buried (*etaphe*) here requires a tomb per se. But the term is neutral—that is, compatible with burial in a grave, pit, or trench, or buried alone or alongside others or in a common grave for criminals, or in a tomb."[1]

Rebuttal 2:
Digging Up Dead Bodies Wasn't Normal Roman Practice

Christian apologists ask why the Roman authorities failed to produce Jesus' corpse when the rumor spread that he had risen from the dead. Vince Hart (Vinny) challenges this apologetic argument in a blog comment. He counters with the following rebuttal that the Romans would have made any effort to refute the apostles' claims seems pretty silly:

1. The way that Rome dealt with troublemakers was to round up a bunch of them and nail them to crosses.
2. The Jewish authorities dealt with heretics by stoning them to death.[2]

Sarcastically, he adds, "If you have any evidence of the Romans ever trying to logically refute their opponents' claims with evidence, I would love to hear it."[3] Historical records demonstrate that the Roman authorities dealt with troublemakers by crucifying them. There is no reason to think either group would have tried to defeat the early Christians by logically refuting their beliefs in the court of public opinion.[4]

Rebuttal 3:
What Pilate Would Have Done Instead

Pilate or other Roman officials would not imagine a resurrection if they believed that people saw Jesus alive after his crucifixion. Instead, they would think that Jesus had survived his execution. This reality being the case, they would have probably undertaken the following actions:

1. The soldiers performing the crucifixion would have been disciplined severely for failing in their duties.

---

[1] Cook, *Modern Jews Engage*, 156.
[2] Hart, "Did First Century Christians Believe."
[3] Hart, "Did First Century Christians Believe."
[4] Hart, "Did First Century Christians Believe."

2. The government would order a search for the re-capture of a dangerous insurrectionist. Acts reported that Jesus remained on earth for at least forty days (contradicting "Luke," who said he ascended to heaven on the day of the resurrection). Also, he was not hiding.
3. The arrest and detention of Jesus' closest followers to ascertain the circumstances of Jesus' re-appearance.

There is no mention in Paul's epistles, the Gospels, or Acts that any of these actions occurred. No record exists to prove that Joseph's empty tomb troubled Pilate. Because Pilate had no interest, there was no attempt to demonstrate that the tomb was empty.

G. M. Lee offers a reason for the lack of controversy and interest in an empty tomb. He proposes that after the Passover festival had ended, Pontius Pilate left Jerusalem and returned to his regular residence in Caesarea. The Jesus affair and the disciples were unimportant to him. Another rebuttal is that Christian apologists assume that the Roman authorities could find (had the capability) and punish those responsible for moving Jesus' body. Even today, in developed nations, with much greater police resources and forensic technology, many murders (and other crimes) remain unsolved.[5]

Rebuttal 4:
The Roman Authorities Showed a Lack of Interest

Numerous challenges exist that reject this seemingly common-sense argument offered by Christian apologists. These challenges include the following points:

1. The Roman authorities would have wanted to avoid the potential for more public upheaval, while the Jewish leadership would have wanted to ensure their Sabbath laws were respected and obeyed. Therefore, they would have wanted to prevent further delays in getting the body buried.
2. There is conjecture that the Roman authorities could not or did not expose the empty tomb because perhaps the body was in a common grave for criminals. If so, the Roman authorities would not have been able to identify Jesus' body from the other bodies if they were all interred in a common grave for fifty or more days.

---

[5] Fodor, "Can a Scientist Believe the Resurrection."

3. Another speculation exists about why Roman officials ignored reports of a resurrected Jesus. The proclamation was after seven weeks after the crucifixion. The Roman authorities knew that someone else could have seized Jesus' body during that time, unbeknown to them, making it impossible to produce his remains. Consequently, the prudent course of action would be to ignore any reports of Jesus being seen alive.

While "Absence of Evidence is not Evidence of Absence," it is noteworthy that there are no known Roman, Jewish, or early Christian writings that state the Romans were concerned about an empty tomb. It seems more likely that the Roman authorities would have dismissed any reports of Jesus being seen alive (if there was a report of such claims) as the incoherent ramblings of a fringe Jewish cult.

In closing, the lack of controversy regarding Jesus' empty tomb by Pilate or other Roman officials provides no support for Jesus' resurrection. Apologists wrongly argue that if belief in Jesus' resurrection was a delusion, lie, or outright conspiracy as proposed by some detractors, then it would have been exposed at that time by the Roman authorities. Hence, that action would have been silenced forever if the tomb were not empty or if the Jewish or Roman leadership could have produced Jesus' body. Apologists fail to present alternative rationales, offering a false dilemma. There are numerous natural and rational explanations for why the Roman leadership did not attempt to expose an empty tomb if it existed. Moreover, if the Romans had produced a body, it would not have stopped Christianity from expanding, as the disciples of Jesus could have plausibly denied that the (by now severely decomposed) body was Jesus. In contrast, **an empty tomb would only prove that a body was not there**.

Why a Lack of Interest in the Tomb by the Jewish Authorities?

Christian apologists argue that if belief in Jesus' resurrection was a delusion, lie, or outright conspiracy, why was it not exposed then by the Jewish religious authorities? Christian apologists ask why these authorities failed to produce Jesus' corpse when rumors spread that he had risen from the dead or why they did not simply open the tomb. As Wilbur Smith, a Christian apologist, says, "The Jewish authorities never questioned the report of the guards. They did not themselves go out to see if the tomb was empty, because they knew it was empty."[1] The inference is that if the Jewish religious authorities had exposed the empty tomb as a falsehood, it would have ended the Christian movement then and there. A confrontation of this Christian defense follows.

Rebuttal 1:
Argument from Silence

Christian apologists claim that the tomb's lack of controversy and interest substantiates its historicity. Since the Jewish officials did not demand an investigation of the tomb, the reason for their inaction demonstrates that the tomb was empty. Furthermore, the rationale presumes the inference that if the Jewish religious authorities had exposed the belief in Jesus' resurrection as a delusion, lie, outright conspiracy, or falsehood; it would have ended the Christian movement then and there. Apologists use a tactic they criticize skeptics for using: an argument from silence. The onus is on them to prove that the Jewish religious authorities never ordered an investigation of the burial site.

---

[1] Smith, *Therefore Stand*, 375.

Rebuttal 2:
Jewish Law Would Render an Investigation a Waste of Time

Public preaching of the resurrection of Jesus did not begin until Pentecost Sunday, more than seven weeks after his death (Acts 2:1, 22–24). Jewish law would have made it a waste of time for the religious authorities to disinter the body of Jesus. The Mishnah and Midrash state that the facial features of a corpse become disfigured in three days and that a body with marks of identification would be *invalid* after three days following death:

1. Mishnah (*Yevamot* 16:3): They must not give evidence [of identity in respect of a dead man] except on [proof afforded by] the full face with the nose, even though there were also marks on its body or on its clothing. No evidence [of a man's death] must be given before his soul has departed, even though they saw him with his arteries cut or crucified or being devoured by a wild beast. They must give evidence [of identification] only during the first three days [after the death. After this period the decay of the corpse makes identification impossible or uncertain.]
2. Midrash Rabbah Genesis C:7 (994) Bar Kappara taught: Until three days [after death] the soul keeps on returning to the grave, thinking that it will go back [into the body]; but when it sees that *the facial features have become disfigured*, it departs and abandons [the body].
3. Midrash Rabbah Genesis LXV:20 (595) You cannot testify to [the identity of a corpse] save by the facial features together with the nose, *even if there are marks of identification in his body and garments: again, you can testify only within three days [of death]* [see Midrash Rabbah Genesis 73:5 (669–670), Midrash Rabbah Leviticus 18:1 (225–226), and Midrash Rabbah Leviticus 33:5.].

Notably, if the Midrash were in effect when Jesus lived, it would invalidate the supposed proof for Thomas to feel the wounds in the apparition that the Gospel of John claims.

Christian apologists argue that had a body been present, it would have disproven the resurrection of Jesus. However, in response to the Jewish authorities' demonstration, believers would have demanded proof that the body was, in fact, that of Jesus. As proven above, Jewish law made this impossible.

Rebuttal 3:
Lack of Interest if There was a Common Grave

A plausible reason for the Jewish authorities not exposing the empty tomb was that the burial of Jesus' body was in a common grave for criminals. Paul, the earliest of all the writers, only declared that Jesus was "buried" (1 Cor. 15:4). Previously mentioned, Michael Cook points out that the Greek word Paul used for 'buried' in the original Greek (*'etaphê'*) lacked specificity. It "is neutral—that is, compatible with burial in a grave, pit, or trench, or buried alone or alongside others or in a common grave for criminals or in a tomb."[2] If Jesus had a burial with other criminals, it would also have been problematic for anyone to identify the body. Presumably, all the criminals would share the telltale marks of crucifixion.

Critical points from A. J. M. Wedderburn's earlier words bear repeating:

1. Such a fate for Jesus' body would also explain how neither the disciples nor the Jewish authorities could subsequently prove anything either way by investigating graves.
2. The relevant one would have held the remains of others so that it would not be empty.
3. However, the fact that it was not empty would only disprove the Christians' claims if Jesus' remains were identifiable.[3]

However, Wedderburn comments, "That would have been extremely difficult (and thoroughly unpleasant and religiously defiling) after any length of time."[4] On the other hand, if the bodies of the crucified criminals had a burial in a lime pit, presumably nothing would be left to identify.

Rebuttal 4:
Political and Theological Intrigue Would Preclude Interest

1. This argument, however, conveniently overlooks the fact that producing the body would have involved the priestly party in taking the resurrection claims of the disciples seriously.
2. With it, the admission that they might have crucified God's Messiah.

---

[2] Cook, *Modern Jews Engage the New Testament*, 156.
[3] Wedderburn, *Beyond Resurrection*, 62.
[4] Wedderburn, *Beyond Resurrection*, 62.

3. It would also have involved them in the admission that they had deliberately deceived Pontius Pilate.
4. They were guilty of the heinous offense of despoiling a grave.

Cumulatively, such a series of admissions would have been psychologically difficult and politically impossible.[5]

Rebuttal 5:
The Women Told Nobody

Mark 16:1–8 informs readers that the women told nobody about the empty tomb. Consequently, at first, no one knew of their experience. If correct, the empty tomb story could have arisen up to forty years after Jesus' execution, at which time the composition of Mark was complete. Therefore, it would have been impossible for the Jewish religious leaders to expose the purported empty tomb as false. As W. F. R. Browning puts it, "If the empty tomb narratives were a late piece of Christian apologetic, then it was too late for the Jews to produce the body in order to refute the story."[6]

Rebuttal 6:
Jerusalem's Destruction Prevented Interest in an Empty Tomb

The story of the empty tomb only appears in the Gospels. Presumably, the final state of the Gospels' composition followed Jerusalem's destruction. By then (70 CE), the city had its inhabitants killed or sold into slavery. Under these circumstances, it would have been impossible to question eyewitnesses. With this in mind, Roy Hoover points out, "By the time the Gospels were written and the empty-tomb story was first 'published,' there was no realistic possibility of checking on whether, or not, Jesus' remains were still in their burial place."[7]

Rebuttal 7:
The Time Factor Prevented Interest in an Empty Tomb

The date of the creed's origin, reported in 1 Corinthians 15, is unknown. Scholars debate what verses made up the creed. Even assuming its development immediately after Pentecost, it would have been impossible

---

[5] Bostock, "Do We Need an Empty Tomb?," 204.
[6] Browning, "Resurrection of Jesus," 321.
[7] Hoover, "A Contest between Orthodoxy & Veracity," 137.

for the Jewish religious leaders to expose the purported empty tomb as false because of Jewish Law (see Rebuttal 2).

Researcher Matti Myllykoski raises an interesting question: did meaningful debates about the empty tomb take place after the burial? He suggests presuming the Jewish religious authorities had Jesus buried that the interval between Jesus' burial and Pentecost (about seven weeks) creates a dilemma. He says, "It is not certain whether they then knew any longer where they had laid the body or whether they would have found it meaningful to try searching and possibly identifying it."[8]

R. R. Bater also offers speculation about the time component. He inquires, "Is it not a distinct possibility that the Gospels and Acts, in their unmistakable vagueness about the whole situation, have telescoped a much longer period into an interval of days?" Therefore, he adds, "It may have been a long time before Christianity was a sufficiently public phenomenon for the question of testing its claims to even arise."[9]

Rebuttal 8:
Grave Robbers Could Have Stolen the Body

There exists a ghoulish explanation for the lack of controversy over or interest in an empty tomb by the religious leaders. If grave robbers wanted body parts and stole from Joseph's tomb the body of Jesus, the Jewish leaders would not be anxious to draw attention to the burial site. Their rationale might have been that the disciples could have claimed that the empty tomb was *prima facie* evidence of Jesus' resurrection.

Rebuttal 9:
An Unknown Person Could Have Removed the Body

An argument from silence engages the missing body. This argument depends upon the burial of a body. If someone else had taken the body, unbeknown to the Jewish religious authorities, it would have been impossible for them to produce Jesus' remains.

Rebuttal 10:
Friedrich Schleiermacher's Sanhedrin Argument

Failure of the Jewish leadership to disprove Jesus' resurrection does not prove that he rose from the tomb. Friedrich Schleiermacher raised a

---

[8] Myllykoski, "What Happened to the Body of Jesus?," 50.
[9] Bater, "Towards a More Biblical View," 56.

thought-provoking idea. He opines that it is very noteworthy that in the first sermon in Acts, the apostles call themselves witnesses of Christ's resurrection uniquely. Peter, for instance, expressly says that Christ had not shown himself to others. Nonetheless, the Sanhedrin, opposing the apostles, remarkably paid no attention to the resurrection. They only commanded the apostles not to preach in Christ's name.

Friedrich Schleiermacher, a German Reformed theologian, philosopher, and biblical scholar, writes, "How easy it would have been to use another method and order the disciples to prove that Christ had risen!" Since it was well-known that Jesus had not shown himself publicly, the Sanhedrin could have ordered the apostles to prove that he was alive, and they would not have been able to do it. He concludes by saying, "They could only produce witnesses from within their own ranks. However, we find no such demand made."[10]

Rebuttal 11:
Matthew's Account of the Jewish Authorities Does Not Hold Water

Some believers in Jesus' resurrection argue that the silent Jewish leadership did not attempt to refute the empty tomb because they knew it was empty. Evan Fales counters this Christian apologetic. The question is not why the Jewish leadership remained silent. The real issue Fales advances is why there was no recorded "wholesale and instantaneous conversion of the Jews—or at the very least, a massive national debate."[11]

Remarkably, it is impossible to understand the reaction of the Jewish authorities to the supernatural events recorded in the Gospels around the time of Jesus' execution. Matthew 27:51 describes an earthquake. If it were a historical event, it would have been severe enough to crack the surrounding rocks in Jerusalem. It would almost certainly have caused damage to the temple's structure.[12] However, no mention of this event appears in Jewish writings. Significantly, this happening is no mere earthquake. This reported geological phenomenon occurred with Jesus' death and other supernatural incidents. The other phenomena that did not affect the Jewish leaders include:

1. The sun remained dark for three hours, from midday until 3 p.m.
2. The tearing of the temple's sixty-foot, four-inch-thick curtain.
3. The opening of an unknown number of tombs.

---

[10] Schleiermacher, *The Life of Jesus*, 459.
[11] Fales, "Successful Defense?," 28; cf. Wolfe, *How the Easter Story Grew*, 114.
[12] Alter, *The Resurrection*, 144–46.

4. An unknown number (many, reported by Matthew) of bodies of saints arose from the dead.
5. These resurrected saints came out of their graves and went into the holy city.
6. The resurrected saints appeared to many people.

Furthermore, after Jesus' death and burial, Matthew relates the guards assigned at the tomb. Allegedly, the rationale for that decision was that the Jewish authorities presumably were aware of Jesus' claim that he would return from the dead after three days. How they knew this information and why the Romans would accede to this strange request are unexplained. Two days later, Matthew 28:2 describes another earthquake, during which an angel of the Lord came down from heaven, rolled away the stone covering the tomb, and then sat on it. The guards then reported *all* these things to the Jewish chief priests (Matthew 28:11).

The Gospel of Matthew reports that the Jewish authorities' reaction to this world-changing event was to cover up the whole incident with a bribe (Matthew 28:12–14). Such a reaction strikes many fair-minded critics as psychologically inconceivable. Readers must judge whether this interpretation is correct.

Rebuttal 12:
An Irrelevant Band of Followers Would Not Generate Interest

The Jewish and Roman religious leaders looked upon the Jesus cult as just another of the many small Jewish sects. They would assume the movement would wither away after its leader's demise. Furthermore, since the disciples did not consider the empty tomb as evidence of Jesus' resurrection, it is unclear why the Jewish leadership would have done so.

Rebuttal 13:
Acts 4 Shows the Jewish Authorities Never Believed the Apostles

The Jewish religious leadership lacked interest in Jesus' tomb. Acts 4 reported the arrest of Peter, John, and the remainder of the apostles a few days after Pentecost. Afterward, they were brought before the Jewish religious authorities and charged with preaching about the resurrection of the dead. Acts record a terse portion of the interrogation. The Sadducees, unlike the Pharisees, did *not* believe in a resurrection. The Jewish authorities decided to command and threaten "them not to speak or teach at all in the name of Jesus" (Acts 4:18, ESV).

Thomas Ralston, a dated source, poses the following situation and rhetorical questions and provides an answer: The apostles face the great council, the Sanhedrin. They, the religious leaders, are the inventors of the story of the stealing of the body. Ralston comments, "How passing strange, that in no one of these instances was the crime of having stolen the dead body of Jesus brought against the apostles!"[13] Next, he asks a series of questions:

1. Why were they not formally accused of this theft?
2. Why were not Joseph of Arimathea and the whole Roman guard instantly summoned and made to confront them?

Ralston adds, "The great question is, the resurrection of Jesus, which the apostles affirm; but not one of the guard is called to confront them. The stealing of the body is not named! And why?"[14] He answers his questions with an intriguing reply, "Because the Sanhedrin *did not believe the story!*" (Italics in original)[15]

Rebuttal 14:
The Accounts were Midrashic

Earl Doherty, a detractor, states that if "the earliest Gospel was not intended to represent history, and for a couple of decades was simply viewed as a piece of midrashic symbolism, no one would have taken the trouble to deny its contents."[16] Midrash is a Hebrew word referring to the exposition, or exegesis, of a biblical text. The word derives from the verb *darosh*, meaning study and investigation of the inner and logical meaning of a particular text as opposed to its plain and literal reading.

Conclusion

Chapter 17 provides its readers with fourteen rebuttals. The readers must judge the effectiveness of the arguments presented. Collectively the rebuttals discussed above provide good reason to doubt the Christian apologetic: if belief in Jesus' resurrection was a delusion, lie, or outright conspiracy, why was it not exposed then by the Jewish religious authorities?

---

[13] Ralston, *Elements of Divinity*, 642.
[14] Ralston, *Elements of Divinity*, 642.
[15] Ralston, *Elements of Divinity*, 642.
[16] Doherty. *Reader Feedback and Author's Response*, RFSet 15.

18

Was There Controversy About the Empty Tomb Among Jesus' Followers?

Christian apologists believe it would have been impossible to preach in Jerusalem that Jesus had risen from the dead if the tomb was not empty.[1] In addition to this assumption, P. B. Fitzwater inquires: "If the resurrection were not real, why should the apostles have made it the very cornerstone of their preaching?"[2] These topics are under investigation in Chapter 18.

Rebuttal 1:
History Confirms the Disciples had No Interest in Jesus' Tomb

Roman authorities and Jewish religious leaders failed to demonstrate concern over or interest in a tomb; *neither* did most of the disciples or the numerous followers of Jesus take notice. The only possible exceptions were Peter (Luke 24:12; John 20:3) and the disciple whom Jesus loved (John 20:3). Not until 326 CE, is it evidenced that Christians were interested in a tomb. That year, Queen Helena, mother of Emperor Constantine the Great, visited Jerusalem, seeking locations associated with Jesus' last days. Years later, the construction of the Holy Sepulcher started on the site that *she* had identified as the place where Jesus had risen. The findings of Charles George Gordon challenged this site arguing for the Garden Tomb as the burial site.[3]

---

[1] Craig, *Reasonable Faith*, 361; "Did Jesus Rise From the Dead?," 151; "The Historicity of the Empty Tomb of Jesus" 59; *Apologetics: An Introduction*, 190; *The Son Rises*, 82; Flood, *The Resurrection*, 45; Habermas, *The Resurrection of Jesus*, 34; Habermas and Licona, *Case for the Resurrection of Jesus*, 70; Keener, *The Historical Jesus of the Gospels*, 704; Morrow, *Welcome to College*, 139–40; O'Collins, "Resurrection and New Creation," 17; Pannenberg, *Jesus, God and Man*, 106; Stein, *Jesus the Messiah*, 264.

[2] Fitzwater, *Christian Theology*, 160.

[3] Barkay, "The Garden Tomb," 40–57; Frantzman and Kark, "General Gordon's Pilgrimage to Palestine," 55–84.

Rebuttal 2:
The Disciples Lacked Knowledge of Jesus' Burial

The presumed burial of Jesus does *not* mean that Joseph buried him in a tomb later discovered empty. The scriptural evidence of the two earliest Gospels, Mark 14:50 and Matthew 28:16, suggest that Jesus' male disciples knew little of the burial location or chose not to make much of it. Only about fifty years after the crucifixion did Luke report Peter examining a tomb. The disciples could not demand an investigation if there was no burial in a tomb or dumping Jesus' body in a common grave.

Rebuttal 3:
Paul Did Not Visit the Tomb Because It Did Not Exist

Paul had visited Jerusalem on at least three occasions. The first recorded visit to Jerusalem is Acts 11:28–30 and Acts 12:25; later in Acts 15:1–30, and finally, Acts 18:21–22. Luke, the presumed author of Acts, omits any record that Paul visited the empty tomb. Why? Paul's epistles also fail to mention a personal examination of the empty tomb. Why? This question is an argument from silence. One speculative possibility is that the story of Jesus' burial and the subsequent discovery of the empty tomb was either deliberately invented or grew out of a legend; if this was the case, the alleged events never occurred. Paul could not have visited it if there had been no burial in a tomb.

Rebuttal 4:
The Disciples Knew Grave Robbers Could Have Stolen Jesus' Body

One rather ghoulish reason why the disciples may not have wanted to visit Jesus' tomb deals with the brisk trade in body parts among grave robbers. Body snatchers were a reality in first-century Palestine and might have stolen the body. Understandably, the disciples would not want to discuss the subject. On the other hand, if the disciples raised questions about the empty tomb, they would need to confront the possibility of their Lord and Master being hacked up and his body parts sold to the highest bidder. In *The Expository Times*, David Whitaker speculates, "The Christians, if they suspected so degrading an end to their Lord and Master, would have every reason to be reticent about it."[4]

---

[4] Whitaker, "What Happened to the Body of Jesus?," 310.

Rebuttal 5:
It is Unknown When the Message was First Proclaimed

Thorwald Lorenzen raises a previously overlooked factor that explains the lack of interest in a tomb burial. He writes that the most persuasive arguments in favor of the historical reliability of the tomb tradition deals with opponents. Lorenzen argues that the Easter message could not have been proclaimed in Jerusalem if the opponents could have invalidated its substance by pointing to the corpse of Jesus in the tomb. Candidly, he admits, "We do not really know as to when the Easter message was first proclaimed in Jerusalem."[5] Analyzing the Gospels, he thinks, "It is unlikely that Mary as a woman, on the basis of her experience with the risen Christ, would have proclaimed the Gospel in Jerusalem."[6] He continues, "The other appearances happened in Galilee; from there, Peter and the disciples had to return to Jerusalem."[7] However, is this chronology viable? Lorenzen elaborates, "That takes time, and the opposition that was directed toward Jesus would also have made his disciples cautious."[8]

Additionally, he points out that the Gospels inform that Peter and the disciples were back in Jerusalem after the Passover Feast. However, there exists a problem. Lorenzen says, "Yet this chronological scheme is a Lukan construct to distinguish between the resurrection of Christ and the coming of the Holy Spirit."[9] Therefore, he concludes his analysis by acknowledging, "We simply don't know when the resurrection was first proclaimed in Jerusalem."[10]

Rebuttal 6:
The Apocalyptic Age was More Important than an Empty Tomb

Another reason for the lack of controversy about a tomb might be that the disciples did not raise the issue. Why? One explanation is that the earliest believers thought they lived in apocalyptic times. They were expecting the imminent final judgment and resurrection of the dead. Furthermore, the day of God's wrath and judgment was at hand. Consequently, God's actions would speak louder than any of their words.

---

[5] Lorenzen, *Resurrection and Discipleship*, 172.
[6] Lorenzen, *Resurrection and Discipleship*, 172.
[7] Lorenzen, *Resurrection and Discipleship*, 172.
[8] Lorenzen, *Resurrection and Discipleship*, 172.
[9] Lorenzen, *Resurrection and Discipleship*, 172.
[10] Lorenzen, *Resurrection and Discipleship*, 171–72.

Conclusion

The lack of interest in the purported empty tomb, whether by the public, the Roman authorities, or the Jewish religious leaders, should raise the proverbial red flag. Do Christian apologists honestly believe meaningful debates about the empty tomb did *not* occur soon after Jesus' burial? Or, do Christian apologists believe that if the guards had said they knew Jesus' disciples carried off the body, they would not have made some arrests and employed false witnesses to convict the accused? The Anglican Bishop of Perth Peter Carnley writes,

> I must confess that I do not understand this argument which suggests that the grave in which Jesus had been laid would have been interesting to Christians had Jesus' body been found in it, but of no continuing interest even as the site of the resurrection if it was found empty."[11]

The lack of controversy over, and interest in, Jesus' tomb by his followers discussed in this issue raises doubt as to the empty tomb's historicity and Jesus' physical, bodily resurrection.

---

[11] Carnley, *The Structure of Resurrection Belief*, 58.

What Were the Consequences of an Empty Tomb?

According to many Christian apologists, the empty tomb is strong evidence of Jesus' resurrection. Their argument centers on the apologetic *conditio sine qua non*, a Latin legal term meaning "without which it could not be." This term refers to a crucial action, condition, or thing. Occupation of a tomb by a body, Christian apologists assert that Jesus' resurrection was impossible to proclaim.[1] The question is whether or not this Christian apologetic is correct. Other writers, to the contrary, argue that even if proven that Jesus' body remained in the tomb, belief in his resurrection probably would *not* have been destroyed.[2]

Rebuttal 1:
The Consequences of an Empty Tomb Presume a Tomb

The consequences of an empty tomb presume the existence of a tomb purportedly belonging to Joseph of Arimathea. For Christianity, the consequences of a nonexistent tomb have enormous ramifications. If there was no tomb:

1. Mark 15:42–47 is omitted. Therefore:
   a. No Joseph of Arimathea.
   b. No tomb or tomb burial.
   c. No stone rolled against the entrance of the tomb.

---

[1] Cambron, *Bible Doctrines*, 106–7; Habermas and Licona, *Case for the Resurrection of Jesus*, 70; O'Collins, "Resurrection and New Creation," 17; Pannenberg, *Jesus, God and Man*, 25; "Did Jesus Really Rise from the Dead?," 134; Richardson, "The Resurrection of Jesus Christ," 153; Samples, *Without a Doubt*, 138; Stein, "Was the Tomb Really Empty?," 25–26.

[2] Goguel, *Jesus the Nazarene*, 236–37; Lüdemann, *The Resurrection of Christ*, 181; Walker, "Christian Origins and Resurrection Faith," 51.

2. Mark 16:1–8 is omitted. Therefore:
   a. No women visit the tomb.
   b. No message is given to the women by the young man.

3. Matthew 27:57–66:
   a. No Joseph of Arimathea.
   b. No tomb or tomb burial.
   c. No big stone rolled against the entrance of the tomb.
   d. No guard at the tomb.

4. Matthew 28:1–15 is omitted. Therefore:
   a. No women visit the tomb.
   b. No earthquake.
   c. No angels at the tomb and their instructions.
   d. No appearance of Jesus with the women grasping his feet.
   e. No guards at the tomb.
   f. No bribes from the chief priests and elders.

5. Luke 23:50–56:
   a. No Joseph of Arimathea.
   b. No tomb or tomb burial.
   c. No women witnessed a tomb or the preparation of the body.

6. Luke 24:1–12:
   a. No women visit the tomb.
   b. No encounter with two angels.
   c. No instructions from the angels
   d. No running to and inspection of the tomb by Peter.

7. John 19:38–42:
   a. No Joseph of Arimathea.
   b. No tomb or tomb burial.
   c. No Nicodemus is purchasing myrrh and spices.
   d. No burial in a garden.

8. John 20:1–18:
   a. No visit by Mary Magdalene to the tomb.
   b. No race to the tomb by Peter or the other disciples.
   c. No discovery of burial cloth.
   d. No encounter between Mary Magdalene and the two angels.
   e. No encounter between Mary Magdalene and Jesus.

The consequences of a nonexistent tomb obliterate a crucial part of the Gospel narratives. Chilton concisely elaborates on the importance. "The critical connection is between Jesus as buried and Jesus as risen: that alone permits identification of the one who is risen with the person who was known by his followers, because he was known to have died."[3] For N.T. Wright, the connection is paramount: "There is no chance that even the most devout of Jesus' former followers would have said he had been raised."[4] It leaves readers with differing appearance stories without a context, undermining the historicity and belief that Jesus rose from death. Without the burial and the empty tomb, the belief in God's saving grace through Jesus' resurrection faces partial destruction.

Rebuttal 2:
An Empty Tomb Did Not
Provide Support for Jesus' Resurrection

What did the empty tomb prove to those who saw it? A review of the Gospel narratives reveals that the consequence of an empty tomb provides *no* support for Jesus' physical, bodily resurrection. In the Gospel of Mark (16:1–8), three things occurred: (1) Mary Magdalene, Mary the mother of James, and Salome found the tomb empty and entered it; (2) afterward, a young man standing inside the tomb explained what happened; and (3) the women fled trembling and amazed, and told no-one.

In the Gospel of Matthew (28:1–8), outside the tomb, the two Marys found an angel sitting on a stone. He informed them that Jesus had risen, and the two women fled the tomb "with fear and great joy" (ESV) and told the disciples what had occurred. After an unspecified amount of time, the eleven disciples saw Jesus in Galilee, but an unknown number doubted it.

Several events transpired in the Gospel of Luke (24:11–12). (1) Mary Magdalene, Joanna, Mary, the mother of James, and other women found the tomb empty and entered it. (2) Inside the tomb, they found two men who explained what had happened. (3) At that point, the women remembered Jesus' words and returned to Jerusalem. (4) Afterward, "they told all these things to the Eleven and to all the others" what they saw and heard. "But these words seemed to them an idle tale, and they did not believe them" (24:9, ESV). (5) After receiving the women's message, "But Peter rose and ran to the tomb; stooping and looking in, he saw the linen

---

[3] Chilton, *Resurrection Logic*, 169.
[4] Wright, *The Resurrection of the Son of God*, 626.

cloths by themselves; and he went home marveling at what had happened" (24:12, ESV).

According to the Gospel of John (20:1–10), several things ensued. (1) When Mary Magdalene saw "that the stone had been taken away from the tomb" (ESV), she immediately ran to Simon Peter and the other disciple whom Jesus loved, saying: "They have taken the Lord out of the tomb, and we do not know where they have laid him" (20:2, ESV). Her last words, "We don't know where they have laid him," refuted any belief in a resurrection. Mary Magdalene's words affirmed her belief that Jesus' body was reinterred elsewhere by a person or persons unknown. (2) Immediately after receiving Mary Magdalene's message, Peter and "the other disciple" raced to the tomb. However, the other disciple arrived first, bending over, "He saw the linen cloths lying there, but he did not go in." (3) John reports, "Then Simon Peter came, following him, and went into the tomb. He saw the linen cloths lying there, and the face cloth, which had been on Jesus' head, not lying with the linen cloths but folded up in a place by itself." Next, the other disciple also went into the tomb. John reports "and he *saw* and *believed*" (v. 9, ESV). Yet in the end, John states, "For as yet they did not understand the Scripture, that he must rise from the dead." (4) Afterward, "Then the disciples went back to their homes" (20:10, ESV). It is noteworthy that several commentators point out that the text does not state what these two disciples believed.[5]

Numerous writers affirm the Gospels' report that the initial investigation of an empty tomb or the message about an empty tomb meant *nothing* to the disciples and was not proof of a physical, bodily resurrection.[6] On the contrary, the empty tomb resulted in perplexity and fear (cf. Mark 16:8; Luke 24:5, 11). The Christian apologist Gary Habermas states, "If Jesus' burial tomb was later found empty, this does not prove that a resurrection occurred. However, it adds credibility to the disciples' claim to have seen the risen Jesus since it both seriously

---

[5] Conway, *Men and Women in the Fourth Gospel*, 189; King, "The New Testament Account of the Resurrection," 29; Koester, "Hearing, Seeing and Believing in the Gospel of John," 344.

[6] Boff, *The Question of Faith*, 35–36; Bulst, *Resurrection, Fundamental Theology*, 328; Corduan, *No Doubt about It*, 222; Fortna, "Mark Intimates/Matthew Defends the Resurrection," 201; Hare, *Matthew*, 329; Hendrickx, *The Resurrection Narratives of the Synoptic Gospels*, 16; Kesich, *The First Day of the New Creation*, 81; Kelly, *The Resurrection Effect*, 140; Ladd, *A Theology of the New Testament*, 361; Léon-Dufour, *Resurrection and the Message of Easter*, 117; MacQuarrie, *Principles of Christian Theology*, 288; McLeman, *Resurrection Then and Now*, 129; O'Collins, *Easter Faith*, 44, *The Resurrection of Jesus Christ*, 20; Patterson, *Beyond the Passion*, 114; Schlier, *On the Resurrection of Jesus Christ*, 35.

complicates the search for a naturalistic hypothesis and indicates that whatever happened most likely involved Jesus' body."[7] That same year, Habermas and Licona said, "It should be noted that the empty tomb, by itself, proves little."[8] It would be remiss, however, not to point out what Habermas and Licona also believe. They say, "The empty tomb does not stand alone."[9] Other factors are required to consider.

Rebuttal 3:
Second Temple Jews Held
Different Beliefs about Resurrection

Christian apologists believe that the prevalent first-century Jewish-Palestinian understanding of "resurrection" precluded the existence of a corpse still lying in the grave. Paul Gwynne points out that this opinion is false:

> Thus, the first Christians could not have preached a resurrected Jesus, and probably would have had deep trouble believing this themselves, if his corpse was known to be still lying in its tomb. This is a potent argument except for the standard objection that there was not one single model of resurrection in first-century Palestine but rather considerable diversity in the way people imagined resurrection, reflecting the complex mix of groups and theological schools that comprised Jewish religious society.[10]

However, not all first-century models of resurrection are the same.

For example, Mark 6:16 demonstrates that in the mind of King Herod, the beheaded prophet, John the Baptist, had risen from the dead and returned as the new prophet Jesus: "But when Herod heard of it, he said, 'John, whom I beheaded, has been raised'" (ESV). Consequently, "At least in Herod's mind, the corpse of John was irrelevant to his resurrection.[11] This event, Christian apologists could counter, more accurately exemplifies reincarnation. (N.B. However, the interval between John's death and Jesus' appearance was such a short reincarnation would not make sense, as there would be no time for a reincarnated Jesus to grow

---

[7] Habermas, "The Case for Christ's Resurrection,"188.
[8] Habermas and Licona, *Case for the Resurrection of Jesus*, 73; cf. Robinson, *Can We Trust the New Testament?*, 123–24.
[9] Habermas and Licona, *Case for the Resurrection of Jesus*, 73.
[10] Gwynne, "The Fate of Jesus' Body," 16–17.
[11] Gwynne, "The Fate of Jesus' Body," 17.

up.) Another text that could support a possible type of resurrection is *Jubilees* 23:31: "And their bones will rest in the earth and their spirit will have much joy." Mark 9:4–5 also reports that Peter, James, and John saw Moses and Elijah, who had long ago died, talking to Jesus.

Rebuttal 4:
Mediterranean Milieu Explains
Their Belief in Jesus' Resurrection

William O. Walker Jr. and others suggest that features of the general religious and theological milieu should be considered, including the following:[12]

1. "First, and this is often overlooked, there never would have been a time when Jesus's followers regarded death as the final and absolute end of Jesus."[13]
2. "Second, as Edouard Schweizer has pointed out, the idea that a 'Righteous One' who humbled himself or voluntarily accepted suffering or death in obedience to God would be rewarded either on earth or in heaven was apparently well established. It appears that the early Christian understanding of Jesus was influenced by this idea."[14]
3. "Third, it was popularly believed that such a Righteous One might escape the usual human experience of death and be assumed bodily to heaven or, perhaps, be assumed to heaven immediately after death;[15] indeed, as James M. Robinson observed, the ascension of dignitaries of the past was "an increasingly popular and detailed motif in first-century Jewish thought (e.g., Enoch, Elijah, Levi, Baruch, Ezra, Moses, Zephaniah, Abraham, Isaiah, Adam, and even Raphael)."[16]
4. "There is ample precedent for the belief that a particularly illustrious figure who had ascended to heaven such as Moses or Elijah, might return to earth to precede or usher in the end time." The primitive Palestinian Church was greatly influenced in its understanding of Jesus by the traditions about Moses and Elijah.[17]

---

[12] Walker, "Christian Origins and Resurrection Faith," 51–52.
[13] Walker, "Christian Origins and Resurrection Faith," 51.
[14] Schweizer, *Lordship and Discipleship*, 21–46.
[15] Schweizer, *Lordship and Discipleship*, 22–28;
[16] Robinson," Ascension," 1:245–47.
[17] Walker, "Christian Origins and Resurrection Faith," 52.

Rebuttal 5:
Rabbinic Literature and Escaping Death

Rolland Wolfe writes, "It should also be noted that rabbinical literature asserts that even minor Old Testament characters were rewarded, for specific acts of meritorious service, by escaping death through being taken alive to Heaven."[18] Several examples include the following "characters":

1. Eliezer, Abraham's faithful steward (Gen. 24);
2. Ebed-Melech, for saving Jeremiah's life (Jer. 38:7–13);
3. Hiram, King of Tyre, for his friendship with King Solomon (1 Kgs. 5);
4. Jabez, for favoring Israel (1 Chr. 4:10);
5. Serah, daughter of Asher (Gen. 46:17; Num. 26:46), for her great wisdom;
6. Pharaoh's daughter, for saving Moses (Exod. 2:5–10).

In *Ancient Near Eastern Texts*, James Pritchard also discusses the idea of reward for meritorious service and being taken to heaven.[19] An example is the Sumerian flood story, where Ziusudra, the hero, is transported to Dilmun, the abode of the gods.

Rebuttal 6:
Multiple Accounts of Empty Tombs
and Disappearing Bodies

Dale Allison details many popular stories of empty tombs and disappearing bodies. Several of these stories include:

1. Moses' mysterious disappearance (Josephus, *Ant.* 9.28);
2. The vain search for the remains of Job's children (*T. Job* 39:1–40:6);
3. The resurrection of the two witnesses in Revelation 11;
4. the failure to find the body of John the Baptist's father (*Prot. Jas.* 24:3);
5. The disappearance of the corpse of the thief who asked Jesus to remember him in his kingdom (*Narratio Jos. Arim.* 4:1);
6. the remains of John the Beloved (*Acts John* 115 Cod. R and V. ed. M. Bonnet; p. 215); and

---

[18] Wolfe, *How the Easter Story Grew*, 145.
[19] Pritchard, *Ancient Near Eastern Texts*, 44.

7. The bodily assumption of Mary, the mother of Jesus (Simon Claude Mimouni, *Dormition et assomption de Marie: Histoire des traditions anciennes* (ThH98; Paris: Beauchesne, 1995).[20]

Allison also includes in his list several unhistorical Greco-Roman analogies:

1. The missing bones of Hercules (Diodorus Siculus 4.38.4–5);
2. The rapture of Ganymede (reputed to be the fairest of mortal men), son of Tros, lord of the Trojans (Homer, *Iliad* 20.234–35);
3. The failure to find Aeneas's body (Dionysius Halicarnassus, *Ant. Rom.* 1.64);
4. The disappearance of Romulus (Ovid, *Met.* 14.805–51; Plutarch, *Romulus* 27.7–28.3);
5. The miraculous exit of Empedocles (Diogenes Laertius 8.67–69);
6. The departure of Aristeas of Proconnesus (Herodotus, *Hist.* 4.14–15);
7. The translation of Cleomedes of Astypalaea (Pausanias, *Descr.* 6.9.6–9); and
8. Various rumors about Apollonius (Philostratus, *Vit. Apoll.* 8:30).[21]

A review of the literature, religious and non-religious, demonstrates multiple accounts of empty tombs and disappearing appearing bodies. Allison comments "Early Christians had the imaginative ability to fabricate fictions on the basis of theological convictions, and on more than one occasion they did so."[22] In his writings, he includes stories about resurrections. Allison writes emphatically, "One of them made up the story in Mt. 27:51b–53. We can also be fairly confident that the narrative about the guard in Mt. 27:62–66, which has no parallel in Mark, Luke, or John, is sheer fiction."[23] Skeptics also challenge what they perceive as invented stories, seen multiple times throughout the Christian Bible: the virgin birth/conception and the ascension forming imaginative bookends, to mention just two.

---

[20] Allison, *Resurrecting Jesus*, 308; *The Resurrection of Jesus*, 138. "Explaining the Resurrection," 123.
[21] Allison, *The Resurrection of Jesus*, 138.
[22] Allison, *The Resurrection of Jesus*, 140.
[23] Allison, *The Resurrection of Jesus*, 140.

Rebuttal 7:
An Empty Tomb Does Not
Lend Credibility to Jesus' Resurrection

Gerd Lüdemann argues that the Christian apologetic of the empty tomb as evidence or proof of Jesus' resurrection is unpersuasive. He reminds his readers of several important facts:

1. Scholars do not know how long after Jesus' death the disciples stayed in Galilee nor when their public appearance in Jerusalem began. By the time they started preaching, the decomposed body of Jesus would no longer have been recognizable.
2. Jesus' burial place, as was the story of Joseph of Arimathea, may well have been a later invention. In other words, researchers cannot be sure that Jesus' tomb was empty or even existed.
   The Jerusalem community, for whatever reason, did not ascribe any significance to the location of Jesus' burial place; had it done so, a tradition about it would, in all likelihood, have arisen early and stayed preserved.[24]

Furthermore, it was not until three centuries afterward that anyone missed the purported tomb and searched for its possible site.

Rebuttal 8:
Bruce Chilton Says
the Empty Tomb Must be Set Aside

With clarity and conciseness, Bruce Chilton writes, "The conventional presentation [empty tomb] has become so prevalent that it needs to be mentioned in order to be set aside because it flies in the face that 'the empty tomb' is a latecomer to the traditions regarding how God raised Jesus from the dead."[25] It is significant that only in the last two canonical Gospels to be written is there a description of an entry into the tomb. Chilton elaborates:

> Both Luke and John go out of their way to say the tomb was *not* empty, since grave clothing was identified. But "the empty tomb," a stock phrase in modern discussion, appeals strongly to apologists of varying

---

[24] Lüdemann, *The Resurrection of Christ*, 181.
[25] Chilton, "The Logic of Jesus' Resurrection"; see also *Resurrection Logic*, 2–3.

kinds: those that demand belief in spite of doubt, those who claim the incontestable authority of the witnesses who visited the tomb, and those who contend that the disciples were mistaken in their belief....

Yet "the empty tomb" persists as if the phrase were necessary to refer to the resurrection; sometimes, those words appear in printed Bibles as a heading to passages in which disciples do not enter the burial cave at all.

When interpreters insist on repeating what they must know is not accurate, something other than exegesis is at issue, something like a myth. In this case, the myth ignores or contradicts the earliest of the sources for the resurrection, composed well prior to the Gospels. Paul says nothing whatever of Jesus' tomb, referring only (1 Corinthians 15:4) to a burial after his death.[26]

Chilton's masterpiece text, *Resurrection Logic: How Jesus First Followers Believed God Raised Him from the Dead*, is a must read.

Rebuttal 9:
An Empty Tomb Proves Nothing

The late Norman Geisler, writing in the *Baker Encyclopedia of Christian Apologetics*, attempts to counter the skeptical hypothesis that none of the disciples ever bothered to check Jesus' tomb after the resurrection appearances: "But no one ever checked the tomb to see if Jesus' dead body actually was there. Why should they, if they had already seen him alive?"[27] Geisler argues that the empty tomb is attested solidly in the Gospels. Several rebuttals to Geisler's apologetic exist. All an empty tomb demonstrates is that it does not contain a body. Nothing is determinable regarding two unknown factors:

1. If the tomb ever contained a body, and
2. If a body was in the tomb, how and when was it removed?

Phillip Wiebe, commenting on the empty tomb in the *Journal of Christian Theological Research*, offers the following opinion:

> While we would reasonably expect a grave to be empty if a resuscitation took place, the converse does not hold. Just because the

---

[26] Chilton, "The Logic of Jesus' Resurrection"; see also *Resurrection Logic*, 2–3.

[27] Geisler, *Baker Encyclopedia of Christian Apologetics*, 645.

place in which a person was buried was found not to contain the corpse, we cannot plausibly assert that the person was resuscitated. Grave robbers have no doubt been found in most places of the world at various times, and reasons exist for exhuming or moving corpses. The Gospel accounts of the Resurrection indicate that questions were raised about whether the body of Jesus had been moved.[28]

John E. Remsburg, a dated source, quoted Lemuel Kelley Washburn as saying: "If Jesus got out of the grave alive, he was put into it alive. If he was put into it dead, he was taken out dead. A depopulated sepulchre is not proof that its former tenant has moved to heaven. It is merely proof that somebody has stolen a dead body."[29] This reinterment theory, or the theory of a body reburial in a different location, was reviewed earlier (i.e., the relocation hypothesis). An obvious objection by apologists is that if the authorities reburied Jesus' body, why did they not produce it to stop the resurrection story from spreading? One potential answer is simple; the body would have been too badly decayed to be identifiable as Jesus' body. The crucial point to remember is that an empty tomb does not offer support for a physical, bodily resurrection.

Conclusion

In closing, all the empty tomb (assuming it even existed) proves is that it was empty; Jesus' body was not inside it. Therefore, the empty tomb provides no proof of how the tomb became empty. To quote Anthony Thiselton, English Anglican priest, theologian, and academic, "The empty tomb could never in itself constitute a 'proof,' for it could be explained in a variety of ways."[30]

---

[28] Wiebe, "Evidence for a Resurrection."
[29] Remsburg, *The Christ*, 245.
[30] Thiselton, *The First Epistle to the Corinthians*, 1197; cf. Edwards, *The Gospel According to Mark*, 494.

Three Alternative Possibilities

> God reveals Himself to people in that way. What we have is the record of Him revealing Himself to the people of Israel. We don't....I shouldn't say we don't have a record because there are other traditions, other than the Jewish traditions in which a divine being reveals himself.
>
> Whether or not that is God, I'm not in a position to judge because remember, Satan is the mimic of God. And Satan can reveal himself the same way God reveals Himself.[1]

Christian apologists believe that Jesus' rising from the grave was a supernatural event proving that he is the Messiah and God Almighty in an absolute sense. However, they often exclusively present that one supernatural option. Another option is possible: miraculous signs that confirm messages from God do happen; however, Jesus' resurrection was *not* one of them. If the supernatural exists, why is it exclusively invoked to support the arguments in favor of Jesus' resurrection? Within the supernatural realm, there are several alternative explanations that pose a real challenge for Christian apologists and theologians. These supernatural alternatives challenge the hypothesis of the death, burial, and a third-day resurrection.

Before discussing Possibility #1, it is necessary to explain the term "skeptical theism." Justin P. McBrayer has written an entire entry on that topic in the *Internet Encyclopedia of Philosophy*. His introduction reads:

> Skeptical theism is the view that God exists but that we should be skeptical of our ability to discern God's reasons for acting or refraining from acting in any particular instance. In particular, says the skeptical theist, we should not grant that *our* inability to think of a good reason for doing or allowing something is indicative of whether

---

[1] Kroll, "Seeing the Glory of the Lord Around Us." N.B. Woodrow Kroll is an evangelical preacher and former radio host and president of the international "Back to the Bible" radio and television ministry.

or not *God* might have a good reason for doing or allowing something. If there is a God, he knows much more than we do about the relevant facts, and thus it would not be surprising at all if he has reasons for doing or allowing something that we cannot fathom.[2]

Possibility #1:
God Deceived the Jewish People
by Sending Jesus of Nazareth

Stephen Law discusses one alternative to the traditional Christian apologetic that Jesus' physical resurrection from the dead is a supernatural sign from God that Jesus is the Messiah. In contradiction to that apologetic, he presents the following line of thought:

> According to skeptical theism, we can't conclude God has no reason to do x just because we can't *think* of a reason for him to do x. For all we know, such a reason exists. But if skeptical theism is true, then, for all we know, God has reason to *lie to us and deceive us in all sorts of ways*. If skeptical theism is true, we can no longer reasonably trust *anything* God says, or might seem to reveal!
>
> Suppose, for example, that God says that all who believe in him will have eternal life. As the philosopher Erik Wielenberg points out, if skeptical theism is true, then for all we know God has a good reason to lie to us about that. So, given skeptical theism, it's not reasonable for us to believe him.
>
> In fact, once we accept skeptical theism, we can no longer reasonably trust our memories and senses at all. If skeptical theism is true then, for all we know, there's a God justifying reason for God to deceive us about both the external world and past. For all we know, God has an excellent reason to dupe us about almost everything!
>
> Or, if a Christian skeptical theist believes that Jesus' resurrection is good evidence for the truth of Christianity, point out that if skeptical theism is true, *then for all they know God has a good reason for starting a false religion by raising Jesus from the dead. How do they know God doesn't have such a reason? And if they're in the dark about whether God has such a reason, then they're in the dark about whether God's deceiving them about Christianity. For all they can tell, Christianity is a divine lie* (italics added).[3]

---

[2] McBrayer, "Skeptical Theism."
[3] Law, "Skeptical Theism"; cf. Hedrick, "Visions, Apparitions, and Other Divine Visitations," 25.

The Hebrew Bible substantiates the hypothesis that God purposely deceives the chosen people. Charles Hedrick points out that the Jewish people were targets in the Hebrew Bible when God sent lying spirits to deceive the prophets (1 Kgs. 22:20–23).[4] Why would God choose to deceive the children of Israel?

One reason is that God Himself could have willed the "apparent" resurrection of Jesus, along with other supposed miracles detailed in the Christian Scriptures, as a test of loyalty to His teachings:[5]

> If a prophet or a dreamer of dreams arises among you and gives you a sign or a wonder, and the sign or wonder that he tells you comes to pass, and if he says, 'Let us go after other gods,' which you have not known, 'and let us serve them,' you shall not listen to the words of that prophet or that dreamer of dreams. *For the Lord your God is testing you, to know whether you love the Lord your God with all your heart and with all your soul.* You shall walk after the Lord your God and fear him and keep his commandments and obey his voice, and you shall serve him and hold fast to him But that prophet or that dreamer of dreams shall be put to death, because he has taught rebellion against the Lord your God, who brought you out of the land of Egypt and redeemed you out of the house of slavery, to make you leave the way in which the Lord your God commanded you to walk. So you shall purge the evil from your midst (italics added, ESV).

The Hebrew Bible proclaims that God alone places both evil and good before every person:

Deut. 30:15 See, I have set before you today life and good, death and evil.

Isa. 45:7 I form the light and create darkness; I make well-being and create calamity; I am the LORD who does all these things.

However, humanity not only has a choice, but it can "hit the mark" and not sin.

---

[4] Hedrick, "Visions, Apparitions, and Other Divine Visitations," 25.
[5] Deut. 13:1–5 = Deut. 13:2–6 in the Hebrew Bible.

Gen. 4:7 If you do well, will you not be accepted? And if you do not do well, sin is crouching at the door. Its desire is contrary to you, but you must rule over it.

Therefore, God places permitted obstacles to challenge humankind to overcome those barriers, improve itself, and grow.

To recap, God, without the use of any angels or intermediaries, could have directly created the illusion of Jesus' supposed miracles, the resurrection, and the post-mortem appearances as a test of the Jewish people's fidelity to Him.

Possibility #2:
Satan Performed the Miracles for Jesus (for God)

Another possible reason for the evils that befall the Jewish people in the Hebrew Bible is a supernatural entity commonly referred to as Satan. In the Hebrew Bible, except for 1 Chronicle 21:1; Satan is not the name of a particular character. Instead, it is a common noun connoting or meaning an adversary.[6]

In the Hebrew Bible, as in mainstream Judaism to this day, Satan never appears as Western Christendom has come to know him, as the leader of an "evil empire," an army of hostile spirits who makes war on God and humankind alike. As he first appears in the Hebrew Bible, Satan is not necessarily evil, much less opposed to God. On the contrary, he appears in the book of Numbers and in Job as one of God's obedient servants—a messenger, or *angel*, a word that translates the Hebrew term for messenger (*mal'āk*) into Greek (*angelos*). In Hebrew, the angels were often called "sons of God" (*benē 'elōhīm*) and were envisioned as the hierarchical ranks of a great army, or staff of a royal court.

In the biblical sources, the Hebrew term *satan* describes an adversarial role. It is not the name of a particular character. Although Hebrew storytellers as early as the sixth century BCE occasionally introduced a supernatural character whom they called the *satan*, what they meant was any one of the angels sent by God for the specific purpose of blocking or obstructing human activity. The root *śṭn* means "one who opposes, obstructs, or acts as adversary." (The Greek term

---

[6] Brown, "The Devil in the Details," 203; De Blois, "How to Deal with Satan?," 302; Farrar and Williams, "Diabolical Data," 40–71; Newsom, "Angels," 251; Rabinowitz, "Satan," 72.

diabolos, later translated as "devil," literally means "one who throws something across one's path.")[7]

Rabinowitz writes: "Nowhere is he in any sense a rival to God....In the New Testament Satan emerges as the very personification of the spirit of evil, as an independent personality, the Antichrist."[8] Satan is one of God's many advocates and trusted servants, all of whom are endowed with special powers by God. Jeffrey Gibson, writing in the *Eerdmans Dictionary of the Bible*, states: "This same Satan seems also to have always been known as one who acts only within and under God's permissive will (note the coordination of divine and satanic purposes in Matt. 4:1) and even in his wickedness functions still as a divine servant, wittingly fostering in the world various aspects of God's righteousness."[9] A pertinent example recorded in the Hebrew Bible is:

> Job 1:12 And the LORD said to Satan, "Behold, all that he has is in your hand. Only against him do not lay your hand." So Satan went out from the presence of the LORD.

As God's advocate, Satan's specific task is to act as an obstacle representing God by testing the Jewish people or other righteous people through temptation: "Then Satan stood against Israel and incited David to number Israel" (1 Chron. 21:1, ESV).

In the case of Jesus, Satan's task may have been to deceive the Jewish people into following a false Messiah and a false god, through his supernatural powers. Why? The reason was to serve as a test of the Jewish people's fidelity. According to Scripture, neither God nor Satan wants the Jewish people to fail this test. Without humankind making a choice, there can be no reward or punishment. Therefore, the miracles and events recorded in the Gospels and Acts were deceptions, but Jesus, his disciples, and later believers were unaware of this fact.

Possibility #3:
Satan Performed the Miracles for Jesus (Against God)

A third alternative is that the miracles of Jesus, the empty tomb, and the post-mortem apparitions of Jesus were all wrought by a supernatural entity referred to as Lucifer, Satan, or the Devil. This supernatural "creature"

---

[7] Pagels, *The Origin of Satan*, 39.
[8] Rabinowitz, "Satan," 72.
[9] Gibson, "Satan," 1170; cf. Brown, "The Devil in the Details," 203–8.

differs from the Jewish view by being a fallen angel with free will and is in open rebellion against God. In the Christian Scriptures,[10] he is styled in many ways:

The Tempter

Matt. 4:3 And the tempter came and said to him, "If you are the Son of God, command these stones to become loaves of bread."

1 Thess. 3:5 For this reason, when I could bear it no longer, I sent to learn about your faith, for fear that somehow the tempter had tempted you and our labor would be vain.

The Evil One

Matt. 13:19 When anyone hears the word of the kingdom and does not understand it, the evil one comes and snatches away what has been sown in his heart. This is what was sown along the path.

1 John 5:18 We know that anyone who has born of God does not keep on sinning, but he who was born of God protects him, and the evil one does not touch him.

The Accuser

Rev. 12:10 And I heard a loud voice in heaven, saying, Now have come the salvation and the power and the kingdom of our God and the authority of his Christ have come, for the accuser of our brothers, has been thrown down, who accuses them day and night before our God.

The Enemy

Matt. 13:39 and the enemy who sowed them is the devil. The harvest is the end of the age, and the reapers are angels.

Luke 10:19 Behold, I have given you authority to tread on serpents and scorpions, and over all the power of the enemy, nothing shall hurt you.

---

[10] cf. Arnold, "Satan, Devil," 1077–82; Brown, "The Devil in the Details," 200–27; Farrar and Williams, "Diabolical Data," 40–71; Gibson, "Satan," 1170; Hedrick, "Visions, Apparitions, and Other Divine Visitations," 25.

The Plaintiff

1 Pet. 5:8 Be sober-minded; be watchful. Your adversary the devil prowls around like a roaring lion, seeking someone to devour.

The Prince of Demons

Mark 3:22 And the scribes who came down from Jerusalem were saying, "He is possessed by Beelzebul," and "by the prince of demons he casts out the demons."

Matt. 9:34 But the Pharisees said, "He casts out demons by the prince of demons."

Matt. 12:24 But when the Pharisees heard it, they said, "It is only by Beelzebul, the prince of demons, that this man casts out demons."

The Ruler of This World

John 12:31 Now is the judgment of this world; now will the ruler of this world be cast out.

John 16:11 concerning judgment, because the ruler of this world is judged.

The Prince of the Power of the Air

Eph. 2:2 in which you once walked, following the course of this world, following the prince of the power of the air, the spirit that is now at work in the sons of disobedience.

Therefore, this "supernatural" entity, through his supernatural powers of craftiness, deception, and guile, could be responsible for the misconceptions regarding Jesus' resurrection. Consequently, just as Satan (although not named such) in the guise of the serpent deceived Eve (Gen. 3:1, 13)—so, too, he misled a portion of humanity regarding Jesus. Peter S. Williams calls this possibility the "Deceptive Deon or Daemon Hypothesis."[11]

---

[11] Williams, "Addendum to Getting at Jesus."

Paul, in his second letter to the Thessalonians 2:9–12, puts forth the notion that Satan has diabolical plans for his evil ends:

> The coming of the lawless one is by the activity of Satan with all power and false signs and wonders, and with all wicked deception for those who are perishing, because they refused to love the truth and so be saved. Therefore God sends them a strong delusion, so that they may believe what is false, in order that all may be condemned who did not believe the truth but had pleasure in unrighteousness. (ESV)

Interactions with Christian Apologists

The late Steve Hays offers the opinion that these and other verses (cf. 2 Thess. 2:9–12; Rev. 13) exemplify divine deceptions that "target the reprobate, while the elect are necessarily excluded."[1] Mark Cambron, writing in defense of Jesus' resurrection, points out that some people think that the tomb was never empty, but to the contrary, Jesus' body was still there. He objects, "Surely common sense would refute this argument, for if Christ had not arisen, the devil would have caused His body to have been found sometime during the last two thousand years."[2]

However, an alternative hypothesis is possible. Suppose that Satan had a more devious objective. What could it be, and what would his plan require? There are at least two possible motives:

1. Satan is God's enemy (not a faithful agent) attempting to prevent the public acceptance of the real Christ, who is yet to come (i.e., the first coming of the real Jewish Messiah).
2. Satan is God's enemy (not a faithful agent) attempting to confuse humanity into accepting Jesus as a false Messiah or God in order to keep humans separated from the true and only God Almighty.

Licona, in his *Resurrection of Jesus: A New Historiographical Approach* offers a relevant definition of the Resurrection Hypothesis (RH) that requires diligent consideration:

> *Following a supernatural event of an indeterminate nature and cause, Jesus appeared to a number of people, in individual and group settings and to friends and foes, in no less than an objective vision and perhaps within ordinary vision in his bodily raised corpse.*" [italics in the original][3]

---

[1] Hays, *This Joyful Eastertide*, 45.
[2] Cambron, *Bible Doctrines*, 103–4.
[3] Licona, *Resurrection of Jesus: A New Historiographical Approach*, 583.

Significantly, in his definition, he offers that the resurrection of Jesus was (1) *"a supernatural event"* and (2) *"of an indeterminate nature and cause."*[4] Unfortunately, he fails to interact and engage with supernatural suppositions relating to the nature and cause of the resurrection. Consequently, Licona's omission makes it impossible to fully engage his text.

The sole supernatural option often offered by Christian apologists in support of Jesus' resurrection is deceptive; in reality, it presents a false dilemma. Alternative supernatural and natural explanations actually exist, even if some of them may appear absurd at first sight. Yet, Christian apologists and theologians rarely make known these options. Once people entertain one supernatural hypothesis, they must be open to *every* supernatural hypothesis.

Christian apologists are asked if it is possible that through supernatural means, Paul, the disciples, the apostles, and later believers "unknowingly" became deceived. Their deceptions include believing Jesus (1) was raised from the dead, (2) appeared many times after death, (3) ascended to heaven and sat at the right hand of God, and (4) was the Messiah and even God. Multiple scriptural citations have been presented from the Hebrew Bible and Christian Bible in this text that lends credence to this speculation. If Christian apologists do not accept this supernatural hypothesis, an explanation is required.

In rebuttal, Hays might object, "Since when is there a burden of proof on your opponent to disprove an artificial example which neither you nor your opponent believes?"[5] The response to this hypothetical charge is that divine intervention in the physical world is possible and that the burden is neither more nor less than the burden Christian apologists place on skeptics regarding the resurrection.

There exist at least two deficiencies with this supernatural hypothesis and the Resurrection hypothesis (that God raised Jesus from death). Both are ad hoc and unfalsifiable. However, the supernatural hypothesis is as equally plausible as the Resurrection Hypothesis.

More than a decade ago, Tim and Lydia McGrew wrote a lengthy and especially noteworthy essay, which appeared in *The Blackwell Companion to Natural Theology*. In the section, "Goal and scope of the argument," they state their objective up-front:

> We intend to focus on a single claim for a miraculous event – the bodily resurrection of Jesus of Nazareth circa A.D. 33 (R). We shall

---

[4] Licona, *Resurrection of Jesus: A New Historiographical Approach*, 583.
[5] Hays, *This Joyful Eastertide*, 31.

argue that there is significant positive evidence for R, evidence that cannot be ignored and that must be taken into account in any evaluation of the total evidence for Christianity and for theism.[6]

Strangely, the McGrews completely neglect to engage with the following alternative hypotheses, a supernatural hypothesis involving a miracle by someone other than the Christian God. The McGrews write:

> **Suppose that we assume, though, that the disciples' visions were experientially exactly as if Jesus had been raised bodily from the dead**, making the objective vision theory phenomenologically indistinguishable from a vivid hallucination theory. It makes no sense to attribute such visions to the power of any other being other than the Judeo-Christian God. Zeus, were he to exist, would have no motive for persuading the disciples of Christ's victory over death. **But equally, it makes no sense for the Judeo-Christian God to give them such visions.** A God who is capable of working miracles – which the God of Abraham and Isaac was certainly conceived to be, and which God would have to be in any event in order to give the witnesses these sorts of visions – and whose followers are strictly enjoined to be truthful **would have no conceivable reason for skipping the physical miracle of a resurrection and befuddling His earnest followers into the bargain**.[7]

In response, the idea of "the Judeo-Christian God" is a modern myth. Although they share many attributes, the God of Judaism and the God of Christianity are not the same. A Jewish God would have had a powerful motive for deceiving the disciples into believing in Christ's victory over death: namely, to test the fidelity of the Jewish people. Would they continue to worship God alone when confronted with such a powerful sign, or would they turn Jesus into an idol? Such a test is perfectly compatible with the character of God, as depicted in the Bible. After all, did not God test Abraham (Gen. 22) and permit Satan to test Job (Job 1)? Moreover, while Christians insist that God would never misdirect his people with supernatural signs, even they have to acknowledge that Satan (whom they regard as "the father of lies") could have had a malicious motive of his own for misleading the disciples into believing that Christ had conquered death. Time and time again, lapses into idolatry have separated the Children of Israel from the true God.

---

[6] McGrew and McGrew, "The Argument from Miracles," 627.
[7] McGrew and McGrew, "The Argument from Miracles," 627.

To summarize, at least three alternative supernatural explanations exist for the visions associated with the post-resurrection appearances of Jesus. These explanations include the following: (1) they were caused directly by God (or gods); (2) they were brought about by an angelic power at the command of God; or, as Jordan Aumann astutely observed in the *New Catholic Encyclopedia* 2nd ed., they (3) "could have been the result of diabolic intervention" by an angel in direct rebellion against God.[8] Therefore, there exist several supernatural explanations for Jesus

1. Appearing dead while on the cross,
2. The alleged empty tomb, and,
3. The alleged post-mortem resurrection appearances.

Skeptics challenge Christian apologists to disprove the supernatural alternatives discussed above.

---

[8] Aumann, "Visions," 14:562.

Conclusion

This volume of *The Resurrection and Its Apologetics: Jesus' Death and Burial* engaged and interacted with the first Minimal Fact that Jesus died by crucifixion. No resurrection could occur if Jesus did not die on the cross. Paul, writing in 1 Corinthian 15:3–4, was unambiguous in explaining the importance of three conjoined events, (1) the death, (2) the burial, and (3) the resurrection of Jesus reports:

> For I delivered to you as of first importance what I also received: that Christ died for our sins in accordance with the Scriptures, that he was buried, that he was raised on the third day in accordance with the Scriptures (1 Cor. 15:3–4, ESV).

Presumably, virtually all Christians believe that Jesus died on the cross by crucifixion. Prominent skeptics also acknowledge this reported event. Nonetheless, excluding people advocating the Christ Myth, there exist skeptics and detractors. The Preface mentions, "The theological position of Islam is often ignored in academia." However, there are approximately 1.9 billion Muslims globally, making Islam the second-largest religion behind Christianity. Significantly, Islamic community members reject the belief that Jesus died on the cross. Moreover, Islam also does not accept the thinking that Jesus is the Son of God as espoused in Christian theology.

Several questions require asking:

1. Does the New Testament account provide sufficient evidence that Jesus was brain-dead while on the cross?
2. On a related point, do the accounts recorded in the New Testament provide sufficient evidence to support the argument that Jesus died from crucifixion?
3. Does the Hebrew Bible provide sufficient evidence through theology (Scripture) that Jesus died from crucifixion for the sins of humanity?

Conclusion 255

4. Equally important, do non-Christian sources outside the New Testament support the first Minimal Fact?
5. Does the Shroud of Turin provide evidence to support the first Minimal Fact?
6. Does the Qur'an provide insufficient evidence that Jesus did not die from crucifixion?

An honest reading of the material in this text identifies numerous reasons for rejecting the argument that Jesus died on the cross because of crucifixion:

1. There exists no New Testament proof that Jesus was brain-dead while on the cross.
2. The New Testament provides insufficient evidence to support the argument that Jesus died from crucifixion (disputed by Christian apologists and theologians). The New Testament contains stories about stories written for apologetical and theological reasons.
3. The Gospels were written by anonymous writers (disputed by Christian apologists and theologians), composed about thirty to seventy years after the events they report, lack multiple independent attestations (Matthew copies Mark and Luke copies Matthew and Mark), exemplify embellishments over time, and contain differences, contradictions, and significant omissions. They may contain kernels of historicity. However, it is impossible to determine where history starts and ends. In the opinion of writers on both sides of the aisle, the accounts cannot be harmonized (refuted by Christian apologists and theologians).
4. A literature review found that the historical evidence composed by non-Christians is less convincing than many argue (e.g., Josephus [the *TF*], Tacitus [*Annals* 15:44], and Mara bar Serapion [Letter]). Biblical scholars and historians question the authenticity and accuracy of these and other works. Their sources are unknown, and perhaps their writings were interpolations, edited or redacted (Josephus), and composed years after the events they reported. Until the fourth century, significantly, Christian writers did not cite Josephus.
5. The Islamic argument primarily focuses on the Hebrew Bible, Christian Bible, and the Qur'an. Its theological basis appears logical and well-grounded (Deut. 21:23; Ezek. 18:20 Prov. 15:29; Psalm 20:6; 28:8; 41:2; and Jonah interacting with Matthew

12:40; Isa. 40:28; 44:6; Jer. 10:10; 1 Tim. 1:17) Obviously, Christians do not accept the Qur'an as Scripture.
6. Even if Jesus died on the cross, the manner of his death disqualified him as a *korban* (offering/sacrifice) or "the Messiah," negating Christian theology (Volume 2).
7. The Shroud of Turin is a controversial topic. Believers (authenticists or shroudies) believe, and skeptics and detractors remain unconvinced. At the moment, scholars have more questions than answers on the origin of the Shroud of Turin.

Part II provides cumulative arguments dispelling numerous apologetics about the burial of Jesus and the existence of an empty tomb. Christian commentators acknowledge many of these findings. Contrary to apologists, there exist logical reasons for denying the body of Jesus experienced a burial in Joseph of Arimathea's tomb:

1. Detractors provide cumulative reasons for the challenge of the historicity of Joseph of Arimathea.
2. It was possible to deny the apologetic that the tomb was empty since its location was well known, and anyone could examine it for himself.
3. The disciples could preach the resurrection in Jerusalem if the tomb in Jerusalem were not empty.

Additionally, it was logical and reasonable to expect there was a lack of controversy or interest in the alleged empty tomb by:

1. The Roman leadership,
2. The religious Jewish authorities, and
3. Jesus' followers.

Moreover, even the *Catechism of the Catholic Church* acknowledges that the empty tomb meant nothing:

> "In itself it is not a direct proof of Resurrection; the absence of Christ's body from the tomb could be explained otherwise (cf. John 20:13; Matthew 28:11–15)."

The empty tomb apologetic is a red herring.

Part III examines a speculative topic frequently omitted by Christian apologists: the Supernatural. If engaging in that topic, their arguments are weak and disingenuous. Numerous examples from Scripture provide evidence that Supernatural explanations challenge the Resurrection Hypothesis: God raised Jesus from death. At least three supernatural explanations can explain the alleged death of Jesus on the cross, his burial, and post-mortem resurrection appearances:

1. God deceived the Jewish people as a test.
2. Satan, acting on behalf of God as an angelic agent, deceived the Jewish people as a test.
3. Satan, acting as a malevolent spirit in opposition to God, deceived the Jewish people.

These arguments are unfalsifiable and unverifiable.

Detractors argue that the cumulative evidence does not support the first Minimal Fact. Given all these unknowns, detractors, doubters, and skeptics argue that Scripture and the literature provide questionable support for believing that Jesus died on the cross or was buried in a tomb later reported empty. Significantly, the tomb was *not* empty. Luke and John report strips of linen lying there, and John adds a head cloth. Moreover, detractors argue that the purported crucifixion event, burial, and alleged post-mortem resurrection appearances do not justify a rationale for converting to Christianity.

Volume II of this series will examine Minimal Facts Two, Three, and Four:

2. Jesus' disciples believed he rose and appeared to them.
3. The church persecutor Paul suddenly changed.
4. The skeptic James, brother of Jesus, was suddenly changed.

Readers must be the final judge to determine whether they believe Jesus died on the cross due to crucifixion and was buried in a tomb later reported empty. Even if Jesus died resulting from crucifixion, his death did not atone for the sins of humanity. The manner of his execution was contrary to Torah. Specifically, it violated God's law (Volume II). Moreover, if Jesus received a burial, refuted by the cultural milieu, it does not support the belief of Christian apologists.

The third-day resurrection (discussed in future volumes) is an unverifiable and unfalsifiable theological claim. Since no person witnessed the resurrection, no person can claim that there was a resurrection on the third day. Equally important, from an Islamic view,

Jesus' death, burial, and resurrection prophesied in Matthew 12:40 does not match Jonah.

In conclusion, Jesus died about two thousand years ago, and Christians eagerly await his return. Nonetheless, the first Minimal Fact is unconvincing and unsubstantiated. The cumulative presentation in Volume 1 is logical and coherent. What happened to the body is only known if the reader accepts the New Testament accounts. The current working position of this text is that Jesus had a dishonorable burial.

This writer would like to thank those who took the time to read this text. You, the reader, could have chosen to do other things with your time. Your time is appreciated and respected.

Bibliography

Allen, Nicholas Peter Legh. *Christian Forgery in Jewish Antiquities: Josephus Interrupted.* Newcastle upon Tyne: Cambridge Scholars Publishing, 2020.
———. "Clarifying the Scope of Pre-5th Century C.E. Christian Interpolation in Josephus' Antiquitates Judaica (c. 94 C.E.)," 2015. https://tinyurl.com/2tu83ahu
Allison, Dale. "Explaining the Resurrection: Conflicting Convictions." *Journal for the Study of the Historical Jesus* 3, no. 2 (2005): 117–33. https://doi.org/10.1177/1476869005060235
———. *Resurrecting Jesus: The Earliest Christian Tradition and Its Interpreters.* New York: T & T Clark, 2005.
———. *The Resurrection of Jesus: Apologetics, Criticism, History.* London: T&T Clark, 2021.
Alter, Michael J. The *Resurrection: A Critical Inquiry.* Bloomsbury, IN: Xlibris, 2015.
———. *A Thematic Access-Oriented Bibliography of Jesus's Resurrection.* Eugene, OR: Resource Publications, 2020.
Alter, Michael J., and Darren M. Slade. "Dataset Analysis of English Texts Written on the Topic of Jesus' Resurrection: A Statistical Critique of Minimal Facts Apologetics." *Socio-Historical Examination of Religion and Ministry* 3, no. 2 (2021): 367–92. https://doi.org/10.33929/sherm.2021.vol3.no2.09
Antonacci, Mark. *The Resurrection of the Shroud.* New York: M. Evans, 2000.
Anyabwile, Thabiti. *The Gospel for Muslims: An Encouragement to Share Christ with Confidence.* Chicago: Moody Publishers, 2010.
"The Apostles' Creed." Apostles Creed, 2004. https://tinyurl.com/37trw8xx
Arnold, Clinton E. "Satan, Devil." In *Dictionary of the Later New Testament & Its Developments*, edited by Ralph P. Martin and Peter H. Davids, 1077–82. Downers Grove, IL: IVP, 1997.
Aumann, Jordan. "Visions." In *The New Catholic Encyclopedia*, edited by Thomas Carson, 14:562–63. Detroit: Thompson-Gale, 2003.
Aus, Roger David. *The Death, Burial, and Resurrection of Jesus, and the Death, Burial, and Translation of Moses in Judaic Tradition.* Lanham, MD: University Press of America, 2008.
Babinski, Edward. "What Is 'Missing' from Conservative Christian Apologetics? the Body of Jesus." Biblical Errancy, n.d. https://tinyurl.com/5buy8vmv

Barclay, John M.G. "The Resurrection in Contemporary New Testament Scholarship." In *Resurrection Reconsidered*, edited by Gavin D'Costa, 13–30. Oxford, England: Oneworld Publications, 1996.

Barclay, William. *Barclay's Guide to the New Testament*. Louisville: Westminister John Knox Press, 2008.

Barkay, Gabriel. "The Garden Tomb Was Jesus Buried Here?" *Biblical Archaeology Review* 12, no. 2 (1986): 40–57.

Barker, Dan. *Godless: How an Evangelical Preacher Became One of America's Leading Atheists*. Berkeley, CA: Ulysses Press, 2008.

Barnett, Paul. *Gospel Truth: Answering New Atheist Attacks on the Gospels*. London: SPCK, 2012.

Bater, R. Robert. "Towards a More Biblical View of the Resurrection." *Interpretation: A Journal of Bible and Theology* 23, no. 1 (1969): 47–65. https://doi.org/10.1177/002096436902300104

Bauckham, Richard. *Jesus and the Eyewitnesses: The Gospels as Eyewitness Testimony*. 2nd ed. Grand Rapids: Eerdmans, 2017.

———. *The Testimony of the Beloved Disciple Narrative, History, and Theology in the Gospel of John*. Grand Rapids: Baker Academic, 2007.

Beecher, H. K. "A Definition of Irreversible Coma. Report of the Ad Hoc Committee of the Harvard Medical School to Examine the Definition of Brain Death." *JAMA: The Journal of the American Medical Association* 205, no. 6 (1968): 337–40. https://doi.org/10.1001/jama.205.6.337

Berry, Colin. "A Masterly Demolition of the Hungarian Pray Manuscript?" Shroud of Turin Blog, June 2, 2012. https://tinyurl.com/62ckm9nv

Birdsall, J. Neville. "The Continuing Enigma of Josephus's Testimony about Jesus." *Bulletin of the John Rylands Library* 67, no. 2 (1985): 609–22. https://doi.org/10.7227/bjrl.67.2.3

Blenkinsopp, Joseph. "Life Expectancy in Ancient Palestine." *Scandinavian Journal of the Old Testament* 11, no. 1 (1997): 44–55. https://doi.org/10.1080/09018329708585105

Bock, Darrell L. *Studying the Historical Jesus: A Guide to Sources and Methods*. Grand Rapids: Baker Academic, 2005.

Bock, Darrell L., and Daniel B. Wallace. *Dethroning Jesus: Exposing Popular Culture's Quest to Unseat the Biblical Christ*. Nashville: Thomas Nelson, 2010.

Bode, Edward Lynn. *The First Easter Morning: The Gospel Accounts of the Women's Visit to the Tomb of Jesus*. Rome: Biblical Institute Press, 1970.

Boff, Leonardo. *The Question of the Faith in the Resurrection of Jesus*. Translated by Luis Runde. Chicago: Franciscan Herald, 1971.

Boi, M. "Pollen on the Shroud of Turin: The Probable Trace Left by Anointing and Embalming." *Archaeometry* 59, no. 2 (2012): 316–30. https://doi.org/https://doi.org/10.1111/arcm.12269

Bondeson, Jan. *Buried Alive: The Terrifying History of Our Most Primal Fear*. New York: Barnes & Noble, 2006.

Borrini, Matteo, and Luigi Garlaschelli. "A BPA Approach to the Shroud of Turin." *Journal of Forensic Sciences* 64, no. 1 (2018): 137–43. https://doi.org/10.1111/1556-4029.13867

Bostock, Gerald. "Do We Need an Empty Tomb?" *The Expository Times* 105, no. 7 (1994): 201–5. https://doi.org/10.1177/001452469410500703

Botelho, Octavio da Cunha. "The Endless Dubiety of the Testimonium Flavium." Academia.edu, June 2020.

Bousset, Wilhelm. *Kyrios Christos: Geschichte Des Christusglaubens*. 3rd ed. Göttingen: Vandenhoeck & Ruprecht, 1926.

Bowman, Robert M. "Tacitus, Suetonius, and the Historical Jesus." Biblical Christianity, February 17, 2017. https://tinyurl.com/5cczvs72

Boyd, Gregory A., and Paul R. Eddy. *Lord or Legend?: Wrestling with the Jesus Dilemma*. Grand Rapids: Baker, 2007.

Broer, Ingo. *Urgemeinde Und Das Grab Jesu Eine Analyse Der Grablegungsgeschichte Im Neuen Testament*. München: Kösel-Verl, 1972.

Broussard, John. "Which Side of Jesus Was Pierced?" The Compass, March 23, 2022. https://tinyurl.com/mvnzsmxn

Brown, Derek R. "The Devil in the Details: A Survey of Research on Satan in Biblical Studies." *Currents in Biblical Research* 9, no. 2 (2011): 200–227. https://doi.org/10.1177/1476993x10363030

Brown, Raymond E. *The Community of the Beloved Disciple*. London: G. Chapman, 1979.

———. *Death of the Messiah*. New York: Doubleday, 1994.

Browning, W.R.F. "Resurrection of Jesus." In *A Dictionary of the Bible*, 320–21. Oxford: Oxford University Press, 1996.

Bruce, F. F. *Jesus and Christian Origins Outside the New Testament*. London: Hodder and Stoughton, 1984.

Bulst, Werner. "Resurrection, Fundamental Theology (Apologetics)." In *Sacramentum Mundi: An Encyclopedia of Theology*, edited by Karl Rahner, 5:328–29. New York: Herder and Herder, 1970.

Butler, Joseph. *The Analogy of Religion, Natural and Revealed, to the Constitution and Course of Nature. to Which Are Added Two Brief Dissertations: I. Of Personal Identity. II. of the Nature of Virtue. by Joseph Butler, LL. D. Now Lord Bishop of Durham*. 3rd ed. London: printed for John and Paul Knapton, at the Crown in Ludgate Street, 1745.

Cambron, Mark G. *Bible Doctrines: Beliefs That Matter*. Grand Rapids: Zondervan, 1954.

Capps, Donald. *Jesus: A Psychological Biography*. St. Louis: Chalice Press, 2000.

Carnley, Peter. *The Structure of Resurrection Belief*. Oxford: Clarendon Press, 1987.

Carrier, Richard. "Josephus on Jesus? Why You Can't Cite Opinions before 2014." Richard Carrier, February 15, 2017. tinyurl.com/mta2sww9

———. *On the Historicity of Jesus: Why We Might Have Reason for Doubt*. Sheffield: Sheffield Phoenix Press, 2014.

———. "The Prospect of a Christian Interpolation in Tacitus, Annals 15.44." *Vigiliae Christianae* 68, no. 3 (2014): 264–83. https://doi.org/10.1163/15700720-12341171

———. "Why I Don't Buy the Resurrection Story." Internet Infidels, August 2006. https://tinyurl.com/vkv72fk6

Carson, D. A. *The Gospel According to John*. Leicester, England: Apollos, 1991.

Carson, D. A., and Douglas J. Moo. *An Introduction to the New Testament*. 2nd ed. Grand Rapids: Zondervan, 2005.

Casabianca, Tristan. "The Ongoing Historical Debate about the Shroud of Turin: The Case of the Pray Codex." *The Heythrop Journal* 62, no. 5 (2021): 789–802. https://doi.org/10.1111/heyj.13929

Casabianca, Tristan, E. Marinelli, G. Pernagallo, and B. Torrisi. "Radiocarbon Dating of the Turin Shroud: New Evidence from Raw Data." *Archaeometry* 61, no. 5 (2019): 1223–31. https://doi.org/10.1111/arcm.12467

Casey, Maurice. *Jesus of Nazareth: An Independent Historian's Account of His Life and Teaching*. London: T & T Clark, 2010.

Catechism of the Catholic Church: With Modifications from the Editio Typica. New York: Doubleday, 2003.

Charlesworth, James H. *An Essential Guide to the Historical Jesus: An Essential Guide*. Nashville: Abingdon Press, 2010.

———. *Jesus within Judaism: New Light from Existing Archaeological Discoveries*. London: SPCK, 1988.

Chilton, Bruce D. "The Logic of Jesus' Resurrection." *The Bible and Interpretation*, October 2019. https://tinyurl.com/bdf582db

———. *Resurrection Logic: How Jesus' First Followers Believed God Raised Him from the Dead*. Waco: Baylor University Press, 2019.

Choi, Charles Q. "Shroud of Turin Is a Fake, Bloodstains Suggest." LiveScience. Purch, July 18, 2018. https://tinyurl.com/4rtt6ta7

Ciccone, Gaetano. "La Truffa Dei Pollini. Il Dossier Completo." La Sindone di Torino, June 22, 2011. http://sindone.weebly.com/pollini1.html

Coale, Ansley J., and Paul Demeny. *Regional Model Life Tables and Stable Populations*. Paris: Academic Press, 1983.

Conway, Colleen M. *Men and Women in the Fourth Gospel: Gender and Johannine Characterization*. Atlanta: Society of Biblical Literature, 1999.

Coogan, Michael D., Carol Ann Newsom, and Marc Zvi Brettler, eds. *The New Oxford Annotated Bible with the Apocrypha*. 5th ed. Oxford: Oxford University Press, 2018.

Cook, John Granger. "Crucifixion and Burial." *New Testament Studies* 57, no. 2 (2011): 193–213. https://doi.org/10.1017/s0028688510000214

Cook, Michael J. *Modern Jews Engage the New Testament: Enhancing Jewish Well-Being in a Christian Environment*. Woodstock, VT: Jewish Lights Publishing, 2008.

Corduan, Winfried. *No Doubt about It: The Case for Christianity.* Nashville: Broadman and Holman, 1997.
Corfield, Richard. "Chemistry in the Face of Belief." Chemistry World, December 22, 2013. https://tinyurl.com/4ywzpz84
Corley, Kathleen E. "Women and Crucifixion and Burial of Jesus." *Forum*, New, 1, no. 1 (1998): 181–217.
Craig, William Lane. *Apologetics: An Introduction.* Chicago: Moody Press, 1984.
———. *Assessing the New Testament Evidence for the Historicity of the Resurrection of Jesus.* Lewiston, NY: Edwin Mellin Press, 1989.
———. "Did Jesus Rise From the Dead?" In *Jesus under Fire*, edited by Michael J. Wilkins and James Porter Moreland, 143–76. Grand Rapids: Zondervan, 1995.
———. "The Historicity of the Empty Tomb of Jesus." *New Testament Studies* 31, no. 1 (1985): 39–67. https://doi.org/10.1017/s0028688500012911
———. "On Doubts about the Resurrection." *Modern Theology* 6, no. 1 (1989): 53–75. https://doi.org/10.1111/j.1468-0025.1989.tb00207.x
———. *Reasonable Faith: Christian Truth and Apologetics.* 3rd ed. Wheaton: Crossway Books, 2008.
———. *The Son Rises the Historical Evidence for the Resurrection of Jesus.* Chicago: Moody, 1981.
Cranfield, C.E.B. "The Resurrection of Jesus Christ." *The Expository Times* 101, no. 6 (1990): 167–72. https://doi.org/10.1177/001452469010100603
Creed, J. M. "The Conclusion of the Gospel According to Saint Mark." *The Journal of Theological Studies* os-XXXI, no. 2 (1930): 175–80. https://doi.org/10.1093/jts/os-xxxi.2.175
Crispino, Dorothy. "The Height of Christ - Shroud," *Studies in Sindonology*, no 1 (1979). https://www.shroud.com/pdfs/ssiheight.pdf
Crossan, John Dominic. *The Birth of Christianity: Discovering What Really Happened in the Years Immediately after the Execution of Jesus / John Dominic Crossan.* New York: HarperSanFrancisco, 1998.
———. *The Cross That Spoke: The Origins of the Passion Narrative.* San Francisco: Harper & Row, 1998.
———. "Historical Jesus as Risen Lord." In *The Jesus Controversy: Perspectives in Conflict*, 1–47. Harrisburg, PA: Trinity Press International, 1999.
———. *Who Killed Jesus?: Exposing the Roots of Anti-Semitism in the Gospel Story of the Death of Jesus.* San Francisco: HarperSanFrancisco, 1994.
Cumming, Joseph L. "Did Jesus Die on the Cross? The History of Reflection on the End of His Earthly Life in Sunni Tarsier Literature." Academia.edu. January 2001. https://tinyurl.com/msks3cy6
———. "Did Jesus Die on the Cross? Reflections in Muslim Commentaries." In *Muslim and Christian Reflections on Peace: Divine and Human Dimensions*, edited by John Dudley Woodberry and Osman Zümrüt, 32–50. Lanham, MD: University Press of America, 2005.

Damon, P. E., D. J. Donahue, B. H. Gore, A. L. Hatheway, and A. J. Jull. "Radiocarbon Dating of the Shroud of Turin." *Nature* 337, no. 6208 (1989): 611–15. https://doi.org/10.1038/337611a0

Danin, Avinoam. "Pressed Flowers Where Did the Shroud of Turin Originate? A Botanical Quest." *Eretz Magazine*, (1997). https://tinyurl.com/4kwf8vr9

De Blois, Kees F. "How to Deal with Satan?" *The Bible Translator* 37, no. 3 (1986): 301–9. https://doi.org/10.1177/026009358603700301

DeLong, Russell V. *Resurrection: Myth or Fact?* Kansas City, MO: Beacon Hill Press of Kansas City, 1980.

Derrett, J. Duncan M. "Financial Aspects of the Resurrection." In *The Empty Tomb: Jesus beyond the Grave*, edited by Robert M. Price and Jeffery Jay Lowder, 383–409. Amherst, NY: Prometheus Books, 2005.

DeSilva, David A. *Introduction to the New Testament: Contexts, Methods, and Ministry*. Downers Grove, IL: Intervarsity Press, 2018.

Di Lazzaro, Paolo. "A Ray of Light on the Shroud of Turin Proc Fiat Lux - Researchgate." Proceedings of the International Conference Fiat Lux - Let there be light" Rome, June 3, 2018. https://tinyurl.com/3scpxt98

———. "Let No-One Who Is Not a Mathematician Read My Principles." *Sidon*, no. 2 (2020): 65–75.

Di Lazzaro, Paolo, Anthony C. Atkinson, Paola Iacomussi, Marco Riani, Marco Ricci, and Peter Wadhams. "Statistical and Proactive Analysis of an Inter-Laboratory Comparison: The Radiocarbon Dating of the Shroud of Turin." *Entropy* 22, no. 9 (2020): 926. doi.org/10.3390/e22090926

Dodd, C. H. *Historical Tradition in the Fourth Gospel*. Cambridge: Cambridge University Press, 1963.

Doherty, Earl. *Jesus: Neither God Nor Man: The Case for a Mythical Jesus*. Ottawa: Age of Reason Publications, 2009.

Drake, Mack, Andrew Bernard, and Eugene Hessel. "Brain Death." *Surgical Clinics of North America* 97, no. 6 (2017): 1255–73. https://doi.org/10.1016/j.suc.2017.07.001

Drews, Arthur. *The Witnesses to the Historicity of Jesus ... Translated by Joseph McCabe from Die Christusmythe.* London: Watts, 1912.

Dunn, James D.G. *The Evidence for Jesus: The Impact of Scholarship on Our Understanding of How Christianity Began*. London: SCM, 1990.

———. *Jesus Remembered*. Grand Rapids: Eerdmans, 2003.

Eddy, Paul Rhodes, and Gregory A. Boyd. *The Jesus Legend: A Case for the Historical Reliability of the Synoptic Jesus Tradition*. Grand Rapids: Baker Academic, 2007.

Edlow, Brian L., and Hannah C. Kinney. "Defining the Boundary between Life and Death: New Insights from Neuropathology." *Journal of Neuropathology & Experimental Neurology* 82, no. 1 (2022): 3–5. https://doi.org/10.1093/jnen/nlac109

Edwards, James R. *The Gospel According to Mark*. Grand Rapids: Eerdmans, 2002.

Ehrman, Bart D. "Could Jews Bury Crucified Victims? Most-Commented Blog Post: #7." The Bart Ehrman Blog, January 1, 2018. https://tinyurl.com/2s4z3h7h

———. *How Jesus Became God: The Exaltation of a Jewish Preacher from Galilee*. New York: HarperOne, 2014.

———. "Women at the Tomb." The Bart Ehrman Blog, April 4, 2014. https://ehrmanblog.org/women-at-the-tomb/

Ercoline, W. R., R. C. Downs, and J. P. Jackson. "IEEE 1982 Proceedings of the International Conference on Cybernetics and Society, October 28, 29 & 30, 1982," 576–79. Seattle, Washington, 1982.

Evans, Craig A. *Jesus and His Contemporaries: Comparative Studies*. Boston: Brill, 2001.

———. "The Resurrection of Jesus in the Light of Jewish Burial Practices." Houston Christian University, May 4, 2016. tinyurl.com/3khj2unv

Fales, Evan. "Successful Defense?" *Philosophia Christi* 3, no. 1 (2001): 7–35. https://doi.org/10.5840/pc2001312

Fanti, Giulo, B. Schwortz, A. Accetta, B. J. Buenaobra, M. Carreira, F. Cheng, F. Crosilla, R. Dinegar, and H. Felzmann. "Evidences for Testing Hypotheses about the Body Image Formation of the Turin Shroud." In *Proceedings of the Third Dallas International Conference on the Shroud of Turin, Dallas, TX*. Dallas, Texas, 2005. shroud.com/pdfs/doclist.pdf

Fanti, Giulo, Emanuela Marinelli, and Alessandro Cagnazzo. "Computerized Anthropometric Analysis of the Man of the Turin Shroud," 1999. https://www.shroud.com/pdfs/marineli.pdf

Farey, Hugh. "British Society for the Turin Shroud Newsletter No. 83," December 2016.

———. "British Society for the Turin Shroud Newsletter, Newsletter No. 79," June 2014.

———. "The Medieval Shroud 2." Academia.edu, January 21, 2019. https://tinyurl.com/2ja73bzt

Farnell, F. David. "Contemporary 21st Century Evangelical NT Criticism Who Do Not Learn from the Lessons of History." Defending Inerrancy, May 30, 2014. https://defendinginerrancy.com/learn-lessons-history/

Farrar, Thomas J., and Guy J. Williams. "Diabolical Data: A Critical Inventory of New Testament Satanology." *Journal for the Study of the New Testament* 39, no. 1 (2016): 40–71. https://doi.org/10.1177/0142064x16660911

Feldman, Louis H. "Josephus (CE 37–c. 100)." In *The Cambridge History of Judaism* 3, edited by William Horbury and W. D. Davies, 3:901–22. Cambridge: Cambridge University Press, 1999.

———. "On the Authenticity of the Testimonium Flavianum Attributed to Josephus." In *New Perspectives on Jewish-Christian Relations in Honor of David Berger*, edited by Elisheva Carlebach and Jacob B. Schacter, 14–30. Leiden: Brill, 2012.

Feldman, Louis H., and Gohei Hata. "Introduction." In *Josephus, Judaism and Christianity*, edited by Louis H. Feldman, 23–67. Detroit: Wayne State University Press, 1987.
Ferguson, Matthew Wade. "Knocking out the Pillars of the 'Minimal Facts' Apologetic." Κέλσος, June 29, 2013. https://tinyurl.com/5n7fu5x2
Fernandes, Phil. *The Atheist Delusion: A Christian Response to Christopher Hitchens and Richard Dawkins*. United States: Xulon Press, 2009.
Filas, Francis L. *The Dating of the Shroud of Turin from Coins of Pontius Pilate*. 2nd ed. Youngtown, AZ: Cogan Productions, 1982.
Fitzwater, P. B. *Christian Theology, a Systematic Presentation*. 2nd ed. Grand Rapids: Eerdmans, 1948.
Flood, Edmund. *The Jesus Story*. New York: Sheed & Ward, 1973.
———. *The Resurrection.* New York: Paulist Press, 1973.
Fodor, James. "'Can a Scientist Believe the Resurrection' by John Lennox: A Critique." The Godless Theist, April 22, 2014. tinyurl.com/5n7esfms
———. *Unreasonable Faith: How William Lane Craig Overstates the Case for Christianity*. S.l.: Hyptia Press, 2022.
Fortna, Robert T. "Mark Intimates/Matthew Defends the Resurrection." *Foundations & Facets Forum* 10, no. 3-4 (1994): 197–218.
Frame, John M. "Apologetics." In *Evangelical Dictionary of Biblical Theology*, edited by Walter A. Elwell, 57–58. Grand Rapids: Baker Books, 1996.
France, R. T. *The Evidence for Jesus*. Downers Grove, IL: InterVarsity Press, 1996.
Frantzman, Seth J., and Ruth Kark. "General Gordon, the Palestine Exploration Fund and the Origins of 'Gordon's Calvary' in the Holy Land." *Palestine Exploration Quarterly* 140, no. 2 (2008): 119–36. https://doi.org/10.1179/003103208x312872
Freeman, Charles. "The Origins of the Shroud of Turin." *History Today*, November 2014. https://tinyurl.com/2u48h9b7
Freer-Waters, Rachel A, and A J Timothy Jull. "Investigating a Dated Piece of the Shroud of Turin: Radiocarbon." Cambridge University Press, July 18, 2016. https://tinyurl.com/63m97wph
Frier, Bruce. "Roman Life Expectancy: The Pannonian Evidence." *Phoenix* 37, no. 4 (1983): 328–44. https://doi.org/10.2307/1088154.
———. "Roman Life Expectancy: Ulpian's Evidence." *Harvard Studies in Classical Philology* 86 (1982): 213–51. https://doi.org/10.2307/311195.
Geisler, Norman L. *Baker Encyclopedia of Christian Apologetics*. Grand Rapids: Baker Books, 1999.
Gibson, Jeffrey B. "Satan." In *Eerdmans Dictionary of the Bible*, edited by Jeffrey B. Gibson and David Noel Freedman, 1169–70. Grand Rapids: Eerdmans, 2000.
Godfrey, Neil. "The Jesus Reference in Josephus: Its Ad Hoc Doctoring and Various Manuscript Lines." Vridar, March 6, 2006. https://vridar.org/2009/03/06/josephus/

Goguel, Maurice. *Jesus the Nazarene- Myth of History?* Translated by Frederick Stephens. New York: D. Appleton, 1926.

Goldberg, Gary J. "The Coincidences of the Emmaus Narrative of Luke and the Testimonium of Josephus." *Journal for the Study of the Pseudepigrapha* 7, no. 13 (1995): 59–77. https://doi.org/10.1177/095182079500001304

———. "Critique of the Argument of Meier in *A Marginal Jew* in Light of the New Evidence." n.d. https://www.josephus.org/meierCrt.htm

———. "Josephus's Paraphrase Style and the Testimonium Flavianum." *Journal for the Study of the Historical Jesus* 20, no. 1 (2021): 1–32. https://doi.org/10.1163/17455197-bja10003

———. "The Mystery of the Testimonium Flavianum." The Mystery of The Testimonium of Josephus, n.d. https://www.josephus.org/testhist.htm

———. "Testimonium-Luke Comparison Table." Testimonium-Luke Comparison Table, n.d. http://www.josephus.org/compTable.htm

Goodyear, Francis R. *Tacitus*. Cambridge: Cambridge University Press, 1970.

Gormley, Rick. "Objections to the Bishops Who Found Evidence That What Is Now the Turin Shroud Is a Fake.' Objections to the D'Arcis Memorandum." Testreligion.com, n.d.

Goulder, Michael. "The Baseless Fabric of a Vision." In *Resurrection Reconsidered*, edited by Gavin D'Costa, 48–61. Oxford, England: Oneworld Publications, 1996.

———. "Did Jesus of Nazareth Rise from the Dead?" In *Resurrection: Essays in Honour of Leslie Houlden*, edited by Stephen C. Barton and Graham Stanton, 58–68. London: SPCK, 1994.

———. "The Empty Tomb." *Theology* 79, no. 670 (1976): 206–14. https://doi.org/10.1177/0040571x7607900404

———. "Jesus' Resurrection and Christian Origins: A Response to N.T. Wright." *Journal for the Study of the Historical Jesus* 3, no. 2 (2005): 187–95. https://doi.org/10.1177/1476869005058195

Gove, Harry E. "Dating the Turin Shroud—an Assessment." *Radiocarbon* 32, no. 1 (1990): 87–92. https://doi.org/10.1017/s0033822200039990

———. "Radiocarbon-Dating the Shroud." *Nature* 333, no. 6169 (1988): 110. https://doi.org/10.1038/333110c0

Grant, Michael. *Greek and Roman Historians Information and Misinformation*. London: Routledge, Taylor & Francis Group, 2006.

Greear, J. D. *Breaking the Islam Code*. Eugene, OR: Harvest House, 2010.

Greer, D. M., P. N. Varelas, S. Haque, and E. F.M. Wijdicks. "Variability of Brain Death Determination Guidelines in Leading US Neurologic Institutions." *Neurology* 70, no. 4 (2007): 284–89. https://tinyurl.com/3xbbm8jx

Groothuis, Douglas. *Christian Apologetics: A Comprehensive Case for Biblical Faith*. Downers Grove, IL: IVP, 2011.

Guscin, Mark. "British Society for the Turin Shroud Newsletter, Newsletter #50," November 1999.

———. *The Oviedo Cloth*. Cambridge: Lutterworth Press, 1998.

Gwynne, Paul. "The Fate of Jesus' Body: Another Decade of Debate." *Colloquium* 32, no. 1 (2000): 3–21.
Habermas, Gary R. *The Resurrection of Jesus*. Grand Rapids: Baker Book, 1980.
Habermas, Gary R., and Michael R. Licona. *The Case for the Resurrection of Jesus*. Grand Rapids: Kregel, 2004.
Hachlili, Rachel. *Jewish Funerary Customs, Practices and Rites in the Second Temple Period*. Leiden: Brill, 2005.
Hachlili, Rachel, and Ann Killebrew. "Was the Coin-on-Eye Custom a Jewish Burial Practice in the Second Temple Period?" *The Biblical Archaeologist* 46, no. 3 (1983): 147–53. doi.org/10.2307/3209825
Hanhart, Karel. *The Open Tomb: A New Approach, Mark's Passover Haggadah (± 72 C.E.)*. Collegeville, MN: Liturgical Press, 1995.
Hare, Douglas R.A. *Matthew*. Louisville: John Knox Press, 1993.
Hart, Vinny. "Did First Century Christians Believe in Miracles Because They Were Pre-Scientific?" Tough Questions Answered, July 30, 2009. https://tinyurl.com/47jmjyhj
Hays, Steve. *The Joyful Eastertide: A Critical Review of the Empty Tomb*, 2006. https://tinyurl.com/mcnmnsv3
Heil, John Paul. *The Death and Resurrection of Jesus: A Narrative-Critical Reading of Matthew 26-28*. Minneapolis: Fortress Press, 1991.
Hedrick, Charles W. "Visions, Apparitions, and Other Divine Visitations." *Fourth R* 22, no. 6 (2009): 25.
Hendrickx, Herman. *The Resurrection Narratives of the Synoptic Gospels*. London: Chapman, 1984.
Hengel, Martin. *Crucifixion in the Ancient World and the Folly of the Message of the Cross*. Translated by John Bowden. London: SCM Press, 1977.
Hillar, Marian. "Flavius Josephus and His Testimony Concerning the Historical Jesus." In *Essays in the Philosophy of Humanism*, 13:1–29, 2005.
Holding, James Patrick. "Refuting 'Remsberg's List.'" In *Shattering the Christ Myth*, edited by James Patrick Holding, 89–94. Xulon, 2008.
Holding, James Patrick. "Tekton Apologetics." Tacitus and Jesus. Christ Myth refuted. Did Jesus exist?, n.d. tektonics.org/jesusexist/tacitus.php
Hoover, Roy W. "A Contest between Orthodoxy & Veracity." In *Jesus' Resurrection: Fact or Figment?: A Debate between William Lane Craig & Gerd Lüdemann*, edited by Paul Copan and Ronald K. Tacelli, 124–46. Downers Grove, IL: InterVarsity Press, 2000.
Hopper, Paul J. "A Narrative Anomaly in Josephus: Jewish Antiquities Xviii:63." In *Linguistics and Literary Studies: Interfaces, Encounters, Transfers*, edited by Monika Fludernik and Daniel Jacob, 147–70. Berlin Germany: De Gruyter, 2014.
Ilan, Tal. *Lexicon of Jewish Names in Late Antiquity*. Tübingen: Mohr Siebeck, 2012.
Imran, Adil Nizamuddin. *Christ Jesus, the Son of Mary: A Muslim Perspective*. Lombard, IL: Book of Signs Foundation, 2009.

Jones, Stephen E. "The Pray Manuscript (or Codex)." The Pray Manuscript (or Codex), January 11, 2010. https://tinyurl.com/u728a89j

Jones, Timothy Paul. "Apologetics: Is It Possible That Jesus' Body Was Left on the Cross?" Timothy Paul Jones, April 6, 2012. tinyurl.com/yzpw2ee6

Joseph, Simon J. "The Shroud and the Historical Jesus Challenging the Disciplinary Divide," 2012. https://www.shroud.com/pdfs/sjoseph.pdf

Josephus, Flavius. *Josephus: Complete Works*. Translated by William Whiston. Grand Rapids: Kregel, 1960.

Keener, Craig S. *The Gospel of John: A Commentary*. Vol. 2. Grand Rapids: Baker Academic, 2012.

———. *The Historical Jesus of the Gospels*. Grand Rapids: Eerdmans, 2009.

Keller, James A. "Response to Davis." *Faith and Philosophy* 7, no. 1 (1990): 112–16. https://doi.org/10.5840/faithphil1990713

Kelly, Anthony. *The Resurrection Effect: Transforming Christian Life and Thought*. Maryknoll, NY: Orbis Books, 2008.

Kesich, Veselin. *The First Day of the New Creation: The Resurrection and the Christian Faith*. Crestwood, NY: St Vladimir's Seminary Press, 1982.

Khan, Arif. "'The Oviedo Cloth by Mark Guscin' Review of Book." The Review of Religions, May 14, 2015. https://tinyurl.com/ywn9e2h5

King, Lauren A. "The New Testament Account of the Resurrection - Is It Credible?" *Quaker Religious Thought* 84, no. 2. (January 1. 1995): 5–30. https://tinyurl.com/33r5hmze

Kirby, Peter. Cornelius Tacitus, 2001. https://tinyurl.com/4ezj7nff

———. "Josephus and Jesus: The Testimonium Flavianum Question." Josephus and Jesus: The testimonium flavianum question, 2001. http://earlychristianwritings.com/testimonium.html

———. "Peter Kirby Tomb Rebuttal1: Rebuttal to Tomb Burial by Joseph of Arimathea." Internet Infidels, n.d. https://tinyurl.com/w4k7ha8s

Koester, Craig A. "Hearing, Seeing and Believing in the Gospel of John." *Biblica* 70, no. 3 (1989): 327–48.

Kohlbeck, Joseph A., and Eugenia L. Nitowski. "New Evidence May Explain Image on Shroud of Turin: Chemical Test Link Shroud to Jerusalem." *Biblical Archaeology Review* 12, no. 4 (1986): 18–29. https://tinyurl.com/2p8r7rxc

Komarnitsky, Kris D. *Doubting Jesus' Resurrection: What Happened in the Black Box?* 2nd ed. Drapper, UT: Stone Arrow Books, 2014.

Kroll, Woodrow. "Seeing the Glory of the Lord Around Us, Part 2." Backtothebible, November 25, 2005. https://www.backtothebible.org/

Köstenberger, Andreas J., L. Scott Kellum, and Charles L. Quarles. *The Cradle, the Cross, and the Crown: An Introduction to the New Testament*. Nashville: B & H Academic, 2016.

Ladd, George Eldon. *A Theology of the New Testament*. Grand Rapids: Eerdmans, 1974.

Lake, Kirsopp. *The Historical Evidence for the Resurrection*. London: Williams & Norgate, 1907.

Lampe, G.W.H., and Donald M. MacKinnon. *The Resurrection: A Dialogue Arising from Broadcasts by G.W.H. Lampe and D.M. MacKinnon.* Edited by William Purcell. London: A. R. Mowbray, 1966.

Lans, Birgit van der, and Jan N. Bremmer. "Tacitus and the Persecution of the Christians: An Invention of Tradition?" *Eirene-Studia Graeca et Latina* 53, no. 1–2 (2017): 299–331.

Lataster, Raphael. *Questioning the Historicity of Jesus: Why a Philosophical Analysis Elucidates the Historical Discourse.* Leiden: Brill, 2019.

———. *There Was No Jesus, There Is No God: A Scholarly Examination of the Scientific, Historical, and Philosophical Evidence & Arguments for Monotheism.* United States: Raphael C. Lataster, 2013.

Lavoie, Gilbert R. *Resurrected Tangible Evidence That Jesus Rose from the Dead; Shroud's Message Revealed 2000 Years Later.* Allen, TX: More, 2000.

Law, Stephen. "Skeptical Theism - Quick Primer for the Uninitiated." Center for Inquiry. Center for Inquiry, May 8, 2015. https://tinyurl.com/a6t5c7av

Lefebvre, Matt. "Arguments for God's Existence-the Argument from Jesus' Resurrection (Part 2)." Warranted Belief, February 10, 2012. https://tinyurl.com/5n6ck5rp

Leidner, Harold. *The Fabrication of the Christ Myth.* Tampa, FL: Survey Books, 2000.

Léon-Dufour, Xavier. *Resurrection and the Message of Easter: Engl. Transl.* London: Chapman, 1974.

Lewis, Ariane, Azza Bakkar, and Elana Kreiger-Benson. "Determination of Death by Neurologic Criteria around the World." *Neurology* 95, no. 3 (2020). https://doi.org/10.1212/wnl.0000000000009888

Licona, Michael R. *Paul Meets Muhammad: A Christian-Muslim Debate on the Resurrection.* Grand Rapids: Baker Books, 2006.

———. *The Resurrection of Jesus: A New Historiographical Approach.* Downers Grove, IL: IVP Academic, 2010.

———. "Using the Death of Jesus to Defeat Islam." *The Journal of the International Society of Christian Apologetics* 2, no. 1 (2009): 87–110.

Loftus, John W., and Robert M. Price, eds. *Varieties of Jesus Mythicism: Did He Even Exist?* USA: Hypatia, 2021.

Loke, Andrew ern tern. *Investigating the Resurrection of Jesus Christ: A New Transdisciplinary Approach.* Abingdon, Oxon: Routledge, 2020.

Lombatti, Antonio. "Doubts Concerning the Coins Over the Eye." *British Society for the Turin Shroud Newsletter*, no. 45 (1997): 35–37.

Lorenzen, Thorwald. *Resurrection and Discipleship: Interpretative Models, Biblical Reflections, Theological Consequences.* New York: Orbis Books, 1995.

Lorusso, Salvatore, Chiara Matteucci, Tania China, and Laura Solla. "The Shroud of Turin Between History and Science: An Ongoing Debate." *Conservation Science in Cultural Heritage* 11, no. 1 (2011): 113–52. https://doi.org/https://doi.org/10.6092/issn.1973-9494/2695.

Lowder, Jeffrey Jay. "Historical Evidence and the Empty Tomb Story: A Reply to William Lane Craig." In *The Empty Tomb: Jesus Beyond the Grave*, edited by Robert M. Price and Jeffery Jay Lowder, 261–306. Amherst, NY: Prometheus Books, 2005.

———. "Jeff Lowder Jury Chap5." Internet Infidels." Internet Infidels, May 15, 2000. https://tinyurl.com/d7bx3btx

Lyons, William. "On the Life and Death of Joseph of Arimathea." *Journal for the Study of the Historical Jesus* 2, no. 1 (2004): 29–53. https://doi.org/10.1177/147686900400200102

Lüdemann, Gerd. "Rebuttal Two." In *Jesus' Resurrection: Fact or Figment?: A Debate Between William Lane Craig & Gerd Lüdemann*, edited by Paul Copan and Ronald K. Tacelli, 60–62. Downers Grove, IL: InterVarsity Press, 2000.

———. *The Resurrection of Christ: A Historical Inquiry*. Amherst, NY: Prometheus Books, 2004.

Lüdemann, Gerd, and Alf Özen. *What Really Happened to Jesus: A Historical Approach to the Resurrection*. Translated by John Bowden. Louisville: Westminster John Knox Press, 1995.

Macquarrie, John. *Principles of Christian Theology*. New York: Scribner, 1977.

Manserigi, Flavia. "Pseudo-Neutral." *Sidon*, no. 1 (September 2020): 20–23. https://tinyurl.com/2bnnkcmt

Margolis, David. "'The Resurrection of Jesus Christ.'" *Debate Between David Margolis and Richard Spencer*. Lecture presented at the Debate Between David Margolis and Richard Spencer, 2006.

Marinelli, Emanuela. "The Question of Pollen Grains on the Shroud of Turin and the Sudarium of Oviedo." Academia.edu, August 28, 2014. https://tinyurl.com/2a6wjrjx

Marino, Joe. "Does the Hungarian Pray Manuscript Indicate the Presence of Jesus' Shroud in the 12th Century? -- an English-Language Bibliography." Academia.edu, November 2022. tinyurl.com/2tsz54zz

———. "Evaluation of the Proposed Existence of Lepton Coins on the Turin Shroud: An Annotated English-Language Bibliography." Academia.edu, January 1, 2021. https://tinyurl.com/2pa683rw

———. "Possible Post-Biblical and Pre-1350s References in History to the Shroud of Jesus - an English-Language Bibliography." Academia.edu, January 1, 2021. https://tinyurl.com/bdhxj73k

Markwardt, Mark. "Modern Scholarship and the History of the Turin Shroud," 2014. https://www.shroud.com/pdfs/stlmarkwardtpaper.pdf

Marshall, I. H. "The Resurrection of Jesus in Luke." *Tyndale Bulletin* 24, no. 1 (1973): 55–98. https://doi.org/10.53751/001c.30642

Mason, Steve. *Josephus and the New Testament*. Grand Rapids: Baker Academic, 2003.

———. *Josephus, Judea, and Christian Origins: Methods and Categories*. Ada, MI: Baker Academic, 2012.

———. "Sources That Mention Jesus from Outside the Circles of Christ-Followers." In *Jesus Handbuch [Guide to Jesus]*, edited by Jens Schröter and Christine Jacobi, 159–70. Tübingen: Mohr Siebeck, 2017.

Massaro, Lucandrea. "This 3D 'Carbon Copy' of Jesus Was Created Using the Shroud of Turin." Aleteia, March 18, 2018. https://tinyurl.com/3ht7tjyr

McBrayer, Justin P. "Skeptical Theism." Internet Encyclopedia of Philosophy, n.d. https://iep.utm.edu/

McCrone, Walter C. "The Shroud of Turin: Blood or Artist's Pigment?" *Accounts of Chemical Research* 23, no. 3 (1990): 77–83. https://doi.org/10.1021/ar00171a004

McDaniel, Spencer. "The Shroud of Turin Is Definitely a Hoax," Tales of Times Forgotten, February 24, 2020. https://tinyurl.com/3wf8u73z

McDowell, Josh. *Resurrection Growth Guide*. San Bernardino, CA: Here's Life Publishers, 1981.

McDowell, Sean. *The Fate of the Apostles: Examining the Martyrdom Accounts of the Closest Followers of Jesus*. Surrey, Eng.: Ashgate, 2015.

McGrew, Timothy, and Lydia McGrew. "The Arguments from Miracles: A Cumulative Case for the Resurrection of Jesus of Nazareth." In *The Blackwell Companion to Natural Theology*, edited by William Lane Craig and James Porter Moreland, 593–662. Chichester, U.K.: Wiley-Blackwell, 2009.

McLeman, James. *Resurrection Then and Now*. London: Hodder and Stoughton, 1965.

Meier, John P. *A Marginal Jew: Rethinking the Historical Jesus, Volume One: The Roots of the Problem and the Person*. New York: Doubleday, 1991.

Mellor, Ronald. *Tacitus*. New York: Routledge, 1993.

Mendell, Clarence W. *Tacitus: The Man and His Work*. New Haven, CT: Yale University Press, 1957.

Mills, David. *Atheist Universe: The Thinking Person's Answer to Christian Fundamentalism*. Berkeley, CA: Ulysses Press, 2006.

Mo, David. "A Masterly Demolition of the Hungarian Pray Manuscript?" Shroud of Turin Blog, June 2, 2012. https://tinyurl.com/62ckm9nv

Montefiore, C. G. *The Synoptic Gospels Volume 1*. London: Macmillan, 1909.

Morini, Mario. "Pontius Pilate's Coin on the Right Eye of the Man in the Holy Shroud, in the Light of the New Archaeological Findings." In *History, Science, Theology and the Shroud," Symposium St. Louis Missouri, June 22-23, 1991*, edited by A. Berard, 276–77. Amarillo, TX: The Man in the Shroud Committee of Amarillo, Texas, 1991.

Morrow, Jonathan. *Welcome to College: A Christ-Follower's Guide for the Journey*. Grand Rapids: Kregel, 2008.

Mosby's Medical Dictionary. 9th ed. St. Louis: Mosby, 2012.

Moss, Candida R. *The Myth of Persecution: How Early Christians Invented a Story of Martyrdom*. New York: Harper One, 2013.

Mykytiuk, Lawrence. "Did Jesus Exist? Searching for Evidence beyond the Bible." Biblical Archaeology Society, April 12, 2022. https://tinyurl.com/5enrex3a

Myllykoski, Matti. "What Happened to the Body of Jesus?" In *Fair Play: Diversity and Conflicts in Early Christianity: Essays in Honour of Heikki Räisänen*, edited by Ismo Dunderberg, C. M. Tuckett, and Kari Syreeni, 43–82. Leiden: Brill, 2002.

Nair-Collins, Michael, and Franklin G Miller. "Do the 'Brain Dead' Merely Appear to Be Alive?" *Journal of Medical Ethics* 43, no. 11 (2017): 747–53. https://doi.org/10.1136/medethics-2016-103867

Newsom, Carol A. "Angels." In *The Anchor Bible Dictionary*, edited by David Noel Freedman, 1248–53. Doubleday, 1992.

Newton, Francis. *The Scriptorium and Library at Monte Cassino, 1058-1105*. Cambridge: Cambridge University Press, 1998.

Nicolotti, Andrea. *The Shroud of Turin: The History and Legends of the World's Most Famous Relic*. Waco, TX: Baylor University Press, 2019.

Nitowski, Eugenia Louise. *The Field and Laboratory Report of the Environmental Study of the Shroud in Jerusalem*. Salt Lake City: Carmelite Monastery, 1986.

Nyet [Romano], Sergy. "The Shroud of Turin and the Pray Codex." Little Green Footballs, March 2015. https://tinyurl.com/mhxm5w77

O'Collins, Gerald. *Easter Faith: Believing in the Risen Jesus*. Mahwah, NJ: Paulist Press, 2003.

———. "Resurrection and New Creation." *Dialog* 38, no. 1 (1999): 15–19.

———. *The Resurrection of Jesus Christ*. Valley Forge: Judson Press, 1973.

O'Collins, Gerald, and Daniel Kendall. "Did Joseph of Arimathea Exist?" *Biblica* 75, no. 2 (1994): 234–41. https://doi.org/10.2143/BIB.75.2.3214870

Office of the Director of National Intelligence. "Assessing Russian Activities and Intentions in Recent US Elections," 2017. https://tinyurl.com/5ew9znpk

Olson, Ken. "A Eusebian Reading of the Testimonium Flavianum." In *Eusebius of Caesarea: Tradition and Innovations*, edited by Aaron P. Johnson and Jeremy M. Schott, 97–114. Cambridge, MA: Center for Hellenic Studies, 2013.

———. "Eusebius and the Testimonium Flavianum." *Catholic Biblical Quarterly* 61, no. 2 (1999): 305–22.

———. "The Testimonium Flavianum, Eusebius, and Consensus (Guest Post) - Olson." The Jesus Blog, August 13, 2013. https://tinyurl.com/ys73359j

O'Neill, Tim. "Is There Evidence Supporting the Validity of the Shroud of Turin? Is There Evidence against It?" *Quora*, 2011. tinyurl.com/bdfm4x98

———. "Jesus Mythicism 1: The Tacitus Reference to Jesus." History for Atheists, December 28, 2021. https://tinyurl.com/38vf67aw

———. "Jesus Mythicism 3: 'No Contemporary References to Jesus.'" History for Atheists, May 18, 2018. https://tinyurl.com/ywnj2xhy

Owen, Richard. "Death Certificate Is Imprinted on the Shroud of Turin, Says Vatican Scholar." breakingchristiannews.com, November 21, 2009. https://tinyurl.com/42ju5tch

Pagels, Elaine H. *The Origin of Satan*. New York: Random House, 1995.

Paget, J. C. "Some Observations on Josephus and Christianity." *The Journal of Theological Studies* 52, no. 2 (2001): 539–624. https://doi.org/10.1093/jts/52.2.539

Pannenberg, Wolfhart. "Did Jesus Really Rise from the Dead?" *Dialog* 4, no. 1 (1965): 128–35. https://doi.org/10.1111/j.1540-6385.1965.tb00226.x

———. *Jesus - God and Man*. Translated by Duane A. Priebe and Lewis L. Wilkins. 2nd ed. Philadelphia: Westminster Press, 1977.

Parsons, Keith. "The Universe Is Probable; The Resurrection Is Not." In *Does God Exist? The Craig-Flew Debate*, edited by Stan W. Wallace, 115–30. Aldershot, Hants, England: Ashgate, 2003.

Patte, Daniel. *The Gospel According to Matthew: A Structural Commentary on Matthew's Faith*. Philadelphia: Fortress Press, 1987.

Patterson, Stephen J. *Beyond the Passion: Rethinking the Death & Life of Jesus*. Minneapolis: Fortress Press, 2004.

Paul, Gregory S. "The Shroud of Turin: The Great Gothic Art Fraud -- Because If It's Real the Brain of Jesus Was the Size of a Protohuman's!" Internet Infidels." Internet Infidels, December 19, 2021. tinyurl.com/4343eef3

Pearce, Jonathan M.S. "Why Was Jesus' Tomb Not Venerated?" A Tippling Philosopher, March 29, 2016. https://tinyurl.com/5bab6bap

Pérez, Alberto Molina. "Brain Death Debates: From Bioethics to Philosophy of Science." *F1000Research* 11 (2022): 195. https://tinyurl.com/4824xxye

Perry, Michael C. *The Easter Enigma: An Essay on the Resurrection with Special Reference to the Data of Psychical Research*. London: Faber and Faber, 1959.

Pervo, Richard I. *Acts A Commentary*. Minneapolis: Fortress Press, 2009.

———. *Dating Acts: Between the Evangelists and the Apologists*. Santa Rosa, CA: Polebridge Press, 2006.

Philonis Alexandrini, *Legatio Ad Gaium*. Translated by E. Mary Smallwood. Leiden: Brill, 1961.

Pines, Shlomo. *An Arabic Version of the Testimonium Flavianum and Its Implication*. Jerusalem: Israel Academy of Sciences and Humanities, 1971.

Porter, Stanley E. "Pauline Authorship and the Pastoral Epistles: Implications for Canon." *Bulletin for Biblical Research* 5, no. 1 (1995): 105–23. https://doi.org/10.2307/26422129.

Prchlík, Ivan. "Auctor Nomini Eius Christus. Tacitus' Knowledge of the Origins of Christianity." *AUC PHILOLOGICA*, no. 2 (2017): 95–110. https://doi.org/https://doi.org/10.14712/24646830.2017.15

Price, Christopher. "Did Josephus Refer to Jesus? A Thorough Review of the Testimonium Flavianum." Did Josephus refer to Jesus, 2004. http://www.bede.org.uk/Josephus.htm

———. "Firmly Established by Josephus: What an Ancient Jewish Historian Knew About Jesus." In *Shattering the Christ Myth: Did Jesus Not Exist?*, edited by James Patrick Holding, 21–54. Xulon, 2008.
Price, Robert M. *The Case against the Case for Christ: A New Testament Scholar Refutes Lee Strobel*. Cranford, NJ: American Atheist Press, 2010.
———. *The Christ-Myth Theory and Its Problems*. Cranford, NJ: American Atheist Press, 2011.
———. *The Incredible Shrinking Son of Man: How Reliable Is the Gospel Tradition?* Amherst, NY: Prometheus Books, 2003.
Pritchard, James B. *The Ancient Near East: Supplementary Texts and Pictures Relating to The Old Testament: Consisting of Supplementary Materials for the Ancient Near East in Pictures and Ancient Near Eastern Texts*. Princeton: Princeton University Press, 1969.
Qasem, Mohamad. *A Closer Look at Christianity*. Al-Islam.org, n.d. https://tinyurl.com/4ee82wyb
Rabinowitz, Louis Isaac. "Satan." In *Encyclopedia Judaica*, edited by Fred Skolnik, 18:72–73. Detroit: Thomson-Gale, 2007.
Rahmani, L. Y. *A Catalogue of Jewish Ossuaries in the Collections of the State of Israel*. Jerusalem: The Israel Antiquities Authority, 1994.
Ralston, Thomas N. *Elements of Divinity*. Edited by Thomas O. Summers. Nashville: Cokesbury, 1924.
Ramm, Bernard L. *Protestant Christian Evidences; a Textbook of the Evidences*. Chicago: Moody Press, 1967.
Remsburg, John. *The Christ: A Critical Review and Analysis of the Evidences of His Existence*. New York: The Truth Seeker, 1909.
Richardson, Alan. "The Resurrection of Jesus Christ." *Theology* 74, no. 610 (1971): 146–54. https://doi.org/10.1177/0040571x7107400402
Riedl, Johannes. "Wirklich Der Herr Ist Auferweckt Worden Und Dem Simon Erschienen (Lk 24:34)." *Bibel und Liturgie* 40 (1967): 81–110.
Rimmer, Sandra. "Shroud of Turin – 1st Century Relic, or Medieval Forgery? 10 Arguments for and Against." Abroad in the Yard, 2021. https://tinyurl.com/mwmxvttd
Robinson, J. M. "Ascension." In *The Interpreter's Dictionary of the Bible*, edited by George Arthur Buttrick, 1:245–47. New York: Abingdon Press, 1962.
Robinson, John A.T. *Can We Trust the New Testament?* Grand Rapids: Eerdmans, 1977.
Rogers, Clement F. *The Evidence for the Resurrection of Christ*. S.P.C.K.: London, 1936.
Rohmann, Dirk. *Christianity, Book-Burning and Censorship in Late Antiquity: Studies in Text Transmission*. Berlin: De Gruyter, 2016.
Samples, Kenneth Richard. *Without a Doubt: Answering the 20 Toughest Faith Questions*. Grand Rapids: Baker Books, 2004.
Samuelsson, Gunnar. *Crucifixion in Antiquity: An Inquiry into the Background of the New Testament Terminology of Crucifixion*. Tübingen: Mohr Siebeck, 2011.

Schleiermacher, Friedrich. *The Life of Jesus*. Edited by Jack C. Verheyden. Translated by S. MacLean Gilmour. Philadelphia: Fortress Press, 1975.

Schlier, Heinrich. *On the Resurrection of Jesus Christ*. Rome: 30Days, 2008.

Schröter, Jens. "The Criteria of Authenticity in Jesus Research and Historiographical Method." In *Jesus, Criteria, and the Demise of Authenticity*, edited by Chris Keith and Le Anthony Donne, 49–72. London: T & T Clark, 2012.

Schweizer, Eduard. *Lordship and Discipleship*. London: SCM, 1986.

Shaw, Brent D. "The Myth of the Neronian Persecution." *Journal of Roman Studies* 105 (2015): 73–100. doi.org/10.1017/s0075435815000982

Shulman, Moshe. Josephus and Jesus, n.d. https://tinyurl.com/5n7356fc

Sigal, Gerald. *The Jew and the Christian Missionary: A Jewish Response to Missionary Christianity*. New York: Ktav, 1981.

———. *The Jewish Response to Missionary Christianity: Why Jews Don't Believe in Jesus*. Createspace, 2015.

———. *The Resurrection Fantasy Reinventing Jesus*. Xlibris, 2012.

Slade, Darren M. "The History and Philosophy of Depicting a Violently Crucified Christ." In *Violence in Art: Essays in Aesthetics and Philosophy*, edited by Darren M. Slade, 117–54. Denver, CO: Inara Publishing, 2022.

Smith, Wilbur M. *Therefore, Stand: A Plea for a Vigorous Apologetic in the Present Crisis of Evangelical Christianity*. Natick, MA: W.A. Wilde, 1959.

Smith, Zach, and Alden Bass. "Questions and Answers [Are There Lost Books in the Bible?]." *Reason & Revelation* 23, no. 12 (December 2003): 105–9. https://tinyurl.com/4m4mk4mh

Spencer, Richard. "Rebuttal to David Margolis's Reframing Resurrection." *Debate Between David Margolis and Richard Spencer*. Address presented at the Debate Between David Margolis and Richard Spencer, 2006.

Stein, Robert H. "The Criteria for Authenticity." In *Gospel Perspectives: Studies of History and Tradition in the Four Gospels*, edited by R. T. France and David Wenham, 1:225–63. Sheffield: JSOT Press, 1980.

———. *Jesus the Messiah: A Survey of the Life of Christ*. Downers Grove, IL: InterVarsity, 2009.

———. *Studying the Synoptic Gospels: Origin and Interpretation*. 2nd ed. Grand Rapids: Baker Academic, 2001.

———. "Was the Tomb Really Empty?" *Themelios* 5, no. 1 (1979): 8–12.

Tabor, James. "Tomography, Talpiot, and Not One but Three Talpiot Tombs." TaborBlog, January 11, 2013. https://tinyurl.com/yxssbfba

Tanford, Alex. Rule 406. Habit; Routine Practice - Indiana University Maurer School of Law, 2020. https://tinyurl.com/5xfc9j9h

Theissen, Gerd, and Annette Merz. *The Historical Jesus: A Comprehensive Guide*. Minneapolis: Eerdmans, 1998.

"This 3D 'Carbon Copy' of Jesus Was Created Using the Shroud of Turin." Aleteia, March 28, 2018. https://tinyurl.com/3ht7tjyr

Thiselton, Anthony C. *The First Epistle to the Corinthians: A Commentary on the Greek Text*. Grand Rapids: Eerdmans, 2000.
Thurston, Herbert. "The Holy Shroud and The Verdict of History." *The Month* 101, no. 463 (January 1903): 17–29. https://tinyurl.com/44tasua9
Torley, Vincent J. "Resurrection Redux I." The skeptical zone, October 31, 2018. http://theskepticalzone.com/wp/resurrection-redux-i/
Tors, John. "The Testimony of Josephus: Powerful Evidence for the Truth of Christianity, or an Interpolated Fraud?" Truth In My Days Ministry, n.d. https://tinyurl.com/4tcpk8ph
Troll, Christian W. *Muslims Ask, Christians Answer*. Translated by David Marshall. New York: New York City Press, 2012.
The Turin Shroud Center of Colorado. "Shroud of Turin: A Critical Summary of Observations, Data and Hypotheses," 2017. https://tinyurl.com/2srft9tj
Tzaferis, Vasillios. "Crucifixion—The Archaeological Evidence." *The Biblical Archaeologist* 11, no. 1 (February 1985): 44–53. tinyurl.com/3zdvpezf
van Gorder, A. Christian. *No God but God: A Path to Muslim-Christian Dialogue on God's Nature*. Maryknoll NY: Orbis Books, 2003.
Van Voorst, Robert E. *Jesus Outside the New Testament: An Introduction to the Ancient Evidence*. Grand Rapids: Eerdmans, 2000.
Verheijde, Joseph L., Mohamed Y. Rady, and Michael Potts. "Neuroscience and Brain Death Controversies: The Elephant in the Room." *Journal of Religion and Health* 57, no. 5 (2018): 1745–63. tinyurl.com/za7vbx4r
Viklund, Roger. "The Jesus Passages in Josephus – A Case Study: Excursus – 'The Emmaus Narrative in Luke.'" Jesus granskad, April 4, 2016. https://tinyurl.com/yc73vd3w
———. "The Jesus Passages in Josephus – A Case Study, Part 2C – 'Testimonium Flavianum': Content and Context; Subjective Methods of Reconstruction." Jesus granskad, February 3, 2011. https://tinyurl.com/4vrzsxvy
———. "The Jesus Passages in Josephus – A Case Study, Part 2T – 'Testimonium Flavianum': The Table of Contents." Jesus granskad, March 25, 2011. https://tinyurl.com/ys9nekmw
Viviano, Benedict. "The Gospel According to St. Matthew." In *The New Jerome Biblical Commentary*, edited by Raymond E. Brown, Joseph A. Fitzmyer, and Roland E. Murphy, 630–74. Englewood-Cliffs, NJ: Prentice-Hall, 1990.
Walker, Wm. O. "Christian Origins and Resurrection Faith." *The Journal of Religion* 52, no. 1 (1972): 41–55. https://doi.org/10.1086/486287
Walsh, Bryan, and Larry Schwalbe. "An Instructive Inter-Laboratory Comparison: The 1988 Radiocarbon Dating of the Shroud of Turin." *Journal of Archaeological Science: Reports* 29 (2020): 102015. https://doi.org/10.1016/j.jasrep.2019.102015
"Was Joseph of Arimathea a Myth?" Christian Worldview Press, June 23, 2013. https://tinyurl.com/ykdnc26u
Wedderburn, A.J.M. *Beyond Resurrection*. London: SCM, 1999.

Wellhausen, Julius. *Das Evangelium Marci*. 2nd ed. Berlin: G. Reimer, 1909.
Wells, George Albert. *The Jesus Legend*. Chicago: Open Court, 1996.
———. *The Jesus Myth*. Chicago: Open Court, 1999.
Whanger, Alan D., and Mary Whanger. "Polarized Image Overlay Technique: A New Image Comparison Method and Its Applications." *Applied Optics* 24, no. 6 (1985): 766–72. https://doi.org/10.1364/ao.24.000766
Whealey, Alice. *Josephus on Jesus: The Testimonium Flavianum Controversy from Late Antiquity to Modern Times*. New York: Peter Lang, 2003.
Whitaker, David. "What Happened to the Body of Jesus?" *The Expository Times* 81, no. 10 (1970): 307–10. https://tinyurl.com/yhpzcxzt
Wiebe, Phillip H. "Evidence for a Resurrection." *Journal for Christian Theological Research* 6 (2001). https://tinyurl.com/33st5dma
Wilcox, Robert K. *The Truth about the Shroud of Turin Solving the Mystery*. Washington, D.C.: Regnery Pub., Inc., 2010.
Wild, R. A. "Shroud of Turin." In *The New Catholic Encyclopedia*, 13:95–97. Detroit: Thomson-Gale, 2003.
Williams, Peter S. "Addendum to Getting at Jesus a Comprehensive Critique of Neo-Atheist ...," August 26, 2019. https://tinyurl.com/5chf7zc7
Wilson, Ian. *The Shroud: Fresh Light on the 2000-Year-Old Mystery*. London: Bantam, 2011.
Wolfe, Rolland. *How the Easter Story Grew from Gospel to Gospel*. Lewiston, NY: E. Mellen Press, 1989.
Wright, N. T. "Resurrecting Old Arguments: Responding to Four Essays." *Journal for the Study of the Historical Jesus* 3, no. 2 (2005): 209–31. https://doi.org/10.1177/1476869005060237
———. *The Resurrection of the Son of God*. Minneapolis: Fortress Press, 2003.
Yamauchi, Edwin M. "Jesus Outside the New Testament: What Is the Evidence?" In *Jesus under Fire*, edited by Michael J. Wilkins and James Porter Moreland, 207–29. Grand Rapids: Zondervan, 1995.
———. "Josephus and the Scriptures." *Fides et Historia* 13, no. 1 (1980): 42–63.
Ydit, Meir. "Disinterment." In *Encyclopedia Judaica*, edited by Fred Skolnik, 5:882–682. Detroit: Thomson-Gale, 2007.
Zara, Erik. "The Chrestianos Issue in Tacitus Reinvestigated," 2009. http://www.diva-portal.org/smash/search.jsf
Zindler, Frank R. *The Jesus the Jews Never Knew: Sepher Toldoth Yeshu and the Quest of the Historical Jesus in Jewish Sources*. Cranford, N.J: American Atheist Press, 2003.
Zukeran, Patrick. "The Resurrection: Fact or Fiction? – a Real Historical Event." Probe Ministries, May 27, 2017. https://tinyurl.com/mryb8rrr

Name Index

A

Abraham, 196, 199–200, 236–237, 252
Adam, 236
Africanus, Sextus Julius, 53, 57
Agrippa, 93, 190
Alexander the Great, 5, 141
Ananus, the High Priest, 32
Anatolius, 58
Ankerberg, John, 194
Antipas, Herod, 68, 196
Apollinaris, 99
Apollonius, 238
Aristeas of Proconnesus, 238
Arius, 211
Arnobius, 58
Athanasius, 211
Athronges the Shepherd, 67
Augustine, 54, 60
Augustus, 86, 145, 187–188
Avigad, N., 142

B

Ballestrero, Cardinal Anastasio, 117
Baruch, 236
Baruch, Uri, 136–137
Beelzebul, 248
Beloved Disciple, 30
Bonnet, Bruno, 120

C

Cappel, Louis, 35
Cassiodorus, 99
Catherine (Saint), 130
Celsus, Aulus Cornelius, 107
Chevalier, Canon, 124
Chrysostom, John, 54, 59
Claudius, 56
Clement of Alexandria, 53, 56, 99
Clement VII (Pope), 120–122
Constantine (Emperor), 227
Corfield, Richard, 131
Courage, Anne-Laure, 144
Cyprian, Bishop of Carthage, 57

D

Danin, Avinoam, 137–138
d'Arcis, Pierre, 120–124
David (King), 65, 177, 210, 246
Dio, Cassius, 97
Diodorus Siculus, 238
Diogenes Laertius, 238
Dionysius of Halicarnassus, 238
Domitian, Flavius, 32
Dubarle, André Marie, 126

E

Ebed-Melech, 237
Eliezer, Abraham's faithful steward, 237
Elijah, 65, 200, 236
Elkanah, 177
Enoch, 200, 236
Enrie, Giuseppe, 145
Eusebius, 33, 36, 46–47, 49, 53–55, 58–61, 64, 74–75, 79–81, 177
Eustathius, 54
Eve, 248
Ezra, 236

F

Faber, Tanaquilius, 35
Felix, Minucius, 53, 57
Fossati, Don Luigi, 134
Frale, Barbara, 144–145
Frei-Sulzer, Max, 136–138

G

Gaius, 190
Gamaliel, 27, 150
Ganymede (rapture of), 238
Garlaschelli, Luigi, 135
Gibson, Mel, 10

H

Hegesippus, 60
Helena (Queen), 186, 227
Hercules, 238
Herod (King), 52, 67, 190, 196, 235
Herodotus, 106, 238
Hippolytus, 54, 57
Hiram, King of Tyre, 237
Homer, 238

I

Irenaeus, 53, 56
Isaac, 196, 252
Isaiah, 53, 30, 165, 186, 197–198, 207, 236
Isidore of Pelusium, 54

J

Jabez, 237
Jacob, 26, 150, 172, 196
James, the brother of Jesus, 32, 57, 63, 166, 233, 257
James, the Just, 57
Jerome, 54, 59, 99
Jesus ben Ananias, 67
Jesus, the son of Saphat, 67
Joanna, 233
John (the apostle/author of the Fourth Gospel, 12, 14, 17–19, 21-22, 29–30, 108, 110–113, 165–167, 170, 180–181, 203, 225, 234, 238–239, 257
John the Baptist, 59, 67–68, 109–110, 196, 235, 237
Jonah, 151, 159–160, 255
Joseph, 26, 150, 172–173
Joseph of Arimathea, 23–25, 30–31, 135, 143–144, 148–149, 154, 163–167, 170–183, 190, 193, 197–198, 204, 226, 228, 231–232, 239, 256
Joseph Smith, 89
Josephus, Flavius, 15, 32–37, 39–41, 43–49, 51–82, 88, 96, 104, 106, 162, 180, 188–190, 197, 237, 255
Judas (Iscariot), 140, 155–156

Judas, the chief of the Jews, 155
Justin Martyr, 55–56
Justinian, 187

K

Kappara, Bar, 220
Killebrew, Ann, 143

L

Lactantius, 58
Lazarus, 199
Levi, 236
Levi–Setti, Richard, 132
Locke, Sir Charles, 133
Lucian, 39
Luke (apostle, author of the third gospel), 15, 19, 22, 46, 62, 104–105, 113, 152, 166–167, 170, 177, 179–180, 197, 200, 217, 228–229, 239, 255, 257

M

Magdalene, Mary, 29, 171, 204, 232–234
Mara bar Serapion, 83–85, 255
Marion, André, 144–145
Mark(s) (apostle, author of the second gospel), 24, 30, 105, 164–175, 178–180, 182–183, 204
Mary, 50–51, 155, 157, 174, 229, 233, 238
Matthew (apostle, author of the first gospel), 22, 29–30, 104–105, 113, 151–152, 162, 165–167, 173, 179–180, 182, 197, 225, 255
Merz, Annette, 35, 79, 173, 196

Methodius, 54, 58
Miese, Benedikt, 35
Minucius Felix, 53, 57
Moroni, Mario, 142
Moses, 43, 64, 160–161, 175–176, 190, 200, 236–237
Muhammad, 113, 148, 160–161
Munro, Douglas, 16
Murra, Daniele, 138

N

Nehemiah, 9
Nernoff, John, 202
Nero, 86, 95, 98–102
Nicodemus, 23, 25–26, 31, 143–144, 148–149, 168, 232

O

Origen, 33, 36, 54, 57–58, 64, 81, 99
Orosius, 54
Osiander, Lucas, 35
Ovid, 238

P

Pamphilus, 79, 81
Paul, 98–99, 104, 148, 167–168, 170–171, 185–186, 197, 200, 210–212, 215, 217, 221, 228, 240, 249, 251, 254, 257
Paulina, 67
Peter, 98–99, 171, 186, 224–225, 227–229, 232–234, 236
Philo, 190
Philostorgius, 54
Philostratus, 238
Phineas, 69

Pilate, 1, 9, 11, 15–16, 22, 31–32, 34–36, 42, 48, 50–52, 56, 58, 67–68, 73, 86–88, 90–91, 95–96, 98, 102, 108–109, 111, 135, 141–142, 150, 173, 189–193, 198, 216–218, 222
Plato, 83, 107
Pliny, 5, 88, 96, 107
Pray, Gyorgy, 124
Plutarch, 238
Pythagoras, 83, 85

R

Raphael, 236
Ricoeur, Paul, 48
Romulus, 238
Romano, Sergey, 129
Rucker, Robert, 119

S

Samuel, 177
St John Chrysostom, 54, 59
Saul, 214
Simon of Cyrene, 2, 11, 156
Seneca, 99
Serah, daughter of Asher, 237
Severus, 99
Sidonius, 99
Simon the Cyrene, 2, 11, 156
Socrates, 83, 85
Solomon, 65, 210, 237
Sozomenus, 54
Spencer, Richard, 174, 183
Suetonius, 97, 99

T

Tacitus, 86–103, 162, 190, 255
Tertullian, 53, 56, 99
Theodore of Mopsuestia, 54
Theophilus, Patriarch of Antioch, 53, 56
Theudus, 67
Thomas, 220
Tiberius, 52, 56, 86–87, 91, 100–101, 141, 144, 190–191
Titanus, 155
Titus, 95
Trump, Donald, 203
Trypho, 54

U

Ulpian, 187–188
Urban VI, Pope, 121

V

Vespasian, 57, 65

W

Washburn, Lemuel Kelley, 241
Wielenberg, Erik, 243
Wilcox, Robert, 115

Z

Zephaniah, 236
Zeus, 252
Ziusudra, 237

Author Index

A

Allen, Nicholas Peter Legh, 35, 52, 55, 61–63, 66–67, 69, 71, 76–77, 81, 89
Allison, Dale C., 203–204, 237–238
Alter, Michael J., 9, 28–31, 104, 109–110, 112, 136, 150, 152, 224
Antonacci, Mark, 115, 138
Anyabwile, Thabiti, 158
Arnold, Clinton E., 247
Aumann, Jordan, 253
Aus, Roger David, 175–176

B

Babinski, Edward, 211–212
Barclay, John M.G., 209
Barclay, William, 105, 167
Barkay, Gabriel, 227
Barker, Dan, 89
Barnett, Paul, 91
Baruch, Uri, 136
Bater, R. Robert, 223
Bauckham, Richard, 30
Beecher, H. K., 6
Berry, Colin, 126–127
Birdsall, J. Neville, 60
Blenkinsopp, Joseph, 181
Bock, 32, 62, 65, 73, 87, 184
Bode, Edward Lynn, 212
Boff, Leonardo, 234
Boi, Marzia, 138–139

Bondeson, Jan, 5, 16, 107
Borrini, Matteo, 135
Bostock, Gerald, 222
Botelho, Octavio da Cunha, 77–78
Bousset, Wilhelm, 212
Bowman, Robert, 86–87, 89
Boyd, Gregory A., 65, 68
Broer, Ingo, 173, 177
Broussard, John, 128
Brown, Derek, 245–247
Brown, Raymond E., 19, 30, 175, 189, 192–193, 204
Browning, W.R.F., 222
Bruce, F. F., 73
Bulst, Werner, 234
Butler, Joseph, 211

C

Cambron, Mark, 231, 250
Capps, Donald, 150
Carnley, Peter, 230
Carrier, Richard, 2, 5, 40, 47, 55, 63, 74–76, 80–81, 95–97, 99–102, 106–107
Carson, D.A., 112, 185
Casabianca, Tristan, 116, 119, 125, 129
Casey, Maurice, 149, 170, 174, 199–200
Charlesworth, James H., 65, 72, 89
Chilton, Bruce D., 233, 239–240
Coale, Ansley J.,
Choi, Charles Q., 135

Ciccone, Gaetano, 136
Conway, Colleen M., 234
Coogan, Michael D., 104
Cook, John Granger, 149, 186, 189
Cook, Michael J., 215–216, 221
Corduan, Winfried, 234
Corfield, Richard, 131
Corley, Kathleen E., 186
Craig, William Lane, 23, 84, 112, 163, 172, 174–175, 177–178, 182, 184, 187, 193–195, 201–202, 227
Cranfield, C.E.B., 209
Creed, J. M., 212
Crispino, Dorothy, 140
Crossan, John Dominic, 1, 178–179
Cumming, Joseph L., 156

D

Damon, P.E., 116–117
Danin, Avinoam, 137–138
De Blois, Kees F., 245
DeLong, Russell V., 209
Derrett, J. Duncan M., 106
DeSilva, David A., 185
Di Lazzaro, Paolo, 116, 119, 134–135, 138, 146
Dodd, C.H., 26, 149
Doherty, Earl, 2, 34, 55, 60, 62–65, 67, 85, 95, 97–99, 102, 226
Drake, Mack, 6
Drews, Arthur, 35, 89, 99
Drews, Robert, 101
Dunn, James D.G., 62, 65, 206

E

Eastlake, Charles Locke, 133
Eddy, Paul R., 35, 59, 65, 68, 84, 94–95, 181
Edlow, Brian L., 6

Edwards, James R., 241
Ehrman, Bart D., 149, 168–169, 191–192
Ercoline, W.R., 139
Evans, Craig A., 35, 84, 187–189

F

Fales, Evan, 163, 224
Fanti, Giulio, 115, 119, 139–140
Farey, Hugh, 116–117, 119–120, 124, 126, 132, 136–139, 141–142
Farnell, F. David, 194
Farrar, Thomas J., 245, 247
Feldman, Louis H., 49, 53–54, 60–63, 74
Ferguson, Matthew Wade, 166
Fernandes, Phil, 184
Filas, Francis L., 141–142
Fitzwater, P.B., 195, 209, 227
Flood, Edmund, 195, 227
Fodor, James, 92, 194, 213–214, 217
Folds, Eric, 115
Fortna, Robert T., 234
Frale, Barbara, 144
Frame, John M.,
France, R. T., 102
Frantzman, Seth J., 227
Freeman, Charles, 128, 131
Freer-Waters, Rachel A., 119
Frier, Bruce, 181

G

Geisler, Norman, 33, 240
Gibson, Jeffrey B., 246–247
Godfrey, Neil, 55–60
Goguel, Maurice, 91, 231
Goldberg, Gary J., 36, 39–41, 44–46, 62–63, 74
Goodyear, Francis R., 93–94

Gormley, Rick, 123
Gove, Harry E., 117–119, 123
Goulder, Michael D., 171–172
Grant, Michael, 93–94, 167
Greer, D. M.,
Greear, J.D., 160
Groothuis, Douglas R., 195
Gove, Harry, 117, 123
Guscin, Mark, 145
Gwynne, Paul, 235

H

Habermas, Gary R., 1–2, 32–33, 65, 83, 86, 103, 152, 184, 193, 195, 205, 209, 227, 231, 234–235
Hachlili, Rachel, 143
Hanhart, Karel, 177, 198
Hart, Vinny, 216
Hays, Steve, 250–251
Hedrick, Charles W., 243–244, 247
Hendrickx, Herman, 234
Hengel, Martin, 149
Heil, John Paul, 198
Hillar, Marian, 62
Holding, James Patrick, 60, 96
Hoover, Roy W., 222
Hopper, Paul J., 33, 47–49, 51–52, 62–63, 74, 80
Housley, R.A., 131

I

Ilan, Tal, 175
Imran, Adil Nizamuddin, 157

J

Jones, Stephen E., 120, 125
Jones, Timothy Paul, 189

Joseph, Simon J., 116, 134
Josephus, Flavius, 15, 32–82, 88, 96, 104, 106, 162, 180, 188–190, 197, 237, 255

K

Keener, Craig, 112
Keller, James A., 213
Kelly, Anthony, 234
Keener, Craig S., 112–113, 195, 227
Kesich, Veselin, 234
Khan, Arif, 145
King, Lauren A., 234
Kirby, Peter, 74, 91, 180–181, 193
Koester, Craig A., 234
Kohlbeck, Joseph A., 132–133
Komarnitsky, Kris D., 185
Köstenberger, Andreas J., 32
Kroll, Woodrow, 242

L

Ladd, George Eldon, 234
Lake, Kirsopp, 198
Lampe, G.W.H., 186
Lans, Birgit van der, 87
Lataster, Raphael, 2, 38, 79, 97, 99–101
Lavoie, Gilbert R., 19
Law, Stephen, 243
Lefebvre, Matt, 178
Leidner, Harold, 69–71
Léon-Dufour, Xavier, 234
Lewis, Ariane, 6
Licona, Michael R., 1–2, 32–33, 35, 65, 77, 83, 86, 103, 108, 113, 148, 151–152, 184, 195, 205, 209, 227, 231, 235, 250–251
Loftus, John W., 2
Loke, Andrew ern tern, 112, 150

Lombatti, Antonio, 142–145
Lorenzen, Thorwald, 185, 212, 229
Lorusso, Salvatore, 145
Lowder, Jeffrey Jay, 93–94, 100, 201–203
Lüdemann, Gerd, 1, 29, 182, 201–202, 231, 239
Lyons, William, 163

M

Macquarrie, John, 234
Manservigi, Flavia, 115
Margolis, David, 163, 174
Marinelli, Emanuela, 116, 119, 136, 139–140
Marino, Joe, 119, 125, 131, 141
Marion, André, 144–145
Markwardt, Mark, 131
Marshall, I. H., 172, 174
Mason, Steve, 34, 55, 62–64, 73–74, 79, 89, 102–103
Massaro, Lucandrea, 140
McBrayer, Justin P., 242–243
McCrone, Walter C., 133–135
McDowell, Josh, 209
McGrew, Timothy, 251–252
McLeman, James, 234
Meier, John P., 32, 34–35, 37, 49, 61–63, 65, 68, 71–76, 87–89, 99, 101, 150
Mellor, Ronald, 93
Mendell, Clarence W., 91–92, 96
Mills, David, 1–2
Mo, David, 129–130
Montefiore, C. G., 198
Morrow, Jonathan,
Moroni, Mario, 89, 142
Mosby's Medical Dictionary, 4
Moss, Candida R., 100
Murra, Daniele, 138
Mykytiuk, Lawrence, 97
Myllykoski, Matti, 179, 223

N

Nair-Collins, Michael, 6
Newsom, Carol A., 245
Newton, Francis, 101
Nickell, Joe, 138
Nicolotti, Andrea, 115, 131
Nitowski, Eugenia L., 132–134, 141, 143–144
Nodet, Étienne, 61
Nyet [Romano], Sergy, 129

O

O'Collins, Gerald, 164
Office of the Director of National Intelligence, 31
Olson, Ken, 33, 39, 46–47, 62–63, 74–75, 80–81
O'Neill, Tim, 87, 90–91, 96, 102, 140
Owen, Richard, 144

P

Pagels, Elaine H., 211, 246
Paget, J. C., 34–36
Pannenberg, Wolfhart, 184, 195, 227, 231
Parsons, Keith, 182
Patte, Daniel, 198
Patterson, Stephen J., 234
Paul, Gregory S., 138–140
Pearce, Jonathan M.S., 206
Pérez, Alberto Molina, 6
Perry, Michael C., 184
Pervo, Richard, 104
Pines, Shlomo, 79
Porter, Stanley E., 185
Prchlík, Ivan, 89
Price, Christopher, 33, 60–63, 65–66

Price, Robert M., 2, 198
Pritchard, James B., 237

Q

Qasem, Mohamed, 157

R

Rabinowitz, Louis Isaac, 245–246
Rahmani, Levy Yitzhak, 142–143
Ralston, Thomas N., 226
Ramm, Bernard L., 184
Remsburg, John, 241
Richardson, Alan, 231
Riedl, Johannes, 212
Rimmer, Sandra, 116
Robinson, J. M., 236
Robinson, John A.T., 235
Rohmann, Dirk, 210

S

Samples, Kenneth R., 209, 231
Samuelsson, Gunnar, 13–14
Schleiermacher, Friedrich, 223–224
Schlier, Heinrich, 234
Schröter, Jens, 92
Schweizer, Eduard, 236
Schwortz, Barrie, 145
Shaw, Brent, 100
Shulman, Moshe, 77
Sigal, Gerald, 174, 176, 197–198
Simionato, A., 139
Slade, Darren M., 12
Smith, Joseph, 89
Smith, Wilbur M., 209, 219
Smith, Zach, 210
Spencer, Richard, 174, 183
Stein, Robert H., 72, 104–105, 166–167, 184, 187, 195, 227, 231

T

Tabor, James D., 165–166
Tanford, Alex, 93
Theissen, Gerd, 35, 79, 173, 196
Thiselton, Anthony C., 241
Thurston, Herbert, 121–124
Torley, Vincent J., 199–200
Tors, John, 61, 65
Troll, Christian W., 158–159
The Turin Shroud Center of Colorado, 111–112
Tzaferis, Vasillios, 14

U

Ugolotti, Piero, 144

V

van Gorder, A. Christian, 160
Verheijde, Joseph L., 6
Verschuuren, Gerand M., 115
Viklund, Roger, 53, 60–61, 78–79
Viviano, Benedict, 198
Voorst, Robert Van, 38–39, 62–63, 65, 81, 83–84, 86, 89–90, 96, 98

W

Walker, Wm. O., 231, 235–236
Walsh, Bryan, 116
Wedderburn, A.J.M., 172, 221
Wellhausen, Julius, 212
Wells, George Albert, 2, 60
Whanger, Alan, 137, 141–142, 144
Whealey, Alice, 36, 79–80
Whitaker, David, 228
Wiebe, Phillip H., 240–241

Wilcox, Robert, 115
Wild, R. A., 146
Williams, Peter S., 248
Wilson, Ian, 111, 115, 125
Wolfe, Rolland, 224, 237
Wright, N. T., 149, 201, 233

Y

Yamauchi, Edwin M., 62
Ydit, Meir, 185

Z

Zara, Erik, 101
Zindler, Frank R., 2, 60, 89
Zukeran, Patrick, 184

Subject Index

A

Ab excess divi Augusti, 86
accelerator mass spectrometry, 118
accursed, 159
accuser, 247
Acts, 24, 29, 31, 104, 128, 148, 152, 167–168, 173, 178, 201, 209, 217, 220, 223–225, 228, 246
ahistorical, 29
aleph, 176
Aleteia, 139
Allah, 154–155, 158–159
allegation (accusation), 101, 117–120
allude (allusion), 93, 100, 109, 150, 197, 205–206
aloes, 26, 144, 149
altered, alteration(s), 35, 72, 81
ambiguity, 14, 49
anachronistically, 98
analogy, 180, 238
Analogy of Religion, 211
anesthesia, 4
angel(s), 24, 89, 124, 131, 170–171, 200, 205, 225, 232–233, 245, 247, 253, 257
 messenger, 245
anthropological, anthropometric, 139–140
Antichrist 98, 246

anti-Jewish motif, 31
Apocalyptic Age, 98, 229
Apocryphon of James, 166
apologetic(s), 17, 33, 38, 80, 94, 99, 112, 114, 128, 151–152, 163–164, 183–185, 193–195, 205, 207, 2010–211, 215–216, 222, 224, 226, 231, 239–240, 243, 256
apologist(s), 32–33, 56–58, 60, 62–63, 66–67, 73, 77, 86, 90, 94, 96, 98, 103–104, 108, 111, 113–114, 148, 151, 154, 162, 164, 169, 172, 178, 181–182, 184–185, 193, 195, 207, 209–211, 213, 215–220, 227, 230–231, 234–235, 239, 241–242, 251, 253, 255–257
apostles, 195, 201, 216, 224–227, 251
apostolic, 51, 195
Apostles' Creed, 50–52
apparition(s), 220, 246
appear(ed/ing), appearance(s), 15, 34–35, 39–40, 42, 45, 51, 58, 62–63, 101, 171, 184–186, 201, 207, 225, 229, 232–233, 235, 238–240, 245, 250–251, 253, 257
aqueduct(s), 67, 190
Arabic, 32–33
aragonite, 132–133
Aramaic, 13, 176–177, 200

archaeology (ists), archaeological, 132, 142–143, 175
Archaeometry, 138
archives, Archive (Vatican), 88, 90–91, 94–96, 144
argument from silence (*Argumentum ex silentio*), 37, 55, 60, 65–67, 184, 186, 207, 209, 211, 219, 223, 228
Arimathea (place), 154, 163–164, 175–178, 182–183
aristocracy, aristocratic, 34, 64, 131
Armatha, 177
armûta, 177
arrest(ed), 3, 169, 203, 214, 217, 225, 230
arson, 101–102
artefacts (artifact), 14, 120, 142, 146
artist(ic), 121–123, 125, 127–130, 133, 135, 139–140
ascended (ascension), 23, 29, 51, 154, 201, 217, 236, 238, 251
assumption(s), 1, 4, 12, 63, 74–75, 90, 107, 114, 130, 155, 174, 180, 185, 227, 238
atone(ment), 8, 158, 257
audience, 49, 63, 103, 135
authenticist (shroudies), 116, 119, 122–123, 125–126, 129, 138, 256

B

bacteria, 202
baptism, 18, 51
battle experience, 21,
beard(ed), 114, 130, 140–141
begotten, 50
beheaded, 235
Bethlehem, 175

betray, 156
Bible, biblical, 1, 32, 62, 65, 112, 152, 155, 157, 159, 161, 172, 175–176, 186, 197–198, 200, 205, 210, 215, 226, 238, 240, 244–246, 251–252, 254
Bible (Lost Books), 210–211
biological children, 8
birds, 149, 192
birthplace, 177
bladder, 3
blame, blaming, 49, 183
blasphemy, blasphemous, 159, 191, 214
bled, bleed(ing), 12, 135–136
blemish, 109
blessed, 13, 159
blindness, 119
blood(y), bloodstains, 2–4, 18–19, 21, 30, 66, 109, 111–114, 126, 128–130, 132–135, 148, 158, 202
body(ies), 16, 21, 26, 31, 108, 135, 149, 169–170, 173, 179, 187–188, 216–217, 221, 225, 237–238
book(end), 27, 35–36, 115, 150, 188, 210–211
born, 3, 33–34, 50–51, 110, 157, 177, 247
botanical, botanist, 136–137
bowel, 3
brain, 4–7, 19–20, 22, 25, 28, 105–106, 112, 139
brain dead (death), 3–6, 19–22, 25, 28, 105–106, 112, 254–255
breathed, breathing, 3, 105–106
bribe(s), bribing, 170, 178, 190, 225, 232
brothers, 160, 199, 247
burden of proof, 36, 71, 209, 251

Burial (Jesus), 149, 173, 176, 186, 188–189, 197, 199, 254
body (linen), 168
body (placement), 168
burials, buried, 5, 50–51, 96, 127, 135, 142–143, 149, 151, 160–161, 164–166, 171–173, 179, 185–190, 192–193, 196–198, 203, 206–208, 215–217, 221, 223, 228, 233, 241, 254, 257
cave, 172, 203, 240
consequences of an empty tomb, 231–241
consequences of no tomb, 207–208, 231–233
dishonorable burial, 206, 208, 258
empty tomb, 24, 40, 124, 163, 166, 168–173, 179, 182, 184–187, 193–197, 199–203, 205, 207, 209–215, 217–219, 221–225, 227–231, 233–235, 237–241, 246, 253, 256
grave robbers could have stolen the body, 223, 228, 241
lack of controversy about or interest in the empty tomb by the Jewish religious authorities, 219–226
lack of controversy about or interest in the empty tomb on the part of Jesus' followers, 227–230
lack of controversy about or interest in the empty tomb by the public, 209–214
lack of controversy about or interest in the empty tomb on the part of Roman authorities, 215–
silence (of the women), 52, 54, 171–172, 207. 211–212, 222
no relationship exists between an empty tomb and preaching, 201
unknown person could have removed the body, 223
entombment, 3, 23, 124, 128, 137, 173
entrance, entry, 164, 168, 231–232, 239
funeral, funerary, 5, 146, 189, 198
grave, graveyard, 22, 135, 149, 165, 173, 185, 192–193, 197, 199, 200, 203, 206, 208, 215–216, 217, 220–222, 225
gravestone ornaments, 129
guard(s), guarding, 155, 170, 194, 203, 219, 225–226, 230, 232, 238
reburied, reburial, 134, 185, 193–194, 241
tomb, 24, 26, 40, 108, 121, 124, 126–127, 131–132, 136–137, 142–143, 149, 151, 154, 160, 163–166, 168–173, 177, 179–182, 184–187, 189, 191–219, 221–225, 227–235, 237–241, 246, 250, 253, 256–257
burn(s), burned, burning, burnt, 86, 99, 126, 188
bury, 159, 179, 182
buttocks, 130
Byzantine artists, 129

C

Caesarea, 80, 217
calibrated(ation), 116, 119, 125
caloric stimulation, 4
Calvary, 13–14
Capernaum, 175
captivity, captured, 83, 190

Subject Index 291

carbon dating, 116–117, 123–125
carpenter, 94, 150
Catechism of the Catholic Church, 50–51, 196, 256
cathedrals, 131
centurion, 19–20, 22, 106, 135
Chrestians, 86, 98
Chrisiano, 98
Christ, Jesus, 2, 12, 33–34, 37, 40, 42–44, 47–50, 58, 61–63, 65, 69–71, 83–84, 86, 89–91, 98, 100, 109, 113, 115, 121, 128–131, 134, 140, 143, 157, 160, 163, 174, 185, 196, 209, 212, 224, 229, 231, 234–235, 239, 241, 247, 250, 252, 254, 256
Christ Myth, 2, 69, 89, 254
Christos, 42, 63, 65
Christus, 86, 98, 102, 190
Christianity, 39, 48, 53, 55–56, 61, 84, 87, 91, 96, 98, 155–157, 158, 162, 184, 199, 206–207, 218, 223, 231, 243, 252, 254, 257
Christians, 32, 34, 39, 44, 46, 48–49, 51–52, 54–55, 58, 60–62, 68, 71, 75, 82, 84, 86–90, 95, 97–102, 155, 157, 171, 173, 178–179, 182, 194–195, 205–208, 214, 216, 221, 227–228, 230, 235, 252, 254–256, 258
Christ Pantocrator, 130
chrysanthemum, 137
Church (Catholic)196, 256
Church Father(s), 53–54, 56, 58–60, 99, 124
clinical death, 3–4
cloth(s), 25–26, 114–116, 118, 120–124, 126, 128, 130, 133–135, 137, 144–146, 232, 234, 257
cognitive dissonance, 203

coin(age), 141–145
coincidence(s), 18, 39, 45, 52
coma(tose), 5, 105
condemn(ation, ed), 33–34, 42, 50, 58, 112, 144, 149, 178, 182, 187–188, 190, 249
condition/state component, 160
confess(es), confession, 8, 63, 122, 230
consciousness, 156
conspiracy, 4, 25–28, 105, 118, 120, 149, 215, 218–219, 226
contamination, 116, 119, 134, 138
contradicted (ing, ion, ory), 8, 10, 29–30, 38, 65, 68, 113, 131, 135, 149, 152, 154, 161, 171–172, 187, 240, 243, 255
conversion, convert(s, ing), 54, 64, 162, 224, 257
convict(ed), 188, 230
corpse(s), 2–3, 128, 135, 142, 149, 151, 165, 184, 195–197, 202–205, 207, 214–216, 219–220, 229, 235, 237, 241, 250
corruption, 190
couched(s) and hedges, 88, 96–97
Council of Nicaea, 211
covered (ing), 21, 73, 96, 101, 112, 128, 133, 143, 206
COVID-19, 203
created, creation, creator, 18, 27, 46, 50, 60, 62, 68, 78, 123, 126, 135, 139, 161, 171, 175, 178–179, 182, 185, 195, 197, 223, 227, 231, 234, 245
creed, 49–52, 185, 222
crime, 54, 189, 226
criminal(s), 16, 96, 173, 179, 185, 188–189, 193, 199, 203, 215–217, 221
criminologist, 136

cross(es), 2–5, 7, 10–12, 14–17, 19–20, 22–24, 27–30, 33–34, 40, 42, 44, 51, 58, 106, 108–112, 128, 130, 135–136, 147–151, 154–160, 162, 168, 173, 185, 190, 192, 216, 253–257
crowd, 52, 190, 207
crown, 12, 130
crucified(ion), 1–3, 5, 7, 10, 12–16, 18, 20–22, 24, 27–30, 32–35, 42, 44, 48–52, 59, 64, 66, 71, 83, 86–87, 89, 91, 94–95, 101, 103, 105–108, 112, 114, 135, 137, 146, 148–157, 159–162, 164–165, 169, 171, 173, 178–179, 184, 186, 189, 192, 201, 204–205, 208, 214–216, 218, 220–221, 228, 254–255, 257
cult, 76, 218, 225
cursed, 154–155, 159
curtain, 224

D

Daemon Hypothesis, 248
Damascus, 175
Daniel 12, 170
darkness, 22, 29, 101, 112, 244
deceit, deceive(r), deception, 9, 115, 121, 146, 197, 222, 243–244, 246, 248–251, 257
Deceptive Deon, 248
defend(ers), 33, 78, 108, 121
deicide, 54
demons, 248
denarii, 143
depict(ion, s), 3, 13–14, 53, 74, 121, 124–125, 128, 140, 207, 252
depression, 4
descendant(s), descent 65, 70, 80–81, 191

detractor(s), 3, 20, 22, 28, 37, 45, 53, 60, 67, 71, 74, 78–79, 87–88, 92, 95, 97, 99–100, 102–103, 105–107, 112–113, 123, 126–127, 129, 147, 151, 161–162, 175, 189, 193, 197, 211, 215, 218, 226, 254, 256–257
Deuteronomy, 159–160, 175–176, 200
devil, 246–248, 250
devoured by wild beast, 205, 220,
diabolic(al), diabolic intervention, *diabolos*, 246, 249, 253
Digesta, 187–188
Diocletian Edict, 211
dirt particles, 132
disappearance, disappeared, 44, 237–238
disciple(s), 9, 16, 29–30, 52, 124, 130, 143, 145, 155–156, 168–172, 178–179, 182–183, 194–196, 198, 201, 203, 209, 211, 214, 217–218, 221, 223–225, 227–230, 232–234, 236, 239–240, 246, 250–251, 256–257
disfigured, 203, 220
divine(ly), 34, 43, 51, 58, 86, 160, 177, 242–243, 246, 250–251
Docetists, 112
doctrine, 157–158, 161
dogs, 149, 192
drug, 4–5, 27

E

earth, 50, 151, 159–161, 170, 200, 217, 236
earthquake, 22, 30, 106, 207, 224–225, 232
Easter, 124, 151, 186, 196, 201, 203–204, 212, 229
eclipse, 29, 207

Subject Index 293

Egypt(ian), 26, 149, 173, 211, 244
electroencephalogram(s), 4–5
elōhīm, 245
embarrassment, 101, 178, 182, 208
embellish(ed), embellishment(s), 19, 26, 61, 106, 149, 152, 180, 255
Emmaus, 13–14, 39–40, 44
Emperor(s), 32, 57, 86, 90, 93, 96, 98, 143–144, 187–188, 191, 211, 227
emplotment, 48, 80
enemies, enemy, 98, 111, 149, 159, 184, 189, 191–194, 205, 247, 250
entomophilous, 137
epistle(s), 99, 185, 210, 217, 228,
epithet, 177, 198
equinox, 110
erroneous, error(s), 5, 12, 14, 92, 119, 134, 156, 161, 171
eschatological, 156
eternal(ly), 50, 113, 158, 196, 243
evangelical, 89, 154, 175, 242
Evangelist(s), 26, 29, 104, 108, 122, 124, 149
evidence(d, s), 3, 17, 23, 28, 32, 34, 38–39, 53, 55, 60–61, 64, 71, 74, 81, 84, 88–90, 92, 96, 100, 102–103, 106, 108, 110, 112, 114, 116, 119–124, 132, 136, 139–140, 142–143, 147, 150, 152, 156, 163, 166, 176, 181, 184, 186, 190, 193, 196, 199, 203–207, 211–212, 214, 216, 218, 220, 223, 225, 227–228, 231, 239, 243, 252, 254–255, 257

execute(d), execution(ers), 1, 13–14, 16, 29, 32, 56, 64, 86–87, 91, 95–96, 99–100, 102, 106, 111–112, 143, 146, 173, 184, 187–193, 204, 216, 222, 224, 257
exegesis, 226, 240
exhume, exhuming, 184, 207, 214, 241
exile, 9, 199
Exodus, 17, 109–110, 173
extrabiblical, 32
eyebrows, 138, 142
eyelids, 142
eyes, 4, 7, 70, 97, 141–144, 170
eyewitness, 21, 33, 93, 104–105, 181, 213, 222
Ezekiel 145, 18, 57

F

fabric, 125, 131–132, 134, 136, 145
fabricate(d), fabrication, 79, 124, 163, 183, 238
fahrenheit, 202
faith(ful), 30, 39, 63, 98, 104, 146, 155, 157–158, 161, 170, 185, 194–196, 199, 237, 247, 250
fake(d), fakery, 78, 120–121, 146, 162
false dilemma, 218, 251
falsifiable, falsification, 47, 79, 120, 163, 183
fanatic, 52
feet, 7, 14–15, 112, 131, 140, 232
festival, 150, 165, 189, 217
fibers, 134–135
fiction(al), 21, 108, 164, 175, 178, 180, 182, 238
finger(s), 114, 125–126, 129, 134, 139

fingerprints, 202
first Minimal Fact, 1, 152, 161, 254–255, 257–258
fish(es), 26, 149, 151, 159–160
flesh, 15, 66, 203–204
flood story, 237
flowers, 136–137
fluid, 19
folded cloth, 126, 234
footprints, 47
forearm, 135, 139
forehead, 138
forensic technology, 217
foretold, 34, 43, 50–51, 58
forgery, forged(r), 35–36, 39, 45–46, 60, 62, 76, 78–80, 96, 99, 120, 133, 146
forgive(ness), 51, 157–158
forsake, 51, 58
fragment(ed), 31, 119, 131, 134, 144, 153
fraud(ulent), 66–67, 79, 101, 122–123
fulfill(ed), fulfillment, 10, 12, 17, 30, 51, 64, 108–110, 151, 159, 165, 186, 197–198, 203
fungal spores, 136

G

Galilee, 29, 52, 68, 70, 87, 171, 205, 229, 233, 239
garments, 220
genital area, genitalia, 128
genre, 48–49
Gentile(s), 8, 34, 39, 50, 58, 64
geological phenomenon, 224
Gerizim (Mt.), 190
ghoulish, 223, 228
glory, glorified, 43–44, 51, glosses, 62, 76
Gnostics, 112

God, gods, godly, 3, 40–41, 45, 47, 51, 62–64, 71, 89, 106, 109–110, 113, 149, 151, 154–161, 165, 170, 177–179, 196, 199–201, 207, 236–237, 239–240, 242–247, 249, 250–254, 257
Gog, 65
Good Friday, 128, 137
Gospel (book), 1–4, 10–11, 14, 19–21, 24, 28–31, 33, 39, 41, 48–49, 52, 68, 82, 89, 104–113, 120, 122, 140, 148–152, 154, 158, 160–161, 163–164, 166–167, 169, 172–175, 178–180, 183, 185, 187–189, 195, 197–198, 203, 206–207, 209, 211–212, 217, 220, 222–229, 233–234, 239–241, 246, 255
gospel (message), 10, 35, 52, 71, 103, 163, 165, 180, 186–187
Gothic, 139
government, 95, 184, 217
governor, governorship, 68, 87–90, 142, 189
grammar, grammatically, 37, 52, 72, 145
grasped, grasping, 14, 197, 232
grass, 137
Great Fire, 97–99
Greek letters, 141
grief, 144
groin, 125
guilt, 86, 158

H

habit evidence, 92–93
hairstyles, 141
hallucination, 252
hands, 7, 12–13, 15, 32, 35, 86, 109, 120, 125, 127–129, 139, 201, 205

hanged, 159
harmonization, harmonized, 152, 255
hearsay, 46, 88, 90, 95
heartbeat, 3, 114
heaven(ly), 3, 50–51, 154, 157, 159, 161, 170, 199–200, 217, 225, 236–237, 241, 247, 251
Hebrew, 7–8, 13, 60, 62, 65, 128, 144, 152, 173, 176–177, 199, 210, 226, 244–246, 251, 254–255
Hedonism, 38
height, 139–140, 176
heresy, heretics, 56, 211, 216
hermeneutic, 151
high priest(s), 32, 63, 69, 131
historian(s), 2, 32–34, 52, 55–57, 59, 63–64, 70, 74, 81, 87–89, 91, 93, 96, 124–125, 255
historicity, historiography, 5, 12, 16, 36–37, 49, 52–53, 59, 70, 91, 93, 95, 99, 102, 107, 110, 153, 169, 211, 226–227, 255
hoax, 182, 184
holes, 125–127, 201
Holy See, 117
Holy Spirit, 50–51, 229
honor(able), 16, 25–26, 149, 173, 182–183, 188, 190–191, 193, 198, 206, 208
hours, 4, 15, 27, 29, 52, 95–96, 112, 128, 136, 150, 165, 224
human, humankind, humanity, 6, 8, 18, 70–71, 112, 121–123, 139, 146–147, 28, 146, 155–158, 161, 236, 244–246, 248, 250, 254, 257
humiliated (ion, ing), 150, 159, 191–192
hypocrites, hypocritical, 156, 205
hypostasis, 155
hypothermia, 4

hysteria, 5, 172

I

icon(ography), 128–131, 140
idol(atry), 142, 252
Iesus Chrestus, 144
Iliad, 238
illusion, 18, 27, 76, 96, 245
imagination, imaginative, imagined, 5, 13–14, 77, 179, 197, 235, 238
impaling, 5
impostor, 190
incarnation, 66, 155
incense, 11, 126
innuendo, 118
inscription, 134, 141–142, 145, 189–190
insurrection(ist), 94, 150, 189, 192, 217
interpolation, interpolator, 33, 35–36, 38, 49, 68–69, 72–75, 82, 87, 97–103, 152, 162, 165, 255
interred, 143, 217
interrogated, interrogation, 52, 88, 96, 225
interview, 135, 139, 194
intoxication, 4
invent(ion), 4, 17–18, 25–26, 31, 108, 112–113, 149–150, 152, 163–164, 166, 168–172, 174–175, 178, 182–183, 194, 207–208, 215, 228, 238–239
irrelevant, 100, 103, 148, 151, 187, 225, 235
Isis cult, 76
Islam(ic), 2, 152, 154–162, 254–255, 257
Israel(ites), Israeli, 1, 7, 10, 26, 42, 63, 65, 109–110, 136–137,

150, 176, 188, 237, 242, 244, 246, 252

J

jaw reflex, 5
Jerusalem, 9, 15, 32, 48, 57, 59, 69, 94, 109, 130–133, 136–137, 143, 170, 173, 175, 177, 181, 184, 193, 195–197, 199, 201–203, 205–209, 212, 217, 222, 224, 227–229, 233, 239, 248, 256
Jerusalem factor, 195
Jesus' Body, 2–3, 5–7, 9, 19–26, 30–31, 112, 135, 148–149, 156, 161, 164, 168–172, 178–179, 182, 184–185, 189, 192–199, 201–209, 212, 215, 217–218, 220–223, 226, 228, 230–232, 234–235, 239–241, 250, 256
  abrasions, 130
  arteries, 150, 205, 220
  bruises, 130
  decay, 118, 195, 205, 220, 241
  heel, 139
  limb, limbed, 3, 140
  lips, 28, 106
  lungs, 5, 21
  wrist, 30, 125, 131
Jesus' Death, 1, 3–7, 9–10, 19, 21–22, 31, 33, 71, 109, 111, 135, 148–149, 151–154, 158, 180–181, 183, 186, 194, 214, 224–225, 239, 254, 258
  asphyxiation, 21
  beaten, beating, 5, 7, 10, 27–28, 114
  Golgotha, 136, 165

Jew(s), 9, 33, 39, 41, 47, 49, 54–55, 58, 61–62, 64–65, 74–75, 83–84, 100, 112, 141, 143, 155, 163, 173, 180, 183, 188–192, 195, 200, 222, 224
Jewish Antiquities (AJ), 32–36, 48–49, 52, 55, 62, 68
Joseph of Arimathea,
  Arimathea was a real place, 175–176
  embarrassing nature, 182
  empty tomb is an unlikely invention, 168–172
  fictional character, 164, 175, 178–181
  historical or theological significance, 177
  member of the Sanhedrin, 178–181
  multiply attested, 164–168
  the name Joseph, 172–175
Josephan style, 35, 38–39, 46, 55, 58–60, 63, 66, 73–75, 80
Josephus controversy, 32–85
Jubilees, 236
Judaea, Judaeans, Judah, Judea, 9, 28, 44, 52, 68, 86–87, 90–91, 95, 100, 142, 189–190, 192
Judaism, 64, 76, 245, 252

K

kingdom, 9, 51, 121, 168, 177, 179, 201, 237, 247
kiss, 140

L

laboratory, laboratories, 116–120
lamb, Lamb of God, 17, 109–110
Laodicea(ns), 58, 210
lashes, 150

Last Supper, 27
law, lawful, lawless, 16, 20, 58, 83, 111, 122, 126, 135, 158, 161, 169, 187, 191, 195, 217, 220–221, 223, 249, 257
Legatio ad Caium, 190
legend(ary), 26, 106, 149, 199, 209, 212, 215, 228
legionaries, 111
leg length, 139
leg break(ing), 16–17, 20–21, 36, 40, 72, 108, 110–111, 173, 201, 203
lie(d), lying, 2, 48–49, 78, 124, 130, 135, 141, 155, 161, 172, 215, 218–219, 226, 234–235, 243–244, 252, 257
lime(stone), 132–133, 149, 221
linguist(ic), 47–48, 74, 145
lion, 7, 248
literal(ly), literalist, 3, 19, 110, 112, 152, 156, 159, 162, 174, 226, 246
literary, 27, 68, 75, 143, 150, 152, 167, 169, 175, 182, 190
Loeb (Classical Library, edition, 69, 106
longhaired, 114
lost books, 210–211
Lucifer, 246
LXX, 177, 198

M

Magnificat, 177
Magog, 65
Manichaeans, 211
manipulation, manipulating, manipulated, 3, 119–120
mannequin, 135

manuscript(s), 32–33, 36, 47, 55, 58, 60, 75, 77–78, 80–81, 99, 101, 124–125, 127, 129, 131, 133
Mara bar Serapion (Letter), 83–85, 255
martyr(dom), 98, 156, 193
Masoretic, 7
Medieval(ists), 119, 123, 125, 128–134, 139–140, 146
Mediterranean, 96, 137, 236
megalomaniac, 192
messiah(ship, messianic), 3, 33, 36–37, 42, 49–53, 55, 62–67, 98, 110, 145, 152, 155, 204, 221, 227, 242–243, 246, 250–251, 256
  anoint(ed), 63, 130, 159, 169, 171, 177
  aspirants, 53
  requisites, 65–66
metaphor(ically), 19, 152, 177
metaphysically, 156
meteorological, 202
microprobe, 132
microscope, 134, 136–137
midday, 207, 224
Midrash(ic), 220, 226
millennium, 120
mimic, 242
Minimal Fact (first), 1, 152, 161, 254–255, 257–258
ministry, 47, 52, 87, 181
miracle, miraculous(ly), 50–52, 64, 120–123, 169, 205, 238, 242, 244–246, 251–252
misdiagnosed, misdiagnosis, 5, 107
Mishnah, 106, 204, 220
misinterpret(ed, s), 110, 148
misleading, misled, 64, 104, 248, 252

missing, missed, 60, 100–101, 133, 151, 199, 212, 223, 238–239
Moab, 175
mocking, 65
modified, modification, 35, 39–40, 55, 73, 118, 187
monastery, 73, 101, 130
monk(s), 120, 211
Mormons, 89
Moroni (angel), 89
mountain, 29, 176
mourners, mourning, 9, 174, 206
moustache, 141
mouth, 73, 75, 113, 142–143, 160, 197
multiple attestation, 11–12, 17, 23, 25, 46, 84, 97, 103–104, 108, 121–123, 149, 164, 166–167, 170, 187, 194, 255
murder(er), 57, 83, 157, 188–190, 199, 217
Muslim(s), 2, 154–161, 254
myrrh, 26, 144, 149, 232
myth(s), 2, 49, 69, 70, 89, 95, 149, 209, 240, 252, 254

N

nail(s), nailed, nailing, 12–14, 23, 131, 154, 216
NASA, 142, 145
Nazarene, Nazareth, 1, 24, 32, 41, 61, 69–71, 76, 99, 144, 146, 150, 171, 174–175, 189, 243, 251
Nebo (Mount), 176
Neofiti (Targum), 176
Neoplatonic, 58
neurological, 4

New Testament, 13–14, 34, 46, 48, 67, 72, 74, 86, 102, 105–106, 109, 113, 148, 153, 157, 161–162, 175, 177, 185, 189, 194, 198, 206, 210, 213, 246, 254–255, 258
Nicene Creed, 49–51
nihilo, 79
Nisan, 110
noon, 29
nudity, 126, 128
numbers, 26, 149

O

obedience, obedient, obey(ing), 21, 111, 158, 217, 236, 244–245
obscure(d), obscurity, 94–95, 127, 133, 143, 163, 177, 179, 193
observance(s), observant, 51, 65, 124, 143
offense, 159–160, 222
offering, 54, 70, 102, 218, 256
ointment, 124
Old Testament, 157, 237
omission(s), omit(s, ted, ting), 4, 9, 22, 29–30, 54–55, 60–61, 70–72, 106, 110, 113, 122, 129, 131, 149, 161, 170, 185, 228, 231–232, 251, 255–256
1 Corinthians 15:1–8, meaning of "He Was Buried," 186, 197, 200–201, 215–216, 222
Paul's knowledge of the tomb, 185–186
problems, 185, 197, 222, 254
one-upmanship, 27, 150
Onqelos (Targums), 176
oozing, 21, 112
opium, 28

organs, 150
ornaments, 129
Orthochromatic film, 145
ossuary (ies), 142–143
oxide, 133–134

P

pagan(s), paganism, 55–56, 80, 85, 141, 145
pain(ful), 4, 18, 55, 112, 179
painting(s), 124, 128, 130, 133, 150
palace, 190
paleness, 3
paleographer, paleontology, 138, 144
Palestine, 1, 108
Palestinian, 10, 106, 141–142, 150, 176, 180, 184, 189, 228, 235–236
palm, 131
palynological, palynologist, palynology, 136–138
papacy, 121
parable, 199
parading zombies, 170
Paradise, 29
paralleled, parallels, 45–46, 68, 80, 166
paraphrase, paraphrasing, 44–45,
parchment, 127
pardons, 158
particles, 47, 132–135
passion, 29, 121, 161
Passover, 10, 17, 109–110, 150, 165, 189, 217, 229
paternity, 70
pathologist(s), 138, 202
patriarchs, 196
pattern(s), 68, 92, 125–127, 135
peasant, 69, 192

pelvic, pelvis, 125, 128
Pentecost, 201, 220, 222–223, 225
peregrinus, 189
persecute, persecution, persecutor, 84, 97–102, 214, 257
personification, 246
Pharisee(s), 34–35, 65, 143–144, 192, 205, 225, 248
physiologic, 4
pierced(s), piercing, 4, 7, 15–18, 21, 108, 110–113, 148, 161, 203
pigment, 133
pilgrims, 13–14, 121, 123, 131
plants, 136–137
poisoning, 4
polemic(s), 52, 55–56, 182
pollen, 136–138
Pope, 120–121, 123–124
possess(ed, ing), 34, 55, 124, 130, 168, 170, 177, 211, 248
pounds, 26, 144, 149
praetorium, 190
Pray Codex, 124–126, 128–130
predicted(ion), 7, 110, 117, 151–152, 170, 200
priests, priestly, 10–11, 29, 32, 34, 42, 44, 59, 63, 69–70, 109, 126, 131, 188, 221, 225, 232
prisoner(s), 20, 96, 191
Proconsul, 97, 187–188
propaganda, 108
prophecy, prophesied, 10, 12, 14, 57, 62, 64, 69, 145, 151–152, 159–160, 165, 186, 197–198, 258
prophet(s), 34, 40–41, 43–44, 50–51, 58, 62, 65, 151, 154, 157, 159–160, 177, 193, 200, 205, 235, 244
Psalm (verses), 109, 126, 159, 199, 255
Psalm 22:17 [16 AV], 12, 14, 30, 161

Pseudo-Eustathius, 54
Pseudo-Hegesippus, 60
Pseudo-Jonathan, 176
Pseudo-Justin, 53
punish, punishment(s), 13, 16, 57, 59, 97, 99, 111, 187–188, 192, 217, 246

Q

Qur'an, 154, 156, 161, 255–256

R

rabbinic, rabbis, 200, 203–204, 237
radiation, 119
radiocarbon, 116–119
rationalize, rationalization, 198, 203, 211
rebellion, rebels, 73, 188, 192, 244, 247, 253
red herring, 256
redacted, 80, 82, 255
redeemed, redeemer, redemption, 42, 65, 157–158, 173, 176, 244
reincarnation, 235
relatives, 121, 143, 187–188, 203–204
relic(s), 117, 120, 124, 131, 134, 146, 162
repentance, 157–158
reprobate, 250
Resurrection (Jesus), 1–4, 6, 8–10, 12, 14–16, 18–20, 22, 24, 26, 28–36, 38–40, 42, 44, 46, 48, 50–52, 54, 56, 58, 60, 62, 64, 66, 68, 70, 72, 74, 76–78, 80, 82, 84, 86–88, 90, 92, 94, 96, 98, 100–104, 106–110, 112, 114, 116, 118, 120, 122, 124, 126, 128, 130, 132, 134, 136, 138, 140, 142, 144, 146, 149–152, 154–156, 158, 160, 162–164, 166, 168, 170–172, 174, 176, 178, 180–188, 190, 192, 194–196, 198–212, 214–246, 248, 250–254, 256–258
  bodily, 170–171, 186, 212, 230, 233–234, 236, 238, 241, 250–252
  third-day resurrection, 32, 35, 40, 43–44, 50–51, 58, 62, 151, 195, 200, 205, 242, 254, 257
Resurrection Hypothesis (RO), 250, 257
resuscitation, resuscitated, 240–241
Revelation, 109, 237
revolt, 143, 188–189, 191
rhetorical, 45, 53, 87, 190, 226
riots, 67, 72
ritual(s), 138, 206
rival, 52, 121, 173, 192, 211, 214, 246
Roman, 11, 16, 20, 23, 31–32, 48, 75, 87, 94–95, 106, 143, 165, 188, 191–192, 216–218, 225, 256
Rome, 48, 55, 62, 64, 70–71, 86, 90–91, 94–95, 97–101, 121, 192, 216
rumor(s), 93, 215–216, 219, 238

S

Sabbath, 31, 134, 148, 165, 173, 217
sacrifice(ing), 8, 109–110, 157–160, 256
Sadducees, 192, 225
saint(s), 22, 30, 51, 56–59, 101, 207, 225
salvation, 50, 52, 109–110, 146, 155, 157, 161, 247

Subject Index 301

Samaritans, 190
Sanhedrin, 52, 143–144, 163–164, 175, 178–183, 206–207, 223–224, 226
Sanhedrist, 178, 182
sarcophagus, 126
Satan, 156, 242, 245–250, 252, 257
  adversary, adversarial, 245, 248
Saviour, 121–122
Scandal(s), 67, 75, 172
scavengers, 192
science, 36, 48, 115, 126, 144, 146
scientific, 6, 29, 115, 118, 138, 146
scientist, 132–133, 135, 138, 144–145
scorpions, 247
scourge(d), scourging, 5, 7, 10–11, 21, 27–28, 112, 128–130, 150
scribe(s), 10, 34, 39, 75, 101, 205, 248
Scripture(s), scriptural, 8, 17, 43, 51, 62, 65–66, 109–110, 112, 128, 152, 155, 157–159, 174, 182, 185, 203, 207–209, 211, 228, 234, 244, 246–247, 251, 254, 256–257
sculpture, 128
sea, 65, 137, 201–202
seal(ed), 155, 160
Second Temple (the temple), 18, 22, 30, 52, 65–67, 70–71, 83, 181, 190–191, 224, 235
sect(s), 34, 49, 95, 102, 225
secular, 83, 154, 190
Seder, 165
sedition(ious), 75, 189, 191, 199
Senate, senators, senatorial, 90, 94, 180

Sepulcher (Sepulchre), Holy, 130, 227, 241
serpent(s), 247–248
servant(s), 23–26, 31, 148, 165, 197–198, 245–246
Shroud of Turin, 111–112, 115–148, 162, 255–256
  agreed testing protocols were not followed, 117–119
  anatomy controversy, 138–140
  artistic evidence, 140–141
  blood stain controversy, 133–136
  coin controversy, 141–144
  d'Arcis Letter controversy, 120–124
  dirt particles controversy, 132–133
  fabric controversy, 131–132
  flower and pollen controversy, 136–138
  Pray Manuscript controversy, 124–132
  radiocarbon dating controversy, 116–120
  Sindonology, 36, 138,
  writing on the cloth controversy, 144–146
Siebeck, Mohr, 13–14
sign of Aries, 110
sin(s), sinner, sinning, 8, 51, 109–110, 157–158, 161, 244–245, 247, 254, 257
sindonists, 130
sitting, 233
skeletal(ton), 78, 134, 203
skeptic(s), 3, 7, 17, 28, 36, 60, 66, 92–93, 97, 108, 120, 122, 129, 139, 145, 147, 149, 154, 162, 170–171, 209, 219, 238, 240, 251, 253–254, 256–257
skeptical theism/theist, 242–243
skepticism, 6, 103

skulls, 142
slavery, 181, 222, 244
soldier(s), 5, 9, 12, 16–17, 20–21, 23–24, 30, 108, 110–112, 148, 170, 190, 192, 216
soul, 6, 156, 158, 204, 220, 244
spear(s), 4–5, 9, 12, 14, 17–18, 21, 30, 110–112, 148, 201, 203
speared, 177,
spices, 26, 31, 149–150, 171, 232
spirit(s), 8, 15, 18, 51, 105, 113, 170, 236, 244–246, 248, 257
spiritual, 8, 170–171
spit, 151, 160
spores, 136
stabbed(ing), 17–18, 111–112, 148
stain(s), stained, 126, 129, 133–134
statue, 83
steal(ing), 9, 226
stone, stoning, 164, 168, 225, 231–234, 247
stoning, 216
storytellers, 169, 245
Styx, 142
substitution, 45, 154–156
suffer(ing), 8, 43, 160, 162, 165, 199, 201, 236
Suffering Servant, 7–8, 165
Sumerian, 237
Sunday, 30, 151, 186, 201, 203, 220
sunlight, 112
sunset, 189
supernatural, 224, 242–243, 245–246, 248, 250–253, 256–257
superstition, 87, 102
survival, survive(d,) surviving, 1, 15–16, 20, 33, 36, 47, 52, 55, 58, 80, 90, 95, 101, 106–107, 114, 150, 181, 207, 211, 216
suspended, 15, 17, 112

suspicious(ly), 100–101, 120
swallowed, 160
sweat, 19
swollen, 130
Swoon (theory), 1, 105, 154
swords, 9
symbol(ism), 18, 109, 112, 160, 226
synagogues, 214
Synoptic Gospels, 104, 110, 166, 204

T

Tacitean scholars, 96
tampered, 73, 77, 95
Targum, 176
temperature, 3, 201–203
temptation, tempted, 246–247
Testimonium Flavianum (TF), 32–82, 88, 255
testimony, 32, 34, 62, 72, 102, 112, 142, 151, 169, 194
tetrarch, 68
theft, 191, 226
theism, 252
theists, 205
theologian(s), 33–34, 56–57, 59–60, 73, 113, 122, 125–126, 161, 193, 211, 224, 241–242, 251, 255
theophany, 59, 75
Thessalonians 2, 249
thief, thieves, 29, 31, 108, 111, 189, 237
time component, 151–152, 160, 223
threat(en), threatening, 180, 189, 192, 225
throat, 5
throne, 170, 200
thumb(s), 114, 125–126, 129–130
titulus, 190

Torah, 65, 257
torture(d, s), 86, 150, 191–192
tradition(s), 27, 39, 63, 84, 89, 96, 150–151, 163, 165–166, 169, 171–173, 176, 179–180, 185–186, 191, 195, 200, 204, 208, 213, 229, 236, 239, 242
translated, translation(s), 7, 9, 38, 50, 59, 121, 176, 212, 238, 245–246
treason, 188–190
treasures, 190
trial(s), 10, 94, 97, 101, 189, 191
tribe, 39, 44, 46–47, 51, 58, 62
Trinity, 155, 157
trope, 47
troublemakers, troublemaking, 73, 189, 216
twin, 2
Tyre, 237

U

unconscious(ness), 4–6
unfalsifiable, 94, 251, 257
unqualified, 35, 103
unresponsiveness, 4, 112
unscientific, 78
unsubstantiated, 211, 258
unverifiable, 18, 73, 93–94, 103, 257
uprising, 72

V

Vatican, 118, 144
veil, 22, 30
veneration(ing), 120, 123–124, 192, 195–196, 205–207
vestments, 124
victims, 14–15, 99, 101, 106, 150, 165

vinegar, 27–28
violate(d), 16–17, 110, 191, 257
violence, 8, 126, 191, 197
virgin, 50, 238
vision(s), 112, 156, 210, 250, 252–253
vocal, voice(s), 145, 160, 213, 244, 247
volunteer(ed), voluntarily, 2, 135, 155, 236
vomiting, 5

W

war, 70–71, 181, 189, 191–192, 245
washing, 149
wealthy, 206
weather, 203
weeks, 9, 195, 202–203, 218, 220, 223
weight, 26, 33, 69, 102, 149, 154
wetted, 63
whatever, 34, 78, 179, 194, 235, 239–240
wisdom, 177, 237
witness(es), witnessed, 21–22, 28, 30, 32–34, 82, 84, 88, 91, 98–99, 112, 129, 151–152, 155, 169, 171–172, 181, 187, 207, 224, 230, 232, 237, 240, 252, 257
women, 14, 24, 40, 45, 124, 150, 169, 171–172, 198, 204–205, 211–212, 222, 232–233
woodworker, 150
worship(ped), 14, 51, 206, 252
wounds, 11, 13–14, 121, 131, 220
wrapped, wrapping, 25–26, 112, 135, 149, 154, 164, 168

Z

Zechariah 12, 9–10, 12, 14, 30, 112, 161

zodiac, 110
zombies, 170

www.ingramcontent.com/pod-product-compliance
Lightning Source LLC
Chambersburg PA
CBHW050837230426
43667CB00012B/2030